Structures of Computing

Egon Börger • Vincenzo Gervasi

Structures of Computing

A Guide to Practice-Oriented Theory

 Springer

Egon Börger
Dipartimento di Informatica
University of Pisa
Pisa, Italy

Vincenzo Gervasi
Dipartimento di Informatica
University of Pisa
Pisa, Italy

ISBN 978-3-031-54357-9   ISBN 978-3-031-54358-6   (eBook)
https://doi.org/10.1007/978-3-031-54358-6

This Springer imprint is published by the registered company Springer Nature Switzerland AG
The registered company address is: Gewerbestrasse 11, 6330 Cham, Switzerland

Paper in this product is recyclable.

Preface: What the Book is About

The Theme of the Book

"Structures of Computing" aims to explain the behavioural meaning of fundamental concepts of computing without referring to any specific computing device or programming language. By defining these concepts in more general and at the same time simpler mathematical terms the book is focused on

cooperating agents that process dynamic structures

where the *data*—stored in abstract memory forming abstract states—are arguments and values of arbitrary functions and relations between objects. These computational structures are dynamic, subject to change due to rule-based *actions* that are performed on the data by algorithm-equipped agents under various forms of cooperation *control*, including in particular the reaction to environmental stimuli.

The book uses the conceptual computational framework of Abstract State Machines (ASMs)—an intuitive form of pseudo-code that operates directly in abstract states (computational structures) and comes with a precise easily defined rule-based meaning—but it does not assume knowledge of ASMs. We explain the small number of basic abstract but operational terms of that framework which suffice to explain the common core of a great multitude of operational concepts and constructs of computing in a uniform way, facilitating their understanding and analysis.

---

[1] I value finding the truth about something, even if inconsequential, more than endlessly speculating about deep questions without reaching anything true.
See [82, pg. 738, footnote 2]. The context of this quote is well described in [63].

A Short Survey of the Book

Roughly speaking, to compute means to execute *algorithmic processes* by a set of *communicating agents* each of which *executes* in a given background structure an *algorithm* assigned to it, interacting with other agents in the given process environment. This calls for an explanation, which we provide from scratch in Part 1, of the triple *data-action-control*, the conceptual constituents of interactive processes:

- **Data** the algorithmic processes operate upon, abstractly described as structured elements, i.e. objects with associated properties, relations and functions (Ch. 1).
- **Actions** (basic algorithmic operations) that affect—create and delete, access (read) and change (write), receive and send—the data *in single execution steps* (Ch. 2).
- **Control** patterns that determine the combination of single (in adaptable systems even run-time-modifiable) steps in

  single-agent sequential or *multi-agent concurrent* or *mixed runs*

  (also called 'executions' or 'computations'), where the algorithm-equipped agents interact with each other and with their environment via communication or other forms of data sharing (Ch. 3-6).

Part 2 investigates the following three themes:

- **Fundamental analysis methods** for the investigation of computations in abstract states at different levels of abstraction/refinement: model inspection, validation and verification (Ch. 7).
- **Classification of principal computational paradigms**, leading from classes of single-agent sequential algorithms to a variety of classes of multi-agent processes with asynchronous or mixed (concurrent or recursive) runs (Ch. 8). This extends the characterizations in Ch. 3-6 of self-modifying reflective algorithms, of synchronous or bulk-synchronous algorithms, of various classes of streaming machines (illustrated by models for spreadsheets or the TCP/IP computer network protocol), etc.
- **Complexity analysis** of the *power* of computations in abstract states and their intrinsic computational *limits* (Ch. 9).

We expect the emerging

Model Theory of Structures of Computing

to contribute to a solid foundation for the practice of computing.

Target Audience and How to Use the Book

The book is addressed to persons who want to understand the conceptual foundation of computing. It does not assume any specific programming experience but only a basic understanding of what are mechanically executable processes and their descriptions. Think of system-control mechanisms, automated service procedures, administrative or business processes and the like which accompany our daily life. To make the book also accessible for non-experts of the theory of computing we avoid any unnecessary formalism and formulate our definitions as much as possible in natural language, using common mathematical notation only where needed to avoid ambiguities.[2] Examples and exercises (coming with solutions in the Appendix) serve as comprehension checkpoints; we insert references to the literature for the reader who is interested in further developments.

The book has been written for self-study but can also be used in teaching, in particular to accompany undergraduate courses or seminars for students who want to understand how the many concepts they learn are intimately linked to each other by a common foundation.

Acknowledgements

We thank the following colleagues who have helped with comments on draft chapters of this book: Giuseppe Del Castillo, Paolo Dini, Flavio Ferrarotti, Uwe Glässer, Albert Fleischmann, Fatemeh Movafagh, Giuseppe Prencipe, Alexander Raschke, Klaus-Dieter Schewe.

Last but not least we thank Ralf Gerstner from Springer for his trust and patience.

Egon Börger and *Vincenzo Gervasi*

Pisa, December 2023

---

[2] We recall in Ch. 1 the few basic concepts we use from classical logic.

Contents

List of Figures

Symbols and Notations

Notations from Logic

not ($\neg$), **and** ($\wedge$), **or** ($\vee$)   -- negation, conjunction, disjunction

iff ($\Leftrightarrow$)   -- logical equivalence: if and only if

forall ($\forall$)   -- universal quantifier

forsome ($\exists$), **thereissome** ($\exists$)   -- existential quantifier

thereisno ($\neg\exists$)   -- negated existential quantifier

ζ -- interpretation of individual variables, see pg. **13**

$eval(exp, \mathfrak{A}, \zeta)$ -- value of exp in state $\mathcal{A}$ with variable assignment ζ

$eval(formula, \mathfrak{A}, \zeta)$ -- formula interpretation, see pg. **15**

$exp(x/t)$ -- result of replacing each free occurrence of x in exp by t

Set/Multiset/List Notation

Nat   -- set of natural numbers $0, 1, 2, \ldots$

Integer   -- set of integers $0, 1, -1, 2, -2, \ldots$

$|A|$ -- cardinality of A

$x \in A$ -- x is an element of A

$A \setminus B = \{a \in A \mid a \notin B\}$ -- difference set

$A \cap B, A \cup B, A \times B$ -- intersection, union, cross product

$A \subseteq B$ -- A is a subset of B

$\mathcal{P}(X) = \{Y \mid Y \subseteq X\}$ -- Power set of X

$\{x \in X \mid P(x)\}$ -- set of all elements of X which satisfy P

$char_R$ -- characteristic function of R

$f\colon A \to B$ -- function f from domain A to range B

$f[a \mapsto b]$ -- denotes f' where $f = f'$ except for $f'(a) = b$

$f_a^b = f[a \mapsto b]$ -- equivalent notation, common in logic

$f(\_) = constant$ -- abbreviates **forall** x $f(x) = constant$

$\epsilon x(P(x))$ -- some x which satisfies P (Hilbert's choice operator)

$\iota x(P(x))$ -- the unique x that satisfies P (Hilbert's ι operator)

$\{\!\!\{\,\}\!\!\}$ -- empty multiset/bag

$\{\!\!\{p_1, p_1, p_2, \ldots, p_n\}\!\!\}$ -- a multiset of $n + 1$ elements

$[]$ -- empty list (or sequence, stream, queue)

$[p_1, \ldots, p_n]$ -- list etc. of n elements, in the given order

$List(Domain)$ -- a list etc. of elements of $Domain$

$head(a)$ -- the first element of a list etc. a

$tail(a)$ -- the list etc. a, except its first element

$concatenate([p_1, \ldots, p_n], [q_1, \ldots, q_m]) = [p_1, \ldots, p_n, q_1, \ldots, q_m]$

$[l \mid l'] = concatenate(l, l')$

$a < b$ -- order relation: a comes before b

$a > b$ -- order relation: a comes after b

ASM Notation

$\mid \mathfrak{A} \mid$ -- superuniverse of $\mathfrak{A}$, see Def. 2

$Upd(M, \mathfrak{A}, env)$ -- update set M computes in $\mathfrak{A}$ with env, see pg. 32

$eval(M, \mathfrak{A}, env)$ -- functional notation for $Upd(M, \mathfrak{A}, env)$

$evalCand(M, \mathfrak{A}, env, U)$ -- nondeterministic relation of $eval$

$Locs(U)$ -- set of locations of updates in an update set U

$\mathfrak{A} + U$ -- sequel state, result of applying to state $\mathfrak{A}$ the updates in U

$\mathfrak{A} \Rightarrow_M \mathfrak{A}'$ -- M can make a move from state $\mathfrak{A}$ to $\mathfrak{A}'$, see Def. 14

$\mathfrak{A} \overset{n}{\Rightarrow}_M \mathfrak{A}'$ -- M moves in n steps from state $\mathfrak{A}$ to $\mathfrak{A}'$, see Def. 14

chooseOneOf (*Rules*)   -- bounded choice **choose** $R \in Rules$ **do** R

M **or** N -- **chooseOneOf** (M, N)

import   -- provides fresh memory, see pg. 36

M **seq** N -- atomic sequence operator, see pg. 53

$U \oplus V$ -- sequential update set merge, see pg. 53

$undef$ -- see Sect. 1.1.2

$\Delta(M, \mathfrak{A}) = step_M(\mathfrak{A}) - \mathfrak{A}$ -- difference set (of fresh updates) see pg. 33

$\Delta(M, \mathfrak{A}) = \{\Delta_M(\mathfrak{A}, \mathfrak{A}') \mid (\mathfrak{A}, \mathfrak{A}') \in step_M\}$ -- see pg. 202

$\mathfrak{A} \downarrow \Sigma$ -- restriction of state $\mathfrak{A}$ to signature Σ

$[M]$ -- the function computed by M, see Sect. **9.1.1**

Part I
Computational Paradigms: Definition

Introduction and Survey of Part 1

The intuitive meaning of the concept of *computing* refers to[3] the

> **mechanical execution of precisely and completely described procedures**
> *by agents which may interact with each other and their environment.*

Procedures are also called programs, agents are often viewed as actors that perform the role defined by the program they execute. Computational *processes* are given by what is called a 'process description' and an entity that performs the 'process execution'. This distinction simplifies dealing with multi-agent processes that come with a large variety of (possibly concrete real-world) process components, executed by corresponding agents. The distinction allows one to use as agents a variety of execution entities: specific physical devices, program interpreters, persons (think about a business process where an employee has to execute precise instructions that may be formulated in natural language, or think about code inspection where the code executor is a person), virtual machines, etc. The distinction also serves to speak about multi-agent systems where different agents may execute simultaneously each a different instance of the same program. When dealing with traditional (single-agent) algorithms we usually suppress the agent.

Instead of mechanical execution also the term algorithmic execution (or simply execution) is used and process descriptions are also called algorithms or algorithmic specifications. By a common abuse of language often the (computational)[4] process descriptions are simply called processes, thereby hiding the underlying execution mechanism where its specifics do not matter. Usually each actor in an algorithmic process can be assumed to execute one algorithm (which may prescribe to perform a finite set of multiple elementary actions simultaneously—in parallel—or in some order).

---

[3] The technical terms that appear in this introductory survey are explained in the main text of the book.

[4] In this book 'process' stands for 'computational process', the only processes we are interested in here.

The execution of an algorithmic process is assumed to depend only on what is specified precisely (without ambiguity) in the process description. In other words, the procedure of an algorithmic process must be 'precise' and its execution performed under the procedure's 'complete' *control* (at the desired level of abstraction). This implies that the *elementary actions* the procedure requires an agent to perform are completely determined by the process description and the current information the agent possesses. This information (also called *data*) may be shared by the agent with its environment (read: other cooperating computing agents). In Ch. 1-6 we investigate these three conceptual constituents of (interactive)[5] algorithms—data, elementary actions and process control—and illustrate them by characteristic examples.

- Ch. 1 describes the **logical structure of the data** algorithmic processes handle. For the sake of generality and simplicity, to refer to computational data, i.e. objects of computations and their current properties and relations, we use logical terms (expressions built up by function symbol applications) and logical combinations of relational statements. In this way an agent's **state**, i.e. its current memory during an execution (read: its data basis or information status), is represented by a mathematical structure (more precisely a first-order structure, i.e. a set with finitely many functions and relations defined on its elements, also called **Tarski structure**). Technically this means that states are defined by an interpretation of the structure's function and relation symbols over a base set; consequently state changes result from assigning new values to some arguments of some functions or relations.

- Ch. 2 describes the **logical structure of the elementary actions** (also called operations) an algorithmic process performs in a single execution step on its data. Due to the most general concept of state introduced in Ch. 1, the elementary actions to create or delete, access (read) or change (write), receive or send data can all be expressed by (conditional) **abstract assignments** of the form $f(t_1, ..., t_n) := t$ which (if the given condition is true in the current state) change the value of the function or relation f for the current values of its argument terms $t_1, ..., t_n$ to the current value of the term t. In every step an agent may execute simultaneously (we also say 'in parallel') finitely many such conditioned (also called 'guarded') assignments that constitute its program. The single-agent version of such *Parallel Guarded Assignment* processes (PGAs) gives rise to the classical concept of sequential run as iteration of single-agent steps, well known from Finite State Machine (FSM) or Turing Machine (TM)

---

[5] For simplicity of wording, in case of a process with only one actor we still consider the process to be interactive; in fact it will interact at least with the environment, e.g. by receiving some input at the start of an execution (the case of Turing machines) or in the simplest case by receiving only a start signal that causes the execution to start. When dealing with a single-agent process (*ag, algorithm*) we often suppress mentioning the executing agent *ag* and speak only about the *algorithm* and the effect of its execution by an agent.

computations. In analogy to FSMs and TMs the PGAs (and various extensions introduced below) are called *Abstract State Machines* (ASMs).

- Ch. 3-6 describe the **logical structure of process control**, i.e. the way single steps are combined in runs of multiple interacting agents. These control structures distinguish different run concepts we illustrate for the following major software control patterns:

  – **Sequential** deterministic and nondeterministic computations, including multiple-agent interleaved or synchronous parallel computations (Ch. 3). Standard examples are runs of imperative procedural (Pascal-like,[6] Sect. 3.2) or structured programs (Sect. 3.3) and of cellular automata (Example 12, pg. 69).

  – **Reflective** algorithmic process runs of dynamic programs, i.e. of programs that can change their definition at run-time (Ch.4). These are processes that during the execution of their algorithm can change this algorithm and continue to execute the modified procedure. We formulate an abstract form of reflective machines and illustrate its refinements for three major programming paradigms: logical (Prolog), functional (Lisp) and imperative (Random Access Machine with Stored Program RASP).

  – **Concurrent** computations (Ch. 5) with their typical context awareness and state separation. We illustrate them by runs of communicating agents (Sect. 5.2), of web browsers (Sect. 5.2.1), of Occam processes (Sect. 5.3) and by multithreaded Java runs (Sect. 5.4.2).

  – **Mixed sequential/concurrent** computations, explained in Ch. 6 by two characteristic examples: Bulk Synchronous Parallel algorithms (Sect. 6.1) and *streaming* machines with three outstanding instances, namely neuronal networks, spreadsheets, and the TCP/IP protocol (Sect. 6.2). Another example with mixed sequential and concurrent executions are recursive computations we investigate in Sect. 8.4.

These together with various other outstanding classes of Abstract State Machines of the kind we explain in Ch. 8 pave the way for a general, Turing machine model independent, ASM-based abstract theory of computation over structures (outlined in Ch. 9) that has the potential to become relevant for the practice of computing.

---

[6] The language Pascal has been created last century by Niklaus Wirth to support good programming practice using structuring of programs and data [165].

Chapter 1
Computational Data, Operations, States

In this chapter we fix the notation we use for first-order logic terms and formulae and their interpretation. We use a common notation so that most readers may immediately jump to Ch. 2 and come back here only should a notational question arise.

Typically, the execution of an algorithmic step implies to perform some *operations* (actions) on some *objects* of computation (that come with their properties and relations, also called data). These fundamental data management items can be represented in full generality, of whatever particular type the data may be, by treating them abstractly, independently of their particular computational nature:[1]

- objects as elements of whatever 'universe of discourse' (a set),[2]
- operations as functions defined over the universe of discourse,
- properties and relations as subsets of the universe of discourse.

Due to algorithmic actions some properties, relations and functions are subject to change so that they are called *dynamic*, in contrast to *static* ones that never change. One therefore has to provide *syntactic* names to denote the items via some name interpretation. This interpretation is subject to change when an algorithmic action is performed on the involved item.

For naming we adopt the usual syntactic terms from classical predicate (first-order) logic. We introduce them in Sect. 1.1 together with their inter-

---

[1] The foundational character of the triple (algorithm, action, object) can be seen from Albert Fleischmann's epistemological observation that the *Subject-Predicate-Object* structure of simple statements *'Subj PerformsActionOn Obj'* in indo-european languages is closely related to the structure of elementary steps of (single-agent) algorithmic processes, namely *AlgorithmicAgent-PerformsActionOn-Objects*; it shows the algorithm-executing agents as the subjects of computational steps, a view that appears *in nuce* already in [78, Sect. 19.7] and explicitly in [79, Sect. 2.6]. The Subject-Oriented Business Process Modeling approach exploits this analogy to smoothly integrate persons as subjects (read: executing agents) of digital business-processing steps.

[2] In the area of *conceptual modeling* the wording 'entities' is used for objects, see `https://conceptualmodeling.org/`

E. Börger, V. Gervasi, *Structures of Computing*,
https://doi.org/10.1007/978-3-031-54358-6_1

pretations (also called their *semantics*), describing how the names denote computational items that constitute what is called the *state* of a computation. To specify conditions under which an algorithmic action is requested to be executed in a state we use mainly standard first-order formulae which for the sake of completeness and to explain the used notation are defined in Sect. 1.2.

1.1 Data and Operations on Data

Functions are the principal operations dealt with in computing. Functions f in the mathematical understanding come mainly with a fixed length of arguments, called their *arity*, and associate with every argument $(a_1, \ldots, a_n)$ (of a given set $A_1 \times \ldots A_n$ of arguments) a unique element b (of a given set B of values); b is called the value of the function for the argument $(a_1, \ldots, a_n)$. The standard notation is $f : A_1 \times \ldots A_n \to B$. Functions can be partial, meaning that for some arguments $(a_1, \ldots, a_n)$ there may be no value defined; this is often expressed by writing $f(a_1, \ldots, a_n) = undef$. A function that is not partial is called total. For a partial function f its *domain* is defined as the set of arguments $(a_1, \ldots, a_n)$ with value $f(a_1, \ldots, a_n) \neq undef$, its *range* as the set of its values.

In mathematics functions usually come with a fixed definition which is independent of any computational action, reason for which they are called *static*. In computing the argument/value association of a function may change for some arguments, due to computational actions that affect the definition of the function values for the involved arguments. This is why such functions are called *dynamic*.

Notational convention for relations. A relation R (also called predicate) is treated in this book as a function with range *true, false, undef*. You may think of $R(a_1, \ldots, a_n) = undef$ as expressing that the type of the arguments is not correct. A relation R is often written as a characteristic function $char_R$ to mark that it is treated as a partial function. A relation can be seen also as a set, namely the set of all elements $(a_1, \ldots, a_n)$ where $R(a_1, \ldots, a_n) = true$. Other standard notations for $R(a_1, \ldots, a_n) = true$ are a relational 'statement' $R(x_1, \ldots, x_n)$ or $R(x_1, \ldots, x_n)$ *is true* or $R(x_1, \ldots, x_n)$ *holds*. The same holds for properties P which we view as relations of arity 1 or sets $\{a \mid P(a) = true\}$.

To simplify the notation we also use the special case of a function with zero arguments as denoting some element, an object that is associated with this function. In logic 0-ary functions are called constants, in contrast to logical variables which are used as auxiliary temporary names to denote any not furthermore specified elements of some set. But since also 0-ary functions may change their value due to computational actions we stick to the wording 0-ary function. We may omit the parentheses for 0-ary functions, writing c instead of $c()$. A dynamic 0-ary function corresponds to a variable of programming.

We now define the syntax (Sect. 1.1.1) and semantics of terms (Sect. 1.1.3) in computational states (Sect. 1.1.2), thereby specifying the logical structure we use to describe data and operations on data.

1.1.1 Naming Objects and Operations (Syntax of Terms)

With the preceding stipulations one can describe any algorithmic action involving any computational item in a uniform way by using *terms* to name computational objects (read: data) on which some operations are performed (by an active entity). Terms are built up from 0-ary function symbols by appropriate function application (Def. 1). To provide the possibility to temporarily name some usually arbitrarily chosen but fixed element of a set we include also individual variables as syntactical names for objects. The semantical interpretation of terms and individual variables assigns values to them, thus constituting what is called an algorithmic *state* (Def. 2). The interpretation of individual variables (Def. 3) appears there as a *variable environment* in which the computation (also called *evaluation*) of functional terms in the state takes place (Def. 4).

Definition 1. (Terms over a Signature) A finite set of function symbols is called a *signature* or *vocabulary*. Since we deal with relations as functions with truth values *true, false, undef* we usually assume without further mention that three special 0-ary function symbols (which we again write as *true, false, undef*) are present in every signature and interpreted in the standard way.

We write f, g, h for function symbols, possibly indexed $f_1, f_2, \ldots$, and indicate their arity n by f^n or $f^{(n)}$ only where necessary to avoid any ambiguity; usually the arity is clear from the context. Sometimes we write $c, c_1, \ldots$ for 0-ary function symbols. For a frugal notation we consider f^n and f^m with $n \neq m$ as different function names, the same for versions of f with different argument types. We write Σ (possibly indexed) for signatures.

We write x, y, z (possibly indexed) for *individual variables* which are special identifiers, used as auxiliary temporary names for arbitrary not furthermore specified elements of a set.

For any signature Σ the *terms* (over Σ) are constructed starting with individual variables x and 0-ary function symbols $f^0 \in \Sigma$ and successively applying any function symbol $g \in \Sigma$ of positive arity n to any already constructed terms $t_1, \ldots, t_n$. Formally the steps of this inductive definition read as follows:

- Every individual variable x and 0-ary function symbol $g^0 \in \Sigma$ is a term (over Σ).
- If $t_1, \ldots, t_n$ are terms (over Σ) and f is an n-ary function symbol (in Σ) for $n > 0$, then $f(t_1, \ldots, t_n)$ is a term (over Σ).

A term which does not contain any individual variable is called a *ground term* or *closed*. We write s, t (possibly indexed) for terms. In computer science they are also called *expressions*, a name which in logic usually refers to formulae as defined below.

Example 1 (Mealy Automaton Signature). As our first example we consider Mealy automata, a frequently used type of machines introduced in [127]. A Mealy automaton consists of a 0-ary function *in* where the input is read, a 0-ary function *out* where the output is written, and a control unit *ctl* (denoting what we call control states) by which the behaviour (read: the execution of specific actions in single steps) of the automaton is managed following a program *pgm*. The program determines how the automaton, reading in its current control state *ctl* some input, produces some output and proceeds to its next control state (for further input reading). The three 0-ary function symbols *in, out, ctl* belong to the signature of a Mealy automaton and denote its architectural components. Their precise meaning (as memory locations) and some more signature elements will become visible when Mealy automaton states and actions are described (see below Example 2, pg. 12).

1.1.2 Generic Notion of States

Definition 2. (States over a Signature) For a given signature Σ a *state* $\mathfrak{A}$ (over Σ) is defined by a non-empty set A and an *interpretation* of each function symbol $f^n \in \Sigma$ by a total function $f^{\mathfrak{A}} : A^n \to A$ which is also called the denotation of f. We assume Σ to contain three elements *true, false*, and *undef* whose denotations are assumed to be fixed (i.e. static) pairwise different elements and different from all other elements in A. We assume Boolean functions and equality to be interpreted in the usual way (see Def. 6, pg. 15).

A is called the *superuniverse* or *base* set of the state $\mathfrak{A}$ and denoted $|\mathfrak{A}|$. We call the elements of the superuniverse also the *elements* of the state. The convention to treat properties and relations by their characteristic functions makes them interpreted in a state as subsets of the superuniverse. Such subsets are also called subuniverses or simply universes.

Comprehensiveness of states. Structures are the most general means mathematical language offers to represent states of affairs of the (part of interest of the) world. As the result of interpretations of given predicate, relation and function symbols they are known in logic as *Tarski structures*

[161, 11] or simply structures and in universal algebra as algebraic structures or simply *algebras* (with static functions). In theoretical computer science they are known as (axiomatically defined) abstract data types. Structures as states support also the view of databases as *relational structures* where every argument for which the relation holds corresponds to a row in the database table for the relation. Allowing some functions in Tarski structures to be dynamic as we exploit in this book provides for the practice of computing a most general but conceptually simple form of computational states. The elements of the superuniverse can be any kind of dynamic structured objects—think about sets, lists, trees, graphs, but also programs (that may even be transformed at runtime), networks of communicating agents, etc.—which can be transformed with the help of corresponding functions that operate on those structures, at whatever desired level of abstraction. In addition, as is further explained in Ch. 2 and exploited throughout in this book:

- functions represent an abstract easy-to-grasp form of memory: every argument of f appears as memory location for f whose content is the value of f for that argument, so that
- any algorithmic action can be described as changing the value of some memory locations, namely the interpretation of those terms that are characteristic for the algorithmic action (read: are at the level of abstraction of that action).

An intuitive representation of functions is by function tables which support the two main views of memory: the abstract view as given by tables and the concrete view as given by single locations (read: table entries), a feature that can be useful for program documentation (see [134, 32]).

A notational convention for 0-ary functions. By Definition 2 dynamic 0-ary functions c play the role of programming variables (or registers) since the denoted element $c^{\mathfrak{A}} \in A$ (or register content) may change from state to state due to some algorithmic action. If c is used as a constant, i.e. as a static function that denotes the same element in every state under consideration, say a natural number $c^{\mathfrak{A}} = 7$, then we sometimes identify the function symbol c with its denotation $c^{\mathfrak{A}} = 7$ and simply write 7 instead of c. This holds in particular for the static constants *true, false* and *undef*. We extend this convention by writing f instead of $f^{\mathfrak{A}}$ when it is clear from the context that not the 0-ary function symbol f, but its interpretation $f^{\mathfrak{A}}$ is meant.

A note on *undef*. By *undef* we denote an undetermined object. It plays the role of the default value of the superuniverse. We use *undef* to handle partial functions as follows. For logical reasons not explained here we require by Definition 2 that the interpretation of a function symbol f in a state associates a value with each element of the state so that it denotes a *total function*. But we want to be able to deal also with *partial functions* that appear frequently in computing. Therefore we permit functions to have *undef* as value and treat the *domain* of functions as the set of all and only those arguments $(a_1, \ldots, a_n) \in |\mathfrak{A}|^n$ for which the function has a 'defined' value

$f^{\mathfrak{A}}(a_1, \ldots, a_n) \neq undef$. As a consequence, by a slight abuse of language we call a function a partial function also in case it has the value $undef$ for some argument. Since we treat relations by their characteristic functions, relations too can be partial so that their range is the set $\{true, false, undef\}$.

Example 2 (Mealy Automaton States). We continue the previous example of a Mealy automaton (see Example 1 above) by modeling a transformation of an input sequence (read from a *tape*) into an output sequence (written to the same *tape*). To this end, we modify the signature by refining the functions *in* and *out* to *tape(head)*, where a 0-ary function *head* represents the position on the *tape* from which the automaton reads the input symbol and to which it writes the output symbol.[3]

More precisely stated: a *tape* is (interpreted as) a (possibly infinite) sequence of squares each of which can bear a letter, constrained by the condition that only finitely many squares are non-empty, i.e. bear a letter that is different from a special value that we identify with *undef* (traditionally called a 'blank'). The segment of a tape that contains all non-empty squares represents a word Mealy automata are interested in, i.e. a finite sequence $a_1 \ldots a_n$ of elements (called 'letters') of a non-empty finite set (called 'alphabet'). Initially all non-empty squares contain a symbol from some *InAlphabet*. As the transformation progresses, such input symbols are replaced by symbols from some *OutAlphabet* (which may or may not coincide with *InAlphabet*).

> *head* : *Square*   -- 0-ary function with values in *Square*
> *tape* : *Square* → *InAlphabet* ∪ *OutAlphabet*

At any time, the control unit is in a *control state* held by a 0-ary function *ctl*; the possible control states are the elements of a non-empty finite set *CtlState*:

> *ctl* : *CtlState*   -- a 0-ary function with values in *Ctl*

The Mealy automaton program *pgm* determines the reaction of the machine when in its current control state *ctl* = *i* it reads an input letter *tape(head)* = *a*: it writes a letter *b* into *tape(head)*, moves the *head* (namely to the next square to the right of the currently visited square), and switches to its next control state *j*. For simplicity of exposition of the moves of the read-and-write *head* we choose *Square* to be (an initial segment of) the set *Nat* of natural numbers so that 'the next square to the right of *ctl*' is *ctl* + 1.

This means that *pgm* is furthermore specified by the following two functions (plus the successor function +1 of *Nat* to determine the next square to the right of *head*):[4]

---

[3] In the literature Mealy automata come with separate input and output tapes. To show below in an explicit manner the subtle relation between Mealy automata and Turing machines we use one *tape* from where input is read and to which output is written.

[4] Alternatively, one can specify *pgm* by one single function *pgm* : *CtlState*× *InAlphabet* → *OutAlphabet* × *CtlState* × *Square*. Here, *Square* is a static successor function that always yields the next *Square* on the right. By omitting *Square*, we obtain the usual notation of *pgm* as a set of instructions of form (i, a, b, j) where the assumed right-move of the *head* remains implicit.

$write : CtlState \times InAlphabet \rightarrow OutAlphabet$

$nextCtl : CtlState \times InAlphabet \rightarrow CtlState$

Thus the superuniverse is the union of *Nat*, the alphabets *InAlphabet*, *OutAlphabet* and the *CtlState* (plus the always assumed 0-ary fixed functions *true*, *false* and *undef*).

The example shows that the further specification of Mealy automata imposes certain constraints on the interpretation of the Mealy automaton signature elements introduced in Example 1 (pg. 10), for example turning the monitored function *in* and the output function *out* into one refined function *tape*. It also adds new signature elements, like for the static program functions *write*, *nextCtl* (usually denoted λ, δ) and the successor function $+1$ together with *head*. In Example 4 (pg. 26) we will conclude the behavioural definition of Mealy automata by specifying also the logical structure of the elementary actions Mealy automata perform in every single step of their computations.

1.1.3 Interpretation (Semantics) of Terms in States

One can compute in every state for each syntactical term a value if an interpretation of the individual variables that occur in the term is given. Such an interpretation consists of an assignment of elements of the superuniverse to finitely many individual variables; such an interpretation is also called (*individual variable*) *environment* of the state.

Definition 3 (Variable environment). Let $\mathfrak{A}$ be a state. A *variable environment* for $\mathfrak{A}$ is a function ζ which binds each of a finite number of individual variables to name ('denote') an element of the superuniverse of $\mathfrak{A}$. We write $\zeta[x \mapsto a]$ for the variable environment that coincides with ζ except that it binds x to denote the element a. $range(\zeta)$ is defined as the set of all elements that occur in the bindings of ζ. Note that the function symbol ζ is not in the signature of an ASM but appears in the ASM framework with the role to keep track of variable bindings where defining the meaning of terms, formulae and machines.

In every state $\mathfrak{A}$ one can compute for every term t a value if a variable environment ζ is given that has a binding for each individual variable that occurs in the term. This term evaluation follows the inductive definition of terms t, evaluating individual variables x as defined by the variable environment and 0-ary functions c as defined by the state. We skip mentioning ζ where the considered terms are without free variables.

Definition 4 (Interpretation of terms in states). Let $\mathfrak{A}$ be a state and t a term of Σ, ζ a variable environment for $\mathfrak{A}$ that defines for each individual variable of t a value.

- $eval(x, \mathfrak{A}, \zeta) = \zeta(x)$ and $eval(c, \mathfrak{A}, \zeta) = c^{\mathfrak{A}}$
- $eval(f(t_1, \ldots, t_n), \mathfrak{A}, \zeta) = f^{\mathfrak{A}}(eval(t_1, \mathfrak{A}, \zeta), \ldots, eval(t_n, \mathfrak{A}, \zeta))$

We say that in state $\mathfrak{A}$ with variable environment ζ the term t *denotes* ('names') the value $eval(t, \mathfrak{A}, \zeta)$ which is also called the *meaning* of t or its *semantics*. By definition only the subfunction of ζ that binds to every individual variable of t a value influences the interpretation of t, a property we formulate for future reference as a lemma. So the evaluation of the variable-free ground terms t depends only on the interpretation of the state signature and one can write simply $eval(t, \mathfrak{A})$.

Lemma 1 (Coincidence Lemma for Term Evaluation). If ζ and η are two variable environments that coincide over t, i.e. satisfy $\zeta(x) = \eta(x)$ for all variables x of t, then also the evaluations of t with those variable environments coincide, i.e. yield the same result $eval(t, \mathfrak{A}, \zeta) = eval(t, \mathfrak{A}, \eta)$.

1.2 State Properties (Syntax and Semantics of Statements)

We definitely want to use any standard mathematical expressions that help to describe the analysis of the behaviour of a computational system, but to formulate the conditions by which typically the execution of any algorithmic action in a state is triggered we need only formulae of predicate logic which we review in this section. As with terms one has to define the syntax and the semantics of formulae.

Since we treat properties and relations by their characteristic functions the only atomic formulae we need to consider are equations between terms. Starting with them arbitrary formulae are syntactically constructed using boolean connectives and quantifiers.

Definition 5 (Formula). Let Σ be a signature. The *formulae* over Σ are constructed inductively:

- Every equation $s = t$ between terms s and t over Σ is a formula, also called an atomic formula.
- Every Boolean composition of formulae φ, ψ is a formula. Boolean compositions are negations **not** (φ), conjunctions $(\varphi$ **and** $\psi)$, disjunctions $(\varphi$ **or** $\psi)$, equivalences $(\varphi$ **iff** $\psi)$, etc.
- The universal and existential quantifications **forall** $x\,(\varphi)$ and **forsome** $x\,(\varphi)$ are formulas if φ is a formula and x an individual variable.

For writing formulae we use the usual notational conventions, in particular when omitting parentheses for better readability. $s \neq t$ stands for **not** $(s = t)$. As usual an individual variable x is called *bound* by the quantifier in a quantification **forall** $x\,(\varphi)$ or **forsome** $x\,(\varphi)$ and its *scope* is the formula φ.

An occurrence of an individual variable x is *free* in a formula if it is not in the scope of a quantifier **forall** x or **forsome** x. By $\varphi(x/t)$ or if x is clear from context $\varphi(t)$ (*substitution*) we denote the result of replacing all free occurrences of the individual variable x in φ by the term t; individual variables that are bound in φ but also occur in t are assumed to be renamed by fresh individual variables.

The interpretation of terms in a state with respect to a variable environment can be extended to formulae, resulting in a truth value that indicates whether what the formula asserts is true in the given state or false. The names of the logical connectives and quantifiers refer to their usual meaning that is used for the evaluation of formulae where the equality sign is interpreted as identity.

Definition 6 (Interpretation of Formulae). Let $\mathfrak{A}$ be a state and φ a formula of Σ and ζ a variable environment that defines a value for every individual variable with some free occurence in φ. By induction on φ we define:

$$eval(s = t, \mathfrak{A}, \zeta) = \begin{cases} true \ \text{ if } eval(s, \mathfrak{A}, \zeta) = eval(t, \mathfrak{A}, \zeta) \\ false \qquad\qquad\qquad\qquad otherwise \end{cases}$$

$$eval(\textbf{not } \varphi, \mathfrak{A}, \zeta) = \begin{cases} true \ \text{ if } eval(\varphi, \mathfrak{A}, \zeta) = false \\ false \qquad\qquad\qquad otherwise \end{cases}$$

$$eval(\varphi \textbf{ and } \psi, \mathfrak{A}, \zeta) = \begin{cases} true \ \text{ if } eval(\varphi, \mathfrak{A}, \zeta) = eval(\psi, \mathfrak{A}, \zeta) = true \\ false \qquad\qquad\qquad\qquad\qquad\qquad otherwise \end{cases}$$

$$eval(\textbf{forall } x\, \varphi, \mathfrak{A}, \zeta) = \begin{cases} true \ \text{ if } eval(\varphi, \mathfrak{A}, \zeta[x \mapsto a]) = true \\ \qquad\qquad\qquad for\ every\, a \in |\mathfrak{A}| \\ false \qquad\qquad\qquad\qquad otherwise \end{cases}$$

etc. as usual

Note that for conceptual economy we use the same name *eval* for the two functions that evaluate terms respectively formulae and thus are distinguished by the type of their arguments. Remember that relations and predicates are treated as functions so that the only atomic formulae we consider are equations. By the preceding definition in every state every formula built up from equations is either true or false. If in a state $\mathfrak{A}$ a formula φ evaluates to true for all variable environments ζ (for φ), this state $\mathfrak{A}$ is called a *model* of φ. As for terms also the interpretation of a formula φ depends only on a subset of any variable environment ζ, namely the values of ζ for the individual variables that have some free occurence in φ. For further reference we formulate this property as a lemma.

Lemma 2 (Coincidence Lemma for Formula Evaluation). If ζ and η are two variable environments for φ that coincide over φ, i.e. satisfy $\zeta(x) = \eta(x)$ for all individual variables x with some free occurence in φ, then also the evaluations of φ with those variable environments coincide, i.e. yield the same result $eval(\varphi, \mathfrak{A}, \zeta) = eval(\varphi, \mathfrak{A}, \eta)$.

For further reference we also formulate here as a lemma that the meaning of any formula φ where an individual variable x has been substituted by a term t can also be obtained by changing the variable environment for the evaluation of the formula to assign the meaning of t to x.

Lemma 3 (Substitution Lemma). Formula evaluation treats variable substitution by terms as variable environment change. To express this more precisely, let $a = eval(t, \mathfrak{A}, \zeta)$. Then

$$eval(\varphi(x/t), \mathfrak{A}, \zeta) = eval(\varphi, \mathfrak{A}, \zeta[x \mapsto a]).$$

Given the above lemma, we will also write $\varphi[x \mapsto t]$ for $\varphi(x/t)$.

Chapter 2
Logical Structure of State-Change Actions

In this chapter we define an abstract form of elementary state-change actions that can be instantiated to describe in a direct, encoding-free manner any concrete **atomic computational step**, at whatever level of abstraction. In Sect. 2.1 we define the underlying **logical memory structure** of states, namely by sets of locations (i.e. function table entries), and classify the interaction type of locations and functions. In Sect. 2.2 we define a generic form of elementary state-change by **updates of locations** via abstract assignments. Iteration of such steps yields a general concept of single-agent computations we investigate further in Ch. 3. In Sect. 2.3 we provide some simple examples how to tailor atomic computational steps to specific abstraction goals, including the important action of increasing the workspace.[1]

2.1 Logical Memory Structure (Locations and Updates)

We consider computational states as Tarski structures, i.e. finite sets of function tables (Def. 2, pg. 10), an abstract form of memory: every function table entry represents a location (Def. 7, pg. 18) where the value of the function for that entry is stored. We explain in this section how every state change (Def. 10), at whatever level of abstraction[2], can be uniformly described by updates (Def. 8) whose application changes the values of the involved locations (Def. 9).

The methodological role of locations and updates. The two crucial contributions of the concept of abstract memory locations are abstraction and localization. The content of locations are data of whatever desired type and can be changed directly (i.e. without any encoding) by operations of what-

---

[1] The reader who knows the concept of ASMs may proceed directly to Sect. 2.3.2 where we explain a constructive Workspace Increase Operation we will use in later chapters of the book.

[2] This will be further expanded upon in Sect. 4.1.

© The Author(s), under exclusive license to Springer Nature Switzerland AG 2024
E. Börger, V. Gervasi, *Structures of Computing*,
https://doi.org/10.1007/978-3-031-54358-6_2

ever appropriate type; this data and operation *abstraction* that is provided by the definition of locations strips away any implementation details that are irrelevant at the involved level of abstraction. By *localization* one can identify the locations at the heart of the algorithmic state where it all happens, stripping away any parts of a state that are irrelevant for a computational step; locations offer to define and analyze any algorithmic step focussing on those and only those data and operations that are relevant for the intended effect of the step. The concept of abstract memory locations offers a tool to realize the major concern of *conceptual modeling*:[3]

> provide the right set of modeling constructs at the right level of abstraction.

The important issue here is not whether a description is *declarative* (i.e. equational or axiomatic) or *operational*[4] but at which level of abstraction it is given, using updates that directly represent the state change action, concentrating on the computational aspects of data and updates that are relevant for a mathematical analysis of dynamic behaviour that changes a state.

Definition 7 (Locations). A *location* of a state $\mathfrak{A}$ is a pair $(f, (a_1, \ldots, a_n))$, where f is an n-ary function symbol and $a_1, \ldots, a_n$ are elements of the superuniverse of $\mathfrak{A}$. The value $f^{\mathfrak{A}}(a_1, \ldots, a_n)$ is called the *content* of the location in $\mathfrak{A}$. The elements of the set $\{a_1, \ldots, a_n\}$ are called the *elements* or the *arguments* of the location. Every location $(f, (a_1, \ldots, a_n))$ is called a location for f or an f-location. $Locs(\mathfrak{A})$ denotes the set of locations of $\mathfrak{A}$. For 0-ary dynamic functions c we usually write c for the location $(c, ())$; usually it is clear from the context whether c is meant to denote the location $(c, ())$ or the value $c^{\mathfrak{A}}$ of the function in a given state $\mathfrak{A}$.

This definition offers to view an entire state $\mathfrak{A}$ as a function that maps every location of $\mathfrak{A}$ to its content so that one can write $\mathfrak{A}(l)$ for the content of the location l in $\mathfrak{A}$. Consequently a state change can be described in a simple and uniform way, whatever items are handled by the investigated computations, by modifying this function $\mathfrak{A}(l)$ (and thereby the functions of $\mathfrak{A}$) via updates of the content of some of its locations l to new values.

Definition 8 (Updates). An *update* for a state $\mathfrak{A}$ is a pair (l, v), where l is a location of $\mathfrak{A}$ and v is an element of the superuniverse of $\mathfrak{A}$. We call the update *trivial* if its value v does not change $\mathfrak{A}$, i.e. if v is identical to the content of l in $\mathfrak{A}$. The elements of an update $((f, (a_1, \ldots, a_n)), v)$ are the elements of the set $\{a_1, \ldots, a_n, v\}$. It has become common usage to call a set of updates an *update set*. If an update set contains some updates with different values for a same location we say that these updates *clash* and that

---

[3] Quoted from https://conceptualmodeling.org

[4] Although we share the experience that the "...idea of describing behavior in terms of mathematical equations works well...where the behavior is fairly simple, it almost inevitably fails whenever the behavior is more complex"[167, pg.3].

the set is *inconsistent* (because it does not determine in an unambiguous way how to change $\mathfrak{A}$); otherwise it is called *consistent*. By *Locs*(U) for an update set U we denote the set of locations in U.

If an update set U is consistent, it describes in a precise way how to change the given state $\mathfrak{A}$. The application of U (we also say to fire U) results in a unique new state we denote by $\mathfrak{A} + U$.

In the new state, the interpretations of those and only those function symbols which appear in *Locs*(U) may be changed.

Definition 9 (Application of updates). The result of applying a consistent update set U to a state $\mathfrak{A}$ is a new state $\mathfrak{A} + U$ with the same superuniverse as $\mathfrak{A}$ such that for every location l of $\mathfrak{A}$

$$(\mathfrak{A} + U)(l) = \begin{cases} v & \text{if } (l, v) \in U \\ \mathfrak{A}(l) & \text{otherwise} \end{cases}$$

$\mathfrak{A} + U$ is called the *sequel* (or *successor state* or *next state*) of $\mathfrak{A}$ with respect to U. If U is inconsistent $\mathfrak{A} + U$ is not defined.

The generality of the concept of state change as application of update sets results also from the following observation that justifies the concept of difference of two states.

Definition 10 (Difference of states). Let $\mathfrak{A}$ and $\mathfrak{B}$ be two states with the same superuniverse and signature. Then $\mathfrak{B}$ can be obtained from $\mathfrak{A}$ by replacing all $\mathfrak{A}$-values $\mathfrak{A}(l)$ that differ from the $\mathfrak{B}$-values $\mathfrak{B}(l)$ by those $\mathfrak{B}$-values $\mathfrak{B}(l)$, in other words by applying to $\mathfrak{A}$ the set of all updates with value $\mathfrak{B}(l)$ that differs from the value $\mathfrak{A}(l)$. This update set $\{(l, \mathfrak{B}(l)) \mid \mathfrak{B}(l) \neq \mathfrak{A}(l)\}$ is called the *difference* of $\mathfrak{B}$ and $\mathfrak{A}$ and written as $\mathfrak{B} - \mathfrak{A}$. By definition $\mathfrak{B} - \mathfrak{A}$ is consistent and $\mathfrak{A} + (\mathfrak{B} - \mathfrak{A}) = \mathfrak{B}$ holds.

Remark on isomorphisms. The definition of updates of memory locations captures the logical structure of state change actions and can be used to uniformly describe state changes at whatever level of abstraction, independently of the specific type of functions and location contents in a state. Furthermore, in a state as defined in Def. 2 (pg. 10) the internal representation of the elements of its superuniverse should play no role, only the functions than can be applied to the elements should count. This can be technically expressed by the algebraic concept of isomorphism. Two *states* $\mathfrak{A}$ and $\mathfrak{B}$ with the same signature are called *isomorphic* if their superuniverses can be mapped to each other one-to-one (say by a function α) in such a way that the interpretations of the functions agree on corresponding elements. This means that for every location $l = (f, (a_1, \ldots, a_n))$ of $\mathfrak{A}$ its content $\mathfrak{A}(l)$ is mapped to the content that $\mathfrak{B}$ assigns to the corresponding location $(f, (b_1, \ldots, b_n))$ (where a_i is mapped by α to b_i). This *homomorphy* condition—first mapping and then interpreting yields the same result as first interpreting and then mapping—is expressed and visualized by the following commutative diagram:

$$(f, args) \overset{\alpha}{\Longrightarrow} (f, \alpha(args)) \qquad \textbf{forall } l \in Locs(\mathfrak{A}) \text{ holds}$$
$$\Downarrow \mathfrak{A} \qquad\qquad \Downarrow \mathfrak{B} \qquad\qquad \alpha(\mathfrak{A}(l)) = \mathfrak{B}(\alpha(l))$$
$$f^{\mathfrak{A}}(args) \overset{\alpha}{\Longrightarrow} f^{\mathfrak{B}}(args)$$

Homomorphisms are extended to locations $loc = (f, (a_1, \ldots, a_n))$ and update sets U by $\alpha(loc) = (f, (\alpha(a_1), \ldots, \alpha(a_n)))$ and $\alpha(U) = \{(\alpha(l), \alpha(v)) \mid (l, v) \in U\}$.

It is reasonable to identify isomorphic states $\mathfrak{A}$ and $\mathfrak{B}$ because every isomorphic mapping between them maps every consistent update set U of $\mathfrak{A}$ to a consistent update set U' of $\mathfrak{B}$ and establishes also an isomorphism between the corresponding successor states $\mathfrak{A} + U$ and $\mathfrak{B} + U'$.

Exercise 1 (Homomorphic Term Value Preservation). Show by induction on terms that every homomorphism α from a state $\mathfrak{A}$ to a state $\mathfrak{B}$ preserves the value of terms t in the sense that $\alpha(eval(t, \mathfrak{A}, \zeta)) = eval(t, \mathfrak{B}, \alpha \circ \zeta)$ holds, where $\alpha \circ \zeta$ denotes the binding of variables x defined in ζ to $\alpha(\zeta(x))$. For ground terms this implies $\alpha(eval(t, \mathfrak{A})) = eval(t, \mathfrak{B})$.

Exercise 2 (Isomorphic State Updates). Check your understanding of update sets and isomorphic states by proving that every isomorphism α between two states $\mathfrak{A}, \mathfrak{B}$ is also an isomophism between the updated states $\mathfrak{A} + U, \mathfrak{B} + \alpha(U)$ for every consistent update set U for $\mathfrak{A}$. For a proof see [58, Lemma 2.4.2].

2.1.1 Interaction Type of Functions and Locations

A practical approach to system analysis and design has to provide means to reflect the important principles of separation of concerns, modularization, information hiding, abstraction and stepwise refinement. The view of states as sets of functions or memory locations allows us to analyze the different roles played by the functions which appear during the evaluation of terms $f(t_1, \ldots, t_n)$ in a given state. Some function may be specifiable independently of the considered computations, e.g. background functions the given algorithm may use in some step but never modify, or input functions the algorithm can only read. Some functions may be accessible for read/write actions only of the considered algorithm and nowhere else in its environment. In this section we define the *interaction type* of functions and locations which classifies their computational role. This interaction type is defined with respect to an algorithm or program M an agent executes and is illustrated by Fig. 2.1.

- A *static* function is defined independently of any computation (of M) so that its argument/value relation does not depend on any states (of M) and therefore never changes during any run (of M). Examples are mathematical functions like addition, multiplication, etc. The definition and

analysis of static functions can be separated from the description of the
system dynamics and may exploit different techniques, depending on the
degree of information-hiding the specifier wants to realize, e.g. explicit or
recursive definitions, abstract specifications using axiomatic constraints,
definitions by a separate program, etc.

- A *dynamic* function may change its argument/value relation as a consequence of some computational action (of M or of any other program-
  equipped agent in the considered computational context). In other words
  the function's argument/value pairs may depend on the computational
  states (of M). Dynamic functions generalize array variables. For dynamic
  0-ary functions c we often identify notationally their name c with their
  interpretation $c^{\mathfrak{A}}$ in a state $\mathfrak{A}$ if the context makes clear what is meant.
- A *controlled* function of M is a dynamic function that can be accessed in
  the considered computational context where M is executed only for read
  and function-changing write actions of M. Controlled functions represent
  the part of the states that is internally and exclusively controlled by M.
- A *monitored* function for M is a dynamic function than can be read
  but not changed by actions of M and is directly updatable only by the
  computational environment of M (e.g. an input device or other program
  executing agents).
- An *output* function (also called *out* function) for M is a dynamic function
  that can be changed but not read by actions of M and is monitored by the
  computational environment of M (e.g. an output device or other program
  executing agents).

Fig. 2.1 Interaction type of functions.
© 2003 Springer-Verlag GmbH Berlin Heidelberg, reprinted with permission

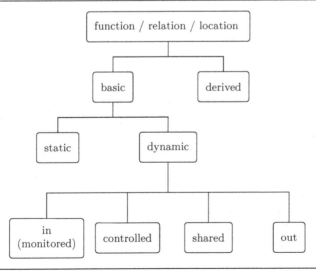

- A *shared* function is a dynamic function that can be read and changed by multiple executing agents. To guarantee the consistency of simultaneous function changes by different agents appropriate interaction (communication) protocols are needed. This helps if one wants to separate internal computation concerns from communication concerns.

This classification of functions extends naturally to the corresponding locations and function symbols. We call functions *external* for M if they are either static or monitored for M. We call shared and input/output functions also *interaction* functions.

For pragmatic reasons we also distinguish *basic* and *derived* functions. Derived functions are dynamic but come with a fixed definition—e.g. by an equation, an abstract specification, a separate algorithm—in terms of other static and/or dynamic functions (read: with an implicit state parameter) so that they are not monitored and cannot be changed but can be read by the considered computational agent. Derived functions are often used to separately describe the behaviour of some system component. Often they are part of what is called the background of sets and functions that can be used to perform state change actions but cannot be modified themselves.

Example 3 (Interaction Type of Mealy Automaton Functions). In Example 2 (pg. 12) *write*, *nextCtl*, $+1$, *CtlState*, *Nat*, *InAlphabet*, *OutAlphabet* are static; *ctl* and *head* are controlled. Furthermore, the set *InAlphabet** of input words is derived (in fact, it is derived from *InAlphabet*, and since the latter is static, *InAlphabet** is also static). The *tape* function is shared with the environment that generates the input (read: the initial *tape* with blank squares except those with letters from *InAlphat*) and receives the output (the non-blank part of the *tape* when the automaton has read all its input.

2.2 Logical Structure of One-Step Actions

We begin the section with a naming convention.

Definition 11. We call an algorithmic process a single-agent process if its execution involves only one agent (not counting the environment); otherwise we speak of multi-agent (interacting) processes we analyze in Ch. 5. The program of a single-agent process is called a single-agent program.

In this section we describe the syntax and the semantics of three 'elementary state-change actions' agents execute in their single steps.[5] The definition comes in a computer and programming language independent abstract form.

---

[5] We say 'execution by a single agent' to distinguish different instances of the same process as executed by different agents with the same process but possibly different data.

It includes the beneficial *simultaneous (synchronous parallel) execution of atomic-step actions* that are independent of each other. This avoids any unnecessary sequentialization of single-step actions in single-agent programs. As a consequence the scheme we define in Def. 12 mentions no sequential control construct.

2.2.1 Single-Agent Algorithmic Steps: Syntax

The view of states as sets of functions or memory locations implies that every single computation step that changes a given state turns out to consist of changing some functions of the state, in practice by changing in one blow the value of some (in practice finitely many) of its memory locations. The standard semantics defined below for an

assignment instruction: $f(t_1, \ldots, t_n) := t$

with any (unless otherwise stated ground) terms t_i, t directly describes the effect of such updates of memory locations $(f, (eval(t_1, \mathfrak{A}, \zeta), \ldots, eval(t_n, \mathfrak{A}, \zeta))$ by $eval(t, \mathfrak{A}, \zeta)$ in states $\mathfrak{A}$ with given variable environment ζ. It is the abstract nature of the terms in an assignment that permits to work directly, without encoding, on arbitrary locations and their contents. Assignment instructions are usually simply called assignments; they represent the elementary state-changing components of structured algorithmic processes that are executed by a single agent.

A basic algorithmic control structure allows one to restrict the execution of an algorithmic process P to states which satisfy a *cond*ition (called a 'guard' of P). The resulting single-agent process (or instruction or program) is called

conditional process: **if** *cond* **then** P

(or guarded process, instruction, program) where *cond* is a logical (unless otherwise stated quantifier-free) formula (Def. 5, pg. 14).

Often various subprocesses P_i of an algorithmic process are independent of each other so that they can be executed in any order without changing the overall behaviour. In such cases it is often convenient to think of these processes as executed simultaneously, in parallel, in one step, by one agent.[6] The resulting process is called a

parallel process: **par** $(P_1, \ldots, P_n)$

or parallel instruction or program.

---

[6] Note that Turing in his epochal paper [162] considered some possible parallelism in a step (called 'move') of his machines from one to the next state (called 'complete configuration'), namely printing, shifting the scanned square to the right/left, and changing the control state (called 'm-configuration').

Definition 12 (Parallel Guarded Assignments). We define *Parallel Guarded Assignment* rules (abbreviated PGA rules or simply PGAs) by induction:

- Every assignment instruction is a PGA rule.
- If P is a PGA rule and *cond* is a quantifier free formula, then also **if** *cond* **then** P is a PGA rule.
- If $P_1, \ldots, P_n$ are PGA rules, then also **par** $(P_1, \ldots, P_n)$ is a PGA rule.

By **PGA** we denote the class of PGA programs.

Each PGA is a restricted form of what in the literature is called an Abstract State Machine (ASM) [58, 50]. We use here the acronym PGA to draw the attention on the three underlying computational core concepts and to distinguish PGAs from the more general ASMs. Abstract State Machines extend PGAs by further computational constructs that are widely used in system design and analysis and exploited in the following chapters of this book. The particular role of PGAs results from a practical experience that eventually became also supported by a theorem:

- A great variety of experiments with well-known, real-world, single-agent sequential computational systems produced the practical experience that such sequential systems can be faithfully modeled, simulated, analyzed and refined to code by specific PGAs. A similar experience has been made with PGAs as sequential components of concurrent systems. For a survey see [58, Ch. 7,9] and https://abz-conf.org/method/asm.
- A theorem we explain in Sect. 8.1 proves that *every* computational process that satisfies three natural postulates for sequential algorithms is in a strong sense computationally equivalent to a PGA.[7]

Terminology and notation. Every PGA can be written in the following theoretically interesting normal form (see the proof of Theorem 7, pg. 200).

Definition 13 (PGA Normal Form).

$$\textbf{if } \varphi_1 \textbf{ then } f_1(s_{1,1}, \ldots, s_{1,n_1}) := t_1$$

$$\vdots$$

$$\textbf{if } \varphi_k \textbf{ then } f_k(s_{k,1}, \ldots, s_{k,n_k}) := t_k$$

where the terms are ground terms and the guards φ_i are boolean combinations of equations between ground terms. The vertical notation hides the **par** operator and indicates the intended simultaneous (synchronous parallel) execution of the horizontally displayed rules (here guarded assignments) in each step.

---

[7] Due to this theorem, in the literature PGAs are somehow misleadingly called 'sequential ASMs' (Gurevich's wording in [93]). But the reader will see below that a) there are forms of sequential algorithms that are not captured by the three postulates of the theorem (Ch. 4), and b) not every PGA is a sequential algorithm in the intuitive understanding of the term (Sect. 3.1.1 and Sect. 8.2).

Sometimes it is technically useful to have a name for a process that performs an empty step. For this purpose we use a special PGA rule **skip**.

The intuitive understanding of PGAs (and generally of ASMs) as pseudocode is supported by their rigorous semantics defined below (Sect. 2.2.2, pg. 31). Therefore we use throughout and without further ado commonly used notational variations and extensions, as long as their meaning is clear and can be expressed by precisely defined core constructs.

For example, if an ASM (for example a PGA) M contains two rules **if** φ **then** M_1 and **if not** φ **then** M_2 we write them also in the shorter form:

if φ **then** M_1 **else** M_2

and call this again a conditional ASM respectively PGA rule. Similarly, we write:

    case exp **of**
      $value_1 \rightarrow rule_1$
      $\vdots$
      $value_n \rightarrow rule_n$

to stand for

    if $exp = value_1$ **then** $rule_1$
      else if ...
      $\vdots$
        else if $exp = value_n$ **then** $rule_n$

There are other kinds of basic algorithmic concepts and corresponding ASM constructs that extend PGAs, in particular call mechanisms (call by value and call by name, see Sect. 2.3.1) to support modular algorithmic structure and two fundamental logical operations (quantification and choice, see Sect. 3.5 and Sect. 3.4). But when it is clear from the context or it does not matter which kind of ASM is considered we use the term ASM rule instead of a more specific name, like PGA rule. An ASM rule is also called *transition rule* or simply ASM although an ASM besides its rule comes with additional features like its signature with interaction type definition, an input/output management for initial/final states, etc. (see Ch. 3). The signature of M contains (and unless otherwise stated is understood to be) the set of all function symbols that occur in a rule of M. For parsimony of names we usually use the same name for an ASM and for any of its instances obtained by different signature interpretations (and possibly associated to different agents when it comes to execution).

To simplify the understanding of rules we often use **where** clauses to separate the specification of particular constraints we impose on some terms that are used in a rule.

We illustrate the definition of PGAs by two well-known examples of sequential algorithmic processes, namely Mealy automata (with the Finite State

Machines variation) and Turing machines. Their control structure suggests a generalization to the class of control state ASMs. Although we define the semantics of PGAs only in the next Sect. 2.2.2, the reader will nevertheless understand the intended meaning of the rules below by reading them as pseudo-code (reading that provides the correct understanding).

Example 4. **Mealy Automata Interpreter**. Example 2 (pg. 12) states in natural language what a Mealy automaton is requested to do in one step; this is formally expressed by the following PGA rule. We indicate some auxiliary functions as parameters of the rule name so that one can define variations of the machine simply by refining (read: specifying furthermore or imposing additional constraints on) those parameters. Remember that for a Mealy automaton +1 as specified in Example 2 is the *right-move* function.

> MEALYAUTOMATON(*write*, *nextCtl*) =
>   *tape*(*head*) := *write*(*ctl*, *tape*(*head*))   -- output function λ
>   *ctl* := *nextCtl*(*ctl*, *tape*(*head*))   -- internal state transition function δ
>   **shift** *head* **to** *right*   -- only one move direction
> **where**
>   **shift** *head* **to** *right* = (*head* := *head* + 1)

This Mealy automaton rule is an abstract Mealy automaton interpreter: once a concrete Mealy automaton program $pgm = write \times nextCtl$ and input *tape* are given, together with an initial value for the *head* position (say 0) and for *ctl*, the interpreter executes for this input the steps required by *pgm*. The abstract Mealy automaton PGA rule stands for the infinite set of all its Mealy automaton instances obtained by instantiating *write* and *nextCtl* by concrete finite functions.

Exercise 3. **A Finite State Machine** (FSM) is a Mealy automaton without output behavior. The variant of a two-way FSM (which is computationally equivalent to one-way FSMs, see [140]) can move its reading *head* to the right or left on the tape, depending on current control state and input symbol. What has to be changed in the above definition of the MEALYAUTOMATON and its signature to refine it to a (two-way) FSM?

Example 5. **Turing Machine Interpreter**. In Sect. 8.1-8.2 we explain the epochal character, for the whole of computer science, of the definition Turing gave of his machines [162]. Here we use them to show how they can be defined by slightly refining the definition given for Mealy automata (which were defined two decades later). In fact, there is a technically rather thin though conceptually crucial line that separates Turing machines (TMs) from Mealy automata. TMs and Mealy automata share the same control structure: the first two rules of MEALYAUTOMATON are the same for the TURINGMACHINE. However, Mealy machines have only one *moveDirection*, namely to move on the tape at every step to the right, and thus can only examine each input symbol once and never re-read what has been written. In contrast, TMs have an additional *moveDirection* *left* that is determined by the current *ctl* and *tape(head)*. As a consequence, *InAlphabet* and *OutAlphabet* collapse into a single set *Alphabet*. To this end, we extend the set of *moveDirec*tions by:

$$moveDir(ctl, tape(head)) \in \{right, left\}$$

Then we can define:

> TURINGMACHINE(*write*, *nextCtl*, *move*) =
>   *tape(head)* := *write(ctl, tape(head))*   -- as for MEALYAUTOMATON
>   *ctl* := *nextCtl(ctl, tape(head))*   -- as for MEALYAUTOMATON
>   **shift** *head* **to** *moveDir(ctl, tape(head))* -- move in indicated direction
> **where**
>   **shift** *head* **to** *right* = (*head* := *head* + 1)
>   **shift** *head* **to** *left* = (*head* := *head* − 1)

In this rule it is crucial that the three updates are executed simultaneously (in parallel), in one machine step, sharing the same values for *ctl*, *head*, *tape(head)* before their updates. Note that we define TM programs by the three static functions *write*, *moveDirec*tion, *nextCtl*.

Look-Compute-Action Pattern. TM instructions incorporate a cycle of three basic sequentially executed actions, namely:

- **Look** up for the values of the state and the environment parameters that are needed to perform the next step, here: read *ctl* and *tape(head)*,
- **Compute** the values of the terms that determine the to-be-executed action, using the parameter values read in the preceding step, here: perform a program table look up to find the to-be-printed letter *b*, the to-be-performed move *m(head)* of the reading head and the to-be-entered next *ctl* state *j*,
- **Action**: perform as last step of the cycle the required proper action with the computed term values, here: perform the three assignments in the rule TURINGMACHINE above.

Instances of this computational Look-Compute-Action pattern (also called Read-Compute-Write pattern) appear in numerous (classes of) algorithms. Prominently the atomic view of ASM steps incorporates this pattern, as becomes visible in the sequential implementation of concurrent ASM steps in Fig. 5.1 (pg. 115). For other examples of the pattern see cellular automata (pg. 69), streaming algorithms (Fig. 6.2 on pg. 156), and Look-Compute-Move algorithms (Sect. 9.2.2).

Exercise 4 (2-dimensional TM). What is needed to extend the TM-interpreter to interpret 2-dimensional Turing Machines? See Appendix B.

Control state ASMs. The control structure of Turing machines underlies a large number of algorithmic processes and is widely used in connection with FSMs and their flowchart visualization. For high-level system design it is useful to raise the level of abstraction from an FSM-notation to an abstract machine notation so that a complex machine M can be composed out of separately specifiable, implementable, testable and verifiable component submachines M_i, one per mode or phase i. Such a modular structure is easily realized by the concept of *control state ASMs*, machines where every component machine M_i splits again into separate guarded submachines, i.e. each one of the following form visualized by the Control State Diagram in Fig. 2.2 (with $i, j_1, \ldots, j_n$ denoting control states and assuming for consistency reasons that the rule guards $cond_j$ are pairwise disjoint)[8] :

> **if** $ctl = i$ **then**
>> **if** $cond_1$ **then**
>>> $rule_1$
>>> $ctl := j_1$
>>
>> $\ldots$
>>
>> **if** $cond_n$ **then**
>>> $rule_n$
>>> $ctl := j_n$

Fig. 2.2 Control State ASM Diagram.
© 2003 Springer-Verlag GmbH Berlin Heidelberg, reprinted with permission

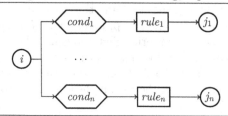

The degree of possible interaction of the guarded submachines of M_i can be controlled by specifying the interaction types of the functions and locations they use. The guarded submachines are often textually written as follows:[9]

> $FSM(i, \textbf{if } cond \textbf{ then } rule, j) =$
>> **if** $ctl = i$ **and** $cond$ **then**
>>> $rule$
>>> $ctl := j$

---

[8] Sometimes instead of pairwise disjoint guards a sequential order is imposed so that each time the first (in the given order) subrule with true guard is executed. An example is the semantics of **if** B_1 $S_1 \ldots B_n$ S_n statements in the programming language Occam [69]: the guards are evaluated in the order $B_1, B_2, \ldots$ in which they appear in the statement and for the first B_i that evaluates to *true* the substatement S_i is executed.

[9] The reader who would like to see a precise mathematical (metamodel) definition of the class of Control State Diagrams (CSD) and a compilation of CSDs to ASMs that define their semantics may consult [50, Ch. 9].

A control state ASM can equivalently be written in the form of a PGA if the component machines *rule_j* are equivalent to PGAs. But the definition works well also for generic ASMs.

Example 6. **Control structure of a transaction operator.**
We illustrate the decomposition potential of control state ASMs by a non-trivial example from transaction control design; to understand the interaction of the given machine M with the transaction control components it should suffice if the reader has some rough idea about the concept of transactional control. In [56] an abstract (programming language independent) transaction controller TACTL is defined together with an operator TA which applied to a family of programs enables them to realize a transactional behaviour in concurrent runs together with TACTL. The transactional control behaviour that results from the application of the operator TA to a program M of the given family appears as control state computation specified in Fig. 2.3: M tamed by TA calls separately specifiable and analyzable (here not further described) components of TACTL for assistance to guarantee that when M FIRES a step (or a sequence of steps) that computation segment is transactional.

Fig. 2.3 Transaction Control Structure of TA(M) (M transformed by TA)

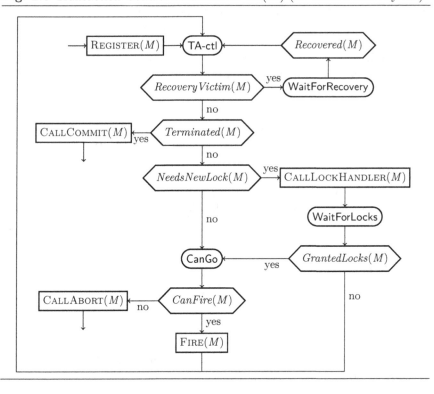

We now explain the control state ASM defined by Fig. 2.3, assuming a rough understanding of the behavior of the diagram components. The diagram shows that once a program M is REGISTEREd with the transaction controller TACTL, its steps are constrained by a series of transactional conditions inserted by the transaction operator TA and to be satisfied by calling the corresponding TACTL components:

- If M has been 'victimized' by the DEADLOCKHANDLER component (which we do not furthermore specify here), then it must wait until the RECOVERY component resolves the deadlock and makes M *Recovered*. The RECOVERY component essentially backtracks some deadlocked programs. Both RECOVERY and DEADLOCKHANDLER are independently definable components that do not appear in the diagram, but their interaction with M behaviour becomes visible in the checks whether M became a *RecoveryVictim* respectively has been *Recovered*.
- If M has *Terminated* its current transactional computation segment— the success case—it calls the COMMIT component, thus completing the current transactional computation segment.
- If M to FIRE its next step needs locks (on shared, monitored or output locations it wants to access) it calls the LOCKHANDLER and can proceed from there only when the LOCKHANDLER has *GrantedLocks* for M.
- If M needs no locks or has been *GrantedLocks* to FIRE its next step but a failure occurred, then M calls the ABORT component to end the failed transactional segment of computation.
- When M does FIRE a step it also executes a RECOVERYRECORDing program (inserted into M by the TA operator) which enables UNDOing the current step upon a RECOVERY step by TACTL.

The interaction structure of the components with the TA-transformed machine M is completely defined by the control state ASM in Fig. 2.3 and permits to specify and analyze those components independently of each other in terms of their behaviour in reaction to input from or output to other components.

For the sake of completeness we define here the component structure of TACTL and refer the reader for their detailed definition and the correctness statement and proof for TACTL to [56].

TACTL =
    LOCKHANDLER
    COMMIT
    ABORT
    DEADLOCKHANDLER
    RECOVERY

Example 7. **Structured Iterated Control State ASMs.** An interesting class of control state ASMs consists of those one can compose in a

Fig. 2.4 Structured Iterated Control State ASM (**while** *Cond M*)

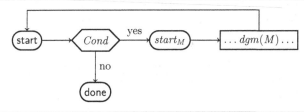

structured way out of flowchart diagrams $dgm(M)$ for basic FSM-like rules $M = \text{FSM}(i, \textbf{if } cond \textbf{ then } rule, j)$ (see Fig. 2.2, pg. 28).

In such diagrams every transition from a current control state i to a successor control state j is considered as one internal machine step, after which the environment can make a step before the next rule is fired in control state j, leading to a next current control state, etc. We illustrate this by Fig. 2.4 where it is assumed that the already defined structured flowchart diagram $dgm(M)$ of M has exactly one initial control state $start_M$ and that each of its final control states (i.e. not connected to any control state in $dgm(M)$) is connected to the initial control state $start$ of the while construct. This constraint catches jumps that would lead out of M and leads them to the initial state of the iteration machine. Such a governed goto-discipline, as is found in various programming languages, helps to avoid what are called spaghetti control structures. To forbid gotos tout court appears as an exaggeration.

Exercise 5 (Register Machine Interpreter). Check your understanding of the above interpreter rules for Mealy automata, Turing machines and control state ASMs by writing a control state ASM which interprets register machines. A *register machine* (RM) M has a finite number of registers r_j to store arbitrary natural numbers and has a program of two kinds of labeled instructions (say labeled by natural numbers): $(i, j, op, i+1)$ (in control state i perform operation op on register r_j and go to the next control state $i + 1$, where $op \in \{+1, -1\}$) and $(i, j, test, l)$ (in control state i test whether the value of r_j is 0: if it is, go to control state l, else go to control state $i + 1$). For a solution see Appendix B.

Exercise 6. Write a control state ASM (e.g. with 2 control states *halting,moving*) for a lift control program. For a solution see [58, Sect. 2.3].

2.2.2 Single-Agent Algorithmic Steps: Semantics

In this section we define the effect—also called the behavioural meaning or the semantics—of the three PGA steps. We formulate the definition in a way that applies also to extensions of PGAs to ASMs with additional one-step actions. Such a generic notion of atomic steps that are executed repeatedly by single-agent algorithmic processes forms the basis for the concept of various (single- or multi-agent) algorithmic process runs investigated in Ch. 3-5.

Definition 14 (Semantics of ASM Rules). In a given state $\mathfrak{A}$ with variable environment ζ an ASM rule M in one atomic step computes (we also say yields) an update set $U = eval(M, \mathfrak{A}, \zeta)$ and—if U is consistent—applies it to $\mathfrak{A}$ to obtain the successor state $\mathfrak{B} = \mathfrak{A} + U$ of $\mathfrak{A}$ as defined in Def. 9 (pg. 19). The evaluation of M is defined by induction on the rules, its result is also called the *yield* of M.

- The evaluation of **skip** yields the empty set: $eval(\textbf{skip}, \mathfrak{A}, \zeta) = \emptyset$.
- The evaluation of an assignment instruction yields a 1-element update set for the location corresponding to the evaluated argument with value obtained by evaluating the right-hand side of the assignment instruction:

$$eval(f(t_1, \ldots, t_n) := t, \mathfrak{A}, \zeta) = \{((f, (\overline{t_1}, \ldots, \overline{t_n})), \overline{t})\}$$
$$\textbf{where } \overline{x} = eval(x, \mathfrak{A}, \zeta).$$

Note that for frugal naming we use the same name for the three evaluation functions of terms (Def. 4, pg. 13) and formulae (Def. 6, pg. 15) and here of machines, distinguishing them by the type of their arguments.

- The evaluation of a conditional ASM yields the update set of the component ASM that must be executed depending on whether the condition is true or not:

$$eval(\textbf{if } \varphi \textbf{ then } M \textbf{ else } N, \mathfrak{A}, \zeta) = \begin{cases} \overline{M} & \text{if } \overline{\varphi} = true \\ \overline{N} & \text{otherwise} \end{cases}$$
$$\textbf{where } \overline{x} = eval(x, \mathfrak{A}, \zeta).$$

Note that we treat the conditional guards φ as formulae so that by the interpretation of formulae in Def. 6 (pg. 15) their meaning is always defined (either true or false).

- Simultaneous evaluation of two ASMs yields the union of their update sets:

$$eval(\textbf{par } (M_1, M_2), \mathfrak{A}, \zeta) = eval(M_1, \mathfrak{A}, \zeta) \cup eval(M_2, \mathfrak{A}, \zeta).$$

If $\mathfrak{B} = \mathfrak{A} + eval(M, \mathfrak{A}, \zeta)$ is defined we say that M *can make a move* (or a step) from state $\mathfrak{A}$ (with variable environment ζ) to $\mathfrak{B}$ and write $\mathfrak{A} \xrightarrow{1}_M \mathfrak{B}$ (or $\mathfrak{A} \xrightarrow{1} \mathfrak{B}$ when M and ζ are clear from the context). We also say that M is (or can be) fired in state $\mathfrak{A}$. The updates in $eval(M, \mathfrak{A}, \zeta)$ are called *internal* updates and are distinguished from updates of monitored locations or from updates of shared locations by the environment (read: by other agents, see Def. 22, pg. 40). The state $\mathfrak{B}$ resulting from internal updates is called successor state, value of the partial *step function* $step_M(\mathfrak{A}) = \mathfrak{B}$ of M on its states, also called transition function. When interactive runs are considered, where also the environment may add further changes of monitored or shared locations, successor states are more precisely called next internal states (see below Def. 22 on pg. 40).

Notation. Note that here again we use *eval* as name for an evaluation function, here of machines in a given state. To emphasize that $eval(M, \mathfrak{A})$ yields an update set sometimes also the notation $Upd(M, \mathfrak{A})$ is used. To prepare the ground for non-deterministic ASMs with a **choose** construct (where in a state more than one update set could be generated, see Sect. 3.4) we write $U = eval(M, \mathfrak{A}, \zeta)$ also as a relation $evalCand(M, \mathfrak{A}, \zeta, U)$. In the literature the relation name *yields* is used instead of *evalCand*. Where the variable environment ζ is empty and the successor state $\mathfrak{B} = \mathfrak{A} + U$ is defined, it has become customary to denote a generated update set U with $eval(M, \mathfrak{A}, U)$ as difference set $\Delta(M, \mathfrak{A}) = (\mathfrak{A} + U) - \mathfrak{A}$.[10]

Exercise 7 (Isomorphic Yields). If M yields U in $\mathfrak{A}$ under a variable assignment ζ, then in every isomorphic $\mathfrak{B}$ M yields $\alpha(U)$ under $\alpha \circ \zeta$ where α is the isomorphism from $\mathfrak{A}$ to $\mathfrak{B}$. Prove this statement.

2.3 Domain-Specific One-Step Actions

The general one-step action concept defined in terms of ASMs in Sect. 2.2 provides the foundation for the ASM refinement method described in Sect. 7.2. In fact, to apply in one step a set of assignments $f(t_1, \ldots, t_n) := t$ implies that the computation of every argument term t_i, t is considered as (part of) one step. Here computing a term can represent any domain-specific complex but well-understood action for given arguments. Furthermore, the ASM update concept makes it easy to define specialized one-step actions where their atomic execution is a helpful abstraction in terms of the given application domain. We illustrate this here for two widely used procedure calling mechanisms (by value and by name, Sect. 2.3.1)) and for workspace creation (Sect. 2.3.2). Other examples of useful one-step action constructs are explained in the following chapters.

---

[10] There is an underlying assumption for the Δ notation. Differently from $\Delta(M, \mathfrak{A})$, the update set U computed by M in $\mathfrak{A}$ may contain a *trivial update*, i.e. some (loc, v) where v is the current value of loc in $\mathfrak{A}$. U is inconsistent if it contains also a non-trivial update for the same location, in which case U does not define a successor state $\mathfrak{B}$. If U contains a trivial update without a conflicting non-trivial one, then this trivial update can be disregarded without loss of generality when applying U to generate the (new part of the) successor state.

2.3.1 Call Step (by Value, by Name)

The **let** construct is often used with advantage to compute once the value of some term t and then use this value in different places, without recomputing the term evaluation in each place. Its usual syntactical form is **let** $x = t$ **in** M (where M denotes any ASM) and its semantics as an ASM rule is defined for any variable environment ζ and state $\mathfrak{A}$ as follows:

Definition 15 (Semantics of let Rules (Call by Value)).

$$eval(\textbf{let } x = t \textbf{ in } M, \mathfrak{A}, \zeta) = eval(M, \mathfrak{A}, \zeta[x \to a])$$
$$\textbf{where } a = eval(t, \mathfrak{A}, \zeta)$$

Remark. The rule **let** $x = t$ **in** M is equivalent to $M(x/t)$ only as long as for each occurrence of x in M that is replaced by t the value of t that is associated with this occurrence of x is the same. This property does not necessarily hold.[11]

The **Call by Name** mechanism applies to a rule M that is defined with some individual variable parameters $x_1, \ldots, x_n$ by a rule body N. When M is called with concrete parameters $t_1, \ldots, t_n$, then the defining rule body N is executed with each x_i replaced by the term (not its value) t_i. Those terms are evaluated when they are used in the rule body N to compute an update set, not necessarily in the state where the rule M is called.

Therefore we extend the syntax of ASMs by rules of the form $M(t_1, \ldots, t_n)$ where M (a rule name of arity n) has been defined by a *rule declaration*, an expression of the form

$$M(x_1, \ldots, x_n) = N$$

where N is an ASM rule whose free variables are among the x_i.

Definition 16 (Semantics of Call (by Name) Rules). Let a rule declaration $M(x_1, \ldots, x_n) = N$ be given. To execute a call $M(t_1, \ldots, t_n)$ execute the rule body N with the call parameters:

$$eval(M(t_1, \ldots, t_n), \mathfrak{A}, \zeta) = eval(N(x_1/t_1, \ldots, x_n/t_n), \mathfrak{A}, \zeta)$$

Note that calls $M(t_1, \ldots, t_n)$ represent a notational abbreviation, they can always be equivalently replaced by a copy of the corresponding body instance $N(x_1/t_1, \ldots, x_n/t_n)$. If the terms t_i are static, then first substituting the terms t_i for x_i in M and then evaluating the machine by $eval(M(t_1, \ldots, t_n), \mathfrak{A}, \zeta)$ generates the same update set as the one obtained by first evaluating the terms t_i for an environment extension $\zeta[x_i \to a_i]$ and then evaluating M under the new environment by $eval(M, \mathfrak{A}, \zeta[x_1 \to a_1, \ldots, x_n \to a_n])$ where $a_i = eval(t_i, \mathfrak{A}, \zeta)$.

---

[11] It may fail for example in the presence of a sequencing operator like **seq** (Def. 24, pg. 53).

Remark. The call by name scheme is sometimes used in a more general form that permits location and rule variables besides the individual variables x_i in Def. 16. At times, by abuse of notation, we use the same scheme to express arbitrary text substitution.

2.3.2 Workspace Increase Operation

To describe how algorithmic processes increase their workspace we introduce an infinite static subset of the superuniverse, a *Heap* of elements machines can **import** to increase their workspace. We treat the *Heap* as 0-ary function symbol in Σ but require that it does not appear in rules because it is only used to define the semantics of ASMs with the **import** construct. We also require that for every machine in each of its initial states $\mathfrak{A}$ the *Workspace*($\mathfrak{A}$) and the *Heap* are disjoint.[12] *Workspace*($\mathfrak{A}$) is defined as follows:

Definition 17 (Workspace). In every state $\mathfrak{A}$ *Workspace*($\mathfrak{A}$) contains besides *true*, *false* and *undef* the elements that for some $f \neq Heap$ appear in state $\mathfrak{A}$ as content $f^{\mathfrak{A}}(a_1, \ldots, a_n) \neq undef$ of a location $(f, (a_1, \ldots, a_n))$ or as element a_i of a location $(f, (a_1, \ldots, a_n))$ whose content is not *undef*.

In the presence of parallelism it is reasonable to require for an **import** operation that two or more simultaneous **import**s yield pairwise distinct elements from the *Heap*. Furthermore, the behaviour of a machine that uses an **import** should not depend on which element of *Heap* is imported, otherwise stated it should not depend on permutations of the *Heap*.

A simple way to achieve this[13] is to guarantee that when computing the updates generated by a parallel rule $M = \textbf{par}\ (M_1, M_2)$ (Def. 14, pg. 32) every **import** that occurs in M_1 or M_2 is *eval*uated separately from the others, in whatever order; keeping track of each element that is **import**ed during the *evaluation* of M permits to select upon the next **import** a *free* element from *Heap*, i.e. one that is distinct from those **import**ed before and neither in the current *Workspace* nor in the *range*(ζ) of the current variable environment. This means that for each machine M and state $\mathfrak{A}$ its *evaluation* procedure $eval(M, \mathfrak{A})$ is refined by an additional parameter η (besides ζ) to generate a pair (U, η) of an update set U (as by Def. 14) together with a set η of those *Heap* elements that during this *evaluation* procedure for M have been committed for an **import** operation. This *evaluation* starts with an initially empty import parameter $\eta = \emptyset$ and an empty variable environment parameter ζ (if M is ground). Each time an **import** subrule of M requests

---

[12] *Workspace*($\mathfrak{A}$) and *Heap* are not complement of each other; elements imported from *Heap* are intended to become workspace elements, but by further machine steps they could loose this property. What does hold is the relation *Workspace*($\mathfrak{A}$)$\cup$ *Heap*$\subseteq |\mathfrak{A}|$.

[13] We define here a constructive evaluation procedure that simplifies the **import** management defined in [58, Sect. 2.4.4] as well as its correctness proof.

to import an element we select a free element $a \in Heap$ to *evaluate* M and
add it to the current value of η.

We formulate the **import** operation with the syntax **import** x **do** M.
We define its semantics as generating for every given M with some **import**
subrules an update set together with a set η of elements imported from *Heap*,
starting the *evaluation* procedure of M with an initially empty η and empty
variable environment ζ (if M has no free variables).

Definition 18 (Semantics of ASM import rule). Let an ASM M be
given together with a state $\mathfrak{A}$ and two parameters for a variable environment
ζ respectively a subset $\eta \subseteq Heap$. We define:

$eval(\textbf{import } x \textbf{ do } M, \mathfrak{A}, \zeta, \eta) = eval(M, \mathfrak{A}, \zeta[x \mapsto \alpha], \eta \cup \{\alpha\})$
where   -- select a free element
$\quad \alpha \in Heap \setminus (Workspace(\mathfrak{A}) \cup range(\zeta) \cup \eta)$

The formulation of the semantics of the other PGA rules on pg. 32 is easily adapted. In the rules M for **skip** and assignment η is passed as fourth
argument of the *eval* function and returned unchanged in the generated pair
$eval(M, \mathfrak{A}, \zeta, \eta) = (U, \eta)$ of an update set U and η; analogously, for conditional instructions we have:

$$eval(\textbf{if } Cond \textbf{ then } M, \mathfrak{A}, \zeta, \eta) = \begin{cases} eval(M, \mathfrak{A}, \zeta, \eta) & \textit{if } Cond^{\mathfrak{A}} \\ (\emptyset, \eta) & \textit{otherwise} \end{cases}$$
$\quad \textbf{where } Cond^{\mathfrak{A}} = (eval(Cond, \mathfrak{A}, \zeta) = true)$

A change appears only for **par** (M_1, M_2) rules and the definition of successor
states.

Definition 19 (par semantics with import).

$eval(\textbf{par } (M_1, M_2), \mathfrak{A}, \zeta, \eta) = (U_1 \cup U_2, \eta_2)$
$\quad \textbf{where}$
$\quad\quad (U_1, \eta_1) = eval(M_1, \mathfrak{A}, \zeta, \eta)$
$\quad\quad\quad\quad\quad\quad$ -- first evaluate M_1 adding imports (if any) to η
$\quad\quad (U_2, \eta_2) = eval(M_2, \mathfrak{A}, \zeta, \eta_1)\}$
$\quad\quad\quad\quad\quad\quad$ -- then evaluate M_2 adding imports (if any) to η_1

Definition 20 (Successor state for ASMs with import). For every state
$\mathfrak{A}$ its successor state $\mathfrak{B}$ computed by a ground ASM M with **import** rules is
defined as follows by a refinement of Def. 14, pg. 32. Note that initially (when
the *evaluation* of M starts) there is no imported element and the variable
environment is empty (if M is ground).

$\quad \textbf{if } eval(M, \mathfrak{A}, \emptyset, \emptyset) = (U, \eta) \textbf{ and } Consistent(U)$
$\quad\quad \textbf{then } nextState_M(\mathfrak{A}) = \mathfrak{A} + U$
$\quad\quad \textbf{else } nextState_M(\mathfrak{A}) = undef$

Notational conventions. We define an operator **new** used in the form
let x = **new** (X) **in** M as an alternative notation for **import** x **do** M.

We write **let** $x_1, \ldots, x_n$ = **new** (X) **in** M for

> **let** x_1 = **new** (X) **in**
>
> $\vdots$
>
> > **let** x_n = **new** (X) **in** M

If **new** does not occur in a formula $\alpha(x)$ and x has only free occurrences
in $\alpha(x)$ we write $\alpha(\textbf{new}\ (X))$ for **let** x = **new** (X) **in** $\alpha(x)$.

For conciseness we also write $c :=$ **new** X for **let** x = **new** (X) **in** $c := x$.

With a slight abuse of terminology, we will at times assume that when
a new element is obtained by **new** for a background that is provided with
an algebra of operations, then this new element is initialized so that the
operations can be applied to the new element with sane results. For example, q =**new** $(Queue)$ would initially satisfy $IsEmpty(q)$, $head(q)$ =$undef$,
$size(q) = 0$, etc. This applies in particular to membership in the domain, i.e.
by $char_{Queue}(q) = true$.

We skip mentioning the $eval$-parameters ζ and/or η where they play no
role or where they are clear from the context.

2.4 Core Actions on Structures (Recap)

Given their fundamental character and for an easy reference we recapitulate
here the three core actions (partial operations) on computational structures
in terms of which we characterize in the rest of the book the major computational paradigms for processing abstract states.

$$apply(\mathfrak{A}, U) = \mathfrak{A} + U$$

This partial function applies to any state $\mathfrak{A}$ and any given consistent update set U to compute a new $\mathfrak{B}$. $\mathfrak{A} = \mathfrak{B}$ is possible.
See pg. 19.

$$eval(M, \mathfrak{A}, \zeta)$$

This function computes the update set machines M without
import subrule generate in state $\mathfrak{A}$ with variable environment
ζ. This set may be inconsistent. See pg. 32.

$$step_M(\mathfrak{A}) = apply(\mathfrak{A}, eval(M, \mathfrak{A}))$$

For every ground M without **import** subrules this partial function is defined in a state $\mathfrak{A}$ if M generates an update set
$U = eval(M, \mathfrak{A})$ that is consistent; in this case M can make

a move in $\mathfrak{A}$ and the function computes what we also call the $nextState_M(\mathfrak{A}) = \mathfrak{A} + U$ by applying the update set U to $\mathfrak{A}$. See pg. 32.

$$eval(M, \mathfrak{A}, \zeta, \eta)$$

For machines that may have some **import** subrule this function computes a pair (U, η') consisting of the (modulo a permutation of *Heap*) same update set U as $eval(M, \mathfrak{A}, \zeta)$ and an extension η' of η by elements imported by M as part of its step (in state $\mathfrak{A}$ with variable environment ζ and set η of already imported elements). See Sect. 2.3.2.

$$step_M(\mathfrak{A}) = apply(\mathfrak{A}, upd(eval(M, \mathfrak{A}, \emptyset, \emptyset)))$$

We write $upd(U, \eta) = U$. For every ground M with **import** subrules this partial function is defined if $eval(M, \mathfrak{A}, \emptyset, \emptyset) = (U, \eta)$ holds for some update set U—in fact the same as $eval(M, \mathfrak{A})$—with a set η of elements imported during the evaluation of M and if U is consistent; when defined the function applies $upd(U, \eta)$ to $\mathfrak{A}$ to determine the successor state. See Def. 20, pg. 36.

Where we are only interested in computed update sets to illustrate a computational issue or where the parameter η is passed unchanged from the argument of an *eval*uation to its value $eval(M, \ldots, \eta) = (U, \eta)$ for some U (as is the case for **skip**, assignment and conditional instructions) we omit mentioning the import of elements from *Heap* during a machine *eval*uation and formulate the investigated issue using $eval(M, \mathfrak{A}, \zeta)$ or $eval(M, \mathfrak{A})$ instead of $eval(M, \mathfrak{A}, \zeta, \eta)$.

Chapter 3
Control Structures of Single-Process Runs

In this chapter we define and investigate in generic terms sequential process runs, also called *sequential algorithmic computations*. They are performed stepwise by a single agent that is equipped with an algorithm it executes and that may interact with an abstract environment (Sect. 3.1). The possible run-time interaction with the environment extends the classical notion of Turing-machine-like algorithmic computations which are input-triggered.[1] Here we illustrate our definition first by runs of imperative procedural Java programs (known as Pascal-like programs, see Sect. 3.2) and then instantiate it to the following widely used specific paradigms of sequential computations.

- In *input-driven output-generating* single-agent sequential runs (Sect. 3.3) the role of the environment is reduced to define by the input the initial state of a computation and to possibly receive some output in a final state.[2] We illustrate this concept of *input/output machines* (abbreviated i/o-machines) by runs of structured ASMs which compute all Turing-computable functions over the natural numbers. Another characteristic example are the components of recursive algorithms we investigate in Sect. 8.4.
- In *nondeterministic* single-agent sequential runs (Sect. 3.4) a step may depend upon some choice that is performed by the executing agent (using a **choose** operator) or by the process environment.[3] We illustrate the use of **choose** for an explanation of the *interleaving* model of parallel computations.
- To describe *truly parallel runs* of multiple synchronized sequential processes (Sect. 3.5) we let one agent execute simultaneously the steps of all

---

[1] In Sect. 8.1.1 this relation is investigated in more detail.

[2] Remember that for single-agent processes, where the attention is focused on a given program to be executed, we do not count the environment as an agent (Definition 11, pg. 22).

[3] Turing [162] already considered 'choice machines' which at certain points 'cannot go on until some arbitrary choice has been made by an external operator'.

© The Author(s), under exclusive license to Springer Nature Switzerland AG 2024
E. Börger, V. Gervasi, *Structures of Computing*,
https://doi.org/10.1007/978-3-031-54358-6_3

involved synchronized agents, expressed by a **forall** construct borrowed from first-order logic.

In Chapter 4 we extend the notion of sequential processes by reflection, an ability of algorithms to change their program at runtime.

3.1 Definition of Single-Process Runs

We view sequential runs of algorithmic processes as executed by a single agent in an abstract process environment. The environment may provide input and receive output via the correspondingly declared interaction type of functions and locations (see Sect. 2.1.1). Such an ongoing interaction of an ASM with its environment turns the machine into a *reactive* process and requires a protocol to avoid any conflict between environment actions and internal actions the agent of the process performs. We adopt here the widely used scheme where environment and process steps alternate. Furthermore, usually computational processes are started in some initial state. For this reason we extend Definition 12 as follows.

Definition 21 (Abstract State Machine). An Abstract State Machine M consists of a signature Σ,[4] a set of initial states over Σ, and a ground ASM rule (i.e. a rule without free variables), called the *main rule* of M, which comes with a finite (possibly empty) set of declarations of rules the main rule may call by name. The main rule and the declared rules are also called machine components. The signature often comes with additional stipulations, e.g. an interaction type classification.

We often use M as name for its main rule and identify the entire machine with this rule if the signature, the declarations and the initial states are clear from the context. The states of M are the Tarski structures of M's signature Σ. We say PGA instead of ASM if the components are PGA rules. To avoid repetitions, definitions which mutatis mutandis apply to every type of ASM are given in terms of not furthermore specified ASMs.

A computation of a single process starts in one of its initial states and repeats (iterates) as long as possible making a move (one step), reacting to interspersed steps of the environment (read: of other agents) which may update some monitored or shared locations.

Definition 22 (Single-Agent Process Run). For an ASM M with signature Σ a single-agent run or computation is a sequence $\mathfrak{A}_0, \mathfrak{A}_1, \ldots$ of states over Σ where $\mathfrak{A}_0$ is an initial state of M and for each natural number n the following holds:

---

[4] In some cases we permit the signature to be infinite. Usually it is requested to be finite.

- either the main rule of M can make a move (see Sect. 2.4, pg. 37) from $\mathfrak{A}_n$ to a next internal state $\mathfrak{A}'_n$ and the environment produces a consistent (possibly empty) update set U of monitored or shared locations such that $\mathfrak{A}_{n+1} = \mathfrak{A}'_n + U$
- or M in $\mathfrak{A}_n$ cannot make any move in which case the run terminates and $\mathfrak{A}_n$ is the last state in the run.

Note that by this definition the environment may override some internal updates of shared locations. In specific applications other protocols can be used to avoid inconsistent updates of shared locations by the involved agents. We adopt the usual wording of *run* or *sequential run* instead of single-agent run where the context prevents any confusion with multi-agent runs. By $\mathfrak{A} \overset{n}{\Rightarrow}_M \mathfrak{B}$ we denote that a single-agent run of M started in $\mathfrak{A}$ leads in n moves to $\mathfrak{B}$. By $\mathfrak{A} \Rightarrow_M \mathfrak{B}$ or $\mathfrak{A} \Rightarrow \mathfrak{B}$ we denote that in a finite number of steps M moves from state $\mathfrak{A}$ to $\mathfrak{B}$. We call a run *internal* if it generates only internal updates (i.e., the environment always generates empty update sets), otherwise it is called an *interactive* run.

In the next sections we illustrate the definition by some characteristic examples. Note that standard Turing machines (Example 5, pg. 26) during their computations do not interact with the environment.

Exercise 8 (Interactive Turing Machine). Refine the concept of TM in such a way that in each step the machine may receive (and react to) some input from the environment and provide an output to the environment. Write an Interactive TM interpreter, refining the TURINGMACHINE defined in Example 5. For a solution see Appendix B.

3.1.1 Relative Computability (Background Concept)

The reader may have wondered that in the signature of an ASM M any function is allowed to appear, even if not computable. This feature is crucial for the freedom of abstraction to design high-level abstract models, in particular to model multi-agent computations. In fact, when using Tarski structures as machine states one can make various constraints or assumptions depending on the considered class of machines. Some are always present to avoid trivial states, e.g. the condition that every state comprises the denotations of *true*, *false* and *undef* which are pairwise different elements and different from all other elements in the state (Definition 2). Others relegate the specification of some well-known and auxiliary features (think about operations on sets, lists, sequences, trees, etc.) or of modules to be done elsewhere. For modularization purposes one can include into the signature of an ASM M some elsewhere defined functions f so that when computing terms of M these functions can just be used without having to compute their values via updates of M.

In logical terms this phenomenon is known as *relative computability*: every step of M is an effective computation step relative to the set of such functions f so that the runs of M represent an algorithmic computation only relative to the computation of such functions f.

A function f may even be non computable but have a precise definition of its values $f(t)$ that are used in the description of the updates generated by a machine. For example, see the one-step ASM computation $out := f(TM)$ where f is the characteristic (total) function of the algorithmically unde-cidable Halting Problem of Turing machines TM (Sect. 9.1.1). Nobody will consider this computation to provide an algorithmic solution of the Halting Problem of Turing machines.

In general, a function symbol f in the signature of an ASM M is a *back-ground* function of M if it appears in (some term in the rules of components of) M but never as outer function symbol f in an assignment $f(s) := t$; this includes all static and monitored functions of M.

Therefore, ASMs can serve for a foundation of relative computability, in-tensively investigated in logic. But be aware that an ASM describes an algo-rithm in the intuitive sense of the term only if all of its background functions are algorithmically computable. This holds even for PGAs so that (contrary to what is suggested in [93]) not every PGA is a sequential algorithm in the intuitive sense of the term, although it satisfies Gurevich's 'Sequential Postulates' (Def. 45, pg. 199). Background restrictions are needed where ef-fectiveness of a computation is an issue.[5]

3.2 Sequential Imperative Procedural Program Runs

Imperative procedural programs constitute a set of sequential processes. Their basic constructs are assignment and sequential control constructs (sequenc-ing, IfThenElse, While, Goto, Call). It is easy to provide a succinct description of their behaviour by a PGA, a program interpreter that reflects directly the intuitions the programming language associates with the program instruc-tions.

However, to make the example convincing for the reader we want to also document its extendability, using the same specification method, to a full-fledged conceptually richer programming language that in particular offers also concurrency (the case of full Java, see Sect. 5.4.2).

For this reason we define an interpreter for the sublanguage of Java that consists of imperative and procedural (neither object-oriented nor multi-threaded) programs. We follow the instructionwise (refinement supporting) platform-independent specification as it has been described and analyzed for

---

[5] Two examples illustrate this phenomenon in this book: the reduction of the background to some undisputedly computable functions for the computation of partial recursive functions (Def. 26, pg. 55) or for the characterization of Turing's thesis (Sect. 8.2).

the entire Java language in [159] and reused in [45] for the description of the ECMA standard of C#. We concentrate the attention here on the dynamics of program execution and refer for the underlying static part of the language (syntax, types, constraints, etc.) to [159, 45] (work that was based on the language manual of that time [89]).

To reflect the traditional distinction of basic imperative method constructs from procedural ones (like call, return) concerning procedures in modules (the class methods in Java), we arrange the instructions in two groups JAVA_I and JAVA_C. Furthermore each group is splitted into a subgroup JAVAEXP_I respectively JAVAEXP_C dealing with the computation of expressions and a subgroup JAVASTM_I respectively JAVASTM_C dealing with the semantics of statements.

$$\text{JAVA}_I =$$
$$\quad \text{JAVAEXP}_I$$
$$\quad \text{JAVASTM}_I$$
$$\text{JAVA}_C =$$
$$\quad \text{JAVAEXP}_C$$
$$\quad \text{JAVASTM}_C$$

The four components are independent of each other and therefore can be developed separately but put in parallel execution because imperative programs describe sequential processes where the program counter enforces to deal at any moment with only one program element. Note that the complete Java interpreter can be defined in a similar way as parallel composition of stepwise extended machines JAVA_I, JAVA_C, JAVA_O (describing Java's object-oriented features), JAVA_E (describing Java's exception handling), JAVA_T (describing concurrency features of Java threads), see [159] .

We adopt the intuitive representation of programs by an annotated abstract syntax tree so that program execution corresponds to a walk through the syntax tree of the current method *body*. A 0-ary function *pos* : *Pos* denotes an abstract program counter: the current position (view it as a node in the tree or as a place in the source code) where the interpreter must compute an expression or a statement. Initially *pos* = *firstPos*, the *firstPos*ition in the *body* of the given method to compute. We write $^\alpha exp$ or $^\alpha stm$ to denote an *exp*ression or a statement *stm* associated with *position* α. At each node the associated pending subcomputation is recorded using a function

restbody : *Pos* → *Phrase*

where initially *restbody*(*firstPos*) = *body*. We write also *restbody*/*pos* for *restbody*(*pos*) denoting the currently to be computed *phrase* at this *position*. The set of *Phrases* contains besides expressions and block statements—the initial values of *restbody*(*pos*) for every *position*—also semi-computed expressions and statements which may contain computed *Values*, some goto information (element of a set of possible reasons for *Abr*uption of the normal control flow) or the word *Norm* denoting that the computation of a statement terminated successfully (read: has been completed without abruption). The interpreter from expressions and statements walks down the syntax tree to first compute the values of the corresponding subexpressions or substatements. Once the pending subcomputation is completed (whether normally or abruptly) the control passes to the parent position we denote by $up(pos)$ so that the *context* of the completed subcomputation becomes the remaining parent's (sub)computation $restbody(up(pos))$.

$up : Pos \rightarrow Pos$ -- parent function of syntax tree
$context(pos) =$
$\begin{cases} restbody(pos) & \text{if } pos = firstPos \text{ or } restbody(pos) \in Bstm \cup Exp \\ restbody(up(pos)) & \text{else} \end{cases}$

where *Bstm* and *Exp* are respectively block statements and expressions, as defined more precisely in Sect. 3.2.1 below.

To record the result of a subcomputation we write:

$yield(result) = (restbody(pos) := result)$

To pass to the parent position the *result* of the subcomputation(s) (or what has to be computed from them at the parent position) we write:

$$yieldUp(result) = restbody(up(pos)) := result$$
$$pos := up(pos)$$

Notational convention. For a succinct and intuitive notation we indicate by $f(\ldots \triangleright t \ldots)$ that the current *pos* is on the subword t of a structured word (sequence of letters) $f(\ldots t \ldots)$. Similarly we write $s = phrase(\triangleright t)$ as abbreviation for $s = phrase(t)$ **and** $pos = \triangleright$ **and** $restbody(pos) = t$. We exploit the flexibility of the ASM framework by adopting here *pattern matching* to write down and execute the rules for JAVA$_I$ and JAVA$_C$—which anyway are sequential rules— so that they are tried out for execution one by one, in the order they are written down.

3.2.1 Imperative Constructs (JAVA$_I$)

The expression evaluation machine JAVAEXP$_I$. The definition follows the inductive syntactical definition of the set of expressions of the imperative sublanguage of Java.

$Exp = Lit \mid Loc \mid Uop\ Exp \mid Exp\ Bop\ Exp \mid Exp\ ?\ Exp : Exp \mid Asgn$
$Asgn = (Loc = Exp)$

Using pattern matching the expression interpreter is defined by the following four sequences described one by one below of case descriptions $e \rightarrow rules$ with *rules* to evaluate the currently visited expression context e:

JAVAEXP$_I$ = **case** *context(pos)* **of**
    LITVAR   -- evaluation of literals and variables
    FCTEXP   -- evaluation of functional expressions
    VARASSIGN   -- evaluation of variable assignments
    CONDEXP   -- evaluation of conditional expressions

The submachines are defined and executed instructionwise in the order of the text. For the meaning of literals and functional expressions we use the definitions provided by the language specification function *JLS* in the reference manual [88, Sect. 3.10]. The value of local variables is given by a function *locals* (that is assumed to be initially undefined):

$$locals : Loc \rightarrow Val$$

Therefore LITVAR has the following two rules:

$lit \rightarrow yield(JLS(lit))$ -- record the meaning of the literal
$loc \rightarrow yield(locals(loc))$ -- record the current variable value

FCTEXP consists of five rules to compute functional expressions formed by unary or binary operators. Note that the Arithmetic Exception division-by-0 case is dealt with in the exception handling component JAVAEXP$_E$ we do not show here.

uop $^\alpha exp \rightarrow pos := \alpha$ -- walk down to compute the *exp*
uop $^\triangleright val \rightarrow yieldUp(JLS(uop, val))$ -- pass computed *value* to parent

$^\alpha exp_1 \ bop \ ^\beta exp_2 \rightarrow pos := \alpha$ -- walk down to compute the left *exp*$_1$
$^\triangleright val \ bop \ ^\beta exp_2 \rightarrow pos := \beta$ -- continue to compute the right *exp*$_2$
$val_1 \ bop \ ^\triangleright val_2 \rightarrow$ -- continue at parent passing computed *val*
    if not $(bop \in divMod$ **and** $isZero(val_2))$ -- exclude division-by-0 case
    then $yieldUp(JLS(bop, val_1, val_2))$

The variable assignment interpreter VARASSIGN is defined by two rules:

$loc = \ ^\alpha exp \rightarrow pos := \alpha$

$loc = \ ^\triangleright val \rightarrow locals(loc) := val$ -- bind *val* to *loc* in local env
                  $yieldUp(val)$

The conditional expression interpreter CONDEXP is defined by four rules:

$^\alpha exp_1 \ ? \ ^\beta exp_2 \ : \ ^\gamma exp_3 \rightarrow pos := \alpha$ -- first compute the condition
if $^\triangleright val \ ? \ ^\beta exp_2 \ : \ ^\gamma exp_3 \rightarrow$ **if** val **then** $pos := \beta$ **else** $pos := \gamma$
                          -- depending on *val* move to compute *exp*$_2$ or *exp*$_3$
$^\alpha true \ ? \ ^\triangleright val : \ ^\gamma exp_3 \rightarrow yieldUp(val)$ -- continue with *val* at parent
$^\alpha false \ ? \ ^\beta exp : \ ^\triangleright val \rightarrow yieldUp(val)$

The imperative statement computing machine JAVASTM$_I$. The definition follows the inductive syntactical definition of the sublanguage of imperative statements of Java.

$Stm = \,; \mid Asgn; \mid Lab : Stm \mid \textbf{break } Lab; \mid \textbf{continue } Lab;$
$\quad \mid \textbf{if } (Exp) \, Stm \, \textbf{else } Stm \mid \textbf{while } (Exp) \, Stm \mid Block$
$Block = \{Bstm_1 \ldots Bstm_n\}$
$Bstm = Type \, Loc \mid Stm$
$Phrase = Exp \mid Bstm \mid Val \mid Abr \mid Norm$

We use pattern matching also for the imperative statement interpreter defined by the following submachines:

JAVASTM$_I$ = **case** $context(pos)$ **of**
   EXPSTM   -- computation of empty and expression stms
   BREAKCONTINUESTM   -- computation of goto stms
   BLOCKSTM   -- computation of block stms
   CONDSTM   -- computation of conditional stms
   WHILESTM   -- computation of while stms

These machines walk through the syntax tree, moving from any structured statement down to compute its substatements and back to the parent statement until the statement has been computed *Norm*ally or an *Abr*uption showed up.

The interpreter EXPSTM for expression statements is defined by four rules:

$;\ \rightarrow yield(Norm)$ -- executing the empty stm terminates normally
$Type \, x; \rightarrow yield(Norm)$ -- a type declaration terminates normally
$^{\alpha}exp; \rightarrow pos := \alpha$ -- an *expression* stm...
$^{\triangleright}val; \rightarrow yieldUp(Norm)$ -- ...terminates normally evaluating *exp*

The interpreter BLOCKSTM for block statements is defined by four rules:

$\{\,\} \rightarrow yield(Norm)$ -- an empty block terminates normally
$\{^{\alpha_1}stm_1 \ldots {}^{\alpha_n}stm_n\} \rightarrow pos := \alpha_1$ -- left-to-right execution strategy
$\{^{\alpha_1}Norm \ldots {}^{\triangleright}Norm \ {}^{\alpha_{i+1}}stm_{i+1} \ldots {}^{\alpha_n}stm_n\} \rightarrow pos := \alpha_{i+1}$
$\{^{\alpha_1}Norm \ldots {}^{\triangleright}Norm\} \rightarrow yieldUp(Norm)$
   -- moves to parent reporting *Norm* if all stm_i terminated *Norm*ally

The interpreter CONDSTM for conditional statements is defined by four rules:

$\textbf{if } (^{\alpha}exp) \ {}^{\beta}stm_1 \ \textbf{else } {}^{\gamma}stm_2 \rightarrow pos := \alpha$ -- first evaluate the condition
$\textbf{if } (^{\triangleright}val) \ {}^{\beta}stm_1 \ \textbf{else } {}^{\gamma}stm_2 \rightarrow \textbf{if } val \textbf{ then } pos := \beta \textbf{ else } pos := \gamma$
$\textbf{if } (^{\alpha}true) \ {}^{\triangleright}Norm \ \textbf{else } {}^{\gamma}stm_2 \rightarrow yieldUp(Norm)$
$\textbf{if } (^{\alpha}false) \ {}^{\beta}stm_1 \ \textbf{else } {}^{\triangleright}Norm \rightarrow yieldUp(Norm)$

The interpreter WHILESTM for while statements is defined by:

$\textbf{while } (^{\alpha}exp) \ {}^{\beta}stm \rightarrow pos := \alpha$ -- first evaluate the condition
$\textbf{while } (^{\triangleright}val) \ {}^{\beta}stm \rightarrow \textbf{if } val \textbf{ then } pos := \beta \textbf{ else } yieldUp(Norm)$
$\textbf{while } (^{\alpha}true) \ {}^{\triangleright}Norm \rightarrow yieldUp(bdy)$ -- iterate the while stm
   where bdy is the program $body(up(pos))$ of the **while** statement

In the imperative sublanguage of Java a statement execution can be abrupted before its normal completion, namely due to the jump statements **break** *lab* or **continue** *lab* which are syntactically constrained to appear in a statement labeled by *lab*. When such an *Abruption* of the normal control flow happens at a node *pos*, the interpreter *yields Break(lab)* or *Continue(lab)* and with this information walks up the syntax tree through all the enclosing statements until it finds a statement labeled with *lab*. All the statements it passes through terminate abruptly. Reaching the statement with continuation label lab_c the execution continutes with the corresponding method *body* (which is avaiable at *pos*). The concept of abruption propagation is defined in such a way that it can be easily refined to other forms of abruption (like return from procedure calls in JAVA$_C$ and handling exceptions in JAVA$_E$). Here it means that every statement except labeled ones propagate the constrained jump statement abruptions in Java programs.

$$propagatesAbr(phrase) \text{ iff } phrase \neq lab : stm$$

This explains the definition of the BREAKCONTINUESTM interpreter:

$lab : {}^{\alpha}stm \rightarrow pos := \alpha$ -- labels do not influence normal execution
$lab : {}^{\triangleright}Norm \rightarrow yieldUp(Norm)$

break $lab; \rightarrow yield(Break(lab))$ -- record abruption of normal ctl flow
continue $lab; \rightarrow yield(Continue(lab))$
$lab : {}^{\triangleright}Break(lab_b) \rightarrow$ **if** $lab = lab_b$
   then $yieldUp(Norm)$ -- jump target stm terminates normally
   else $yieldUp(Break(lab_b))$ -- propagate abruption upwards
$lab : {}^{\triangleright}Continue(lab_c) \rightarrow$ **if** $lab = lab_c$
   then $yield(body(pos))$ -- proceed iterating *body*
   else $yieldUp(Continue(lab_c))$ -- propagate abruption upwards
$phrase({}^{\triangleright}abr) \rightarrow$ **if** $pos \neq firstPos$ **and** $propagatesAbr(restbody(up(pos)))$
   then $yieldUp(abr)$ -- *up(pos)* is not a labeled stm

3.2.2 Procedural Constructs (Class Model JAVA$_C$)

JAVA$_C$ is the extension of JAVA$_I$ by class (also called static) fields, methods and initializers, traditionally called global variables, procedures (subroutines) and module initializers. Correspondingly the syntax of JAVA$_C$ adds to the syntax of JAVA$_I$ (indicated by ...) expressions with global variables and procedure calls (method invocations), as statements method return and trigger of static initializers.

$Exp = \ldots \mid Class.Field \mid Invk$
$Asgn = \ldots \mid Class.Field = Exp$

$Invk = Class.meth(Exps)$
$Exps = Exp_1 \ldots Exp_n$
$Stm = \ldots \mid Invk; \mid \textbf{return } Exp; \mid \textbf{return};$
$Phrase = \ldots \mid \textbf{static } Block$

To describe the dynamics of these class concepts we refine $JAVA_I$ by enriching the state for $JAVA_C$ and adding corresponding new expression evaluation and statement execution rules grouped in $JAVAEXP_C$ and $JAVASTM_C$.

Class related state elements for $JAVA_C$. As for $JAVA_I$ we refer for the static part of $JAVA_C$ to the literature and mention here only those static state functions that appear directly in the new rules. One of them is the function $super(C)$ which yields the direct superclass of a given class. A function $body$ associates with each method $C/msig$ of a given signature in a given class its body. $C/MSig$ denotes the set of method signatures declared in C, i.e. method names with arity and argument types.

$super : Class \rightarrow Class$
$body : Class/MSig \rightarrow Block$

$globals : Class/Field \rightarrow Val$ records the current value of class variables.

The currently executed method is denoted by $meth$ with values in $C/MSig$. We use a stack of method $frames$: when the current $method$ makes a call, its frame—consisting of $meth$, the $restbody$, the current $position$ and $locals$— is pushed on the stack and will be resumed once the called method has terminated.

$Frame = (Class/MSig, Phrase, Pos, Locals) \qquad frames \in Frame^*$

Concerning its initialization a class can be in one of four states: the class is *Linked* but its initialization did not start yet, its initialization is *InProgress*, the class is *Initialized* or *Unusable* (due to an initialization error). The initialization must be performed at the first use of a class (or interface). Being *InProgress* is considered as being *initialized* because during the execution of a static initializer the access to class variables or calls of class methods do not count as a first use of the class.

$ClassState = \{Linked, InProgress, Initialized, Unusable\}$
$classState : Class \rightarrow ClassState$
$initialized(c) \textbf{ iff } classState(c) \in \{Initialized, InProgress\}$

We now apply to $JAVA_C$ the definition scheme introduced above for $JAVA_I$.

Class expressions evaluation machine $JAVAEXP_C$. The new expression evaluation rules are defined instructionwise:

$JAVAEXP_C = \textbf{case } context(pos) \textbf{ of}$
    GLOBALVAR   -- evaluation of global variables
    GLOBALASSIGN   -- assignments to global variables
    METHCALL   -- execution of method calls
    SEQEXP   -- evaluation of sequences of expressions

GLOBALVAR differs from recording values of local variables in the LITVAR subrule of JAVAEXP$_I$ not only by using *globals* instead of *locals*, but also because the recording takes place only when the class of the global variable is *initialized*. If it is not, first the interpreter must INITIALIZE(c), using the submachine defined below. This explains the following rule GLOBALVAR.

$$c.f \rightarrow \textbf{if } initialized(c) \textbf{ then } yields(globals(c/f)) \textbf{ else } \text{INITIALIZE}(c)$$

GLOBALASSIGN refines VARASSIGN in JAVAEXP$_I$ the same way.

$$c.f = {}^{\alpha}exp \rightarrow pos := \alpha$$

$$c.f = {}^{\triangleright}val \rightarrow \begin{array}{l} \textbf{if } initialized(c) \textbf{ then } \begin{array}{l} globals(c/f) := val \\ yieldUp(val) \end{array} \\ \textbf{else } \text{INITIALIZE}(c) \end{array}$$

When executing METHCALL first the sequence of arguments must be evaluated. Only then can the interpreter proceed to INVOKEMETHOD with the computed parameter values, preparing the return from that call to the parent position $up(pos)$ in the caller method. In case the method's class is not yet *initialized*, first the initialization must be performed. This explains METHCALL.

$$c.m^{\alpha}(exps) \rightarrow pos := \alpha$$
$$c.m^{\triangleright}(vals) \rightarrow \textbf{if } initialized(c)$$
$$\qquad\qquad \textbf{then } \text{INVOKEMETHOD}(up(pos), c/m, vals)$$
$$\qquad\qquad \textbf{else } \text{INITIALIZE}(c)$$

The rules in SEQEXP to evaluate a sequence of expressions follow the left-to-right strategy used in Java.

$$() \rightarrow yield([\,]) \qquad\qquad\qquad\qquad\qquad \text{-- no parameters}$$
$$({}^{\alpha_1}exp_1 \ldots {}^{\alpha_n}exp_n) \rightarrow pos := \alpha_1 \qquad\qquad \text{-- left-to-right evaluation order}$$
$$({}^{\alpha_1}val_1 \ldots {}^{\triangleright}val_i \, {}^{\alpha_{i+1}}exp_{i+1} \ldots {}^{\alpha_n}exp_n) \rightarrow pos := \alpha_{i+1}$$
$$({}^{\alpha_1}val_1 \ldots {}^{\triangleright}val_n) \rightarrow yieldUp([val_1 \ldots val_n]) \qquad \text{-- pass } vals \text{ to parent}$$

It remains to define the submachine INITIALIZE(c). It calls the static initializer $c/<clinit>$ (without parameters and with return position pos, to proceed upon return where the initialization was triggered), assigns the default values to the global variables and sets $classState(c)$ to *InProgress*, value that is replaced by *Initialized* at the exit from the static initializer method.

INITIALIZE(c) =
  if $classState(c) = Linked$ **then**
    $classState(c) := InProgress$
    forall $f \in staticFields(c)$ $globals(f) := defaultVal(type(f))$
    INVOKEMETHOD($pos, c/<clinit>, [\,]$)

The submachine INVOKEMETHOD pushes the current frame on the frame stack *frames* and defines a new current frame for the execution of the invoked method's body. The argument values are bound in *locals* to the method's formal parameters.[6]

$$\text{INVOKEMETHOD}(nextPos, c/m, values) =$$
$$frames := push(frames, (meth, restbody, nextPos, locals))$$
$$meth := c/m$$
$$restbody := body(c/m) \qquad\qquad \text{-- syntax tree initialization}$$
$$pos := firstPos(body(c/m)) \qquad \text{-- start at the root of the syntax tree}$$
$$locals := ((x_1, v_1) \dots (x_n, v_n)) \qquad\qquad \text{-- binding values to params}$$
$$\textbf{where } (x_1, \dots, x_n) = argNames(c/m) \textbf{ and } (v_1, \dots, v_n) = values$$

Notice that in this refinement, *firstPos* — which has been so far a pre-initialized static value — becomes a dynamic function; previous occurrences can be interpreted as $firstPos(body(meth))$ with *meth* initialized to *initialClass*/main.

Class statements execution machine JAVASTM$_C$. The new procedural statements are triggering a STATICINITIALIZER to be executed and RETURNSTMs, including the report of normal method body execution to the caller.

$$\text{JAVASTM}_C = \textbf{case } context(pos) \textbf{ of}$$
$$\text{STATICINITIALIZER}$$
$$\text{RETURNSTM}$$

Before executing a static initialization statement the STATICINITIALIZER must check whether the superclass of the current class c (if it exists, i.e. if $c \neq Object$) is already *initialized*. If not, the initialization of the superclass must be called. The return from the static initializer triggers a new kind of abruption, namely *Return* which will trigger to EXITMETHOD (see below). This explains the following definition of STATICINITIALIZER.

$$\textbf{static } {}^{\alpha}stm \to \textbf{let } c = className(meth)$$
$$\textbf{if } c = Object \textbf{ or } initialized(super(c)) \textbf{ then } pos := \alpha$$
$$\textbf{else } \text{INITIALIZE}(super(c))$$
$$\textbf{static } {}^{\alpha}Return \to yieldUp(Return)$$

There are two new reasons for abruption, namely *Return* and *Return(val)* occurring upon execution of **return** statements. Therefore the *Abruptions* set now contains four kinds of abruption:

$$Abr = Break(lab) \mid Continue(lab) \mid Return \mid Return(val)$$

The **return** from a *method* triggers an abruption to exit from the current *method*. Instead of transfering the control directly back to the caller

---

[6] We skip here the submachine INVOKENATIVE that plays a role only in the concurrent extension JAVA$_T$.

of the *method* we refine the abruption mechanism of JAVA$_I$ and propagate the *Return* abruption up to the *firstPos* of the current method body to EXITMETHOD there. This prepares a simple refinement of the propagation mechanism to include the execution of what is called finally code which may be present in the *method* and is dealt with in the exception handling module JAVA$_E$ of Java we do not show here. Return from class initializers is dealt with by a STATICINITIALIZER rule and therefore is excluded from this propagation. Thus *propagatesAbr* is refined as follows:

$$propagatesAbr(phrase) \text{ \textbf{iff} } phrase \neq lab : stm \text{ \textbf{and} } phrase \neq \textbf{static } stm$$

RETURNSTM =
    return $^{\alpha}exp; \rightarrow pos := \alpha$ -- evaluate returned *exp*
    return $^{\triangleright}val; \rightarrow yieldUp(Return(val))$ -- throw abruption to parent
    return; $\rightarrow yield(Return)$
    $lab :^{\triangleright} Return \rightarrow yieldUp(Return)$ -- propagate abruption upwards
    $lab :^{\triangleright} Return(val) \rightarrow yieldUp(Return(val))$
    $Return \rightarrow$ **if** $pos = firstPos(body(meth))$ **and** $frames \neq [\,]$
                    -- *meth* terminated normally and there is a caller
        then EXITMETHOD(*Norm*)
    $Return(val) \rightarrow$ **if** $pos = firstPos(body(meth))$ **and** $frames \neq [\,]$
        then EXITMETHOD(*val*)

    $^{\triangleright}Norm; \rightarrow yieldUp(Norm)$ -- pass normal termination upwards

It remains to define the EXITMETHOD(*result*) submachine. It reestablishes the invoker's frame popped from the *frames* stack passing also the *result* in case the terminated method is not a class initialization method, otherwise it updates the *classState* of the initialized class to *Initialized*.

EXITMETHOD(*result*) =
    let (*oldMeth, oldRestBdy, oldPos, oldLocals*) = *top(frames)*
    method := *oldMethod*
    pos : *oldPos*
    locals := *oldLocals*
    if *methName(meth)* = " < *clinit* > " **and** *result* = *Norm* **then**
        restbody := *oldRestBdy*
        classState(className(meth)) := *Initialized*
    else
        restbody := *oldRestBdy*[*oldPos*/*result*]
    frames := *pop(frames)*
    where *oldRestBdy*[*oldPos*/*result*] is obtained by replacing
            the value of *oldRestBdy* at argument *oldPos* by *result*

This ends the instructionswise platform-independent definition of the procedural sublanguage of Java, refining the imperative component JAVA$_I$ (with assignment and sequential control constructs seq, if, while, goto) by adding

JAVA$_C$ rules which define the semantics of procedural language concepts. Using the same method this model has been extended in [159] by modeling object-oriented features (JAVA$_O$), exception handling (JAVA$_E$) and concurrency (thread model JAVA$_T$), covering the entire Java language of the time. This model JAVA has been reused in [45] to formulate a rigorous model for the ECMA standard of C#. In Sect. 5.4.2 we explain a general context-sensitivity-based method to pass from single-agent sequential to multi-process concurrent runs. We illustrate it by defining the multithreaded JAVA$_T$ component and using it to pass from the single-thread interpreter JAVA to a multi-core-inspired model with truly concurrent runs of Java threads.

3.3 Input Driven Sequential Runs

Definition 22 (pg. 40) of sequential runs makes it possible to use ASMs directly as reactive processes. If in a sequential run of a machine the interaction with the environment is reduced to define the initial state we say that the run (or the machine) is *input-driven*. In such runs, once they are started, the machine does not interact any more with the environment (except for possibly generating some output the environment can read).

The number computations performed by Turing's original machines in [162] are input-driven runs: they all start with the empty tape and in a non-terminating run output bitwise each an infinite 0-1-sequence that represents the computed real number in binary decimal notation. The huge variety of algorithms to compute functions perform input-driven output-generating runs, coming with a notion of final state where their computations may terminate and output the function value for the input. We call them *i/o-algorithms* or machines.

Definition 23 (i/o-algorithm). An *input/output algorithm* $\mathcal{A}$ (or machine) is an input-driven output-generating sequential algorithm, meaning that the role of the environment in runs of $\mathcal{A}$ is reduced to define the initial state of a computation—dynamically by assigning input to monitored locations and/or statically via the definition of a class of initial states—and to possibly receive some output (usually if and when the computation terminates in some final state). We call also such runs to be input-driven and output-generating. The signature of such algorithms $\mathcal{A}$ is the disjoint union $\Sigma = \Sigma_{in} \cup \Sigma_{ctl} \cup \Sigma_{out}$ of monitored functions that are used only for the initial *input*, of controlled (read: local) functions and of output functions. We say that *initial states are input-dependent* if they are defined by the input in monitored locations (with content *undef* in the other locations).

To follow standard notation, when investigating i/o-machines we sometimes use as locations also variables which appear as input resp. output parameters, although the parameters are not (0-ary) function symbols.

We now illustrate runs of i/o algorithms by runs of structured ASMs which compute the computable number-theoretic (also called partial recursive) functions.

3.3.1 Computable Functions (Input/Output Machines)

It is often claimed that using equations to compute functional values is less error prone than computing these values by (programs executed by) machines. This seems to be a question about the structure of the terms that are involved in the computation steps and about the level of abstraction where the computation is formulated. We define in this section a class of i/o ASMs whose compositional structure reflects a widely used ordering for the computation of subterms of functional terms that purely equational definitions do not show. In fact this order appears as 'natural' to us because we have learnt it at school and have been drilled to follow it.

We use two well-known structured sequential programming operators **seq** and **while** and apply them to inductively define structured i/o ASMs, starting with assignment instructions. To illustrate the flexibility for choosing the desired level of abstraction of a specification we define **seq** and **while** hiding all internals—all the intermediate steps which appear explicitly in the control state ASM flowchart notation for the machine components, see Fig. 2.4 of Example 7, pg. 31—so that executing M **seq** N appears in a black-box view as one (called a macro-) step; the same for **while** *cond* **do** M. It implies that during a macro step the environment is assumed to make no step.[7]

Definition 24 (ASM Operator seq). For ASMs M, N with signature Σ we define M **seq** N so that for every state $\mathfrak{A}$ over Σ, first M computes its update set U in $\mathfrak{A}$ to construct its successor state $\mathfrak{B} = \mathfrak{A} + U$ (if U is consistent) and then N computes its update set V in state $\mathfrak{B}$ to construct the M **seq** N-successor state of $\mathfrak{A}$ (if V is consistent). Since N may overwrite some updates of M, the update set M **seq** N computes consists of V plus all those updates in U that are not overwritten by N. It is the update set which appears for the outside world as produced by M **seq** N in one atomic step.[8]

$eval(M \textbf{ seq } N, \mathfrak{A}) = eval(M, \mathfrak{A}) \oplus eval(N, \mathfrak{A} + eval(M, \mathfrak{A}))$
where
$$U \oplus V = \begin{cases} U & \text{if } U \text{ is inconsistent} \\ V \cup \{(loc, val) \in U \mid loc \notin Locs(V)\} & \text{otherwise} \end{cases}$$

---

[7] Similarly we assume for logical reasons not explained here (but see [58, Sect. 8.1.4]) that these machines are deterministic, i.e. that they do not use the **choose** construct added to ASMs in Sect. 3.4.

[8] We skip mentioning the variable environments ζ because the ASMs we consider here are without free variables.

By this definition when U is inconsistent, neither $\mathfrak{A} + U$ nor $\mathfrak{A} + (U \oplus V)$ (because of $U \oplus V = U$) are defined so that the computation gets stuck.

Exercise 9. Convince yourself that the **seq** operator is associative. This property justifies the parenthesis-free notation of machines composed by **seq**.

Consider now iterations (read: successive firings) of an ASM M, starting in some state $\mathfrak{A}$. We write M^n for n iterations of M, i.e. $M^0 = \textbf{skip}$ and $M^{n+1} = M^n \, \textbf{seq} \, M$.

Definition 25 (ASM Operators iterate and while). The iteration of M started in a state $\mathfrak{A}$ is computed by the sequence of states

$$\mathfrak{B}_0 = \mathfrak{A} \qquad \mathfrak{B}_{i+1} = \mathfrak{B}_i + eval(M, \mathfrak{B}_i)$$

that is said

- to *terminate* at the first integer n where $eval(M, \mathfrak{B}_n)$ is either $\emptyset$ (in which case the iteration is said to terminate with *success*) or inconsistent (in which case the iteration is said to terminate with *failure*), if there is such an n.[9] If the iteration terminates, then

$$eval(\textbf{iterate } M, \mathfrak{A}) = (\mathfrak{B}_n - \mathfrak{A}) \oplus eval(M, \mathfrak{B}_n)$$

- to *diverge* else.

In the success case we say that $\mathfrak{B}_n$ is the successor state of $\mathfrak{A}$ computed by **iterate** M.

The **iterate** operator has the effect of executing M repeatedly across multiple steps, until a step produces either an empty or an inconsistent update set. However, such steps and corresponding intermediate states $\mathfrak{B}_i$ are internal to the execution of the **iterate**, whereas from the point of view of the outer machine, only a single step is performed, which produces all the updates needed to reach the final state of the iteration (see Fig. 3.1 where we have $U_i = eval(M, \mathfrak{B}_i)$). Notice that this cumulative update set will be consistent if the iteration terminated in success, or inconsistent if it terminated in failure. If the iteration diverges, then the result of its evaluation is undefined (and in fact, there is no successor state).

The **while** operator can then be defined as an instance of **iterate**:

while *cond* **do** $M = $ **iterate** (**if** *cond* **then** M)

Remark. Such **while** computations terminate with success upon the first encounter of a state where the *condition* is false. However, the computation

---

[9] Including the case of an update set that does not change the given state, i.e. $\mathfrak{B}_n + eval(M, \mathfrak{B}_n) = \mathfrak{B}_n$, is an alternative termination criterion we do not use here. When using ASMs to compute functions a natural alternative $Stop(S)$ criterion is that an initially undefined $output$ location is for the first time defined in state S. We use this criterion below for structured input/output ASMs.

also succeeds if in some of the iteration steps M yields an empty update set; furthermore the computation fails if in some of the iteration steps M yields an inconsistent update set. So to obtain **while** steps with the usual meaning the iteration body M should be designed not to yield an empty or any inconsistent update set.

Fig. 3.1 Internal and external steps of an **iterate** that terminates in success

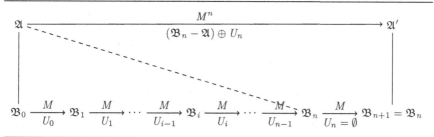

Exercise 10. Consider Fig. 3.1, which depicts the case of a **iterate** terminating with success. $\mathfrak{A}'$ denotes the state that results from a move of M^n in state $\mathfrak{A}$. Convince yourself that the definition of $eval(\mathbf{iterate}\ M, \mathfrak{A})$ is sound also in the case in which U_n is inconsistent (the case for termination with failure), even if in that case the states $\mathfrak{B}_{n+1}$ and $\mathfrak{A}'$ are of course not defined.

Exercise 11. Check your understanding of **while**: determine whether the following ASMs started in a state $\mathfrak{A}$ terminate with or without success or diverge. See Appendix B for the answer.

> **while** $cond$ **do skip**   **while** $false$ **do** M **while** $true$ **do** $a := a$
> **while** $true$ **do** $\begin{array}{l} a := 1 \\ a := 2 \end{array}$

In the following definition we tailor the signature of ASMs for computing partial recursive functions.[10] The encapsulation properties of **seq** and **while** are then exploited to literally paraphrase each application of an equation defining a partial recursive function by one step of those machines.[11]

Definition 26 (Structured Input/Output ASMs). A structured input/output ASM M (used to compute computable functions over Nat and

---

[10] The definition comes from [58, Ch. 4] and will be reused for Def. 46 (pg. 203) of the Arithmetical State Postulate.

[11] In [58, Sect. 4.1.3] it is shown that each step of such a 'turbo'-ASM M can be computed by an ASM MicroStep(M) which (starting with M and an empty update set) step-by-step computes the update set accumulated so far by M and the still to be executed rules of M.

therefore a deterministic ASM) is defined as an ASM with a signature consisting of only one monitored (a 0-ary) function in_M (to store input sequences of natural numbers), only one output (a 0-ary) function out_M (to store a natural number), a finite number of controlled functions and of some clearly computable so called initial functions of recursion theory (see below). In its initial states every dynamic function except in_M is undefined. Its rule is built from unguarded assignment instructions applying finitely often **seq**, **while** and **par**.

M computes a partial function $f : Nat^n \rightarrow Nat$ if for every argument $x \in Nat^n$ the machine, starting an input-driven run in the initial state with $in_M = x$, reaches after a finite number of steps a state where out_M gets updated for the first time, namely to $out_M = f(x)$, if and only if $f(x)$ is defined.

The *initial functions* of recursion theory are the following functions of natural numbers: $+1$, the projection functions $U_i^n(x_1, \ldots, x_n) = x_i$, the constant functions $C_i^n(x_1, \ldots, x_n) = i$ and the characteristic functions of the predicate $= 0$ and of the smaller-than relation $<$.

Theorem 1 (Structured Programming). *Every partial recursive function f on natural numbers can be computed by a structured input/output ASM* STRUCTINOUT(f).

Proof. We use Kleene's [112] equational definition of the partial recursive functions which starts from the initial functions of recursion theory and applies finitely often equations for simultaneous substitution, primitive recursion and the minimal-zero-point operator.[12] So one can define STRUCTINOUT(f) by induction on the definition of f.

Basis of the induction. Each initial function f is computed by an assignment instruction that reflects the defining equation for f:[13]

$$\text{STRUCTINOUT}(f) = (out_f := f(in_f))$$

Inductive step. By the functional notation $M(x)$ we indicate the program we intend to use for an input-driven run of M to compute the functional value for input x:

Abbreviation. $M(x) = ((in_M := x) \textbf{ seq } M)$

To transfer the output value computed by $M(x)$ from out_M to a different location *result* we write:

Abbreviation. *result* $\leftarrow M(x) = (M(x) \textbf{ seq } result := out_M)$

---

[12] In recursion theory this operator is called μ-operator and partial recursive functions are also called μ-recursive functions.

[13] As shorthand we index the in/out functions with the function name f to stand for the longer rule name STRUCTINOUT(f).

Case 1: substitution. Let f be defined by simultaneous substitution of functions h_i into a function g, i.e. $f(x) = g(h_1(x), \ldots, h_m(x))$. Then $f(x)$ can be computed by first computing for every h_i its value for input $x = in_f$, independently of each other so that these subcomputations can be done in parallel,[14] and then the value of g for the computed intermediate values $(out_{H_1}, \ldots, out_{H_m})$. This order of using the given equations to compute f is made explicit by the following definition of a structured input/output ASM STRUCTINOUT(f). Let $G, H_1, \ldots, H_m$ be structured input/output ASMs which compute respectively $g, h_1, \ldots, h_m$ by induction hypothesis.

STRUCTINOUT$(f) =$
   par $(H_1(in_f), \ldots, H_m(in_f))$ **seq** $out_f \leftarrow G(out_{H_1}, \ldots, out_{H_m})$

The structure of STRUCTINOUT(f) reflects the structure of the term on the right side of the defining equation for f: simultaneous substitution reveals its nature of a parallel computation step followed by one 'equational' step.

Case 2: primitive recursion. Let f be defined by primitive recursion from g, h, i.e.

$$f(x, 0) = g(x), \quad f(x, y+1) = h(x, y, f(x, y))$$

Let G, H be structured input/output ASMs which compute respectively g, h by induction hypothesis. To computate $f(x, y)$ one can start with computing $f(x, 0)$ as first intermediate value $ival$, using the first equation for f, and setting the recursor to 0; then one can iterate the computation of $f(x, rec+1)$, using the second equation for f and increasing the recursor, until $rec = y$: in this moment $ival = f(x, y)$ so that the result can be copied to the output location.

STRUCTINOUT$(f) =$
   let $(x, y) = in_f$
      par $(ival \leftarrow G(x), rec := 0)$ -- basis: run G, initialize recursor
      seq while $rec < y$ **do**
         par $(ival \leftarrow H(x, rec, ival), rec := rec + 1)$ -- a recursion step
      seq $out_f := ival$ -- output final intermediate value

Note that it is only for better readability that we use the **let**-notation instead of writing $U_i^{n+1}(in_f)$ for x_i with $(1 \leq i \leq n)$ and $U_{n+1}^{n+1}(in_f)$ for y where $in_f = (x_1, \ldots, x_n, y)$.

The structure of STRUCTINOUT(f) makes this order for applying the defining equations for f explicit: first perform the basis step—computing the right-hand side of the equation with recursion parameter 0—and then use step-by-step the right-hand side of the equation with positive recursion parameter until this parameter reaches the recursor value y of the input of f.

---

[14] For simplicity of exposition but without loss of generality assume that the function computing submachines have pairwise disjoint signature.

Exercise 12. Define a structured input/output ASM for the case of primitive recursion where the computation of $f(x, y)$ uses the defining equations in the following order:

$$f(x, y)$$
$$= h(x, y - 1, f(x, y - 1))$$
$$\vdots$$
$$= h(x, y - 1, h(x, y - 2, \ldots h(x, 0, f(x, 0)) \ldots))$$
$$= h(x, y - 1, h(x, y - 2, \ldots h(x, 0, g(x)) \ldots))$$

Compare this order with the simpler sequence $(ival_i)_{i \leq y}$ that is computed by the above machine STRUCTINOUT$(f))$ to compute $f(x, y)$:

$$ival_0 = g(x) \qquad ival_{i+1} = h(x, i, ival_i)$$

Case 3: minimal-zero-point operator. Let f be defined by the μ-operator from g, i.e. $f(x)$ is the smallest y such that $g(x, y) = 0$. The equational definition suggests to perform the computation of $f(x)$ as follows: start with computing $g(x, 0)$ and setting the recursor to 0; then iterate the computation of values $g(x, rec + 1)$ until the value 0 shows up in which case the current recursor value $rec = f(x)$ can be copied to the output location.

The structure of the following definition of STRUCTINOUT(f) makes this order explicit. Let G be a structured input/output ASM which computes g by induction hypothesis.

> STRUCTINOUT$(f) =$
> **par** $(G(in_f, 0), rec := 0)$
> **seq while** $out_G \neq 0$ **do par** $(G(in_f, rec + 1), rec := rec + 1)$
> **seq** $out_f := rec$

Remark. The definitions of STRUCTINOUT represent patterns

$$\text{FCTSUBST}(G, H_1, \ldots, H_m), \text{PRIMRECURSION}(G, H), \text{MINZEROPOINT}(G)$$

to compose structured input/output ASMs out of components that appear as parameters $G, H, H_1, \ldots, H_m$. An occurrence of **par** indicates where any sequentialization of the involved simultaneous steps yields the same result. In purely functional notations this operator is suppressed and it is implicitly assumed that some sequentialization of the involved independent steps is chosen for their execution. Note that the PGA normal form (Def. 13, pg. 24) is structurally flat. Nevertheless, in a sequential context it is easy to simulate **seq** and **while** machines by PGAs.

Exercise 13 (PGAs for seq and while). Define PGAs that simulate M **seq** N and **while** *cond* **do** M. Use this to write PGA rules for each of the three ASM schemes FCTSUBST$(G, H_1, \ldots, H_m)$, PRIMRECURSION(G, H), and MINZEROPOINT(G) to see what is gained by the abstraction. See Appendix B for a solution.

Exercise 14 (Random Access Machine). The RAM is a refinement of the register machine model (pg. 261), equipped with an explicit input/output mechanism. It comes close to the Harvard computer architecture model and is often used as reference model to investigate complexity properties of arithmetical algorithms.

Data from an input tape can be copied into registers and the content of any register (or some integer) can be written to an output tape. All other data (not *ctl*) manipulations happen only involving a special register called the *accumulator*: register transfers—from other registers into the *accumulator* and from there into other registers applying to its content some operation— and operations involving as one argument the content of the *accumulator*. The second argument is either an integer or taken from other indirectly addressable registers *reg* in *main memory*. Those registers serve only as containers of data that can be loaded into the *accumulator*, be modified there and stored from *acc* into *reg*.

The main memory is a (potentially infinite) set of registers r_n (with $n \in Nat$ and $acc = r_0$) whose *contents* are integers, in initial states assumed to be 0 (unless otherwise stated). The finite instruction memory where the to-be-executed program *pgm* is stored is separated from the (potentially infinite) main memory in the sense that during the execution of the program its instructions can be read and executed but not modified. In other words *pgm* is static, i.e. the execution of the program cannot change the program. A RAM program is a finite sequence of labeled instructions *instr* with pairwise different labels *lab(instr)*, an *opCode(instr)* and (except the *Halt* instruction) an *operand(instr)* on whose interpretation—together with the *accumulator* content as first argument (except for jump instructions)— the assembly-like operation code is executed.

To simplify the presentation but without loss of generality we use as labels natural numbers $0 \leq l \leq m$ for some natural number m; 0,1 are usually written and interpreted as *start* respectively *halt* label. We write $instr_l$ or $instr(l)$ for the instruction with label l so that the currently executed instruction can be defined by $instr(ctl)$. The commands that can appear as $opCode(instr)$ are of the following kinds:

- *Load* and *Store* for data transfer (between the *accumulator* and any other register),
- *Add*, *Sub*, *Mult*, *Div* for the basic functions $+, -, \times, /$ of integers to be applied to the content of *acc* and a second operand (an integer or the content of another register),
- *Jump*, *Jump*(> 0), *Jump*(= 0) and *Halt* for the management of an instruction counter *ctl*,
- *Read* (from the finite input tape into a register) and *Write* (an integer or a register content to the potentially infinite output tape).

The *operands* of instructions are of three types:

- A *Halt* instruction has no operand.
- For jump instructions the *operand* is a label indicating where to jump to if the jump condition (if any) is satisfied.
- For memory transfer or functional *opCode* the *operand* and its interpretation *operandVal* is defined for the following three cases:

  - *int i*: denotes an integer constant i (except for *Store*)[15]
  - *reg n* (for $n \in Nat$): denotes the content of register r_n
  - *addr n*: denotes the content of the register whose address (also called index) i is the content of register r_n. If $i < 0$ the machine halts.

$$operandVal(int\ i) = i$$
$$operandVal(reg\ n) = content(r_n)$$
$$operandVal(addr\ n) = \begin{cases} undef & \text{if } content(r_n) < 0 \\ content(r_{content(r_n)}) & \text{else} \end{cases}$$

The definition of *operandVal(addr n)* reflects that only natural numbers are used as register index. If in a computation step an operand *addr n* appears where $content(r_n) < 0$, then the computation is required to halt (due to a register address error). The same for divisions by 0. Note that the function *operandVal* has an implicit state parameter, referring to register contents.

Define a PGA rule that interprets the behaviour of the RAM, refining the RM-rule of the solution for Exercise 5 (pg. 261). For a solution see pg. 263 in Appendix B.

3.4 Nondeterminism and Interleaving

For a computational or a proof step it often suffices to perform the step for an arbitrary element a belonging to some set A, without exploiting any specific property of the chosen element or any relation it shares with other elements of the set. Such a selection can be expressed using a choice function ϵ which applied to a set X provides an element $\epsilon x(X)$ of X if there is at least one. If there is none $\epsilon x(X)$ is undefined so that the function is a partial function; as an alternative a default value *undef* can be used.

Hilbert [99] and Ackermann [4] (see also [101, vol. II]) defined and axiomatized this choice operator and used the resulting epsilon-calculus in a foundational context. For example, first-order logic can be dealt with in terms of quantifier-free reasoning involving the ϵ operator:[16]

forsome $x\ P(x) = P(\epsilon x(P(x)))$ **forall** $x\ P(x) = P(\epsilon x(\text{not } P(x)))$.

---

[15] For *Store* a number operand *int i* makes no sense.

[16] See [8] for foundational and proof-theoretic work using the ϵ operator.

The quantifier elimination capability of Hilbert's and Ackermann's ϵ operator is exploited in some contemporary proof engines. In the extensional version of the epsilon-calculus the epsilon operator assigns the same witness to equivalent formulae, i.e. **if forall** x $(\alpha(x)$ **iff** $\beta(x))$ **then** $\epsilon x(\alpha) = \epsilon x(\beta)$ holds. But there are other possibilities to correlate different choices, in particular in computing where multiple choices made in a dynamic context appear. In a run a choice operator can be used to express an interface condition φ under which the next step is performed, e.g. an abstract property an element is required to satisfy to be used for the next step in the run, abstracting from how such elements are computed. We follow that approach and define the syntax of the **choose** construct by the following ASM rule, called **choose** rule:

choose x **with** φ **do** M

Its meaning is to select—due to the presence of **import** rules not in the superuniverse $|\mathfrak{A}|$ but in the current $Workspace(\mathfrak{A})$—an element a that satisfies the choice condition phi and to execute M with this element a, bound by the variable environment to x. In this way the **choose** rule offers to continue the computation with any one among possibly many update sets M computes in state $\mathfrak{A}$ with individual variable environment $\zeta[x \mapsto a]$ for any chosen element $a \in X$ satisfying φ. Technically, to extend the semantics of ASMs by a semantics for **choose** rules it suffices to replace the $eval$uation function, which provides a unique update set $U = eval(M, \mathfrak{A}, \zeta)$, by an evaluation candidate relation

$evalCand(M, \mathfrak{A}, \zeta, U)$

expressing that the evaluation of M in state $\mathfrak{A}$ with variable environment ζ offers U as one update set candidate to continue the computation.

Definition 27 (Semantics of choose rules). We extend the class of ASMs inductively by **choose** rules, i.e. rules of the form **choose** x **with** φ **do** M (where M is an ASM). We define their semantics by extending Def. 14 (pg. 32) as follows: replace in Def. 14 $eval(M, \mathfrak{A}, \zeta) = U$ by the evaluation candidate relation $evalCand(M, \mathfrak{A}, \zeta, U)$ and add the following inductive clause to define this relation for **choose** rules :

    if $range(x, \varphi, \mathfrak{A}, \zeta) = \emptyset$ -- there is no element to choose
        then $evalCand($**choose** x **with** φ **do** $M, \mathfrak{A}, \zeta, \emptyset)$ holds
                                  -- generates empty update set
    else
        forall $a \in range(x, \varphi, \mathfrak{A}, \zeta)$ **and forall** U
            if $evalCand(M, \mathfrak{A}, \zeta[x \mapsto a], U)$ holds
                then $evalCand($**choose** x **with** φ **do** $M, \mathfrak{A}, \zeta, U)$ holds
        where
            $range(x, \varphi, \mathfrak{A}, \zeta) =$
                $\{a \in Workspace(\mathfrak{A}) \mid eval(\varphi, \mathfrak{A}, \zeta[x \mapsto a]) = true\}$

In the presence of **imports** import parameters are passed without change from $evalCand(M, \ldots, \eta, (U, \eta'))$ to $evalCand(\textbf{choose } x \textbf{ with } \varphi \textbf{ do } M, \ldots)$.

ASMs with **choose** rules are nondeterministic machines. In their sequential runs each time they execute a **choose** rule this may offer multiple update sets U (to continue the run by one more step if U is consistent), namely all those update sets U_a that for an element $a \in range(x, \varphi, \mathfrak{A}, \zeta)$ satisfy the relation $evalCand(M, \mathfrak{A}, \zeta[x \mapsto a], U_a)$. Thus the corresponding run can have multiple continuations $\mathfrak{A} + U_a$, each computable in single M-steps $\mathfrak{A} \xrightarrow{1}_M \mathfrak{A} + U_a$. This means that the $step_M$ function of deterministic ASMs is refined to a relation of state pairs $(\mathfrak{A}, \mathfrak{A} + U_a)$ where a is an element of $range(x, \varphi, \mathfrak{A}, \zeta)$ and U_a is a consistent update set for which the relation $evalCand(M, \mathfrak{A}, \zeta[x \mapsto a], U_a)$ holds. We summarize this by the following definition.

Definition 28 (Successor State Relation for ASMs with choose).
For every state $\mathfrak{A}$ its (possibly multiple) successor states computed by any M in the presence of **choose** (and **import**) rules are defined as follows, refining the $step_M$ function in Def. 14 (pg. 32) to a relation:

> **forall** U, η
> > **if** $evalCand(M, \mathfrak{A}, \emptyset, \emptyset, (U, \eta))$ holds **and** $Consistent(U)$
> > > **then** $nextState_M(\mathfrak{A}, \mathfrak{A} + U)$ holds

In most applications the **choose** construct is used only with non-empty sets to choose from. To catch error situations where there is no $a \in Workspace(\mathfrak{A})$ satisfying φ a good discipline is to use the construct always together with a dedicated **ifnone** N clause; if such a clause is provided, and there is no (a, U) satisfying the conditions above, then for every update set U' such that $evalCand(N, \mathfrak{A}, \zeta, U')$ holds also

$$evalCand(\textbf{choose } x \textbf{ with } \varphi \textbf{ do } M \textbf{ ifnone } N, \mathfrak{A}, \zeta, U') \text{ holds.}$$

Notational remark. When the choice condition φ is restricted to being an element of a set X we simply write **choose** $x \in X$ **do** M. We use other familiar notational shorthands without further explanation; for example, with power sets we write **choose** $A \subseteq B$ instead of **choose** A **in** $\mathcal{P}(B)$.

Example 8. **Nondeterministic Turing Machine**. A nondeterministic Turing machine differs from its deterministic version by some choice, for example in updating the control state *ctl*. Refining the function *nextCtl* in Example 5 (pg. 26) to a function with range $PowerSet(Ctl)$ instead of Ctl yields the following behavioural description of nondeterministic TMs:

> NONDETERMINISTICTURINGMACHINE(*write*, *nextCtl*, *move*) =
> > $tape(head) := write(ctl, tape(head))$ -- read and write on the tape
> > $head := move(ctl, tape(head))(head)$ -- move reading device
> > **choose** $c \in nextCtl(ctl, tape(head))$ **do**   -- choose next control state
> > > $ctl := c$ -- go to the chosen control state

Note that this choice in Turing machines is bounded, i.e. it offers only a finite number of choices that depends only on the program and the alphabet.

Exercise 15. How can a NONDETERMINISTICTURINGMACHINE be configured and specified to become able to choose also for the writing and move actions?

Non determinism occurs frequently in computing, but it not necessarily increases the computational power. For example, deterministic Finite State Machines (see Exercise 3, pg. 26) and their non-deterministic variant compute the same class of languages [140]; also every non-deterministic Turing machine can easily be simulated by a deterministic TM (Exercise 16). But restricting TM computations by a polynomial time bound leads to two classes P respectively NP of sets—those decidable by polynomial-time-bounded deterministic respectively non-deterministic Turing machines—for which it is a longstanding open problem whether they coincide. See Sect. 9.1 for more on this theme.

Exercise 16. Explain how every non-deterministic Turing machine can be simulated by a deterministic Turing machine.

As one justification for the definition of PGA rules (Def.12, pg. 24) we mentioned the axiomatic sequential process characterization that leads to an ASM version of Turing's thesis, as we will explain in Sect. 8.1. With some small changes the characterization remains valid if a 'bounded choice' is allowed in sequential process descriptions. To capture this we define bounded-choice PGAs.

Definition 29 (Bounded-choice PGAs). Bounded-choice PGAs are defined by adding to the inductive definition of PGAs (Def. 12, pg. 24) a clause that applies **choose** to a finite number of (already defined bounded-choice PGA) rules M_i:

> **choose** $M \in \{M_1, \ldots, M_n\}$ **do** M

Notationally we write such a rule also as **chooseOneOf** $\{M_1, \ldots, M_n\}$ or M_1 **or** ... **or** M_n. Bounded-choice PGAs have the following normal form:[17]

> **if** φ_1 **then choose** $rule \in \{rule_{1,1}, \ldots, rule_{1,l_1}\}$ **do** $rule$
>
> $\vdots$
>
> **if** φ_k **then choose** $rule \in \{rule_{k,1}, \ldots, rule_{k,l_k}\}$ **do** $rule$
> **where**
> $rule_{i,j}$ consists of finitely many parallel assignment instructions

---

[17] See the proof of Corollary 1 (pg. 202).

Example 9. **Alternative and Repetitive Guarded Commands.** Dijkstra proposed in [67] what he called an 'alternative construct' *if* $G0 \to S0 \mid G1 \to S1... \mid Gn \to Sn$ *fi* and a 'repetitive construct' *do* $G0 \to S0 \mid G1 \to S1... \mid Gn \to Sn$ *od* of sequential program statements Si whose execution is guarded by boolean expressions Gi. Both constructs describe some non-deterministic sequential program behaviour. Their semantics can be easily defined by non-deterministic PGA-ASMs as follows, bypassing Dijkstra's weakest pre-condition approach. Let $cond_i$ be Boolean expressions, M_i PGA-ASMs and ABORT a description of Dijkstra's abort command.

ALTERNATIVECMD$((cond_i, M_i)_{i \leq n}) =$
    choose $i \in \{0, \ldots, n\}$ **with** $cond_i$ **do** M_i
    ifnone then ABORT
  where
    ifnone = **if thereisno** $i \in \{0, \ldots, n\}$ **with** $cond_i$

The repetitive construct repeats the choice until a state is reached where no more choice is possible.

REPETITIVECMD$((cond_i, M_i)_{i \leq n}) =$
    while forsome $i \in \{0, \ldots, n\}$ $cond_i$ **do**
      choose $i \in \{0, \ldots, n\}$ **with** $cond_i$ **do** M_i

Note that the behaviour of REPETITIVECMD in case **ifnone** is that of **skip** (by Def. 27, pg. 61), as required by Dijkstra's definition. The same holds if instead of the macro-step **while** operator the control state *while cond M* construct of Example 7 (pg. 30) is used.

We generalize the choice among different actions from Dijkstra's guarded commands to arbitrary ASMs M_i with the following notation:

  chooseOneOf $(\{M_0, \ldots, M_n\}) =$
    choose $i \in \{0, \ldots, n\}$
    M_i

Correspondingly we adapt the graphical representation of control state ASMs from Fig. 2.2 (pg. 28) to the following Fig. 3.2 (where for the sake of notational succinctness we write **choose** instead of **chooseOneOf**):

Example 10. **Alternative Statement in Occam.**
    The programming language Occam [69] has an alternative command **alt** $(G_1 \ S_1 \ldots G_n \ S_n)$ that instantiates the if-part of Dijkstra's ALTERNATIVECMD but replaces the else-part ABORT by a waiting mechanism; this mechanism is specified in the guards to wait for a communication with other agents to happen or for a state property or a time constraint to be satisfied.
    Consider Occam programs as executed by agents a which walk through the flowchart representation of their program; each of them carries its own *env*ironment (internal state in which to evaluate expressions $eval(exp, env(a))$

Fig. 3.2 Choose Control State ASM Diagram

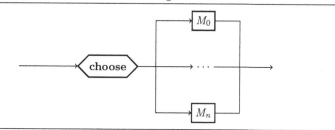

and to $bind(id, env(a))$ identifiers id to a variable or channel) and is positioned at each moment on its currently visited node $pos(a)$. We abbreviate $bind(id, env(a))$ to $\overline{id}$ when $env(a)$ is clear from the context. Each *node* is decorated by a to-be-executed command $cmd(node)$. A *node* with alternative (guarded) command **alt** $(G_1, \ldots, G_n)$ has possible successor nodes $next(node, i)$ decorated by command S_i, see Fig. 3.3.

Fig. 3.3 Occam alt $(G_1 \ S_1 \ldots G_n \ S_n)$ statement diagram

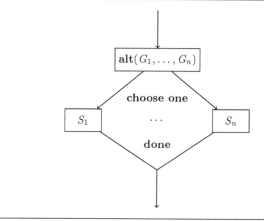

Guards come in three forms:

- A *StateGuard* G_i consists of a *StateCondition* $cond_i$ that is requested to evaluate to true.
- A *TimeGuard* has the form $G_i = cond_i : time?after \ t$ requesting besides the *StateCondition* also a *TimeCondition* the clock of the executing agent a has to satisfy, namely $timer(a) > eval(t, env(a))$.
- A *ComGuard* has the form $G_i = cond_i : chan_i \ ? \ v_i$ with an additional communication request $chan_i \ ? \ v_i$ to be satisfied by a *ComCondition* (in addition to the *StateCondition*), expressing that the executing agent a

wishes to receive for its variable v_i some data via the channel $\overline{chan_i}$ (to which $chan_i$ is bound) and that there is another agent b with command $c!t$ ready to communicate its value of t via the channel $\overline{c} = \overline{chan_i}$.

To execute an alternative command for some i the StateCondition $cond_i$ must evaluate to true in the requestor's environment. If G_i is a StateGuard, the truth of $cond_i$ suffices to let agent a proceed to execute S_i. Similarly in case G_i is a TimeGuard for which $timer(a) > eval(t, env(a))$ is satisfied. To satisfy in addition the ComCondition, in case G_i is a ComGuard, agent a and some other agent b must agree on the channel (i.e. both must bind the channel identifier $chan_i$ respectively c in their respective environment to the same channel). If this is true for some i and b, the data transmission (if chosen) can take place, agent a proceeds to execute S_i and the communication partner b proceeds to execute its next statement.

This explains the following definition of **alternative** commands in Occam.[18] For $i = 1, \ldots, n$ let G_i be $cond_i$ or $cond_i : chan_i ? v_i$ or $cond_i : time?after\ t$.

$$\text{ALT}_0(a, (G_1, \ldots, G_n)) =$$
$$\quad \textbf{if } a \textbf{ does alt } (G_1, \ldots, G_n) \textbf{ then}$$
$$\quad\quad \textbf{choose } i \in \{1, \ldots, n\} \textbf{ with } Ready(G_i) \textbf{ do}$$
$$\quad\quad\quad pos(a) := next(pos(a), i) \qquad \text{-- } a \text{ proceeds with } i\text{-th alternative}$$
$$\quad\quad\quad \textbf{if } ComGuard(G_i) \textbf{ then} \qquad\qquad \text{-- com partner requested}$$
$$\quad\quad\quad\quad \textbf{let } b, c, s \textbf{ with } b \textbf{ does } c!s \textbf{ and } \overline{chan_i} = \overline{c}$$
$$\quad\quad\quad\quad\quad v_i := eval(s, env(b)) \qquad\qquad \text{-- data transfer to the variable}$$
$$\quad\quad\quad\quad\quad pos(b) := next(pos(b)) \qquad \text{-- } b \text{ proceeds with next command}$$
$$\quad\quad \textbf{where}$$
$$\quad\quad\quad Ready(G_i) =$$
$$\quad\quad\quad\quad (StateGuard(G_i) \textbf{ and } StateCond(G_i))$$
$$\quad\quad\quad\quad \textbf{or } (ComGuard(G_i) \textbf{ and } StateCond(G_i) \textbf{ and } ComCond(G_i))$$
$$\quad\quad\quad\quad \textbf{or } (TimeGuard(G_i) \textbf{ and } StateCond(G_i) \textbf{ and } TimeCond(G_i))$$
$$\quad\quad\quad StateCond(G_i) = (eval(cond_i, env(a)) = true)$$
$$\quad\quad\quad ComCond(G_i) = \textbf{forsome } b, c, s \quad b \textbf{ does } c!s \textbf{ and } \overline{chan_i} = \overline{c}$$
$$\quad\quad\quad TimeCond(G_i) = timer(a) > eval(t, env(a))$$
$$\quad\quad\quad a \textbf{ does } instr =$$
$$\quad\quad\quad\quad a \in Agent \textbf{ and } mode(a) = running \textbf{ and } cmd(pos(a)) = instr$$

Example 11. **Interleaving.** Often, in particular for machine assisted proofs of properties of multiprocess algorithms, as computational model *interleaving* is used where in each step an arbitrary process among those which can make a step is chosen to be executed on one processor (read: by one agent). For

---

[18] Note the usual assumption on Occam programs that any two agents are connected by a *parent* chain (see Example 13 on pg. 116 with the Occam PAR rule) if in any states they could both input or both output on the same channel (*Occam Channel Assumption*). This implies that in a same state they cannot be both in *running* mode both trying to communicate with the same agent on the same channel.

every set of *Process*es and a notion of being *ReadyToExecute*—that is deliberately left abstract to be refinable by scheduling schemes of interest—one can describe this interleaving paradigm by the following scheme:

Interleav(*Process*) =
    choose $M \in Process$ **with** $ReadyToExec(M)$ **do** M

The Interleaving machine specifies by its nondeterministic sequential runs the *multitasking view* of runs of multiple sequential processes on one processor: the processor switches between the multiple tasks to execute them. Interleav(*Process*) as formulated here switches step by step, but it suffices to refine the choice condition *ReadyToExec* to obtain the usual time-sharing versions and also sophisticated cooperative or preemptive multitasking schemes as they appear in operating systems. Since we explain below in detail the relation between the states of concurrent processes (Sect. 5.4) we do not enter here the issue that every process switch typically implies also a context switch whereby the state of the to-be-switched process is saved and the state of the next to-be-executed process is reloaded.

In case the interleaved processes do not work on completely separated states but interact via input/output and shared locations the question is which of the 'sequential multiprocess runs' of Interleav(*Process*) should be considered as *sequentially consistent*, given that the interaction creates an access order to shared locations which may result in dependencies between the component processes. Here are two natural constraints (discovered in [116]):

- in the sequential multiprocess run for each agent a its moves appear in the order in which they appear in its given sequential run (property called *preservation of sequentiality* of the component processes);
- each time in the sequential multiprocess run a component process reads a location, the value read is the most recently written value in the multiprocess run (property called *read-freshness*).

For a generalization of sequential consistency to ASM runs the read-freshness property must include the effect of environment moves which by Def. 22 (pg. 40) alternate with internal moves. This means that one can allow any interleaving where between two successive moves m_n, m_{n+1} of an agent a, the moves of other agents can be arranged in any sequentiality preserving order as long as their execution computes the effect of the environment move between m_n and m_{n+1}, as perceived by agent a. This leads to the following definition.

Definition 30 (Sequentially Consistent Interleavings). Let *Process* be a set of pairs $(a, asm(a))$ of agents $a \in A$ each equipped with a PGA $asm(a)$. A run R of Interleav(*Process*) is called sequentially consistent if it preserves the sequentiality of the component processes $(a, asm(a))$ and satisfies the read-freshness property.

More precisely stated, for every agent $a \in A$ its moves $m_n(a)$, coupled in its given single-agent sequential run $\mathfrak{A}_0(a), \mathfrak{A}_1(a), \ldots$ with the environment moves $m_n(environ(a))$, appear in the same order in R (restricted to the signature Σ_a of a). Furthermore, for each location a reads in state $\mathfrak{A}_n(a)$—to make its move $m_n(a)$ leading to its next internal state $\mathfrak{A}'_n(a)$ with successor state $\mathfrak{A}_{n+1}(a)$—the value a reads is the last-written value into that location in R.

Note that the states $\mathfrak{A}_n$ in a sequentially consistent run are not states any single agent a can see. a sees only the restriction $\mathfrak{A}_n \downarrow \Sigma_a$ to its own signature. It is for reasons of analysis that we speak about *viewing* INTERLEAV(*Process*) as a multiprocess system. For a truly concurrent (not only multitasking) computation model the single processor which manages the interleaving must be replaced by multiple processors (see Ch. 5).

Internal versus external choice. Often the choice performed by the **choose** x **with** φ **in** M construct is called an *internal* choice, to be distinguished from an *external* choice **let** $x = select(\{y \mid \varphi(y)\})$ **in** M expressed by a background function *select* that is assumed to provide an element that satisfies φ (if there exists one). External *selection* functions may be static (in which case the run of the agent becomes deterministic) or dynamic (thus preserving non-determinism, in a way that may be constrained by background stipulations as usual).

3.5 Synchronous Parallel Step Control

The **par** construct for ASMs expresses a bounded parallelism, namely the simultaneous one-step execution of a fixed finite number of processes. For high-level specifications, in particular in connection with modeling the behaviour of hardware or other synchronous processes, it is often very useful to work with an unbounded parallelism the universal quantifier from logic helps to express. The ASM construct **forall** x **with** φ **do** M, called **forall** rule, generates in $\mathfrak{A}$ the union of all update sets (one per instance) which are generated in state $\mathfrak{A}$ by the instances of M that interpret x by an $a \in Workspace(\mathfrak{A})$ satisfying φ.

Definition 31 (Semantics of forall rules). We extend the class of ASMs (with **choose** and **import** rules) inductively by **forall** rules, i.e. rules of the form $M' = $ **forall** x **with** φ **do** M (where M is an ASM). Its semantics is defined (in mathematical terms, borrowing some notation from the ASM framework) by the following clause that generalizes the semantics of **par** rules in the presence of **import** and **choose** rules (Def. 19, pg. 36).

Let ζ, η_0 be two parameters given in the context where the **forall** rule is evaluated, and let the set of elements x satisfying φ be defined as

$$range(x, \varphi, \mathfrak{A}, \zeta) = \{a \in Workspace(\mathfrak{A}) \mid eval(\varphi, \mathfrak{A}, \zeta[x \mapsto a]) = true\}.$$

We define:

if $range(x, \varphi, \mathfrak{A}, \zeta) = \emptyset$ **then**
  $evalCand(\textbf{forall } x \textbf{ with } \varphi \textbf{ do } M, \mathfrak{A}, \zeta, \eta_0, (\emptyset, \eta_0))$ holds
else
  $evalCand(\textbf{forall } x \textbf{ with } \varphi \textbf{ do } M, \mathfrak{A}, \zeta, \eta_0, (U, \eta))$ holds
  where
    $\{a_1, a_2, \ldots\}$ is any enumeration of $range(x, \varphi, \mathfrak{A}, \zeta)$[19]
    $evalCand(M, \mathfrak{A}, \zeta[x \mapsto a_n], \eta_{n-1}, (U_n, \eta_n))$
      holds for every a_n with some (U_n, η_n)
    $U = \bigcup_n U_n$ **and** $\eta = \bigcup_n \eta_n$

Why we restrict choose/forall to quantify over the current *Workspace*, besides for implementation reasons, can be explained here: without the restriction a rule like **forall** x **with** $true$ **do** $f(x) := 1$ would turn each *Heap* element into an argument of the function f with value $1 \neq undef$ and thereby into a *Workspace* element. That would exhaust the capacity of *Heap* to provide free elements for further **imports**.

With the **forall** construct one can specify the synchronous parallel control behaviour paradigm for any set of *Processes* as follows:

SYNCPAR(*Process*) = **forall** $P \in Process$ **do** P

An interesting combination of interleaving with synchronous parallelism is implemented in CoreASM [64]—an ASM interpreter—where in each step not only one but a finite number of agents can be chosen to simultaneously make a step. We call this computational paradigm *parallel interleaving*. It provides an interesting sequential implementation of concurrent runs (Ch. 5) and at the same time coincides with concurrency of communicating processes (Sect. 5.2) where the information exchange between agents is provided by a communication medium with an appropriate protocol so that there are no shared locations that could create update conflicts in concurrent runs. Another example appears in runs of Look-Compute-Move algorithms (Sect. 9.2.2.3).

Definition 32 (Parallel Interleaving Paradigm).

PARINTERLEAV(*Process*) =
  choose $\mathcal{P} \subseteq Process$ **with forall** $M \in \mathcal{P}$ $ReadyToExec(M)$
    forall $M \in \mathcal{P}$ **do** M

Example 12. **Cellular Automata** are an intensively studied computing device (see [109] for a survey) that uses the **forall** construct for its behavioural definition. These automata can be defined by refining the Finite State Machine rule FSM—that is executed by a single agent (see Exercise 3, pg. 26)—to

---

[19] We assume that every superuniverse $|\mathfrak{A}|$ is enumerable.

an even simpler CELLRULE of just one control state assignment that is executed in every step simultaneously by all agents of a discrete d-dimensional space *Cell*, say of all (or a finite subset of) d-tuples of integers viewed as actors. So the overall behaviour of a CELLAUTOMATON working on a (possibly infinite) structure of connected agents is defined by the following ASM (not any more a PGA!) rule:

> CELLAUTOMATON =
>   **forall** $c \in Cell$ **do** CELLRULE(c)

The refinement of the FSM rule to the CELLRULE is obtained by replacing input reading by reading at each cell c the *ctl* state of each neighbour of c. More precisely:

- in the FSM rule $ctl := nextCtl(ctl, in(head))$ replace reading the input $in(head)$ by reading at each cell c the *ctl* states of its finitely many neighbour cells $neighb_i(c)$ ($0 \leq i \leq n$ for some $n > 0$) where for notational convenience we include c as one of its neighbours, say $neighb_0(c) = c$. We call each n-tuple $(ctl(c), ctl(neighb_1(c)), \ldots, ctl(neighb_n(c)))$ a *neighbourhood configuration* of c.

This implies to delete the FSM reading *head* (together with its assignment rule and *move* function) and to refine the dynamic 0-ary FSM function *ctl* to a unary function $ctl : Cell \to CtlState$ where *CtlState* is the usual finite set of FSM control states.

Thus each CELLRULE performs an atomic action that represents an instance of the Look-Compute-Action paradigm (pg. 27) of the following form. As usual **self** denotes the currently considered cell (the executing agent).

> CELLRULE =
> $ctl(\textbf{self}) := nextCtl(ctl(neighb_0(\textbf{self})), \ldots, ctl(neighb_n(\textbf{self})))$.

For every CELLAUTOMATON a state consists of the dynamic function $ctl : Cell \to CtlState$ plus the space Cell with static $neighb_i$ and $nextCtl$ functions. Runs are ASM runs of an agent executing program CELLAUTOMATON without further interaction with the environment (see Definition 22, pg. 40), i.e. a synchronizer of all local agents c each of which computes its instance CELLRULE(c) of the CELLRULE. Note that in every step the update set of all updates computed for every location (ctl, c) by the local CELLRULE is obviously consistent.

The multitude of CELLRULEs is provided by different rule specific interpretations of the finite and static local-update function $nextCtl$ that specifies for every cell c and for each of its finitely many possible neighbourhood configurations the next value of $ctl(c)$.

The constituents of a cellular automaton—the local rule and function instances (CELLRULE(c), $neighb_i(c)$, $ctl(c)$) and $nextCtl$—are rather simple. This holds in particular for what in the literature is known as *elementary cellular automata*, the 1-dimensional case with integer cells ($Cell = \mathcal{Z}$) and only two control states $0, 1$ where every cell c has only its direct *leftNeighb*our and *rightNeighb*our; so per cell there are only $2^3 = 8$ neighbourhood configurations ($ctl(c-1), ctl(c), ctl(c+1)$) resulting in $2^8 = 256$ possible *nextCtl* functions in CELLRULEs. Despite of this simplicity some elementary cellular automata A are computation universal in the sense that for every Turing machine computation C there is an initial state of A such that A starting its run in this initial state simulates C [167, Ch. 11: Sect. 4-6]. This reflects the power of cooperation that results from connecting elementary component processes in nets that provide specific interaction structures. In Sect. 9.2.2 we illustrate a similar example: the distributed Look-Compute-Move automata whose components are connected in an underlying discrete graph or Euclidean space where they can also change their position in the structure, moving along an edge in the graph or following a computed trajectory in the given space. The universality phenomenon is explained in more detail in Sect. 9.1.2 and Sect. 9.2.1; here we point only to the following rule of a concrete computation universal elementary cellular automaton, rule 110 in Wolfram's notation with *ctl* represented by *color*, control state 1 by *black* and 0 by *white* (see [167, Ch. 11: Sect. 8]):

> CELLRULE110 =
>   **if** *color*(**self**) = *color*(*leftNeighb*(**self**)) = *color*(*rightNeighb*(**self**))
>   **or** (*color*(*leftNeighb*(**self**)) = *black* **and**
>   *color*(*rightNeighb*(**self**)) = *color*(**self**) = *white*)
>   **then** *color*(**self**) := *white*
>   **else** *color*(**self**) := *black*

Computations of cellular automata with small dimension (for example 1 or 2), a small number of control states and (possibly near) neighbors when started with not too complicated initial states can be efficiently visualized in the plane representing control states by colors. This has been exploited intensively in investigations of the behaviour of cellular automata and revealed a new kind of behavioural complexity, namely the complexity of (either static or dynamically evolving) structural patterns that are generated by (segments of) cellular automata computations started in specific initial states. See for example [166, 167] and the rich catalogues [132] of patterns generated from initial states by the best known particular cellular automaton: Conway's (computation universal 2-dimensional) Game of Life.

Exercise 17 (Conway's Game of Life). Consider the 2-dimensional Game of Life where a cell with 3 *alive* neighbours becomes (or remains) *alive* and a cell with less than 2 or more than 3 neighbours becomes (or remains) *dead*. Have a look at [132] for interesting patterns this simple rule generates from initial states.

As a further example of 2-dimensional cellular automata, with *neighbours* consisting of the cell itself plus the 4 cells directly above, below, left or right of it, consider the following CELLRULE:

CELLRULEDIAMOND =
   if thereissome $x \in neighbours(\textbf{self})$ **with** $color(x) = black$ **then**
      $color(\textbf{self}) := black$

which, starting from a single black cell, produces an ever-growing diamond shape of black cells. Figure 3.4 shows the first few generations of the automata (with the new black cells at each step highlighted in a darker shade).

Fig. 3.4 Successive generations of the CELLRULEDIAMOND automata

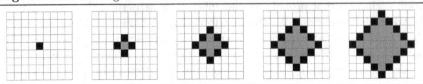

Chapter 4
Dynamic Sequential Step Control

In this chapter we explain the basic ingredient of self-modifying (also called adaptive) sequential algorithms, namely their ability to change their own behaviour at runtime. This reflectivity feature extends the classical notion of Turing-machine-like algorithmic computations which are input-triggered and follow a fixed static program.

In Sect. 4.2 we analyse the intuitive concept of reflectivity which directs our definition of an abstract notion of sequential deterministic reflective algorithms in Sect. 4.3. As characteristic examples for the practice of reflective programming we specify the reflective behaviour of programs in three concrete (logical, functional and imperative) languages: Prolog (Section 4.4), LISP (Section 4.5), and the reflective version RASP (Random Access Stored Program Machine) of the RAM (Section 4.6). In Sect. 4.6.1 we show an example of a reflective machine at work, namely a RASP simulation of indirect addressing. The simplicity and the expressive power of our generic concept of reflective machines are also highlighted by using reflectivity to define a computationally universal abstract machine (Sect. 9.1.2.1, pg. 228). In Sect. 4.7 we compare the reflectivity features of the mentioned languages with our definition of reflective ASMs and relate them with the closely related concept of reification of programming features, a different reflectivity style offered for example by Java.

In this chapter by reflective algorithms we mean deterministic sequential algorithms with reflection and use as abstract model an extension of PGAs (unless otherwise stated). We use the occasion to illustrate a practical and rather general mechanism to handle domain-specific extensions of a given language or machine. As example we use an extension of PGAs by a conceptually simple but general scheme for program change instructions. This scheme allows one to modify (at run time) a complex structured object (here: a program) by an appropriate combination into one 'global' update of multiple 'local' updates of parts of this object. The generic character of this construct relies upon a partial update technique we explain in Section 4.1.

E. Börger, V. Gervasi, *Structures of Computing*,
https://doi.org/10.1007/978-3-031-54358-6_4

The hurried reader may skip this section and go directly to the discussion of reflectivity in Sect. 4.2.

4.1 Partial Updates of Structured Objects

When operating on structured objects one might wish to permit the independent specification of two or more 'local' updates in parts of the structure that are then combined ('aggregated') into one 'global' update of the structure, possibly also mediating conflicts that could occur among the given local updates. This consideration applies in full generality to multiple so-called *partial updates* for any structured objects, like sets, functions, graphs, trees, programs, and also to multiple assignments to shared locations in concurrent runs, e.g. a counter where updates by different agents may be intended to be applied cumulatively (see Example 13, pg. 116).

The update-based ASM framework lends itself to deal with partial updates computed by appropriately tailored update instructions (to be distinguished from assignment instructions, see pg. 23), also called partial assignment instructions or partial assignments. They extend regular updates of a given *location* that has structured content in such a way that one can specify the desired update of *loc* by a set of updates of parts of the structure of the content of *loc*, 'partial' updates that will be aggregated using some *action* to become executable as one regular update of the (structure in the given) *location*. For example, one may wish to handle two simultaneous requests of a *count*er increase, say $count := count + 1$ and $count := count + 2$, not as generating in any state $\mathfrak{A}$ two inconsistent regular updates $(count, count^{\mathfrak{A}} + 1)$ and $(count, count^{\mathfrak{A}} + 2)$ but as an action that will *addCumulative*ly the two addition requests, expressed by two partial updates $(count, count^{\mathfrak{A}} + 1, addCumulative)$ and $(count, count^{\mathfrak{A}} + 2, addCumulative)$ that are combined to result in one regular *count*er update $(count, count^{\mathfrak{A}} + 3)$.

The syntax we use for partial updates adds to assignment instructions $f(t_1, \ldots, t_n) := t$ the *action* by which the *val*ue in the generated partial update $(loc, val, action)$ is combined with the values of possibly further generated (occurrences of) partial updates of the same *location*, possibly also with a different action (for example $(count, count^{\mathfrak{A}} - 1, subtractCumulative)$:

$$f(t_1, \ldots, t_n) :=_{action} t$$

Correspondingly, the semantics of ASMs is extended to compute two kinds of updates:

- Usual updates we continue to simply call updates (or also regular or genuine updates), i.e. location/value pairs (l, v) which form an update set U as described in Definition 14 (pg. 32).
- Possibly multiple occurrences of *partial updates* $(loc, val, action)$. They result from the evaluation of a partial assignment instruction, i.e. with

$loc = (f, (eval(t_1, \mathfrak{A}, \zeta), \ldots, eval(t_n, \mathfrak{A}, \zeta))), val = eval(t, \mathfrak{A}, \zeta)$ and the indicated *action*. For every *location* these partial updates must be transformed together with a computed regular update (loc, v) (if any) into a unique update of loc.

The semantics of partial updates is therefore defined as follows:

Definition 33 (Semantics of update instructions). It suffices to extend the basis of the induction in Definition 14 (pg. 32), the inductive cases remain the same (but use partial update multisets instead of update sets, given that possibly multiple occurrences of one update are intended to be taken into account, for example two occurrences of $(count, count^{\mathfrak{A}} + 1, addCumulative)$ could be treated to yield the update $(count, count^{\mathfrak{A}} + 2))$.

$$eval(f(t_1, \ldots, t_n) :=_{action} t, \mathfrak{A}, \zeta) = \{(loc, val, action)\}$$
where
$$loc = (f, (eval(t_1, \mathfrak{A}, \zeta), \ldots, eval(t_n, \mathfrak{A}, \zeta)))$$
$$val = eval(t, \mathfrak{A}, \zeta)$$

The triples (loc, val, act) generated in state $\mathfrak{A}$ form a partial-update multiset $PartUpd_{loc}$. For each *location*, from those triples together with a regular update (loc, v) generated in state $\mathfrak{A}$ (if any) a unique update $(loc, newVal)$ has to be computed which contributes to form the successor state $\mathfrak{A} + U$ (if any) as described in Def. 9 (pg. 19).[1] This computation is performed by a separately specified machine AGGREGATE that depends on the (type of the) structure of the content of the involved *location* (e.g. a set), on the used *actions* (e.g. insertion or deletion of some elements), and on the *value*[2] that contributes to the update. Therefore here we have to leave this machine abstract, its specification is possible once the structure of the content of loc and the corresponding kinds of *action* are known.

For notational economy, in the following we assume that the $+$ operator (the application of updates to a state, Def. 9 pg. 19) is extended to support partial updates.

Remark. This treatment of partial updates is supported by the ASM interpreter CoreASM, see [128, 73, 74] and [50, Ch. 8]. If there are dependencies among updates of different locations—e.g. when in a structured object the value of one location l_1 determines the value of another location l_2—the specification of the AGGREGATE machine must include a compatibility analysis.[3]

---

[1] Note that if one does not want to combine a regular update (loc, v) generated in state $\mathfrak{A}$ with the partial updates generated for the same *location* in state $\mathfrak{A}$, then the update (loc, v') resulting from the combination of those partial updates in $PartUpd_{loc}$ must be consistent with the regular update (loc, v) to be applicable to form the successor state. One could also give priority either to the regular (a 'global') update or to the update resulting from the combination of the partial ('local') updates.

[2] This is without loss of generality; if multiple parameters are needed to specify a certain *action*, we can assume the *value* to be a tuple of such parameters.

[3] For the analysis of some sophisticated compatibility criteria investigated in terms of an alternative treatment of partial updates see [154].

Partial Update Instruction Notation. Instead of partial assignments $container :=_{addCumulative} container + c$ we often use an equivalent update instruction notation (preferring a mixfix natural-language based syntax for readability) such as

add c **to** *container*

(or ADDCUMULATIVE(c, *container*)) with an indication of the partial updates the instruction is intended to generate in a state $\mathfrak{A}$. For example, we may stipulate that **add** c **to** *container* generates triples (*container*, c^*, *addCumulative*) where c^* does not stand for the new value that would result for the *container* by the assignment $container := container + c$; instead it stands for the element $eval(c, \mathfrak{A}, \zeta)$ that is intended to-be-added to the *container* (maybe together with other elements, depending on what AGGREGATE will compute to combine the partial *container* updates). The *container* may stand for say a (0-ary function) *counter* or *set* or *list* or *stack* with structured content as indicated by the names. The computation of the AGGREGATE machine for the *addCumulative* action depends on this structure of the *container* elements: *addCumulative* is interpreted as the cumulative version (possibly using some ordering of the local operations) of the following operations:

- number operation $+$ if the *container* is a *counter* with values in say *Nat*,
- set union $\cup$ if the *container* contains sets,
- *insert* (at an indicated position) if the *container* contains lists,
- *push* if the *container* contains stacks, etc.

Similarly for update instructions **remove** c **from** *container* describing the effect of $container :=_{remove} c$ (as it is often the case that such update instructions come in families, providing various operations of a coherent algebra of partial updates).

4.2 Intuitive Meaning of Reflectivity

Before proceeding to the definition of the language **ReflectPGA** of reflective PGAs we investigate the intuitive concept of reflective algorithms which directs our definition.

Reflective processes support a double view on the functionality of their algorithm: an execution view and a data view.

- At the 'object-level' an algorithm is seen as description of the updates the algorithm performs in a given state S on some of its data, excluding the algorithm itself. The instructions of the algorithm are *read*, *interpreted* as actions the algorithm requires to perform, and *executed* on the involved data, but they are not changed (cannot be written).
- At the 'meta-level' instructions of an algorithm are seen as *data that can be modified by runtime writes*, i.e. as location(s) (data container(s)) where

to store at runtime a possibly new value which determines the execution step that will be performed in the successor state S'. For this view the algorithm must be included in its modifiable data space.

This is the main characteristic of reflexive algorithms: they can be both executed and updated by the algorithm. Therefore, to find a general but precise reflectivity concept that can be instantiated to explain the behaviour of reflective programs of concrete programming languages we have to investigate two questions:

- Can one define in a general, precise and simple form how to incorporate into states $\mathfrak{A}$ an algorithm that is executed in $\mathfrak{A}$ such that the execution step may include to perform some updates that modify the algorithm itself, resulting in a new algorithm that is executed in the next state (if there is a next state)?
- Can one define a precise, general and simple form for instructions that manipulate reflective programs?

To answer these two questions for sequential and deterministic algorithms we use PGAs. The first question has a simple answer: introduce into the state of a PGA a **dynamic program location** pgm where to store the current value of the PGA rule, more precisely a 0-ary dynamic function pgm whose value $pgm^{\mathfrak{A}}$ in a given state $\mathfrak{A}$ first of all defines the step function $step_{(pgm^{\mathfrak{A}})}$, i.e. it drives the execution of the PGA rule to compute the successor state $step_{pgm^{\mathfrak{A}}}(\mathfrak{A}) = \mathfrak{A}'$ (if it is defined). But in addition this step of the PGA with program $pgm^{\mathfrak{A}}$ may also generate an update $(pgm, rule)$ whose execution modifies $pgm^{\mathfrak{A}}$ to a new PGA rule $rule = pgm^{\mathfrak{A}'}$ that is executed in the successor state $\mathfrak{A}'$ to compute the next $step_{pgm^{\mathfrak{A}'}}(\mathfrak{A}')$.

To answer the second question we must analyze the structure of programs which determines which parts of this structure are appropriate for being updated. For example, in the logic programming language Prolog a program is a sequence of instructions (called clauses) that can be inserted and deleted. In the functional programming language LISP a program is an expression all of whose terms can be modified. In the imperative RASP (Random Access Stored Program) language a program is a sequence of instructions that come with two components, an operation code and an operand both of which are stored in registers that can be modified when the current program executes a step. In the structure of PGA rules we find all of these three features: a rule can be inserted or deleted from the program, a logical expression that appears as condition of a guarded rule can be modified, and all the terms that appear in an assignment can be modified.

This suggests to consider pgm update instructions at the level of PGA rules, of conditional expressions and of terms as candidate for a general form of instructions tailored to manipulate reflective programs.

A question that remains concerns the signature: in a reflective algorithm the fixed signature Σ of PGAs must become dynamic to reflect that in updates of pgm new functions may be introduced, maybe together with some initialization code. This is easily specified by the **import** construct of ASMs which allows one to introduce new functions and specify their initialization.

4.3 Reflective PGAs

As explained in the preceding section we start with the following simple definition.[4]

Definition 34 (Reflective PGA). We call an ASM M a reflective PGA if it is an extension of a PGA (Def. 12, pg. 24) by the following two properties:

- The signature of M contains a 0-ary dynamic function pgm together with a 0-ary dynamic signature function Σ such that the runs of M start in initial states where the value of pgm is the main rule of M and in every state $\mathfrak{A}$ the executed step is a step of $pgm^{\mathfrak{A}}$ computing the successor state $step_{(pgm^{\mathfrak{A}})}(\mathfrak{A})$. pgm is required to have the same value in every initial state of M, called its initial program.
- Besides the original PGA rules M uses program update instructions (Def. 35 below) and also the **import** construct, added to the inductive definition of PGA rules to express extensions of the signature Σ.

By **ReflectPGA** we denote the class of reflective PGAs.

For simplicity of exposition but without loss of generality, in this definition we assume every call-by-name $N(t_1, \ldots, t_n)$ in M to be replaced by the corresponding body instance $N'(x_1/t_1, \ldots, x_n/t_n)$ of the declaration of N so that we have to consider for the pgm only the program of the *main* component of M.

The structure of PGAs suggests three kinds of **specific program update instructions**, namely to insert/delete rules (read: instructions) and to modify formulae (which occur as guards of conditional instructions) or terms (which occur in assignment instructions). This can be expressed by corresponding update instructions that contribute to modify the program value of pgm.

Rule replacement. To express that a particular occurrence of a PGA *rule* in a given PGA *program* should be replaced by some PGA *rule'* we label all occurrences of the to-be-replaced *rule* in the *program*, say by $rule_1, \ldots, rule_n$ (using number indices as labels). This allows us to formulate the desired rule replacement by an update instruction of the following form:

---

[4] The section is inspired by [153] where the authors provide an axiomatic definition of reflective sequential algorithms with a proof that the latter are captured (in the sense defined in Ch. 8, pg. 195) by an appropriate class of sequential ASMs. These ASMs use for the program manipulation a tree algebra background we replace by a conceptually simple partial program assignment construct that provides a practical definition of reflective ASMs—in terms of Sect. 7.1 a *ground model* for the above reflectivity requirements.

REPLACERULE $rule_i$ **by** $rule'$ **in** $program$

The effect of this REPLACERULE is defined to generate a partial update

$$(program, (rule_i, rule', program), replaceRule)$$

the AGGREGATE$_{PgmUpd}$ machine will try to perform by replacing in the given $program$ the indicated $rule_i$ occurrence by $rule'$. Note that the labeling is assumed to be made (in the background) for a given program where needed to name a rule one wants to replace.

Rule deletion. The deletion of a rule occurrence $rule_i$ in a $program$ is a special case of rule replacement so that it can be defined as follows:

DELETERULE $rule_i$ **from** $program$ =
REPLACERULE $rule_i$ **by skip in** $program$

Rule insertion. The insertion of a $rule$ makes sense only in case $rule$ becomes a **par** companion of some rule occurrence in $program$. Therefore it can be defined as follows:

INSERTRULE $rule'$ **at** $rule_i$ **into** $program$ =
REPLACERULE $rule_i$ **by par** $(rule_i, rule')$ **in** $program$

Formula and term update instructions. The same technique can be used for update instructions that modify rule guards (i.e. logical formulae) or terms in a PGA $program$:

- REPLACEFORMULA $cond_i$ **by** $cond'$ **in** $program$ is defined to generate the partial update triple $(program, (cond_i, cond', program), replaceFormula)$.
- REPLACETERM t_i **by** t' **in** $program$ is defined to generate the partial update triple $(program, (t_i, t', program), replaceTerm)$.

Definition 35 (Program Update Instructions). We call REPLACERULE, INSERTRULE, DELETERULE, REPLACEFORMULA, and REPLACETERM pgm update instructions of reflexive PGAs.

Note that the AGGREGATE$_{PgmUpd}$ machine for the handling of partial $program$ updates is tailored to try to combine partial updates generated to modify rules, guards and terms of $program$ into a regular update of $program$ (if the partial updates are compatible). In this way the detailed specification and implementation of how to apply multiple partial updates to a $program$ is pushed for a refinement (i.e. a more detailed specification or an implementation) to the background (in CoreASM to a plugin), an example of separation of concerns. Also the update of the labeling of the items of interest (rules, guards, terms) in the updated $program$ is computed in the background.

Remark on program representation. The abstract program update instructions of reflexive PGAs hide the details of program representation, access and change and indicate the place for their refinement and implementation in the AGGREGATE$_{PgmUpd}$ machine. These update instructions work not only for a representation of ASMs as code (as obtained by their inductive definition, see pg. 24) but also for other widely used program representations, including visual ones. A standard example is the definition by annotated parse trees, see Fig. 4.1, Fig. 4.2, Fig. 4.3 and Fig. 4.4, by which program manipulation is realized by operations on (sub)trees.

Fig. 4.1 Tree representation of assignment instructions $f(t_1, \ldots, t_n) := t$

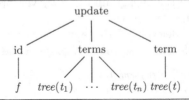

Fig. 4.2 Tree representation of update instructions $f(t_1, \ldots, t_n) :=_{action} t$

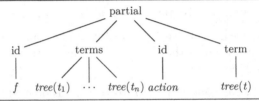

Fig. 4.3 Tree representation of **if** *cond* **then** M and **par** $M_1, \ldots, M_n$ rules

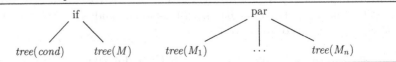

Fig. 4.4 Tree representation of **let** $x = t$ **in** M and **import** x **do** M rules

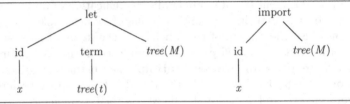

The visualization often helps to find easy-to-comprehend definitions of intricate program behaviour. A typical example is the definition of a Java interpreter in [159] the procedural part of which we have used in Sect. 3.2 to illustrate the sequential imperative programming paradigm. Using that technique the labeling of rule occurrences—introduced above to have a distinct name $rule_i$ for every occurrence of $rule$ in $program$—comes for free: in the $parseTree(program)$ representation use the labeling of tree nodes by $\alpha, \beta, \ldots$ to refer to $rule_i$ by the unique α that labels the root of the subtree that represents $rule_i$ (in $parseTree(program)$). Therefore the corresponding program update instruction becomes (for example) REPLACERULE α **by** $rule'$ **in** $parseTree(program)$. For another example where the parse tree structure helps see Fig. 9.6–Fig. 9.8 in Sect. 9.2.1 for the construction of a universal ASM over fixed signature.

However, for the formulation of partial updates of reflective $programs$ the two representations are equivalent. The important point here is the abstraction obtained by the Program Update Instructions defined above (Def. 35) for reflective PGAs (Def. 34). These instructions abstract from the complex technical details that are involved when parse trees (or program texts) for ASMs are treated as terms to which the basic term $eval$uation function is applied, as done in [153] to define reflectivity.

Extensions of ReflectPGA. To let the essential part of the computational reflectivity notion come out explicitly we have defined it by a technically simple extension of deterministic PGAs, namely by letting the given program that computes the $step$ function be value of part of the memory, for simplicity value of a location pgm. In terms of PGAs the execution view and the data view of a reflective pgm stand out explicitly as follows:

- pgm appears as parameter of the $step$ function whose application to a state $\mathfrak{A}$ executes the step that leads from $\mathfrak{A}$ to the successor state $step_{pgm^{\mathfrak{A}}}(\mathfrak{A})$.
- pgm can appear in updates of part of the memory where pgm is stored, namely in (partial updates that are aggregated into) an update of $pgm^{\mathfrak{A}}$ to $pgm^{\mathfrak{A}'}$.

Technically this is obtained by using the $eval(M, \mathfrak{A}, \zeta)$ function to determine the update set deterministic PGAs apply to compute the successor state of the given state $\mathfrak{A}$. Using instead the nondeterministic version $evalCand(M, \mathfrak{A}, \zeta, U)$ (Def. 27) integrates reflectivity in a natural way into nondeterministic ASMs. It provides reflectivity also in the presence of other constructs or for multi-agent concurrent ASMs we investigate in the next chapter.[5]

---

[5] Also the characterization of reflexivity in [153] starts with PGAs. Whether this characterization can be extended to work for ASMs with unbounded choice and/or parallelism has not yet been investigated.

4.4 Backtracking and Reflection (Prolog)

The logic programming language Prolog offers dedicated instructions to change the program at runtime. We explain in this section from scratch an abstract precise definition of an interpreter for dynamic Prolog programs; the definition is given in ASM (even PGA) terms, the way that has been used to formulate the entire ISO Prolog standard [66] and to perform a rigorous analysis of the various proposals to decide upon for the specification of the ISO standard semantics of program updates [30, 42].

We use the occasion to illustrate by a circumscribed but concerning the reflectivity phenomenon complete example how to construct a language interpreter out of components for groups of instructions, using the same instruction wise composition method as in Sect. 3.2. The interpreter is defined as a parallel composition of independent but interacting modules which directly reflect the organization of Prolog instructions into the following groups:

- Pure Prolog, consisting of the cut-free part without built-in predicates. This group has been proven to be correct but not complete with respect to SLD resolution.
- Logic Control, including cut and catch-and-throw.
- Dynamic Program Management
- Solution Collecting Predicates, including findall, bagof, setof.
- Error Handling.
- Box Model Debugger.

We concentrate our attention here on the core machine for Pure Prolog— which explains the by itself interesting computational *backtracking paradigm* by four simple rules—and its extension by a machine for the management of dynamic code. For the remaining components and their proven to be correct implementation to virtual machine code by a dozen of proven to be correct stepwise refinement steps the interested reader is refered to the literature [51, 52] and [149]. The last mentioned work is an interesting and for the ASM framework typical example for implementing a detailed proof-engine version of a mathematical proof, obtained by splitting the proof details into a series of independently verifiable stepwise ASM refinements (see Sect. 7.2).

4.4.1 Interpreter for Pure Prolog

A Prolog computation represents a systematic search through a space of possibly multiple solutions to an initially given problem, called *initialQuery*, where each time the currently tried out solution alternative fails a backtracking mechanism directs the search engine to try the next alternative (if available). The search is naturally modeled using a dynamically built tree structure of a dynamic set of *Nodes*:

$$parent : Node \setminus \{root\} \rightarrow Node \qquad root : Node$$

Each node (except the *root* and its *initialQuery*-node child, see the initialization condition below) represents computation states that correspond to one solution-computing alternative provided by the *pgm*. The search engine is a sequential machine so that in every moment it visits a unique node we denote by a 0-ary dynamic function *currnode*. Each node is associated with a sequence of its to-be-resolved *Goals* that come with (we say are 'decorated' by) their backtracking information in presence of the Prolog-specific crucial tree-pruning operator *cut*. Each goal is a sequence of user-defined or built-in terms. This explains the following functions that serve to record state information (we skip the explanation of the role of *Marks* because they are needed only for some built-in predicates we do not explain here):

$$Goal = Term^* \qquad Decgoal = Goal \times Node$$
$$decgoalseq : Node \rightarrow (Decgoal \cup Mark)^*$$
$$currnode : Node$$
$$currdecgoalseq = decgoalseq(currnode)$$
$$currgoal = first(first(currdecgoalseq))$$

At *currnode* with a user-defined to-be-resolved term *first(currgoal)*, called *activator*, the search engine can do two things:

- LAYOUTALTERNATIVES: if in *mode = layoutAlts* lay out the possible solution alternatives for the current *activator* by extending the tree by a list *cands(currnode)* of children of *currnode*, one candidate for each to-be-tried-out code alternative provided by the *pgm*, and switch to *mode = tryNextAlt*,
- TRYNEXTALTERNATIVE: in *mode = tryNextAlt*, try to RESOLVE the *activator* by one of the code alternatives if there is still some candidate available, otherwise BACKTRACK.

The user-defined terms in elements of *Goal* are called *literals*. When a *literal* appears as *activator* at *currnode* the Prolog engine retrieves via a function *procdef* from its current program *pgm* the *Code* sequence of all occurrences of *Clauses* of form *Head ← Body* whose *Head* is formed by the same predicate symbol as *lit* (so that it may be unifiable with *lit*); in other words *procdef(lit, pgm)* retrieves from *pgm* the candidate clause occurrences for *lit*.[6] *lit* can be successfully computed by first unifying it with the *Head* of the alternative *clause(clauseOcc(child))* of at least one child in *cands(currnode)* and then computing with success the subgoal represented by the *Body* of such a clause. We use a dynamic function *clauseOcc* to record the association of one code alternative with each new child node in *cands(currnode)*.

Since Prolog has an error handling mechanism and supports termination of programs the rules we explain here have in their guard the following *OK* condition:

---

[6] *nil* in the range of this function is needed for the PROLOGDBMODULE defined below which handles dynamic changes of Prolog *pgms*.

$OK = (stop = 0$ **and** $error = 0)$

This explains the following four rules for Prolog's basic backtracking mechanism. The logical unification-based RESOLVE procedure is explained below.

LayOutAlternatives =
  if $UserDefined(activator)$ **and** $mode = layoutAlts$ **and** OK **then**
    ExtendTreeBy $node_1, \ldots, node_m$ **with**   -- state alternatives
      forall $i = 1, \ldots, m$ $clauseOcc(node_i) := c_i$
                     -- one per to-be-tried-out solution alternative
    $mode := tryNextAlt$ -- switch to compute the alternatives
    where $[c_1, \ldots, c_m] = procdef(activator, pgm)$ -- solution alternatives

The signature elements and the auxiliary macro are defined as follows:

$activator = first(currgoal)$ -- currently to-be-resolved term
$procdef : Lit \times Program \rightarrow Code^* \cup \{nil\}$ -- yields solution alternatives
$clauseOcc : Node \rightarrow Code$ -- records associated code line
                -- candidate clause occurrence of candidate child node
$clause : Code \rightarrow Clause$ -- clause at code line
ExtendTreeBy $node_1, \ldots, node_m$ **with** $M =$
  let $n_1, \ldots, n_m = $ **new** $(Node)$ **in**
    forall $i = 1, \ldots, m$ **do**
      $parent(n_i) = currnode$
      $cands(currnode) := [n_1, \ldots, n_m]$
      M

TryNextAlternative =
  if $UserDefined(activator)$ **and** $mode = tryNextAlt$ **and** OK
    then if $cands(currnode) = [\,]$ -- no alternative resolved $activator$
    then Backtrack
    else Resolve
  where Backtrack =
    if $parent(currnode) = root$ **then** $stop := Failure$
    else $currnode := parent(currnode)$

Observe that when the engine BACKTRACKs to $parent(currnode)$ it finds there all necessary state information (attached to the node by the functions that record the state information) to continue the computation with possibly remaining alternatives that may resolve the $activator$.

The GoalSuccess rule expresses that once the $currgoal$ has been successfully computed the engine PROCEEDs to compute the rest of its current $decgoalsequence$, popping the call stack. [7]

---

[7] PROCEED is refined by an additional rule to express special actions that have to be taken for certain built-in predicates we do not explain here.

GOALSUCCESS =
   if $currgoal = [\,]$ **and** OK **then** PROCEED
   where
     PROCEED $= (decgoalseq(currnode) := rest(currdecgoalseq))$

The QUERYSUCCESS rule expresses that once all goals have been computed the computation terminates with success.

QUERYSUCCESS =
   if $currdecgoalseq = [\,]$ **and** OK **then** $stop := success$

These four rules describe the backtracking-based computational paradigm of Prolog. For the initialization of Prolog computation trees we stipulate that initially the tree consists only of two nodes: the *root* node (on which no function is defined) and its unique child *currnode*; the latter comes with the one-element-list with *initialQuery* goal and with the backtracking node *root*, matching the condition $parent(currnode) = root$.

PUREPROLOG =
   LAYOUTALTERNATIVES
   TRYNEXTALTERNATIVE
   GOALSUCCESS
   QUERYSUCCESS

Exercise 18 (BACKTRACKSCHEME). Abstract from the particular Prolog features in PUREPROLOG and extract a generic BACKTRACKSCHEME for alternative machines whose execution is supposed to terminate with or without success and may recursively call alternative submachines to be tried out for execution. See Appendix B for a solution.

Prolog programs are sequential and deterministic. In fact at each moment at most one PUREPROLOG rule can be applied at the uniquely determined *currnode* because the rules have pairwise disjoint guards: if the *UserDefined(activator)* guard is true, then *currgoal* and with it *currgoalseq* are not the empty list. $currgoal = [\,]$ implies that *currgoalseq* is not empty; if *currgoalseq* is empty then *currgoal* $=undef$.

Exercise 19 (Prolog rule NEXTSOLUTION**).** Define an additional stop rule that continues the search for another solution if requested (by the user) in case $stop = success$. See Appendix B for a solution.

It remains to specify the RESOLVE mechanism.[8] It involves the logical concepts of term unification (most general unifier *mgu* of terms) and substitution (of free variables by terms) we assume the reader to know. We use the following functions:

---

[8] The reader who is not interested in the logical details of the resolution procedure may proceed directly to the interpreter rules for reflective Prolog.

$mgu : Term \times Term \to Substitution \cup \{nil\}$ -- most general unifier

$t \circ sub$ -- postfix notation for application of sub to t

$sub_1 \circ sub_2$ -- postfix notation for composition of substitutions

$sub : Node \to Substitution$ -- current substitution in a state

$term' = rename(term, vi)$ -- variables renamed at variable index vi

RESOLVE tries to unify the given $UserDefined(activator)$ with the renamed $Head'$ of the clause $Head \leftarrow Body$ that is associated with the first candidate $fstcand = first(cands(currnode))$. Whether the unification fails or not, the engine updates $cands$ to the remaining candidates (having tried the alternative $firstcand$). But if there is a unifying substitution $s = mgu(activator, Head')$, then the machine in addition updates at $fstcand$ the $decgoalseq$ to a new one—obtained by replacing in the current one the $activator$ by the renamed $Body'$ (with cutpoint information) and applying the substitution s, extends the current $sub(currnode)$ (to continue with at $fstcand$) by s, increases the variable renaming index vi, switches to $mode = layoutAlts$ and moves to $fstcand$ to continue the computation there by trying to resolve the new first goal defined by $Body' \circ s$.

RESOLVE =
    let $fstcand = first(cands(currnode))$ -- look at next alternative
    let $Hd \leftarrow Bd = clause(clauseOcc(fstcand))$ -- find its clause
    let $s = mgu(activator, Hd')$ **in**   -- try to compute a unifier
        $cands(currnode) := rest(cands(currnode))$ -- that is all if $s = nil$
        if $s \neq nil$ **then**   -- if unification is possible
            $decgoalseq(fstcand) := newdecgoalseq$
            $sub(fstcand) := sub(currnode) \circ s$ -- extend current substitution
            $vi := vi + 1$ -- increase variable renaming index
            $mode := layoutAlts$ -- move to try out goal Bd' under s
            $currnode := fstcand$ -- at next candidate child node
    where
        $newdecgoalseq = [(Bd', parent(currnode)) \mid continuation] \circ s$
        $continuation = [(rest(currgoal), cutpoint) \mid rest(currdecgoalseq)]$
        $cutpoint = snd(first(currdecgoalseq))$

4.4.2 Interpreter for reflective Prolog

Prolog has six so-called database operations[9] four of which are instructions to modify and the other two to read the pgm at runtime. $asserta(clause)$ and $assertz(clause)$ are deterministic instructions that simply $inserta$ (at the beginning) respectively $insertz$ (at the end) of the current pgm a new occurrence

---

[9] The in the Prolog community usual wording database db refers to what we denote by pgm.

of their argument *clause*. *retract*(*clause*) and *abolish*(*P*) allow one to (try to) delete a clause in the *pgm* which via unification matches *clause* respectively all clauses whose head is a literal with predicate symbol *P*. In addition Prolog also offers a read version *clause* of *retract* and *currentPredicate*(*P*) of *abolish*(*P*) both of which coincide with their *pgm* updating version except for the deletion operation. We therefore first analyse the behaviour of *retract* and *abolish*.

Since in every state a Prolog program can execute at most one of its *pgm* related instructions no partial updates are needed to specify the semantics of those instructions. Furthermore, the tree structure we considered for the general case of reflective *pgms* (Sect. 4.3) is reduced here to a list with corresponding list functions. So the two *assert* instructions immediately succeed, using the corresponding list *insert*ion function to insert a new occurrence of the given clause *Head* ← *Body* at the begin respective the end of *pgm*. Prolog operations on *pgm* are applied only if the user-defined predicate symbol that occurs in the head of the involved clauses is declared as *Dynamic*. This requirement implies that when an *assert* instruction is executed the predicate symbol *P* in the clause head must have been declared as *Dynamic*.[10]

ASSERT =
    if *activator* = *assert*(*H*, *B*) **and** *Dynamic*(*H*) **and** *OK* **then**
        pgm := *insert*(*H*, *B*, *pgm*)
        decgoalseq(*currnode*) := *continuation*-- *assert* succeeds immediately
    where
        continuation = [(*rest*(*currgoal*), *cutpoint*) | *rest*(*currdecgoalseq*)]
        cutpoint = *snd*(*first*(*currdecgoalseq*))

Prolog has the two instances ASSERTA and ASSERTZ of ASSERT, defined with the corresponding functions *inserta* and *insertz*.

The behaviour of *retract* and *abolish* has the same structure as the behaviour of user-defined predicates described in the two PUREPROLOG rules LAYOUTALTERNATIVES and TRYNEXTALTERNATIVES. For the Lay-Out *retract*(*Head*, *Body*) rule it suffices to refine LAYOUTALTERNATIVES by two replacements which constitute a pure data refinement:

- in the guard replace *UserDefined*(*activator*) by the two conditions *activator* = *retract*(*Head*, *Body*) **and** *Dynamic*(*Head*),
- replace *procdef*(*activator*, *pgm*) by *clauseList*(*Head*, *Body*, *pgm*).

The *clauseList*(*Head*, *Body*, *p*) of program *p* for clause terms *Head*, *Body* is the restriction of *procdef*(*Head*, *p*) to occurrences in *p* of candidate clauses *Hd* ← *Bd* whose predicate symbols in their literals coincide with the corresponding ones in *Head* ← *Body* (so that these clauses might be unifiable with the clause *Head* ← *Body*. This explains the first *retract* rule.

---

[10] So the signature extension rule EXTEND(Σ, *P*) boils down to a declaration statement.

LAYOUTRETRACTALTERNATIVES =
   if $activator = retract(Head, Body)$ **and** $Dynamic(Head)$
    and $mode = layoutAlts$ **and** OK
  then
    EXTENDTREEBY $node_1, \ldots, node_m$ **with**   -- solution alternatives
      forall $i = 1, \ldots, m$ $clauseOcc(node_i) := c_i$
    $mode := tryNextAlt$
  where
    $[c_1, \ldots, c_m] = clauseList(Head, Body, pgm)$
    $clauseList : Term \times Term \times Program \to Code^* \cup \{nil\}$

Similarly we can define the TryNext $retract(Head, Body)$ rule as a refinement of TRYNEXTALTERNATIVES. It suffices to make the same guard refinement as for the LayOut $retract(Head, Body)$ rule and two further refinements, an operation refinement of RESOLVE and a data refinement:

- add to RESOLVE the update of pgm by deleting the $clauseOcc(fstcand)$,
- refine the unification $mgu(activator, Hd')$ to unify the entire $activator$ clause $Head' \leftarrow Body'$ with the entire $clause(clauseOcc(fstcand))$ (instead of only its Hd'),
- refine $newdecgoalseq$ to the $continuation \circ s$ (because a retraction succeeds immediately without introducing any new subgoal).

TRYNEXTRETRACTALTERNATIVE =
   if $activator = retract(Head, Body)$ **and** $Dynamic(Head)$
    and $mode = tryNextAlt$ **and** OK
  then if $cands(currnode) = [\,]$ **then** BACKTRACK
  else
    RESOLVE
    if $s \neq nil$ **then** $pgm := deleteClauseOcc(clauseOcc(fstcand), pgm)$
  where
    $s = mgu(Head' \leftarrow Body', clause(clauseOcc(fstcand)))$
    $newdecgoalseq = continuation \circ s$
    $deleteClauseOcc : Code \times Program \to Program$

The function $deleteClauseOcc$ deletes a code line $c \in Code$ in pgm so that after the deletion c does not appear any more as member of any $clauseList$ (with whatever terms) of the modified program $deleteClauseOcc(c, pgm)$.

The clause reading rules LAYOUT/TRYNEXTCLAUSEALTERNATIVES— with $clause$ instead of $retract$—are identical to the corresponding $retract$ rules except for the missing clause deletion update of pgm.

The structural identity of $retract$ rules to the corresponding rules for user-defined predicates holds also for the $abolish(P)$ instruction of Prolog and its read version $currentPredicate(P)$. $abolish(P)$ deletes from the current pgm all clause occurrences with the predicate symbol P in their head. It works the same way as $retract$ but using functions $predicateList$ (instead of $clauseList$)

and *deletePredOcc* (instead of *deleteClauseOcc*). Similarly for the reading version *currentPredicate(P)* of *abolish(P)*.

The function *predicateList* : *Program* → *PI** yields for a program p the sequence of code lines in p that are associated with a clause whose head is formed by a predicate symbol, code lines we call predicate indicators which form a subset *PI* of *Code*. Thus for an n-ary predicate symbol $P^n \in predicateList(p)$ if and only if the *clauseList* of p contains a code line with associated clause with head $P(t_1, \ldots, t_n)$ for some terms t_i and some body B. For n-ary predicate symbols P the function *predicateList(P, p)* is the restriction of *predicateList(p)* to clauses whose head is formed with P.

LAYOUTABOLISHALTERNATIVES =
  if *activator = abolish(P)* **and** *Dynamic(P)*
    and *mode = layoutAlts* **and** *OK*
  then
    EXTENDTREEBY $node_1, \ldots, node_m$ **with**   -- solution alternatives
      forall $i = 1, \ldots, m$ $clauseOcc(node_i) := c_i$
    mode := tryNextAlt
  where
    $[c_1, \ldots, c_m] = predicateList(P, pgm)$
    predicateList : *PI* × *Program* → *PI**

Similarly the TryNext *abolish(P)* rule is structurally identical to the TryNext *retract(Head, Body)* rule. A pure data refinement replaces *delete-ClauseOcc* by *deletePredOcc* and unifies the *activator* parameter P with the (predicate symbol of the clause associated with the) code line *clause-Occ(fstcand)*.[11]

TRYNEXTABOLISHALTERNATIVE =
  if *activator = abolish(P)* **and** *Dynamic(P)*
    and *mode = tryNextAlt* **and** *OK*
  then if *cands(currnode) = [ ]* **then** BACKTRACK
  else
    RESOLVE
    if $s \neq nil$ **then** *pgm := deletePredOcc(clauseOcc(fstcand), pgm)*
  where
    $s = mgu(P, clauseOcc(fstcand))$
    newdecgoalseq = continuation ∘ s
    deletePredOcc : *PI* × *Program* → *Program*

The function *deletePredOcc* deletes a code line $c \in PI$ in *pgm* that is associated with a predicate symbol so that after the deletion this predicate symbol (here P) does not appear any more as element of the *predicateList* (see the Definition above) of the modified program *deletePredOcc(c, pgm)*.

---

[11] The word unification is used for notational uniformity reasons. What is checked here is the equality of the predicate symbols in two predicate symbol occurrences.

$P \notin predicateList(deletePredOcc(c, pgm))$

Thus all clauses whose head is formed with P are deleted from pgm.

The two rules for the reading version $currentPredicate(P)$ of $abolish(P)$ are identical to the corresponding $abolish(P)$ rules except for the missing predicate-symbol-deletion update of pgm.

The rules presented in this section constitute the reflective PROLOG-DBMANAGMT module, obtained by refining LAYOUTALTERNATIVES and TRYNEXTALTERNATIVE of PUREPROLOG to structurally identical rules for runtime pgm management. PUREPROLOG and PROLOGDBMANAGMT interact with each other without conflicts, given that their rules have pairwise disjoint rule guards.

> PROLOGDBMANAGMT =
>   ASSERT
>   LAYOUTDBALTERNATIVES
>   TRYNEXTDBALTERNATIVE
> **where**
>   ASSERT =
>   ASSERTA
>   ASSERTZ
>   LAYOUTDBALTERNATIVES =
>   LAYOUTRETRACTALTERNATIVES
>   LAYOUTCLAUSEALTERNATIVES
>   LAYOUTABOLISHALTERNATIVES
>   LAYOUTCURRENTPREDICATEALTERNATIVES
>   TRYNEXTDBALTERNATIVE =
>   TRYNEXTRETRACTALTERNATIVE
>   TRYNEXTCLAUSEALTERNATIVE
>   TRYNEXTABOLISHALTERNATIVE
>   TRYNEXTCURRENTPREDICATEALTERNATIVE

Historical remark. The PROLOGDBMANAGMT rules guided the detailed comparative ASM-model-based analysis (see [30, 42]) of various proposals for the ISO Prolog standard [66] and led to the decision to define the so-called *logical view* [122] of Prolog pgm operations as the ISO standard view, recognized as the best one concerning comprehension, rigorous design and efficient implementation.

Remark on separation of concerns. Our Prolog interpreter illustrates two natural and expressive ways by which the ASM framework supports the important concept of *separation of concerns* in system design: one consists in decomposing a system into independent modules, characterized by making the relevant parameters together with the operations on them explicit in an abstract reusable form; another one is the introduction of appropriately parameterized functions to independently specify various actions within a module. An example is the definition of RESOLVE with differently instantiatable parameters, namely *mgu*, *newdecgoalseq* and the deletion functions *deleteClauseOcc* and *deletePredOcc*. Another example is the separation of layout and try phase to compute an *activator*, coupled with the introduction of *procdef*, *clauseList* and *predicateList* to operate on user-defined or retract or abolish *activators*; this yields the independent but structurally isomorphic (thereby reusable) rules that lay out and successively try out the alternatives for computing the given *activator* in the corresponding module. The introduction of *deleteClauseOcc* and *deletePredOcc* with appropriate constraints illustrates how to separate the definition of their effect from the specification of the rules where they are used.

4.5 Reflection in LISP

The handling of reflectivity in Reflective ASMs (Sect. 4.3) and in Prolog (Sect. 4.4) is based on replacing the current value of *pgm* with a new value, typically obtained by manipulating the previous one. A different and more localized approach applies to languages which have a uniform by-reference semantics.

The **LIS**t **P**rocessing language **LISP** [126] is a prime example of what is called a homoiconic language, in that LISP programs are LISP data structures—namely lists made up from atoms by a pairing function—which can be dynamically manipulated in the language and executed. In this section we describe the part of LISP that suffices to explain its distinctive reflective list manipulation and execution features.

A LISP program is a sequence of *Expressions* (also called *S-expressions* for "symbolic expressions") rather than statements; consequently to execute the program means to EVALUATEEXPRessions of such a sequence (that is technically defined as a list, see below). Depending on the execution environment, the sequence can be provided interactively (e.g., by a user typing in a terminal) or as one or more textual source file (or, in certain implementations, as compiled file). The result of the evaluation of the last expression in a program is considered to be the result of the whole program. Therefore, to distill the reflective properties of LISP programs we can concentrate our attention on what a LISP interpreter EVALUATEEXPR does to execute one expression, abstracting from how the execution environment organizes the execution (i.e. evaluation) of the entire sequence of expressions.

The set of LISP *Expressions* is inductively defined from *Atoms* and *Constructs*.

The elements of *Atom* are individual values: numbers, strings denoted by a sequence of characters enclosed in double quotation marks, or symbols. Each string literal produces a new instance of the string, whereas number and symbol literals produce a reference to a unique instance. Symbols can be

alphanumeric sequences (e.g., if or let), but can also use a wide variety of
characters from the available character set (e.g., + or pair? are valid symbols
and thus valid identifiers).

Constructs are equipped with two functions *head* and *tail* in terms of which
complex data structures can be defined. We call the elements of the abstract
set *Cons* simply *cons* and write them with lower case 'c'.

$$Atom = Number \cup String \cup Symbol \qquad \text{-- disjoint union}$$
$$Expr = Atom \cup Cons \qquad\qquad\qquad \text{-- disjoint union}$$
$$head : Cons \rightarrow Expr$$
$$tail : Cons \rightarrow Expr$$

We will freely use predicates such as *isAtom*, *isSymbol*, *isCons* to indicate
the characteristic functions of the various sorts.

Using *head* and *tail* one can express a *List* element by a *cons* representing
the structure of a finite sequence of given *cons* c_i for $1 \leq i \leq n$, in particular
singly-linked lists defined from a cons l by the equations $(*)$ and denoted as
usual by $(e_1 \ldots e_n)$; the special atom NIL indicates the end of a list (an empty
list) and *tail* is required to be defined on *List* with values in $List \cup \{NIL\}$.

$$(*) \quad \textbf{forall } i = 1, \ldots, n, \quad e_i = head(tail^{i-1}(l)) \quad \textbf{and} \quad tail^n(l) = NIL.$$

To access the elements of such a list $l = (e_1 \ldots e_n)$ we use the notations
$item(l, i) = e_i$, $length(l) = n$, $range(l) = \{1, \ldots, length(l)\}$.

The use of parentheses to denote lists, and the prefix notation with function symbols preceding the arguments, give LISP its instantly recognizable
and remarkably regular syntax. As an example,

```
(if (= (mod (read) 2) 1)
   (print "odd")
   (print "even")
)
```

is an expression which reads a value (hopefully a number) from whatever
input is provided, computes the modulo 2 of that value, compares the results
for equality to the atom 1, and prints "odd" or "even" depending on the
outcome. The *Cons*-based representation of the above program S is given in
Figure 4.5 (where $\times$ stands for a reference to NIL). In the figure, each cons
c is represented as a pair of cells, with the left one representing $head(c)$ and
the right one representing $tail(c)$.

At any given moment our interpreter will be evaluating a specific expression pointed to by a 0-ary *position* function, which we will consider initialized
by an unspecified top-level loop[12] to the top-level expression to evaluate. The
results of the evaluation will be given as the value of a function $value(\cdot)$ which
is initially undefined everywhere; we use a predicate $done(\cdot)$ to check whether

---

[12] Such a loop can be of the form (loop (print (eval (read)))), hence the acronym
REPL for read-eval-print-loop.

Fig. 4.5 Program representation in LISP

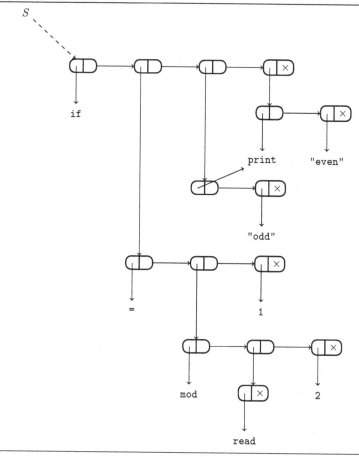

value(·) is defined. Two other auxiliary functions, *return*(·) and *result*(·) will hold, respectively, the continuation that is to be taken once the evaluation at a given *pos* is completed, and the result returned from that evaluation, which will be then accessed via *value*(·).

It should be noted that, in general, LISP programs may be graphs, not necessarily trees. An example is Figure 4.5, where the symbol `print` is referenced by multiple cons, but the same is true more generally: while the parser will always generate a tree up to symbol sharing from a textual representation of a program, as in Figure 4.6(a), the program itself may modify its contents — as we will show below — and produce arbitrary program structures such as the one in Figure 4.6(b), which requires the same sub-expression (`read`) to be evaluated twice. In addition, a program may request the evaluation of expressions that are dynamically constructed (e.g. via `cons`) or read from I/O (e.g., via `read`), and which are thus not part of any "source file". To support these features, as well as to implement recursion, each evaluation of an expression takes place in a corresponding *context*. We model a context by a value of sort *Ctx*; a variable (dynamic 0-ary function) *ctx* will hold at any moment the current context, with context nesting expressed via a function *parentCtx* : *Ctx* → *Ctx*. The initial value for *ctx* is a distinguished ctx_0 element of the sort, corresponding to the top-level evaluation.

Fig. 4.6 (a) LISP program structure as produced by the parser for the program (`print (read) (read)`). Notice how the arguments to `print` are two distinct lists. (b) Another structure with the same effect: Here, the arguments to `print` are the same list (`read`), referenced twice.

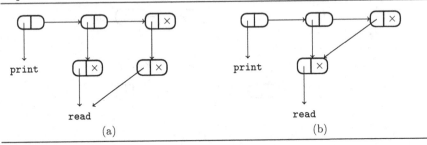

(a)   (b)

For navigating the expression being evaluated, we define two macros: PROCEEDAT(p, k) instructs the interpreter to proceed to evaluating the expression at (that is, referenced by) p, after preparing a new context *nc* for the evaluation. The new context establishes where to store the result (in *result* at key k of the invoking context) and where to continue the evaluation (via *return* of the invoked context). Different keys will be used to store results from possibly many subexpressions of the same expression (e.g. in FULLEVALFORM defined below). YIELD(v) instructs the interpreter to store the computed value v in the appropriate *result* of the invoking context, and continue executing from the associated continuation in *return*.

Accordingly, we define our signature and basic navigation operations as follows:

pos : *Expr* initialized by pos_0 -- current *position* of the interpreter
ctx : *Ctx* initialized by ctx_0 -- current context of the interpreter
parentCtx : *Ctx* → *Ctx*
key : *Ctx* → *Key*   -- key used to store intermediate value
result : *Ctx* × *Key* → *Expr*   -- storage for intermediate values
return : *Ctx* → *Expr*   -- continuation

PROCEEDAT(p, k) =   -- evaluate p, store result in k
  let *nc* = **new** *Ctx* **in**
    parentCtx(*nc*) := *ctx*

$key(nc) := k$
$return(nc) := pos$
$ctx := nc$
$pos := p$

$\text{YIELD}(v) =$ -- evaluation complete, return v as result
    let $pc = parentCtx(ctx)$ **in**
    $result(pc, key(ctx)) := v$
    $pos := return(ctx)$
    $ctx := pc$

We also use the following two derived functions:

$value(k) = result(ctx, k)$
$done(k) = (value(k) \neq undef)$

To EVALUATEEXPR LISP uses various forms of global or local bindings (e.g. `let`). We model a set of *bindings* as a function that in a given
*Env*ironment interprets given *Symbols* by some *Expr*essions. To model nesting of scoping, each environment has a *parentEnv*ironment, and one distinguished environment env_0 is assumed to hold all pre-defined (library) bindings
in the system. At any moment, the 0-ary global function env refers to the
current environment; we assume env to be initialized by env_0. This explains
the following functions:

$env : Env$ initialized by env_0
$parentEnv : Env \rightarrow Env$
$binding : Env \times Symbol \rightarrow Expr$ -- a partial function

It should be noted that the same symbol can be bound to different values
in different environments. As usual in programming languages, a shadowing
convention prescribes that more recent bindings take precedence over previous ones. We model this convention by defining the following function:

$$envVal : Env \times Symbol \rightarrow Expr$$

$$envVal(e, s) = \begin{cases} binding(e, s) & \text{if } binding(e, s) \neq undef \\ envVal(parentEnv(e), s) & \text{if } binding(e, s) = undef \text{ and} \\ & \quad parentEnv(e) \neq undef \\ undef & \text{otherwise} \end{cases}$$

LISP dialects differ in whether they implement dynamic or static scoping;
some use both forms. Our definition above models dynamic scoping (as in
Emacs Lisp). In any given implementation, the top-level scope will include
a number of well-known symbols (e.g., `+`) that are bound to corresponding
well-known functions (e.g., addition). Some of these well-known functions are
part of the definition of the language (the historical term for such functions

is *special forms*), while others are provided by a given implementation as a standard library, for the convenience of programmers.

The evaluation of a LISP expression consists in the repeated execution of EVALUATEEXPR in the state established by an appropriate invocation PROCEEDAT (to indicate the *pos* to evaluate and the key k where the result will be stored).

The EVALUATEEXPR procedure includes the following cases we formalize below by PGA rules:

1. If an expression is a number or a string, the result is the number or string itself.
2. If an expression is a symbol for which a binding exists in the current scope, the result is the value bound to the symbol.
3. If an expression is a list, then:

   a. If the first element of the list is a special form symbol, corresponding special processing EVALUATESPECIALFORM is performed;
   b. otherwise, all elements in the list are evaluated by EVALUATELIST and the function indicated by the first element of the list is invoked.

4. Other cases may vary depending on the specific dialect, but are generally regarded as an error.

The corresponding PGA rules are thus:

> EVALUATEEXPR =
>   **if** *isNumber(pos)* **or** *isString(pos)* **then**
>   YIELD(*pos*)   -- numeric and string literals evaluate to themselves
>   **if** *isSymbol(pos)* **then**
>   YIELD(*envVal(env, pos)*)   -- symbols looked up in the environment
>   **if** *isCons(pos)* **then**
>   **if** *isSpecialForm(head(pos))* **then**
>   EVALUATESPECIALFORM   -- forms with special semantics
>   **else**
>   EVALUATELIST   -- any other list

EVALUATELIST handles the evaluation of lists that are not special forms. It evaluates all items in the list (in whatever order) and APPLYs the function expressed by the first item to the arguments provided by the remaining items. The result of the function invocation is the result of the evaluation.

> EVALUATELIST =
>   **choose** $i \in range(pos)$ **with not** *done(i)*
>   PROCEEDAT(*item(pos, i), i*)   -- evaluate *i*-th element
>   **ifnone**   -- if all list elements are evaluated
>   APPLY   -- apply function

The APPLY macro describes the process of invoking a function (given by the first item) with the actual parameters provided by the subsequent items. Note that the usual mathematical notation $f(x_1, \ldots, x_n)$ is written in LISP as the list $(f\ x_1\ \ldots\ x_n)$. We expect[13] the function to be a lambda expression which is itself a special form. Most commonly, the first element will be a symbol that has been bound to a lambda expression, but it could also be a literal lambda expression, or any expression that evaluates to a lambda expression. To bind formal parameters (named in the lambda definition) to actual parameters (provided by the invoking form), we create a new local environment. Notice this is a form of dynamic scoping, as e.g. in newLisp or Emacs Lisp, whereas other dialects (e.g. Scheme) prefer static scoping. Finally, the body of the lambda is evaluated in the new environment, and the result of the evaluation of the body (as stored in the key call) provides the result of the invocation.

APPLY =
   let $f = value(1)$,   -- will be $f =$ (lambda *(formals) body*)
      $formals = item(f, 2)$,   -- list of formal arguments symbols
      $body = item(f, 3)$ in   -- body of function
   if not $done$(call) then   -- pass arguments to *body*
     let $ne =$ new *Env* in
       forall $i \in range(formals)$ do
         $binding(ne, item(formals, i)) := value(i + 1)$ -- bind args
       $parentEnv(ne) := env$ -- nesting of *env*
       $env := ne$ -- make callee env current
       PROCEEDAT(*body*, call)   -- compute *body* in callee env
   else
      $env := parentEnv(env)$ -- reestablish invocation env
      YIELD(*value*(call))   -- return computed function value

Special forms start with one of a set of well-known symbols (e.g., if, let, car), and they have a semantics specified by the language; most importantly, they do not follow the usual rules for evaluation of lists. The need for, and utility of, special forms in LISP has been analyzed in detail in [136]. We focus here only on those special forms that are essential to provide the capabilities for reflection.

We distinguish two classes of special forms: those that evaluate only part of the arguments before applying the function expressed by the initial symbols (PARTIALEVALFORMS) and those that evaluate all arguments before application (FULLEVALFORMS). A prime example of the first class is if, whose

---

[13] We choose to not model error handling since it contributes nothing specific to the reflectivity features of LISP. The original LISP did check that the *head* of the function definition was the literal symbol lambda; later versions used symbol properties instead, to better integrate with compiled code.

entire point is to evaluate either the second or the third argument, depending on whether the first argument evaluated to true or false. Evaluating both
the "then" and the "else" part before checking the condition would of course
defeat the purpose. Similar reasoning applies to other forms, e.g. **and** and
or which guarantee short-circuit evaluation. An example of the second class
is **cons**, which evaluates both the second and third argument (the *head* and
tail of the new cons to be built), but then applies special processing (i.e.,
allocating new memory from the machine's heap) that cannot be expressed
via standard LISP. Most LISP primitive operations, including input/output
primitives, belong to this class.

> EVALUATESPECIALFORM =
>   **if** *isPartial(head(pos))* **then**
>   PARTIALEVALFORM
>   **else**
>   FULLEVALFORM

The evaluation of FULLEVALFORMs consists in evaluating all arguments
(e.g., the second to last element in the list), and then applying specific semantics according to the symbol (the first element). The order of evaluation
is irrelevant so that we leave it unspecified using the **choose** construct. Some
LISP dialect (e.g. CommonLISP) specify leftmost-innermost order, whereas
others (e.g. Scheme) explicitly leave the order unspecified.

> FULLEVALFORM =
>   **choose** $i \in range(pos)$ **with** $i > 1$ **and** **not** *done(i)*
>   PROCEEDAT(*item(pos, i), i*)   -- evaluate chosen unevaluated item
>   **ifnone**   -- if argument list fully evaluated
>   **case** *item(pos, 1)* **of**
>   cons →
>   **let** $c =$ **new** *Cons* **in**   -- construct a new pair
>   *head(c) := value(2)*   -- assign *head* value
>   *tail(c) := value(3)*   -- assign *tail* value
>   YIELD(*c*)   -- return new *cons*
>   car → YIELD(*head(value(2))*)   -- access *head* value
>   cdr → YIELD(*tail(value(2))*)   -- access *tail* value
>   setcar →   -- set *head* value of a cons and return it
>   *head(value(2)) := value(3)*
>   YIELD(*value(3)*)
>   setcdr →   -- set *tail* value of a cons and return it
>   *tail(value(2)) := value(3)*
>   YIELD(*value(3)*)
>   set →   -- mutate a binding
>   *binding(env, value(2)) := value(3)*
>   YIELD(*value(3)*)
>   eval →   -- evaluates the value of the argument

> **if not** *done*(eval) **then**
> PROCEEDAT(*value*(2), eval)
> **else**
> YIELD(*value*(eval))
> . . .

We need to specify FULLEVALFORMs such as `cons` to show how new parts of the program can be dynamically constructed at runtime, and `eval` to show how to execute such a part. We also need a way to prevent the immediate execution of parts of a program, which is obtained by the `quote` special form. `quote` is handled by PARTIALEVALFORM, and in fact its entire purpose is to return its argument unevaluated. So, for example, `(quote (+ 1 2))` evaluates to `(+ 1 2)` — which can be used to build a new part of the program — whereas an evaluating form such as `(print (+ 1 2))` would print 3. The special form `if` needs no further discussion, except to observe that its rather cumbersome specification is in part due to the need to accommodate both the if-then and if-then-else variant.

It is more interesting to comment the `let` special form. It has two arguments; the first is a list of declarations, with each declaration being a pair (*symbol expr*), whereas the second is the body, i.e. an expression to be evaluated in an environment where the declarations are in effect. To evaluate a `let`, we evaluate all the *exprs* and bind them to the corresponding *symbols* in the declaration list, and finally evaluate the body in the environment by establishing the new bindings. The result of a `let` is the result of its body.

The last remaining capability we need is that of defining `lambda`. This is particularly simple, because in our model the value of a `lambda` expression is the `lambda` expression itself (in other words, `lambda`s are always implicitly quoted, and a `lambda` expression is essentially a literal constant). Notice that the actual application (i.e., invocation) of a `lambda` has been described in APPLY above.

PARTIALEVALFORM =
  case *item*(*pos*, 1) **of**
    quote → YIELD(*item*(*pos*, 2))   -- return arg unevaluated
    lambda → YIELD(*pos*)   -- return (implicitly quoted) lambda-exp
    if →
      if not *done*(2) **then**
        PROCEEDAT(*item*(*pos*, 2), 2)   -- evaluate guard
      else
        if *value*(2) ≠ *NIL*[14] **then**   -- if guard true
          if not *done*(3) **then**
            PROCEEDAT(*item*(*pos*, 3), 3)   -- compute the then-case

---

[14] Historically, the global symbol T or *T* is used in LISP to denote the canonical *true*, but any non-NIL value is also considered as *true*. NIL denotes not only the empty list, but also the canonical *false*.

$$\mathbf{else}$$
$$\qquad \text{Y{\scriptsize IELD}}(value(3)) \qquad\qquad\qquad \text{-- return then-case result}$$
$$\mathbf{elseif}\ item(pos, 4) \neq undef \qquad\qquad \text{-- there is an else-case}$$
$$\qquad \mathbf{if\ not}\ done(4)\ \mathbf{then}$$
$$\qquad\qquad \text{P{\scriptsize ROCEED}A{\scriptsize T}}(item(pos, 4), 4) \qquad \text{-- compute the else-case}$$
$$\qquad \mathbf{else}$$
$$\qquad\qquad \text{Y{\scriptsize IELD}}(value(4)) \qquad\qquad\qquad \text{-- return else-case result}$$
$$\mathbf{else}$$
$$\qquad \text{Y{\scriptsize IELD}}(NIL) \qquad\qquad \text{-- if guard false and no else-case}$$

$\mathbf{let} \rightarrow \qquad\qquad$ -- will be (let $((x_1\ e_1)\ \ldots\ (x_n\ e_n))$ body)

$\quad \mathbf{let}\ decls = item(pos, 2), body = item(pos, 3)\ \mathbf{in}$

$\qquad \mathbf{choose}\ i \in range(decls)\ \mathbf{with\ not}\ done(\text{init}_i)$

$\qquad\qquad \text{P{\scriptsize ROCEED}A{\scriptsize T}}(item((item(decls, i), 2), \text{init}_i)$

$\qquad \mathbf{ifnone} \qquad\qquad\qquad$ -- all declarations evaluated

$\qquad\qquad \mathbf{if\ not}\ done(3)\ \mathbf{then}$

$\qquad\qquad\qquad \mathbf{let}\ ne =\mathbf{new}\ Env\ \mathbf{in}$

$\qquad\qquad\qquad\qquad \mathbf{forall}\ i \in range(decls) \qquad$ -- bind x_i to computed values

$\qquad\qquad\qquad\qquad\quad binding(ne, item(item(decls, i), 1)) := value(\text{init}_i)$

$\qquad\qquad\qquad\qquad parentEnv(ne) := env \qquad\qquad$ -- record env

$\qquad\qquad\qquad\qquad env := ne \qquad\qquad$ -- continue with new env

$\qquad\qquad\qquad\qquad \text{P{\scriptsize ROCEED}A{\scriptsize T}}(body, 3) \qquad\qquad$ -- evaluate body

$\qquad\qquad\qquad \mathbf{else} \qquad\qquad$ -- evaluation of body terminated

$\qquad\qquad\qquad\qquad env := parentEnv(env) \qquad\qquad$ -- reestablish parent env

$\qquad\qquad\qquad\qquad \text{Y{\scriptsize IELD}}(value(3)) \qquad\qquad$ -- return computed body value

$\ldots$

We now have all the ingredients LISP provides for reflectivity in a homoiconic language:

1. symbols, bound via `let` or `lambda` to lists which are valid program fragments, provide a way to identify and refer to parts of the existing program;
2. `cons` and various list manipulations provide a way to construct new parts and modify existing parts of the program;
3. application of a `lambda`, or using `eval`, provide a way to cause the execution of such parts;
4. `quote` provides a way to prevent the immediate evaluation of parts of the program.

Of course, a *practical* language may well provide additional facilities, such as `defun` (defining a function and binding it to a name), `defparameter` and `defconstant` (binding variable or constant symbols in env_0), `print` and `read` (input/output operations), `setf` and `setq` (modifying the value of a binding), `do` and `loop` (iterative statements), etc. However, these are either primitives that must be implemented in native code, or short-hands for more complex forms that can be defined on the basis of the special

forms we have specified. For example, (setq x 3) is an abbreviation for
(set (quote x) 3), whereas (defun f (x y) (+ x y)) is an abbreviation
for (set (quote f) (lambda (x y) (+ x y))) (the specification of set is
found in FULLEVALFORM above). The same goes for more advanced features
(e.g., class/object systems, namespaces, macros) that have been implemented
in various concrete LISP variants [103] but do not contribute additional elements to the reflectivity features of LISP.

4.6 Reflective RAM

As third concrete example we investigate reflectivity in an imperative language. As characteristic example we consider the language of Random Access
Machine programs. The RAM model has been described on pg. 59 and by the
RAMINTERPRETER (pg. 263). The Random Access Stored Program Machine
RASP is a reflective version of the RAM, with the same instructions and
their meaning, but without indirect addressing (because indirect addressing
can be programmed on the RASP, see Sect. 4.6.1 below).

To become reflective the RASP needs that its program instructions are
part of its state. The RASP has no explicitly named pgm memory, but for
simplicity, in its usual definition (see for example [6, Ch. 1.4]), the pgm the
machine executes is contained in a known part of the main memory, say in
the consecutive registers $r_2\ r_3 \ldots r_p$ for some program space number $p \in$
Nat. Technically this is achieved via an instruction Gödelization[15] $\overline{instr(l)} =$
$r_{2l+2}\ r_{2l+3}$ using two adjacent registers to contain (a Gödel number of) the
operation code respectively the operand of the instruction. Given the labeling
convention that the label l of an instruction $instr_l$ is a natural number $l \leq m$
(for some natural number m) this Gödelization occupies the first registers
$r_2\ r_3 \ldots r_p$ (where $p = 2m + 3$) (see Fig. 4.7).

More precisely, $\overline{pgm}$ is defined as a sequence $\overline{instr(0)} \ldots \overline{instr(m)}$ of pairs
of adjacent registers $\overline{instr(l)} = r_{2l+2}\ r_{2l+3}$ that contain a Gödel number of
the $instr$uction's command (called $opCode$) respectively of (the address of)
its argument (called $operand$):

> **let** $instr(l) = (l, cmd, arg)$ **in**
>   **if** $arg = int\ i$ **then** $r_{2l+2} = \overline{cmd\ int}$ $r_{2l+3} = i$
>   **if** $arg = reg\ n$ **then** $r_{2l+2} = \overline{cmd\ reg}$ $r_{2l+3} = n$
>   **if** $arg = label$ **then** $r_{2l+2} = \overline{cmd}$ $r_{2l+3} = label$ --jump cmd
>   **if** $cmd = Halt$ **then** $r_{2l+2} = \overline{cmd}$

---

[15] The method of Gödelization was invented in [84] to algorithmically relate logical
concepts and operations (e.g. deductions) in axiomatic systems to computations on
numbers. We use it here to encode non-numeric algorithmic instructions by natural
numbers.

Fig. 4.7 Architectures of RAM and RASP machine compared

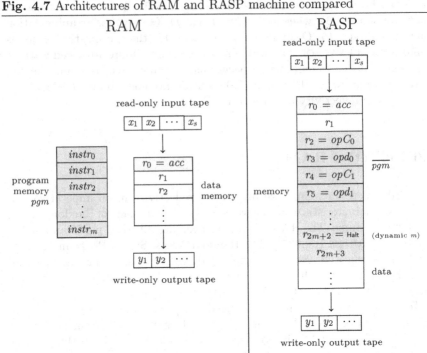

Without loss of generality we assume that the *Halt* instruction is the last one in any given program (with label m) so that it marks the end of the *pgm* Gödelization in the main memory. In this way it is easy to decode in each state of a RASP computation the currently executed program *pgm* from the content of the registers $r_2, r_3, \ldots, r_{2m+3}$ where r_{2m+2} contains the Gödel number of (the *opCode* of) the *Halt* instruction. The program counter *ctl* in the RASP model takes values in the set of register addresses $\{2, 4, \ldots, 2m + 2\}$: in each state it is the address of the first of the two consecutive Gödelization registers of the currently executed instruction. Therefore the *next* function of the RAM interpreter is refined for its RASP interpreter version to $next(l) = l + 2$.

Having RASP programs in the updatable and executable part of the memory permits to program in RASP the insertion, deletion, or modification of instructions. In the specific case here we have the sequence $\overline{pgm}$ of instruction registers as modifiable description—by updating, deleting or inserting adjacent register pairs $r_{2x+2}\ r_{2x+3}$— of the currently executed RASP program *pgm*. $\overline{pgm}$ is conceptually similar to the *db* memory of Prolog.

4.6.1 Reflectivity at Work (Indirect Addressing)

As noted in the preceding section there is no indirect addressing in RASP instructions. The reason is that RAM instructions with indirect addressing can be programmed by small RASP programs that exploit the reflectivity capability, modifying some instruction registers in some execution step. We show this in this section by an ASM refinement (of mixed types ($(1,1)$ and $(1,6)$)) of any RAM program M by a RASP program M^* defined as follows:

- First we refine each RAM $instr(l)$ of M that does not use indirect addressing by an equivalent RASP instruction $instr(l)^*$. This is a step-by-step refinement, a pure data refinement of refinement type $(1,1)$.
- Then we refine each instruction $instr(l)$ with indirect addressing in its *operand* by an equivalent RASP program $instr(l)^*$. This is an ASM refinement of type $(1,6)$ where one M-step of the RAM is refined by a program of 6 successive M^*-steps of the RASP.

By RAM/RASP steps we refer to the steps of the RAMINTERPRETER with program M respectively its RASPINTERPRETER version with program M^*. The latter is the same interpreter but without the indirect addressing operands $addr\ n$ in the instructions and without the rules that interpret them. The (dynamic part of) states of a RAM/RASP program consists of the current values of the instruction counter and the registers:

$$(ctl_M, Reg_M) \textbf{ with } Reg_M = r_{0,M}, r_{1,M}, \ldots \text{ the same for } M^*.$$

For notational uniformity, in Reg_M we do not list the static RAM registers (for example $\overline{r_0}, \ldots, \overline{r_m}$) where the program M is stored. To simplify the notation we write ctl and r_n without the index M or M^* where from the context it is clear to which machine the location belongs.

A pair (S, S^*) of corresponding M and M^* states consist of a state S where M makes a step and a state S^* where M^* starts the simulation of that M-step. We define the to-be-defined simulation to be correct if in runs of the two programs corresponding states satisfy the correspondence of their locations of interest in the following sense:

- Accumulator correspondence: acc_M in state S and acc_{M^*} in S^* have the same content.
- Register correspondence: for every n the registers $r_{n,M}$ in state S and r_{s+n,M^*} in state S^* have the same content. The offset s is defined to satisfy that the encoding of the RASP program M^* fits in the RASP registers $r_0, r_1, \ldots, r_s$. Remember that for the simulation of M-runs we do not need to consider the static RAM memory registers.
- Instruction counter correspondence: $ctl_M = l$ in state S and ctl_{M^*} in state S^* correspond to each other as follows: if M executes in state S the $instr(l)$ with label $ctl_M = l$, then M^* in state S^* starts to execute the simulation code $instr(l)^*$ at its start address, so that $ctl_{M^*} =$

$startAddrSimCode(l)$. The function $startAddrSimCode(l)$ defined below denotes the address of the first register of the register segment that Gödelizes the simulation code $instr(l)^*$.

For the initialization we define $startAddrSimCode(0) = 2$ (i.e. the Gödelization of the first instruction of M^* begins in the RASP register r_2). We stipulate that the two accumulators acc_M and acc_{M^*} contain 0, the same for all M-registers r_n and for all M^* registers r_n with $n > s$.[16] We assume that the two programs start with the same input tape and a blank output tape.

The computation of the simulation code $instr(l)^*$ uses the RASP *accumulator*. Therefore we must reserve one register (say r_{1,M^*}) where M^* when starting the execution of the simulation code $instr(l)^*$ can temporarily save its current *accumulator* content.

We define $instr(l)^*$ by induction on the labels of M-instructions $instr(l)$. There are two cases to distinguish.

Case 1: $instr(l)$ does not involve indirect addressing, i.e. its operand is not of type $addr\ n$. In this case M^* is defined to execute the same instruction with parameters adapted. More precisely, $instr(l)^*$ is the instruction with the same $opCode(instr(l))$ and the same type (*int* or *reg* or jump label k) of the $operand(instr(l))$ but with appropriately incremented address $s + n$ in case the operand is $reg\ n$ (for some $n \in Label$) and with jump target label $startAddrSimCode(k)$ in case the $operand(instr(l))$ is a jump label k. Initially (where $l = 0$)—the same in case 1 of an induction step—this $instr(l)^*$ is Gödelized in the two consecutive RASP registers with index $startAddrSimCode(l) + 2$ and $startAddrSimCode(l) + 3$. Consequently, if M has a next instruction (with label $l + 1$) we define $startAddrSimCode(l + 1)$ as $startAddrSimCode(l) + 2$.

Case 2: $instr(l)$ does involve indirect addressing so that it has an $operand(instr(l)) = addr\ n$. Let cmd be the $opCode(instr(l))$. To simulate such an $instr(l)$ by RASP instructions the idea is to supply the content of r_n in the RAM, say the index $i_M \in Nat$, as operand $reg\ i_M$ to the execution of the cmd by M^*. This involves a code manipulation and is achieved by letting M^* execute sequentially the following instruction sequence. We define this sequence by its Gödelization (in the RASP registers starting with the register labeled $l^* = startAddrSimCode(l)$) and explain for each instruction the behaviour of M^* when it executes the considered instruction.

---

[16] The RASP registers $r_2, \ldots r_s$ are occupied by the simulation code M^*, the RAM registers $\overline{r_0}, \ldots, \overline{r_m}$ by the static to-be-simulated M-code.

label	opcode	operand	behaviour	
l^*	*Store reg*			save acc into register 1
$l^* + 1$		1	$r_1 := acc$	
$l^* + 2$	*Load reg*			load address i_M from $r_{n,M}$
$l^* + 3$		$s + n$	$acc := r_{s+n}$	using $r_{n,M} = r_{s+n,M^*}$
$l^* + 4$	*Add int*			compute M^*-address i_{M^*}
$l^* + 5$		s	$acc := acc + s$	adding M^*-offset to i_M
$l^* + 6$	*Store reg*			store i_{M^*} as operand for
$l^* + 7$		$l^* + 11$	$r_{l^*+11} := acc$	the (cmd reg)-instruction
$l^* + 8$	*Load reg*			retrieve the stored acc
$l^* + 9$		1	$acc := r_1$	
$l^* + 10$	*cmd reg*		RASPINTERPRETER	
$l^* + 11$		r_{l^*+11}		where $r_{l^*+11,M^*} = r_{n,M}$

- Step 1. $r_1 := acc$: save the current accumulator content by placing it into register r_1.
- Step 2. $acc := r_{s+n}$: load the *address* of the indirectly addressed *RAM*-register M operates with when executing its $instr(l)$. This address is the current content of $r_{n,M}$ and can be retrieved by M^* from register r_{s+n,M^*}.
- Step 3. $acc := acc + s$: add to the retrieved *address* used by M the offset s to obtain the address used by M^* to execute the cmd of $instr(l)$ by the code sequence $instr(l^*)$.
- Step 4. $r_{l^*+11} := acc$: store the computed address in the address register r_{l^*+11} of the M^*-instruction defined by the encoding registers r_{l^*+10} and r_{l^*+11}. This is the step where M^* makes use of the possibility to modify at run time the (encoding of the) program it is currently executing.
- Step 5. $acc := r_1$: retrieve the content of the *ac*cumulator saved in Step 1 of the simulation code.
- Step 6. Execute cmd of $instr(l)$ (with the computed parameter i_{M^*}). Due to Step 4, M^* performs this cmd with the operand reg i_{M^*} where the number i_{M^*} that is stored in the RASP register r_{l^*+11} equals the content of the RAM register r_n in the state where M executes the $instr(l)$.

Given that M^* needs 6 steps to simulate the given $instr(l)$-step of M, starting in $l^* = startAddrSimCode(l)$ we define $startAddrSimCode(l+1)$ as $l^* + 12$ (if M has a next instruction with label $l + 1$).

Exercise 20. Show that every RASP program can be simulated by a RAM program. Use indirect addressing to decode and simulate RASP instructions that are stored in the RAM-memory. For a solution see [6, Sect. 1.4].

4.7 Reflectivity Styles

In Section 4.3 we tried to find a precise, conceptually simple but general definition that captures the intuitive concept of sequential reflective processes. Given the characterization of a large class of sequential algorithms by PGAs we searched for a natural extension of the latter by some generic easily refinable construct that makes them reflective. This led us to describe self-modifying ASM programs as executable content of a dedicated updatable part of memory. For the sake of generality we have chosen to represent the latter by a 0-ary dynamic function *pgm* whose content in each step is read and evaluated for execution and whose function can be easily refined to concrete reflection mechanisms in various programming languages. Note that the parallelism of ASMs permits to nevertheless perform meta-level *pgm* updates simultaneously with 'ordinary' object-level updates. When searching for appropriate generic and easily refinable operations on ASM rules their well-known parse tree structure offered a useful intuitive support, namely to use without loss of generality just one abstract but well-known background operation: rule-tree replacement. This operation covers the full spectrum from single assignment rules $s := t$—an abstract version of the single instruction view in programming languages—to arbitrarily complex ASM rules, including a replacement of the entire current program. In addition, to permit reflection also in a parallel (or even concurrent) context we wanted simultaneous replacements in different parts of the program to be supported, a requirement that could be easily satisfied using the partial update technique of ASMs. Therefore, in the ASM ground model for reflectivity a program can manipulate its own structure at any point, from term manipulations in assignment instructions to a complete program change.

A background that supports this approach is a tree structure where one can define a rather generic single operation to *replace* a program by another one. We could have chosen a different program representation. We have chosen the parse tree representation mainly because the tree substitution can be easily refined to many forms of concrete program updates, covering a wide spectrum of different realizations of reflectivity using different program structures and different (computed and/or background) operations on them.

Above we have illustrated concrete versions of reflection for three characteristic programming paradigms: logical (Prolog), functional (Lisp) and imperative (RAM) programming. In this section we compare the different styles and their relation to the abstract concept of reflective PGAs.

Prolog (Sect. 4.4) has an explicit separation of meta-level and object-level ('ordinary') steps. In object-level steps a Prolog program performs only operations that do not affect the given program, a list of clauses that is called database *db*. In each meta-level step a Prolog program applies either one of two kinds of *db*-read instructions (which trigger no update of *db*) or one out of four kinds of dedicated, at the level of clauses atomic operations that do change *db*. Each such step refines a reflective ASM *pgm* assignment step of form *pgm* := *replace*(...) so that *db* directly instantiates the *pgm* of a reflective ASM. No partial updates are needed because in each meta-level step a Prolog program performs at most one (an atomic) *db* operation. In this way the abstract *replace* operation is instantiated by the respective concrete clause insertion, deletion (or inspection). New predicate symbols must be declared as *Dynamic*. So the Prolog reflectivity model is an instance of the ASM reflectivity model.

Lisp (Sect. 4.5) program states are given by the set of *Expressions* (with its subsets *Atom*, *Cons* and functions *head*, *tail*), the *Env*vironment (with its associated functions) and the graph traversal functions *pos*, *result*, *return*. There is no explicitly defined separate *pgm* memory. Instead, the program the LISP interpreter EVALUATEEXPR executes currently (in a program graph traversal, see Figure 4.5) is distinguished as *pos*. Note that every syntactically correct list expression represents a program the LISP interpreter can execute (read: evaluate). The only functions that can modify a given list expression are *head* and *tail* so that one can view these two functions as representing a global reflective *pgm*; otherwise stated, the meta-level operations on list expressions are those that update or inspect *head* or *tail* or both, like (`setcar` c_2 c_3), (`setcdr` c_2 c_3), (`cons` c_2 c_3) for updating, and (`car` c_2), (`cdr` c_2) for inspecting.

The execution of an expression that modifies *head* or *tail*, resulting in a modified expression that is going to be evaluated, can be seen as a refinement of the updates to *pgm* in our reflective ASM model; in fact, one way to make the refinement explicit would be to assume that *pgm* maps to the pair (*head*, *tail*).

No partial updates are needed since due to the sequential character of LISP computations a LISP program executes in each step exactly one (whether object or meta level) operation.

RASP, the reflective version of the RAM, has no explicitly named *pgm* memory, but in its usual definition (see for example [6, Ch. 1.4]) the *pgm* the machine executes is contained in its (updatable) registers r_2 $r_3 \ldots r_s$ for some $s \in Nat$ (via a Gödelization $\overline{instr(l)}$ as described in Sect. 4.6). Therefore, as long as the register labeling of this encoding is respected when instructions are added or deleted one can consider the sequence $\overline{pgm}$ of those first registers r_2 $r_3 \ldots r_s$ as description of the current RASP *pgm* memory, similarly to the *db* memory of Prolog. In this way a RASP program is in main memory and can be changed during a run by updating, deleting or adding register pairs r_{2x} r_{2x+1} containing instruction data.

Clearly, there is a price to pay for a precise comprehensive explanation of the intuitive program reflectivity phenomenon by a conceptually simple and epistemologically satisfying extension (of a provably generic model) of sequential algorithms. If one is interested in the detailed reflectivity features of a particular programming language one is well advised to construct an

ASM ground model directly for the given language, instead of investigating it as refinement of reflective PGAs. We illustrated this for the three technically different cases Prolog (for logic programming), Lisp (for functional programming) and the reflective RAM (RASP for imperative programming). The resulting ASM ground models come with specific reflectivity backgrounds which can serve as basis for a direct investigation and comparison of the reflectivity model of the given languages. They all show that there is nothing magic in reflectivity, contrary to a widespread belief: whatever new program shows up at run time is result of a computation that has been programmed (and hopefully well thought through!) before.

This is the place to mention another practical approach, exemplified by the Java language, where the program itself cannot be manipulated, but the language provides a set of utilities that afford *reification* of programming concepts. Thus, in Java, one could have for example an instance of the library class `java.lang.reflect.Method` whose properties describe a concrete method of some concrete class. However, that `Method` instance is *not* the method itself, but only a concrete representation (i.e., a reification) of the method, as a data object. The `Method` may well provide its own methods to cause actions on the method it represents (e.g., `invoke()`), but these rely on private conventions of the virtual machine. Java also provides ways to dynamically create new classes, e.g. by implementing a custom `ClassLoader`, but that entails providing the bytecode for the body of the method. Essentially, the programmer is required to implement a compiler in order to modify (in limited[17] ways) the running program.

Such forms of reification are different from genuine reflection in the sense explored in this chapter, as from a computational point of view they do not substantially differ from the case in which a program writes a text file with some source code S, then causes the external compilation of S and thereafter the execution of the compiled program $C(S)$. An external compilation that occurs concurrently (or possibly interleaved) with the execution of the main program is also the case of Just-In-Time (JIT) compilers, such as those implemented in most virtual machines (including many of those available for executing Java, LISP and Prolog). In JIT compilation, the running program is reflectively modified by an embedded compiler, which only uses two reflective operations: (1) inspecting the source code, in order to compile it into native executable, and (2) replacing the first instruction in the body of a method by a *jump* to the first instruction of the compiled version of the body. This process could be modeled by a minor change to the various interpreters we have specified in this chapter. For example, to specify the typical behaviour of a function-level JIT compiler it suffices to refine in the APPLY macro of our LISP model (pg. 97) the line

---

[17] Among the limitations: while new classes can be generated on the fly, they are isolated "inside" their original class loader for security reasons; moreover, entire new classes can be created and added to the program, but existing classes cannot be removed from the running program, nor dynamically modified.

PROCEEDAT($body$, call)

by the conservative extension

> **if** $compiled(body) \neq undef$ **then**
>   PROCEEDWITHRASP($compiled(body)$, env, call)
> **else**
>   **if** $runCount(body) > JITThreshold$
> $compiled(body) := JITCompile(body)$
> $runCount(body) := runCount(body) + 1$
>   PROCEEDAT($body$, call)

The interested reader may want to consider the following rather difficult

Exercise 21. Define an ASM model for the *JITCompile(expr)* function and the PROCEEDWITHRASP(*memory, env, key*) macro used above. The compiler would need to traverse the *expr*ession, but instead of applying the evaluation to the interpreter state immediately, it would emit RASP instructions to the same effect. It can be assumed that in the RASP program, jumping to certain well-known *label*s will cause the execution of specific rules of the LISP interpreter (i.e., the RASP program can call back on the LISP virtual machine if needed). The PROCEEDWITHRASP rule would start the execution of the code produced by the *JITCompiler*, establishing some convention on the use of registers to implement parameter passing and to collect and return the result of the execution (to be stored in the provided *key* as usual).

Chapter 5
Control Structures of Multi-Process Runs

In this chapter we explain the concept of true concurrency (Sect. 5.1), i.e. of runs of multi-agent interacting algorithmic processes where the single (usually sequential) agents compute their steps under a genuine form of *concurrent asynchronous control*. As first illustrative examples we use in Sect. 5.2 computations of *communicating processes* and describe a stepwise refined high-level model of a web browser running JavaScript programs. In Sect. 5.3 we explain Occam program runs where concurrency comes together with communication and choice. We illustrate some typical provably correct stepwise refinements of such runs towards an implementation.[1]

In Sect. 5.4 we study the context awareness property of concurrent processes. For this we explain in Sect. 5.4.1 a simple framework to parameterize ambient-sensitive processes. We apply it in Sect. 5.4.2 to define a precise model of concurrent multithreaded Java runs that has been used for concurrency analysis for Java and mutatis mutandis for C# programs. Another interesting application is in Sect. 9.2.2 where we use parameterization to define teams of communicating Look-Compute-Move robots which operate over graphs to solve various classical graph problems, each robot executing its instance of a same ambient-sensitive protocol.

5.1 What are Concurrent Runs

Many reactive processes consist of multiple sequential processes that run asynchronously, truly concurrently (not in synchronous parallelism and not in interleaving manner), each at its own pace, and interact autonomously with each other via interaction locations, i.e. input/output and shared locations, without any designated controlling agent (read: there is no global clock and

---

[1] For these rather simple proofs the precise definition of the general ASM-refinement concept is not needed but it is defined in Sect. 7.

© The Author(s), under exclusive license to Springer Nature Switzerland AG 2024
E. Börger, V. Gervasi, *Structures of Computing*,
https://doi.org/10.1007/978-3-031-54358-6_5

no agent has a full global view of the decentralized system). This breaks the synchrony feature of parallel actions in atomic steps. In Def. 22 (pg. 40) we could enrich the merely input-driven interaction of sequential processes with their environment (see Sect. 3.3) by a simple alternation scheme for updates of interactive locations that is rather useful in practice, but already for multitasking as described in the interleaving Example 11 (pg. 66) the notion of interaction with the environment is more complex, though still based upon synchronous atomic read-and-write steps of a single processor (see Def. 30, pg. 67 of sequentially consistent interleavings).

The crucial question is how to obtain, without introducing any explicit synchronous control, read-cleanness for interaction locations, those whose values become 'globally visible' in the concurrent view of runs of multiple agents. Read-cleanness means that when a reading and a writing of a location by different agents overlap, still the reading yields a well-defined value, either taken before the writing starts or after the writing is finished [115, 117]. The ASM framework offers a solution by splitting in concurrent runs $S_0, S_1, \ldots$ the atomic read-and-write of interaction locations, at whatever level of abstraction, into a pair of two separate atomic actions, a read in a state S_n (needed to compute an update set without applying it already) followed in some later state S_m with $m > n$ by a write, which is an application of the computed update set. The case $m = n$ describes the sequential atomic read-and-write step semantics of ASMs (Def. 14, pg. 32). The case $n < m$ reflects the concurrent refinement of this behaviour where each agent reads and writes its locations at its own pace.

We therefore require[2] that in every state of a concurrent run every agent that is ready to make an interaction step can be in global or in local *mode*: in global mode it can choose whether to *GoGlobal*—i.e. perform an atomic read/write GLOBALSTEP and stay in global mode—or to move into *local mode*, locally recording (say by a subprogram COPYINTERACTDATA) the current values of the interaction locations. From local *mode* the agent may switch back to global *mode*, contributing (say by a WRITEBACK subprogram) its computed updates for interaction locations to the global interaction state.

Definition 36 (Concurrent ASM Runs). Let $\mathcal{A}$ be a finite set of pairs $(a, pgm(a))$ of agents $a \in A$ with PGA rule $pgm(a)$, called a multi-agent ASM. A *concurrent run* (or computation) of $\mathcal{A}$ is a sequence $S_0, S_1, \ldots$ of states (started in an initial state S_0) together with a sequence $A_0, A_1, \ldots$ of subsets of A such that[3] each state S_{m+1} is obtained from S_m by applying to S_m simultaneously for each agent $a \in A_m$ that chooses to *GoGlobal* the update set computed by $pgm(a)$ in state S_m. An agent $a \in A_m \setminus GoGlobal$ in *mode* = global that does not want to *GoGlobal* is required to switch to local *mode*, recording the current interaction location values (by a subprogram

---

[2] The idea is taken from [54]

[3] One can permit the set A to be (potentially) infinite. This includes the case of dynamically increasing sets of agents.

COPYINTERACTDATA). In local *mode* $pgm(a)$ starts a local subcomputation (a submachine LOCALSTEP); in this subcomputation it may eventually enter a write back *mode* = wb (and from there again the global *mode*), executing a subprogram that does WRITEBACK to the interaction state sequence the values the submachine of $pgm(a)$ has computed for (some of) its interaction locations. The run terminates in state S_m if the updates computed by the agents in A_m are inconsistent.

This is expressed as follows (see also Fig. 5.1). The equation is a refinement of the equation for deterministic single-agent steps (Def. 22, pg. 40):

$$S_{m+1} = S_m + \bigcup_{a \in GoGlobal} eval(pgm(a), S_m)$$

$GoGlobal = \{a \in A_m \mid$
$\quad (mode(a) = \text{global and } (mode, \text{local}) \notin Upd(pgm(a), S_m))$
$\quad \text{or } mode(a) = \text{wb}$ -- write back mode
$\textbf{if } a \in A_m \setminus GoGlobal \textbf{ and } mode(a) = \text{global then}$
$\quad Upd(pgm(a), S_m) = \{(mode, \text{local})\} \cup CopyInteractData$
$\textbf{where}$
$\quad CopyInteractData = \text{the updates generated by COPYINTERACTDATA}$

Def. 36 is a scheme we use often with other single-agent component machines instead of PGAs. For example, with non-deterministic PGAs (Def. 29, pg. 63) *evalCand* is used instead of *eval* so that in a state S there may be different continuations S_{m+1} of the concurrent run. We leave it as an exercise to define S_{m+1} for nondeterministic PGAs.

Exercise 22. Define S_{m+1} for nondeterministic ASMs. See Appendix B.

Remark on the *pgm* refinement. Note that with multi-agent machines the 0-ary *pgm* function we used to define reflective machines (Def. 34, pg. 78) is refined to a unary function $pgm(a)$ whose arguments are agents. To make these machines reflective it suffices to treat $pgm(a)$ as a location so that in each state $\mathfrak{A}$ the program $pgm(a)^{\mathfrak{A}}$ is executed and (possibly) modified. This is at times used to alter during execution the program associated to an agent; see Sect. 5.2.1 for an example of application. In executable implementations the *pgm* function is often called *program*.

Making single-agent steps concurrency-aware. Def. 36 above captures asynchronous behavior in the ASM framework by allowing every agent to compute and apply at its own pace the update sets it contributes to a concurrent run. The pairs of read-only and successive write-only steps each agent makes in a concurrent run for its interaction locations can be implemented by refined single-agent steps. The refinement preserves the—via the **par** construct—synchronous parallel state-based ASM computation model at the level of single autonomous agents. In fact, by separating reads of interaction locations from writing them every agent a can be viewed to perform a globally visible read-and-write step of its $pgm(a)$ in a concurrency-aware manner by first a) only reading (and locally recording) in some state S_n the current values of its interaction locations, then b) locally emulating at its own pace its update computation step triggered by those interaction data, and eventually c) writing back its own new interaction data. WRITEBACK(a) means that a submits the locally computed updates of interaction locations to a global state S_m where they become 'globally visible' (i.e. readable by other agents) in the successive state S_{m+1}, with $n \leq m$ ($n < m$ reflecting the asynchrony). Such a sequential three-steps-refinement CONCURSTEP(a) of the one-step $pgm(a)$ relates the abstract concurrent view of $pgm(a)$-steps in a given concurrent run to a sequential implementation view, making the underlying Look-Compute-Action Pattern (pg. 27) explicit, in the following way (see Fig. 5.1 below):

- In global *mode* agent a can choose to perform one atomic GLOBALSTEP(a) by executing its $pgm(a)$ as a normal atomic ASM read-write-step.
- In global *mode* agent a may also choose to perform three successive (and further refinable, see Exercise 24, pg. 116) local substeps which emulate the concurrent step of its $pgm(a)$:

    - first COPYINTERACTDATA(a), coupled with a switch to local *mode*,
    - then emulate GLOBALSTEP(a) by
        · executing a LOCALSTEP(a) on copies of interaction locations,
        · followed by a WRITEBACK(a) and switching back to global *mode*.

The CONCURSTEP(a) components implement the concurrent run steps of the given $pgm(a)$ as expressed by the following proposition.

Proposition 1 (Implementing Single-Agents' Concurrent Steps). *Let $\mathcal{A}$ be a multi-agent ASM of pairs $(a, pgm(a))$ of agents $a \in A$ with bounded-choice PGA rule $pgm(a)$. Each concurrent run R of $\mathcal{A}$, say with states $S_0, S_1, \ldots$ and subsets $A_0, A_1, \ldots$ of A, can be implemented by a parallel interleaving run R' where each $pgm(a)$-step in R is simulated in R' either directly by an atomic combined read-and-write GLOBALSTEP(a) or by a sequence of moves COPYINTERACTDATA, LOCALSTEP (local emulation of the write-step of $pgm(a)$), WRITEBACK agent a performs in R' at the pace and with the same choices as in R.*

```
CONCURSTEP(a) =
    if mode = global then
        choose R ∈ {GOLOCAL, STAYGLOBAL} do R
    if mode = local then
        LOCALSTEP(a)                          -- emulate pgm(a)-step
        mode := wb
    if mode = wb then
        WRITEBACK(a)
        mode := global
```

Fig. 5.1 CONCURSTEP: Component Steps in Concurrent Runs

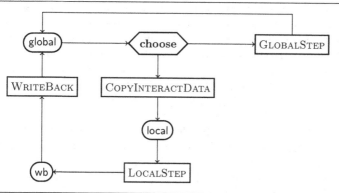

where
STAYGLOBAL = GLOBALSTEP(a) = $pgm(a)$
GOLOCAL =
  COPYINTERACTDATA(a)
  $mode :=$ local

- COPYINTERACTDATA(a) executes for all interaction locations $(f, args)$ of $pgm(a)$ in the given state (with shared or monitored function symbol f) an update $((f', args), f(args))$.
- LOCALSTEP(a) is a local copy of GLOBALSTEP(a), namely the result of replacing in $pgm(a)$ every interaction function symbol f by a new function symbol f' controlled by $pgm(a)$.
- WRITEBACK(a) is defined similarly by copying back to f the new locally computed values $f'(args)$ for every shared or output function f.

Exercise 23. Check your understanding of the proposition by proving it via an induction on concurrent runs.

Concurrent versus Parallel Interleaved Runs. Def. 36 of concurrent runs leaves it to scheduling refinements to determine how the subsets A_m of agents are formed that happen to be ready to simultaneously execute a write step in state S_m. If in Def. 36 in every state S_m all involved agents always perform an atomic read-and-write step in S_m, then the concurrent run coincides with a parallel interleaved run (as defined at the end of Sect. 3.5). A concrete example are runs of communicating processes (Sect. 5.2) or more generally of processes with disjoint states (Sect. 5.4).

Note that in Definition 36 every state and every state transition from S_m to S_{m+1} represents a 'snapshot of the run' provided by those agents which we see to interact by simultaneously applying to S_m the update set they computed (maybe earlier) as read part of the concurrent implementation of a read-and-write $pgm(a)$-step. Obviously the states of major interest for an analysis of concurrent run behaviour are those where some agents perform a GLOBALSTEP(a) or a WRITEBACK(a) step because in those steps the interaction locations are updated, whereas the other steps are of purely local single-agent nature. The components GLOBALSTEP(a) and WRITEBACK(a) are also the only ones that may generate an inconsistent update set due to update disagreements of different agents that become visible in the concurrent state view; to COPYINTERACTDATA from global to local state view and to perform LOCALSTEPs does not become visible in the concurrent state view.

Exercise 24 (CONCURSTEP **with local loop**). Refine CONCURSTEP such that agent a in local *mode* can decide whether it wants to make further internal steps before performing the WRITEBACK. The solution in Appendix B (pg. 266) exhibits a scheme for implementing atomic actions by a sequence of micro-steps, e.g. functional specifications by state-based behavioural descriptions.

Remark on Atomicity. As stated above, to not loose the expressiveness coming with atomic one-step abstract machine actions we deliberately treat reading and writing in concurrent runs as possible atomic operations which provide a clear result for every read or write operation. Doing this we trade the read-freshness property for read-cleanness: when in local *mode*, an agent may use a value of an interaction location that has already been updated by another process. This means that in particular we abstract from possibly overlapping reads/writes as they occur in relaxed memory models. Modeling such features is a question of further detailing the atomic view at refined levels of abstraction. For an example see the Location Consistency Memory Model in [164].

Example 13. **Partial Updates in Concurrent Runs**. This example illustrates the use of update instructions to handle simultaneous cumulative updates of shared locations by different agents in concurrent computations in Occam.

As already explained in Example 10 (pg. 64), in an Occam run the agents walk through the flowchart representation of their program. To execute a **par**($S_1 \ldots S_n$) statement an agent a creates n new agents a_i ($i = 1, \ldots, n$) as its children and initializes them to enter the computation of S_i, see Fig. 5.2. Furthermore a sets a *counter* to the number of created children and goes to sleep at its *nextCtl* node. Every child agent a_i works in an asynchronous manner, independently of the other agents; upon the termination of its subcomputation it decreases its parent's *counter* and deletes itself. When the *counter* becomes 0 all children have terminated their program and their parent agent a becomes *running* again. This explains the following rule; remember that it may happen that some agents terminate simultaneously.[4]

---

[4] For conceptual simplicity we use the **forall** construct though the parallelism in Occam programs is bounded so that an explicit description without **forall** could be given.

Fig. 5.2 Occam **par** $(S_1 \ldots S_n)$ statement diagram

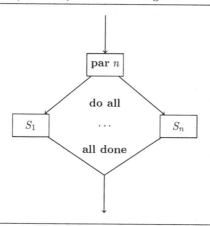

$\text{PAR}(a, n) =$
    if a **does par** n **then**
        forall $i = 1, \ldots, n$ **do**
            let $a_i =$ **new** $(Agent)$ **in**
                $env(a_i) := env(a)$ -- initialize the state of a_i
                $pos(a_i) := next(pos(a), i)$ -- assign the subprogram S_i to a_i
                $parent(a_i) := a$
                $mode(a_i) := running$ -- set a_i to run
                $count(a) := n$ -- set running-children counter
                $pos(a) := next(pos(a))$ -- move to next node
                $mode(a) := sleeping$ -- wait for children to terminate

This rule needs two auxiliary rules: one describing the last step of a child agent and one wakeup rule for the parent agent. The CHILDTERMINATION may be executed simultaneously by more than one child b of a same parent agent a, each of them wishing to subtract one from $count(a)$. Therefore we use an update instruction with an *accumulate* action that turns k occurrences of partial updates $((count, a), count(a) - 1, accumulate)$ generated simultaneously by children b of a into one update $((count, a), count(a) - k)$.

$\text{CHILDTERMINATION}(a) =$ -- simultaneous termination
    choose $agents^5 \subseteq \{b \in children(a) \mid$ -- of some children
        $mode(b) = running$ **and** $cmd(pos(b)) = end\}$
    forall $b \in agents$ **do**   -- report termination and terminate
        $count(a) :=_{accumulate} count(a) - 1$
        $\text{DELETE}(b, Agent)$ -- garbage collection: back to *Reserve*

---

[5] This abbreviates **choose** x **in** $\mathcal{P}(children(a)$ **with forall** $b \in x$ holds $mode(b) = running$ **and** $cmd(pos(b)) = end$.

PARENTWAKEUP(a) =
  if $mode(a) = sleeping$ and $count(a) = 0$ then
    $count(a) := undef$
    $mode(a) := running$

5.2 Communicating Processes

In the definition of concurrent runs (pg. 112) the interaction locations (input/output or shared) provide a direct form of process communication that is independent of any specific communication medium. However this abstraction makes it difficult to specify forms of process communication that deliberately avoid shared memory and rely upon an underlying communication mechanism for the design and analysis of message passing, corruption, failure, security, etc. We therefore define here a class of multi-agent processes which come with disjoint states and perform besides local actions only some inter-process communication. We leave this communication scheme abstract so that it can serve as refinable model for the major message passing systems used in computing.[6]

Concretely we distinguish in communicating processes two types of single computation steps, excluding any other external steps:

- *internal* steps which involve only internal data (controlled locations),
- *communication* steps we treat as atomic update instructions to SEND, RECEIVE or CONSUME messages. Their interpretation involves a communication medium through which messages are sent and for each communicating agent a mailbox where messages are *Received*.

Definition 37 (Communicating ASMs). A system of communicating ASMs is a multi-agent ASM $\mathcal{A}$ with triples $(a, pgm(a), mailbox(a))$ of agents $a \in A$, PGA (or more generally ASM) rule $pgm(a)$ and a $mailbox(a)$ satisfying the following conditions:

- the agents' signatures are pairwise disjoint so that each agent a has its own *internal state*, also called its *local state*, where to be distinguishable every function symbol f may be (implicitly) parameterized as f_a,
- each program $pgm(a)$ of agent a can contain the abstract communication actions (technically atomic one-step actions) SEND(msg), RECEIVE, CONSUME(msg) and a $Received(msg)$ predicate. Using $Received(msg)$ is a means to leave any particular feature of the RECEIVE action for further refinement.

With the communication constructs we deliberately abstract from details like communication channels, constraints on messages (e.g. their sender, type,

---

[6] A well-known example the reader may wish to look at are *actor systems* [98, 5] that are closely related to Communicating ASMs.

content, sending time, multitude of sent/received messages), the way they are transmitted (reliably or not) and delivered (corrupted or not), the way the destination RECEIVEs them, etc. The constructs are used with the following intended (refinable) interpretation:

- SEND(m, **to** a) transfers the message (m, **from self, to** a) to the communication medium which is supposed to deliver it to $mailbox(a)$ (note that there is no handshake requirement between sender and receiver of a message),
- $Received(msg) = (msg \in mailbox(\textbf{self}))$ means that the msg has been delivered to the mailbox of the destination, where unless otherwise stated $mailbox$ is treated as a set,
- RECEIVE = **choose** $msg \in mailbox$ **do** HANDLEMSG. This rule may include CONSUME(msg)
- CONSUME(msg) = DELETE($msg, mailbox(\textbf{self})$).

A complete message has the form (m, **from** a, **to** b) with message content m (also called *payload*), *sender* a and *receiver* b. When it is clear from the context, we omit notationally the sender or receiver of messages or write (m, a, b) instead of (m, **from** a, **to** b).

Definition 36 (pg. 112) of concurrent runs applies to communicating ASMs where—since there are no interaction locations but only local states—one can assume that $lastGlobalRead(a, m) = m$ holds for every write move of every agent $a \in A_m$ in state S_m, so that these runs are also parallel interleaved runs. One of the best known examples of a system of communicating processes is *WhatsApp*. It illustrates well that the components (the registered cellular phones) work autonomously, each at the pace of its user, performing each send or receive step possibly simultaneously with a step of some other users but without being synchronized by any global clock. Due to their abstract character concurrent runs of communicating ASMs can be refined to describe frequently used communication patterns and serve for a rigorous analysis of distributed algorithms; for some characteristic examples see [50, Ch. 3.3, 4.4], [124, 36].

5.2.1 Web Browser Model

To show a concrete Send/Receive pattern example we sketch in this section the structure of a simple browser model with three refinements (by layers describing successively environment, transport and stream details) which describe the concurrent behaviour triggered by a web browser that runs Javascript programs.[7]

---

[7] The specification is taken from [83] where in a similar way the Request/Reply pattern of a web server is specified at various levels of abstraction.

5.2.1.1 Browser User Layer

The top level of a browser model is where the interaction between the user and the browser takes place, e.g. when the user opens or closes the browser (or a new window or tab) and when the browser shows some documents to the user. Windows or tabs within windows visualize a browser environment we call browser context. Most browsers can work with a set of multiple independent contexts which appear in an (initially empty) subset *currContexts* of an abstract set *Context*. We describe only three basic user commands, just to illustrate by a few characteristic concrete examples the kind of rules that appear at this level in a complete model. We use two submachines STARTBC and STOPBC to start or stop a browser context. These submachines together with the notion of *Context* are refined in the context layer below.

> BROWSER =
>   STARTCONTEXT   -- includes start of the browser
>   CLOSECONTEXT
>   CLOSEBROWSER

The three submachines are triggered by *userInput*. We keep it abstract here, together with the related CONSUME concept. There are various possible refinements, notably by events in an *eventQueue* (provided by the window manager or a graphical user interface tool or the operating system). See the context layer below.

> STARTCONTEXT =
>   **if** *userInput* = startContext **then**
>   **let** *newContext* = **new** (*Context*)
>   STARTBC(*newContext*)
>   INSERT(*newContext, currContexts*)
>   CONSUME(*userInput*)   -- event consumption
> CLOSECONTEXT =
>   **if** *userInput* = (closeContext, *context*) **then**
>   STOPBC(*context*)
>   DELETE(*context, currContexts*)
>   CONSUME(*userInput*)
> CLOSEBROWSER =
>   **if** *userInput* = closeBrowser **then**
>   **forall** *context* ∈ *currContexts* **do**
>   STOPBC(*context*)   -- stop every element of *currContexts*
>   DELETE(*context, currContexts*)   -- empty entire set *currContexts*
>   CONSUME(*userInput*)

As a side note, most implemented browsers in fact execute an initial STARTCONTEXT on startup (this is equivalent to assuming that *userInput* is startContext in the initial state).

5.2.1.2 Browser Context Layer

Here we define the notion of browser *Context* and the meaning of starting/stopping a browser context to run. A browser context is characterized by the following five elements:

- the current document that is presented to the user, a tree called DOM (Document Object Model),
- the stack of documents the user has visited (in the given browsing context), called *session history*,
- a *window* where the current document is presented and where the interaction with the user takes place,
- a RENDERER that produces the user-visible graphical representation of the current document,
- an EVENTLOOP that receives and processes the local browser input (read: operating system applied events).

Since we want to illustrate here the concurrent browser behaviour we concentrate our attention on the EVENTLOOP, leaving the *window* and the work of the RENDERER abstract and assuming that the user interaction with the window is handled by the operating system. For the same reason we skip modeling the *session history*.

For the definition of $\text{STARTBC}(k)$ and $\text{STOPBC}(k)$ note the context parameter k which identifies the corresponding request/response pair. Upon starting a new browsing context the $DOM(k)$ is initialized by an *initialDOM* (whose definition is provided by the implementation) and two agents are created to execute independently the RENDERER respectively the EVENTLOOP program for the given browsing context. These two agents contribute to the concurrent browser run.

$\text{STARTBC}(k) =$
    let $a, b =$**new** $(Agent), q =$**new** $(Queue)$ **in**
        $pgm(a) := \text{RENDERER}(k)$
        $pgm(b) := \text{EVENTLOOP}(k)$
        $DOM(k) := initialDOM$
        $eventQueue(k) := q$ -- initially empty
        $agents(k) := \{a, b\}$

To stop a running browsing context its agents and DOM are canceled:

$\text{STOPBC}(k) =$
    forall $agent \in agents(k)$
        $pgm(agent) := undef$
    $DOM(k) := undef$
    $agents(k) := \emptyset$

A stated above we keep the RENDERER abstract. So we only require that there is a (system dependent) *renderingTime(k)* at which the RENDERER will $\text{GENERATEUI}(DOM(k), k)$ if no other agent has a lock on the $DOM(k)$.

RENDERER(k) =
    if $renderingTime(k)$ **and not** $Locked(DOM(k))$ **then**
      GENERATEUI($DOM(k), k$)

The EVENTLOOP(k) agent is created when the browsing context k is created. Its role is to handle the events in the *eventQueue* of the browsing context k.[8] For the sake of illustration we define the behaviour for two typical request/response pattern events, a new url request and a form submission request. Other event types can be specified similarly.

EVENTLOOP(k) =
    if $eventQueue(k) \neq empty$ **then**
      let $e = head(eventQueue(k))$ **in**
        DEQUEUE($e, eventQueue(k)$)
        if $UrlRequestFromUser(e)$ **then**
          HANDLEURLREQ(e, k)
        if $FormSubmission(e)$ **then**
          HANDLEFORMSUBMISSIONREQ(e, k)
      $\vdots$ -- rules for other event types

If the user provides a new url (e.g. by typing it in the browser's address bar or by selecting a bookmark), by a PAGELOAD that starts an asynchronous GET TRANSFER the browsing context is navigated to that url and a new DOM is created to keep the data of the requested document. PAGELOAD comes with three parameters besides k: the GET *method*—other methods are POST, PUT, HEAD, and some more we do not discuss—an *url* and no *data* (some other components come with data, e.g. HANDLEFORMSUBMISSIONREQ below). The TRANSFER machine used by PAGELOAD has an additional callback parameter *proc* denoting the process that should handle the expected response to the given request, namely the HTMLPROCessor defined in the stream layer below. It contains an HTMLPARSER component whose mode must be set to Parsing. This explains the following definitions. The TRANSFER machine is defined at the transport layer below.

HANDLEURLREQ(e, k) = PAGELOAD($GET, url(e), \langle \rangle, k$)
where
    PAGELOAD($method, url, data, k$) = [9]
      TRANSFER($method, url, data,$ HTMLPROC$, k$)
      $htmlParserMode(k) :=$ Parsing
      let $d =$ **new** (DOM) **in**
        $DOM(k) := d$
        $curNode(k) := root(d)$

---

[8] Therefore in the browser layer $userInput = x$ is treated as an event, i.e. it is refined to $head(eventQueue(k)) = (userInput = x)$ and CONSUME($userInput$) is refined to DEQUEUE($userInput = x, eventQueue$).

[9] Here is the place for a session history rule.

If an event e is about the submission of a form, the machine computes from it the relevant data and an url to send out a request to the new url (MUTATEURL) or to submit the data computed for the form (SUBMITBODY). This explains the following definition where the vertical dots refer to GET and POST methods of other schemas like ftp, javascript, data, mailto we do not describe here.

HANDLEFORMSUBMISSIONREQ$(e, k) =$
   let $f = formElement(e), m = method(f), a = action(f),$
      $data = encodeFormData(f), u = resolveUrl(f, a)$ **in**
      case $(schema(u), m)$ **of**
         $(\mathsf{http}, \mathsf{GET})$: MUTATEURL$(u, data, k)$
         $(\mathsf{http}, \mathsf{POST})$: SUBMITBODY$(u, data, k)$
         $\vdots$

where
   MUTATEURL$(u, data, k) =$
      let $u' = u \cdot \text{``?''} \cdot data$ **in**   -- compute new url
        PAGELOAD$(\mathsf{GET}, u', \langle\rangle, k)$
   SUBMITBODY$(u, data, k) =$ PAGELOAD$(\mathsf{POST}, u, data, k)$

5.2.1.3 Browser Transport Layer

This layer describes the HTTP Request/Response data exchange structure between agents residing on different hosts. We define here the TRANSFER machine to initiate a complete HTTP request/response data exchange, as used for example in the context layer PAGELOAD machine above. The TRANSFER machine uses a submachine SEND which does the eventual TCPSENDing of a request but also activates a RECEIVE machine instance which processes the expected response stream. These three machines are defined at this level of abstraction.

As we have seen in the context layer, TRANSFER comes with five parameters $method, url, data, callBackProc, k$ (the latter being the *Context* of the transfer). It records the first three parameters in corresponding context locations and then performs the specific actions foreseen by the specific protocol of the given *url*. We only describe the actions for the HTTP protocol: first the cookies that match the *url*—they are stored by the RECEIVE component below—are retrieved using the function *cookiesFor(url)* to compute by the *makeHeader* function the HTTP header of the message to be sent (that depends also on *method* and *url*). Then the request body is formatted applying the function *makeData* to the parameter *data* and the destination host address is computed by the function *addressFor(url)*. This explains the following definition.[10]

---

[10] Note that we leave it to further refinements to specify aspects concerning transmission reliability or quality of received data (e.g. being virus or advertisement free).

$\text{TRANSFER}(method, url, data, callBackProc, k) =$
  $meth(k) := method$
  $url(k) := url$
  $data(k) := data$
  $\textbf{if } protocol(url) = \text{http } \textbf{then}$
    $\textbf{let } cookies = cookiesFor(url),$
      $header = makeHeader(method, url, cookies),$
      $bodyData = makeData(data),$
      $host = addressFor(url) \textbf{ in}$
        $\text{SEND}(host, header, bodyData, callBackProc, k)$

    $\vdots$ -- other transfer forms, e.g. file, ftp, etc.

To send request data to a host using the HyperText Transfer Protocol (HTTP, which we will later refine as HTTP over TCP/IP [60]) some format constraints must be satisfied which we represent by an abstract *header* concept; it includes a request line (indicating a *method*, protocol versioning information, etc.) and a possibly empty header sequence of (*key*, *value*) pairs followed by an empty line followed by a (possibly empty) data body to be processed by the receiver of the request. To record the communication data we use *Buffers*. The SEND machine besides constructing the HTTP request and sending it to the destination host (using the actual TCPSEND) also creates an agent a—which contributes to the concurrent browser run—and a new *buffer* managed by this agent to process the response, using the RECEIVE program with the callback process determined by the initiator of the TRANSFER in the given context k. This explains the following definition.

$\text{SEND}(host, header, bodyData, callBackProc, k) =$
  $\textbf{let } buffer = \textbf{new } (Buffer), a = \textbf{new } (Agent) \textbf{ in}$
    $ag(k) := a$
    $buf(k) := buffer$
    $\text{TCPSEND}(host, header \cdot emptyline \cdot bodyData, buffer)$
    $mode(k) := \text{expectStatus}$
    $pgm(a) := \text{RECEIVE}(callBackProc, k)$

We specify the RECEIVE(*callBackProc*, k) machine only with a characteristic frequent example for headers, namely a cookie header.

$\text{RECEIVE}(callBackProc, k) =$
  $\textbf{if } mode(k) = \text{expectStatus } \textbf{then}$
    $\textbf{if } IsLine(head(buf(k))) \textbf{ then}$
      $\textbf{let } l = head(buf(k)) \textbf{ in}$
        $status(k) := l$ -- *status* determines type of response code
        $mode(k) := \text{expectHeader}$
        $\text{DEQUEUE}(l, buf(k))$
  $\textbf{if } mode(k) = \text{expectHeader } \textbf{then}$
    $\textbf{if } IsLine(head(buf(k))) \textbf{ then}$

> **let** $l = head(buf(k))$ **in**
> $\textsc{Dequeue}(l, buf(k))$
> **if** $EmptyLine(l)$ **then** $mode(k) :=$ expectData
> **if** $SetCookie(l)$ **then**
> $\quad$ **forall** $cookie \in l$ $\textsc{Record}(cookie, url(k))$
>
> $\vdots$ $\qquad\qquad\qquad\qquad$ -- processing other headers
>
> **if** $mode(k) =$ expectData **then**
> $\quad callBackProc(k)$

Remark on locks in concurrent browser runs. Since in a concurrent browser run multiple tranfers may occur simultaneously, the access to cookies must be constrained by a locking mechanism, as we assume here using abstract functions to access and modify cookies.[11]

Remark on program switch. In the last if-clause of $\textsc{Receive}$, one could also have written $pgm(\textbf{self}) := callBackProc(k)$. However, in that case we would not have been able to change $mode(k)$ after entering expectData, which could have been useful to handle, say, network errors — which we omit here.

5.2.1.4 Browser Stream Layer

At this level of abstraction we describe three typical stream processors that are used for the call back processes invoked by the $\textsc{Transfer}$ browser component, namely for HTML, script and image streams.

We start with the $\textsc{HtmlProcessor}$. We specify three typical cases. Depending on the response code $status$ in the given context the processor parses an HTML document and builds the corresponding DOM (in case of $SuccessCode$) or will $\textsc{RestartTransfer}$ (with a new url provided by the response in case of $RedirectCode$) or in case of $ErrorCode$ handles the error (notifying the user that a requested page loading failed).

> $\textsc{HtmlProc}(k) =$
> $\quad$ **if** $SuccessCode(status(k))$ **then** $\textsc{HtmlParser}(k)$
> $\quad$ **if** $ErrorCode(status(k))$ **then** $\textsc{HandleHtmlError}(k)$
> $\quad$ **if** $RedirectCode(status(k))$ **then** $\textsc{RestartTransfer}(k)$
>
> $\vdots$ $\qquad\qquad\qquad\qquad$ -- rules for other return codes

We concentrate our attention on three (among many other) aspects of the HTML parsing process which are important for the execution of web applications, namely to build the DOM tree, to $\textsc{LoadResources}$ and to

---

[11] One could also apply the method described in [56] to embed the critical browser components into an abstract control scheme that turns their concurrent behavior into a transactional one. See Fig. 2.3. A similar remark applies in the stream layer below where we specify details of operations on the DOM.

EXECSCRIPTS. The structure of this little parser is determined by three components detailed below. For brevity we write in the following again k to denote any context.

> HTMLPARSER(k) =
> **if not** $paused(k)$ **then**
>   PARSETEXT(k)   -- if $head(buf(k))$ is a piece of text
>   PARSETAG(k)   -- if $head(buf(k))$ is a tag
>   FINISHPARSING(k)   -- if $buf(k)$ is Finished

If the head of the $buf(k)$ is a piece of text (if the buffer is not empty), this text is dequeued and appended to the contents of $curNode(k)$ in the DOM, the parent node of the content that is currently parsed. This describes the behaviour of the PARSETEXT(k) parser component where we use a controlled function $curText(node)$ to store the accumulated text at the $node$.

> PARSETEXT(k) =
>   **if** $buf(k) \neq [\ ]$ **then let** $t = head(buf(k))$ **in**
>   **if** $IsText(t)$ **then**
>   APPENDTEXT(t, $curNode(k)$)   -- write to DOM
>   DEQUEUE(t, $buf(k)$)
> **where**
>   APPENDTEXT($text$, $node$) =
>   **if** $curText(node) = undef$ **then** $curText(node) := text$
>   **else** $curText(node) := curText(node) \cdot text$

The PARSETAG(k) component is triggered if $head(buf(k))$ is a tag. It has a subrule to OPENTAGS and a subrule to CLOSETAGS. Both are applied if the tag in question is both opening and closing.

- In case of an opening tag the DOM tree is extended by a new child node of $curNode(k)$; the $curNode(k)$ moves there if the tag is only opening and not also closing. If the tag requires background loading of further resources—as characteristic examples we consider three cases: a script, an image or a stylesheet—OPENTAG will STARTLOADRESOURCE calling the corresponding TRANSFER component with the appropriate callback process (in our examples SCRIPTPROC, IMAGEPROC or STYLESHEETPROC). These background transfers run concurrently with the transfer of the main HTML page, managed by the agent created to RECEIVE the expected resource (see the SEND component defined together with TRANSFER in the transport layer).
- In case of a closing tag that is not also opening the $curNode(k)$ moves back to its parent node. At this point some post-processing may be required. We consider the example of a closing SCRIPT tag </SCRIPT>. In this case a script execution component SCRIPTEXEC triggers the (synchronous immediate, asynchronous or deferred) execution of the loaded code. This explains the following definition of PARSETAG(k) and its components whose behaviour we describe below.

PARSETAG(k) =
    let $t = head(buf(k))$ **in**
      if $IsTag(t)$ **then**
        OPENTAG(t, k)
        CLOSETAG(t, k)
        DEQUEUE($t, buf(k)$)

The components of PARSETAG(k) are defined as follows. Other cases we do not consider here can be specified in an analogous way.

OPENTAG(t, k) =
    if $IsOpening(t)$ **then**
      let $n = $ **new** ($Node$) **in**
        ADDCHILD($n, curNode(k)$)
        if not $IsClosing(t)$ **then** $curNode(k) := n$
        STARTLOADRESOURCE(t, n)
    where
      ADDCHILD($n, node$) =
      $parent(n) := node$
      if $firstChild(node) = undef$
        then $firstChild(node) := n$
        else $nextSibling(lastChild(node)) := n$

For STARTLOADRESOURCE(t, n) we consider only the cases of script code, images and style sheets with their call back processes we describe in more detail below.

STARTLOADRESOURCE(t, n) =
    case t **of**
      <SCRIPT src=url> :
        TRANSFER(GET, $url, \langle\rangle$, SCRIPTPROC, n)
      <IMG src=url> :
        TRANSFER(GET, $url, \langle\rangle$, IMAGEPROC, n)
      <LINK rel=rl src=url> :
        if "stylesheet" $\in rl$ **then**
          TRANSFER(GET, $url, \langle\rangle$, STYLESHEETPROC, n)
      $\vdots$ -- other cases requiring background transfer

For the possible post-processing to be done upon closing a tag we consider only the script execution case. The invoked SCRIPTEXECution component manages the three kinds of execution of loaded code: immediate (synchronous) execution, asynchronous execution (that is also started immediately) and execution that is deferred (with information enqueued in $Deferred(k)$) to be performed for each element in $Deferred(k)$ when the component FINISHPARSING is activated.

CLOSETAG(t, k) =
  if $IsClosing(t)$ then
    if not $IsOpening(t)$ then $curNode(k) := parent(curNode(k))$
    case t of
      </SCRIPT> : SCRIPTEXEC
      ⋮   -- other cases requiring post-processing
  where
    SCRIPTEXEC =
      if $IsAsync(curNode(k))$ then
        STARTASYNC($curNode(k), k$)
      elseif $IsDeferred(curNode(k))$ then
        ENQUEUE(($curNode(k), k), Deferred(k)$)   -- store for later exec
      else
        RUNIMMEDIATE($curNode(k), k$)   -- start exec now

FINISHPARSING(k) =
  if $Finished(buf(k))$ then   -- loading and parsing finished
    if $Deferred(k) \neq [\,]$ then
      RUNDEFERRED(k)   -- see below
  else
    FINALIZELOADING(k)
    $pgm(\mathbf{self}) := undef$ -- parser program can be deleted

It remains to specify the execution of script components encountered in a
page. The synchronous (also called immediate) execution pauses the HTML
parser and inserts into the interpreter call parameters also the current context
with a callback component RUNCOMPLETED to restart the parsing once the
immediate code execution terminates. The reason for pausing the parser is
that HTML content can be injected into the page under construction from a
script, typically using the `document.write()` method. We leave the detailed
specification of this for a further refinement step and assume here that output
generated by `document.write()` or `document.writeln()` during a script
execution is collected in an ordered $documentWriteBuffer(k)$ and prepended
to $buf(k)$ just before resuming the parsing. Accordingly, we define:

RUNIMMEDIATE($node, k$) =
  $paused(k) := true$
  case $type(node)$ of
    text/javascript :
      ECMASCRIPTINTERPRETER($node,$ RUNCOMPLETED, k)

    ⋮   -- other language interpreters
  where
    RUNCOMPLETED(k) =
      $buf(k) := documentWriteBuffer(k) \cdot buf(k)$
      $paused(k) := false$

The main difference of asynchronous with respect to immediate execution is that the asynchronous script execution is concurrent to parsing (subject to locking for shared data access, typically concerning the DOM) so that the HTML parser is not *paused* and no callback is performed when the called interpreter terminates.

STARTASYNC(*node*, *k*) =
   case *type*(*node*) **of**
     text/javascript :
       ECMASCRIPTINTERPRETER(*node*, NOOP, *k*)
       ⋮
                         -- other language interpreters
   where
     NOOP(*k*) =**skip**

As the name suggests deferred execution postpones the execution of a script, namely until the entire page is loaded. Therefore a queue *Deferred*(*k*) is used to store the information about the pending scripts and to execute them managed by RUNDEFERRED before executing FINALIZELOADING. We skip specifying FINALIZELOADING that is about some final events fired by the parser (see [163, Sect. 8.2.6]) and further operations for malformed documents.

RUNDEFERRED(*k*) =
   if *Deferred*(*k*) ≠ [ ] **then**
     let *node* = *head*(*Deferred*(*k*)) **in**
       RUNIMMEDIATE(*node*, *k*)
       DEQUEUE(*node*, *Deferred*(*k*))

It remains to specify the processors which process script and image streams. The rules that describe their behaviour are structurally the same as the rule specifying HTMLPROC.

Script streams. Script streams appear when the browser loads script code from a remote url; this happens when the HTML parser component STARTLOADRESOURCE defined above processes an element of form <SCRIPT src=*url*>. When an error occurs the SCRIPTPROCessor does not notify the user but assigns an empty *programText*.

SCRIPTPROC(*k*) =
   if *SuccessCode*(*status*(*k*)) **then** SCRIPTPARSER(*k*)
   if *ErrorCode*(*status*(*k*)) **then** *programText*(*k*) := " "
   if *RedirectCode*(*status*(*k*)) **then** RESTARTTRANSFER(*k*)
   ⋮
                           -- rules for other return codes

For the sake of simplicity of exposition we formulate the parsing of script source code in terms of text, using the same abstract functions used already in the PARSETEXT(*k*) component above. When the parsing of the content of $buf(k)$ is *Finished* the context is notified that the to-be-executed code is *Complete* and the parser program can be deleted.

SCRIPTPARSER(k) =
    if not *Finished*($buf(k)$) **then**
        let $t = head(buf(k))$ **in**
            programText(k) := *programText*(k) · t -- build the script code
            DEQUEUE(t, $buf(k)$)
    if *Finished*($buf(k)$) **then**
        Complete(k) := *true*   -- signal that code is complete
        pgm(**self**) := *undef*

Note that the execution of script code can start while the script is still loading, but the interpreter can terminate only when the full program text has been loaded and parsed (i.e. when *Complete*(k) has become true.)

Image streams. IMAGEPROCessor and IMAGEPARSER have a similar rule structure to that of the HTML and script processors and parsers. Therefore we do not formulate it here although the incremental loading behaviour has interesting image specific features (e.g. progressive image rendering with different quality).

5.3 Concurrency, Communication, Choice (Occam)

In this section we illustrate concurrent runs—and some of their proven to be correct stepwise refinements towards the Transputer implementation—by executions of programs of the programming language Occam where concurrency comes together with communication and choice. Such refinement correctness proofs are methodologically important to produce reliable software-intensive systems (see Sect. 7.2), although in this book we can only sketch the proof method and refer for detailed proofs to [44].

5.3.1 Occam Ground Model

The ALT$_0$ and PAR commands (Examples 10, pg. 64 and 13, pg. 116) together with the COMmunication instruction we add here describe already the conceptual core of an Occam ground model (in the sense explained in Sect. 7.1). Channel communication requires one reader and one writer. At this level of abstraction we assume the synchronous view of instantaneous channel communication: if only one communication partner is ready it stands still until also the other partner becomes ready.[12]

---

[12] For a more detailed definition and analysis of such bilateral synchronous communication models as used in operating systems see [40, 65]. In Sect. 6.2.1 (pg. 154) the reader

$\text{COM}(a, c, v; b, d, t) =$
  if a does $c?v$ **and** b does $d!t$ **and** $\bar{c} = \bar{d}$ **then**
    write $eval(t, env(b))$ to a at v
    $\text{PROCEED}(a)$
    $\text{PROCEED}(b)$
    where
      write α to a at $v = (\bar{v} := \alpha)$
      $\bar{v} = bind(v, env(a))$
      $\bar{c} = bind(c, env(a))$
      $\bar{d} = bind(d, env(b))$

For the sake of completeness we add the following rules for the set SEQCMDS of basic sequential commands of Occam.

$\text{ASSIGNMENT}(a) = $ **if** a does $v := t$ **then**
  write $eval(t, env(a))$ to a at v
  $\text{PROCEED}(a)$
$\text{TIME}(a) = $ **if** a does $time?v$ **then**   -- time request
  write $timer(a)$ to a at v -- record the current local time
  $\text{PROCEED}(a)$
$\text{IF}(a, cond) = $ **if** a does $cond$ **then**
  if $eval(cond, env(a)) = true$
    then $pos(a) := yes(pos(a))$ **else** $pos(a) := no(pos(a))$
$\text{SKIP}(a) = $ **if** a does $skip$ **then** $\text{PROCEED}(a)$
$\text{STOP}(a) = $ **if** a does $stop$ **then** $mode(a) := sleeping$

Putting these rules together we obtain the following ground model for Occam (the rules CHILDTERMINATION and PARENTWAKEUP have been defined together with the PAR rule, see pg. 117):

$\text{OCCAM}_0 =$
  SEQCMDS
  COM
  ALT_0
  PAR
  CHILDTERMINATION
  PARENTWAKEUP
where
  SEQCMDS =**par** (ASSIGNMENT, TIME, IF, SKIP, STOP)

---

finds an asynchronous communication model where each communication channel has a writer and a reader which access the channel independently of each other. Every bilateral Send/Receive pattern can be defined as composition of refinements (see Sect. 7.2) of two abstract ASM communication models SENDPATTERN(m) and RECEIVEPATTERN(m), similarly for multilateral communication models with ASMs ONETOMANYSEND and ONEFROMMANYRECEIVE and their composition, see [10] and [50, Sect. 4.4].

It is called *ground model* because it tries to capture the intuitive understanding of the semantics of the programming language. Consequently inspection of this model must establish that it correctly reflects the design goals for Occam (and its Transputer implementation [105, 104]) because a mathematical verification of the desired language properties is possible only with respect to a mathematical definition of the language. Here we illustrate some first refinement steps, moving towards the implementation. Since the ground model and its refinements represent mathematical objects, properties of the refinement steps which show their correctness can be mathematically proved, adding to the reliability of the implementation. These two issues are explained further in Ch. 7.

The successive refinement steps we are going to explain now replace the synchronous by an asynchronous communication (via external Transputer channels) (Sect. 5.3.2), optimize the communication by shared locations (internal Transputer channels) (Sect. 5.3.3), then proceed to a sequential implementation (Sect. 5.3.4) and prevent divergence (Sect. 5.3.5).

To simplify the exposition of the refinement steps we split the rule ALT_0 into three rules $\text{ALTRULE}_0(G_i)$, one per type of the guards: type *StateCondition* for $G_i = cond_i$, type *TimeCondition* for $G_i = cond_i : time?after\ t_i$ and type *ComCondition* for $G_i = cond_i : chan_i\ ?\ v_i$. So ALT_0 assumes the following form:

$\text{ALT}_0(a, (G_1, \ldots, G_n)) =$
  if a **does alt** $(G_1, \ldots, G_n)$ **then**
    choose $i \in \{1, \ldots, n\}$ **do** $\text{ALTRULE}_0(G_i)$
  where
    forall $i \in \{1, \ldots, n\}$
    $G_i \in \{cond_i, cond_i : time?after\ t_i, cond_i : chan_i\ ?\ v_i\}$

We simply collect for each guard parameter type (element of $\{StateCond, TimeCond, ComCond\}$) the conditions for the rule to be fireable and the effect of its application, resulting in three different parameterized rules $\text{ALTRULE}_0(guard)$, one per type of *guard*.

$\text{ALTRULE}_0(cond_i) =$
  if $eval(cond_i, env(a)) = true$ **then**   -- StateCond
    $pos(a) := next(pos(a), i)$

$\text{ALTRULE}_0(cond_i : time?after\ t_i) =$
  if $eval(cond_i, env(a)) = true$ -- StateCond
    and $timer(a) > eval(t_i, env(a))$ -- TimeCond
  then
    $pos(a) := next(pos(a), i)$

$\text{ALTRULE}_0(cond_i : chan_i\ ?\ v_i) =$
  if $eval(cond_i, env(a)) = true$ **and** $ComCond(G_i)$ **then**
    $pos(a) := next(pos(a), i)$

> **let** b, c, t **with** b does $c!t$ **and** $\overline{chan_i} = \overline{c}$
> write $eval(t, env(b))$ to a at v_i -- data transfer
> $\textsc{Proceed}(b)$
> **where**
> $ComCond(G_i) = \textbf{forsome } b, c, t \ \ b \text{ does } c!t \textbf{ and } \overline{chan_i} = \overline{c}$

5.3.2 Refining Sync to Async Communication

The idea of this refinement step is to split the synchronization of input request $c?v$ and output offer $d!t$ via channel condition $\overline{c} = \overline{d}$ into 3 independent asynchronous steps. This needs some new auxiliary functions:

- agents first register as *reader/writer* at a (now active) *Channel*:

  $reader, writer : Channel \to Agent \cup \{nil\}$

- then they wait (go to sleep)
- until the channel agent fires to transmit its *mssg* to the indicated *place* (a variable identifier):

  $mssg : Channel \to Value \quad place : Channel \to Id$

We therefore define a reader rule IN, a writer rule OUT and a CHAN rule to asynchronously simulate the synchronized ground model communication $\textsc{Com}(a, c, v; b, d, t)$. For reasons explained below such a communication must be distinguished from a communication via an $\textsc{AltRule}_0$ (with communication parameters $(cond_i : chan_i \, ? \, v_i)$). Therefore we introduce a communication version c_mode of the $mode$ function

$c\_mode : Agent \to \{altRunning, altSleeping, input\}$

so that a refined 'ordinary' communication (not via an alternative choice) can be distinguished by c_mode $input$ of the reader.[13]

$\textsc{In}(a, c, v) = \textbf{if } a \text{ does } c?v \textbf{ then}$
$\quad reader(\overline{c}) := a$
$\quad place(\overline{c}) := v$
$\quad c\_mode(a) := input$
$\quad \text{put } a \text{ asleep at } next(pos(a))$
$\textsc{Out}(b, d, t) = \textbf{if } b \text{ does } d!t \textbf{ then}$
$\quad writer(\overline{d}) := b$
$\quad mssg(\overline{d}) := eval(t, env(b))$
$\quad \text{put } b \text{ asleep at } next(pos(b))$

---

[13] Rules IN and OUT need no check that when an agent accesses the involved channel there is not yet a defined reader resp. writer. This follows from Occam's Channel Assumption we do not explain further here: if two agents in some states both access a same channel by rules IN or OUT then they are connected by a parent chain.

$\text{CHAN}(C) =$ -- executed by channel agent
    if $Ready(C)$ **and** $c\_mode(reader(C)) = input$ **then**
      write $mssg(C)$ to $reader(C)$ at $place(C)$
      $\text{WAKEUP}(reader(C))$
      $\text{WAKEUP}(writer(C))$
      $\text{CLEAR}(C)$
where
    $Ready(C)$ **iff** $reader(C) \neq nil$ **and** $writer(C) \neq nil$
    $\text{CLEAR}(C) =$
      $reader(C) := nil$
      $writer(C) := nil$
    $\text{WAKEUP}(a) = (mode(a) := running)$

For the refined ALTRULE_1 we must guarantee that choosing an alternative with communication parameter $cond_i : chan_i ? v_i$ can result in a data exchange step only when both a reader and a writer are registered at $\overline{chan_i}$. Therefore when an agent a starts to execute an alternative command with some communication alternative, it can only announce at the relevant channel its own readiness to choose that communication alternative. So a registers itself at all involved channels as potential reader with true $cond_i$ (REGISTER) and then will have to wait (in communication $c\_mode = altSleep$) for a writer. This case implies the need to wake up a (switch to $c\_mode(a) = altRunning$) when $TimeCond$ (TIMEWAKEUP) or $ComCond$ (CHANWAKEUP) become true. In case upon REGISTERing at some channel already a writer is registered and $ComCond$ is true or the minimal $TimeCond$ition and $StateCond$ition is already satisfied, a directly PROCEEDs in $c\_mode = altRunning$. This explains the following refinement of the flowchart for an alternative command and the ALTREGISTRATION rule.

For simplicity of exposition we assume for the flowchart and the formulation of the ALTREGISTRATION rule that $\overline{G} = \ldots G_i \ldots$ is grouped into com/time/state segments:

- $cond_i : chan_i ? v_i$ for $i = 1, \ldots, k$ and $0 \leq k$
- $cond_i : time?after\, t_i$ for $i = k+1, \ldots, k+l$ and $0 \leq l$
- $cond_i$ for $i = k+l+1, \ldots, k+l+m$ and $0 \leq m$

$\text{ALTREGISTRATION}(a, \overline{G}) =$
    if a does **altRegister**$(\overline{G})$ **then**
      forall $1 \leq i \leq k$ $\text{REGISTER}(\overline{chan_i}, cond_i, a)$ -- where $cond_i$ holds
      $minTime(a) := t_{min}$
      if $StateCond$ **or** $TimeCond$ **or** $ComCond$ **then**
        $\text{PROCEED}(a)$ -- to execute the selection cmd **altSelect**
        $c\_mode(a) := altRunning$
      else
        put a asleep at $next(pos(a))$
        $c\_mode(a) := altSleep$ -- wait for $TimeCond$ or $ComCond$

Fig. 5.3 Occam$_1$ **alt** $(G_1 \ S_1 \ldots G_n \ S_n)$ statement diagram

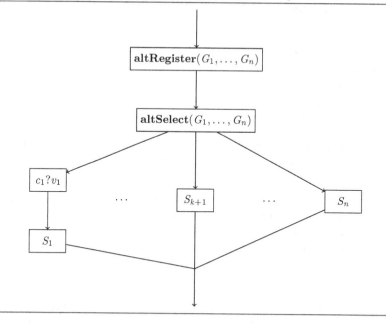

where
    REGISTER$(C, cond, a) =$
    if $eval(cond, env(a))$ **then** $reader(C) := a$
$$t_{min} = \begin{cases} min(T) & \text{if } T \neq \emptyset \\ \infty & \text{otherwise} \end{cases}$$
    where
      $T = \{eval(t_j, env(a)) \mid k+1 \leq j \leq k+l$ **and**   -- minimal time
                     $eval(cond_j, env(a)) = true\}$ -- with $cond_j = true$
      $StateCond = (m > 0)$ -- some guard has no time or channel cond[14]
      $TimeCond = (timer(a) > t_{min})$
      $ComCond =$ **forsome** $1 \leq i \leq k$
        $eval(cond_i, env(a)) = true$ **and** $writer(\overline{chan_i}) \neq nil$

Two new rules are needed to wakeup agents waiting in $c\_mode(a) =$ *altSleep* for *ComCond* or *TimeCond* to become true. CHANWAKEUP(C) serves to wake up an agent registered at a channel and waiting for a writer at that channel to satisfy *ComCond*. TIMEWAKEUP(a) serves to wake up an agent that is waiting for a *TimeCond* to become satisfied.

---

[14] Whether a pure state condition $cond_i$, i.e. without additional time or channel requirements $(k + l + 1 \leq i \leq k + l + m)$, is true is checked when executing the selection command **altSelect**. Obviously to be **altSelect**able such a guard must become true.

$\textsc{ChanWakeup}(C) =$ -- channel agent rule
   if $Ready(C)$ **and** $c\_mode(reader(C)) = altSleep$ **then**
     $\textsc{Wakeup}(reader(C))$
     $c\_mode(reader(C)) := altRunning$
$\textsc{TimeWakeup}(a) =$ -- Occam agent rule
   if $timer(a) > minTime(a)$ **and** $c\_mode(a) = altSleep$ **then**
     $\textsc{Wakeup}(a)$
     $c\_mode(a) = altRunning$
  where $\textsc{Wakeup}(a) = (mode(a) := running)$

For the refinement $\textsc{Alt}_1$ of $\textsc{Alt}_0(a, (G_1, \ldots, G_n))$ there are three subrules $\textsc{AltRule}_1$ each of which refines the corresponding subrule $\textsc{AltRule}_0$ of $\textsc{Alt}_0$.

$\textsc{Alt}_1(a, (G_1, \ldots, G_n)) =$ -- same as $\textsc{Alt}_0$ for cmd **altSelect**
   if a **does altSelect** $(G_1, \ldots, G_n)$ **then**
     choose $i \in \{1, \ldots, n\}$ **do** $\textsc{AltRule}_1(G_i)$
     where forall $i \in \{1, \ldots, n\}$
     $G_i \in \{cond_i, cond_i : time?after\ t_i, cond_i : chan_i\ ?\ v_i\}$

The state or time conditioned subrules $\textsc{AltRule}_1$ are structurally identical to their abstract companions $\textsc{AltRule}_0$: the **alt** command is replaced by **altSelect** and the agent is required to be in $c\_mode(a) = altRunning$.

$\textsc{AltRule}_1(cond_i) =$
   if a **does altSelect** $(G_1, \ldots, G_n)$ **and** $G_i = cond_i$
     and $c\_mode(a) = altRunning$ **then**   -- waiting for $cond_i$
     if $eval(cond_i, env(a)) = true$ **then**   -- StateCond satisfied
       $pos(a) := next(pos(a), i)$ -- enter the choice

$\textsc{AltRule}_1(cond_i : time?after\ t_i) =$
   if a **does altSelect** $(G_1, \ldots, G_n)$ **and** $G_i = cond_i : time?after\ t_i$
     and $c\_mode(a) = altRunning$ **then**
     if $eval(cond_i, env(a)) = true$ -- StateCond satisfied
       and $timer(a) > eval(t_i, env(a))$ -- TimeCond Satisfied
     then
       $pos(a) := next(pos(a), i)$ -- enter the choice

The communication conditioned $\textsc{AltRule}_1$ differs from its abstract companion by the fact that the data transfer cannot happen directly but only after the choice, via an execution of a communication command $c_i?v_i$ by the reader (see Fig. 5.3 where the command $c_i\ ?\ v_i$ is placed before S_i for $i = 1, \ldots, k$). Therefore to execute the **altSelect** command with channel parameter $chan_i\ ?\ v_i$ the agent only enters the alternative command and $\textsc{UnRegisters}$ from the channel. $\textsc{UnRegister}$ makes sure that the communication (and therefore becoming $reader$ at the involved channel) takes place only after the choice (with parameters of the chosen alternative, redoing rule $\textsc{In}$).

$\text{ALTRULE}_1(cond_i : chan_i ? v_i) =$
    if a **does** **altSelect** $(G_1, \ldots, G_n)$ **and** $G_i = cond_i : chan_i ? v_i$
      and $c\_mode(a) = altRunning$ **then**
        if $eval(cond_i, env(a)) = true$ **and** $ComCond(G_i)$ **then**
          $pos(a) := next(pos(a), i)$ -- enter the choice
          forall $i = 1, \ldots k$ $\text{UNREGISTER}(\overline{chan_i}, cond_i, a)$
    where
      $ComCond(G_i) = (writer(\overline{chan_i}) \neq nil)$
      $\text{UNREGISTER}(C, cond, a) =$
        if $eval(cond, env(a))$ **then** $reader(C) := nil$

The result of this refinement of OCCAM_0 (by introducing the external Transputer channels [137]) is the following machine OCCAM_1. To make the refinement explicit we indent the new rules that replace the OCCAM_0 rule COM respectively ALT_0.

$\text{OCCAM}_1 =$
  SEQCMDS
  $\Big[$ IN
     OUT   -- 3 parallel rules that refine COM
     CHAN
  $\Big[$ ALTREGISTRATION
     CHANWAKEUP
     TIMEWAKEUP   -- 4 parallel rules that refine ALT_0
     ALT_1
  PAR
  CHILDTERMINATION
  PARENTWAKEUP
  where
    SEQCMDS = **par** (ASSIGNMENT, TIME, IF, SKIP, STOP)

Theorem 2 (Refinement By External Channels). OCCAM_1 *is a correct and complete refinement of* OCCAM_0 *by external channels.*

Proof. The explanations of the refined rules show that and how each abstract step in a concurrent OCCAM_0 run can be simulated by corresponding concrete steps in a concurrent OCCAM_1 run (completeness). For the correctness proof we map OCCAM_1 runs to equivalent OCCAM_0 runs as follows:

- If in state S_i the rule R an agent $a \in A_i$ executes is the last step in a run segment containing all concrete steps that simulate an abstract R^*, then we map R to R^* (using $R = R^*$ for homonymous rules).

State and time conditioned OCCAM_1 rules are mapped to their homonymous OCCAM_0 companion. Denote by ALTSTATE_i the rule ALTRULE_i with parameter $cond$ (for $i = 0, 1$), analogously for ALTTIME_i and ALTCOM_i. We map ALTSTATE_1 to ALTSTATE_0 and ALTTIME_1 to ALTTIME_0. For applications of the CHAN rule there are two cases.

- Case 1. If CHAN is reached in the given run via corresponding rules IN and OUT (in any order) in states before S_i, this application of CHAN is mapped to COM.
- Case 2. If otherwise CHAN is reached in the given run via some of the *AltComRules*, where

$$AltComRules =$$
$$\{\text{IN}, \text{OUT}, \text{ALTREGISTRATION}, \text{ALTCOM}_1\}$$
$$\cup\{\text{CHANWAKEUP}, \text{TIMEWAKEUP}\}$$

  then this application of CHAN is mapped to an application of a corresponding communication conditioned ALTCOM_0.
- All other rules that are not in $AltComRules \cup \{\text{ALTSTATE}/\text{TIME}_1, \text{CHAN}\}$ are mapped to themselves.

For a detailed proof see [44, Sect. 4.1].

5.3.3 Optimized Communication

The Transputer supports concurrent execution of multiprocesses on one processor. To reflect this we add to the PAR rule a *processor placement update* $processor(a_i) := proc$. Concentrating the attention on one processor, communication can be optimized via *internal* channels which are implemented in the Transputer by shared locations. Shared channels permit to let the communicating *agents* (instead of a CHANnel agent) directly perform the data transfer when accessing an internal not idle channel.

To achieve this by a refinement of OCCAM_1 we refine the signature and some rules. For the signature:

- we merge the two functions *reader, writer* into one function *agent*,
- we replace the domain *Channel* of the functions *msg, place* by *Agent*.

For the operational refinement we refine the IN/OUT rules to the corresponding rules INIDLE/OUTIDLE for accessing idle internal channels and add a companion rule INREADY respectively OUTREADY which when accessing a not idle internal channel immediately does the data exchange work of CHAN. Furthermore, we incorporate the work of the CHANWAKEUP rule into a new rule ALTOUTWAKEUP.

To define the refined rules for internal channels we let $\text{INIDLE}(a, c, v)$ do the work of $\text{IN}(a, c, v)$ for internal channels where no writer showed up yet: a makes itself waiting in $c\_mode(a) = input$ for input from a writer.

$\text{INIDLE}(a, c, v) = $ **if** a does $c?v$ **and** $Internal(\bar{c})$ **and** $Idle(\bar{c})$ **then**
    $agent(\bar{c}) := a$
    $place(a) := v$
    $c\_mode(a) := input$
    put a asleep at $next(pos(a))$

INREADY(a, c, v) does the work of CHAN($\bar{c}$) for internal channels where a writer is waiting to communicate its data to a reader.

INREADY(a, c, v) =
  if a does $c?v$ **and** $Internal(\bar{c})$ **and not** $Idle(\bar{c})$ **then**
    write $mssg(agent(\bar{c}))$ to a at v
    WAKEUP($agent(\bar{c})$)
    PROCEED(a)
    CLEAR($\bar{c}$)

Analogously OUTIDLE(a, c, t) does the work of OUT(a, c, t) for internal channels where no reader showed up yet: a records its data and makes itself waiting for a reader to communicate with.

OUIDLE(a, c, t) = **if** a does $c!t$ **and** $Internal(\bar{c})$ **and** $Idle(\bar{c})$ **then**
  $agent(\bar{c}) := a$
  $mssg(a) := eval(t, env(a))$
  put a asleep at $next(pos(a))$

OUTREADY(a, c, t) does the work of CHAN($\bar{c}$) for internal channels where a reader is waiting in $c\_mode(a) = input$ to receive input from a writer:

OUTREADY(a, c, t) =
  if a does $c?v$ **and** $Internal(\bar{c})$ **and not** $Idle(\bar{c})$
    and $c\_mode(agent(\bar{c})) = input$ **then**
      write $eval(t, env(a))$ to $agent(\bar{c})$ at $place(agent(\bar{c}))$
      WAKEUP($agent(\bar{c})$)
      PROCEED(a)
      CLEAR($\bar{c}$)

When the *ComCondition* a reader is waiting for becomes true one must wake up the reader. In OCCAM$_1$ this is done by CHANWAKEUP. Here the writer must do it and wait that the ALTCOM$_2$ rule in question will be chosen. So we incorporate CHANWAKEUP into the rule OUTALTWAKEUP to make the writer ready for the communication (if chosen).

OUTALTWAKEUP(a, c, t) =
  if a does $c!t$ **and** $Internal(\bar{c})$ **and not** $Idle(\bar{c})$
    and $c\_mode(agent(\bar{c})) \neq input$ **then**   -- a reader is waiting
      if $c\_mode(agent(\bar{c})) = altSleep$ **then**   -- CHANWAKEUP
      WAKEUP($agent(\bar{c})$)   -- wake up reader
      $c\_mode(agent(\bar{c})) := altRunning$
      $mssg(a) := eval(t, env(a))$ -- record data to transmit
      $agent(\bar{c}) := a$ -- record writer
      put a asleep at $next(pos(a))$ -- wait for com choice

As a result we obtain the refinement OCCAM$_2$ of OCCAM$_1$.

$\text{OCCAM}_2 =$
  SEQCMDS
  PAR
  CHILDTERMINATION
  PARENTWAKEUP
  $\begin{bmatrix} \text{INIDLE} \\ \text{OUTIDLE} \end{bmatrix}$ -- rephrased IN/OUT
  $\begin{bmatrix} \text{INREADY} \\ \text{OUTREADY} \end{bmatrix}$ -- simulating work of CHAN
  $\begin{bmatrix} \text{OUTALTWAKEUP} \end{bmatrix}$ -- simulating work of CHANWAKEUP
  ALTREGISTRATION
  TIMEWAKEUP
  ALT_1

Theorem 3 (Refinement by Internal Channels). OCCAM_2 *with internal channels is a correct and complete refinement of* OCCAM_1.

Proof. The explanations of the refined rules show that and how each abstract step in a concurrent OCCAM_1 run can be simulated by corresponding concrete steps in a concurrent OCCAM_2 run (completeness). For the correctness proof we map $Occam_2$ runs to equivalent $Occam_1$ runs as follows, using the same technique as for the correctntess of OCCAM_1 with respect to OCCAM_0:

  (IN/OUT)IDLE are mapped respectively to IN/OUT
  (IN/OUT)READY are mapped respectively to
      IN/OUT followed by CHAN
  OUTALTWAKEUP is mapped to OUT followed by CHANWAKEUP

Every other OCCAM_2 rule R is mapped to the homonymous rule R from our previous OCCAM_1 model.

NB. This mapping preserves the set of agents, their states (environment, position), communication traces, termination, deadlock, divergence. For a detailed proof see [44, Sect. 4.2].

5.3.4 Sequential Implementation

Consider any sequential *Processor* with an *agentQueue* of *active Agents* a processed by $P = processor(a)$ which share the external *timer*(*processor*(a)) (a data refinement of *timer*(a)) and are executed by the unique *currAgent* whose value is at any time either some of the agents placed on processor P or *nil*.

The introduction of a unique active agent whose task is to serve an *agentQueue* of processes subject to some time requirements requires three kinds of data and operation refinements we are going to explain in this section, concerning *mode* (becoming a question of being in the *agentQueue*), concerning *minTime* (which becomes a list of time conditions t_{min} of agents in the *agentQueue*), and concerning the sequential implementation of parallelism (refined rules for PAR, CHILDTERMINATION and the removal of the PARENTWAKEUP rule).

Refinement concerning *mode*. The crucial data refinement is the refinement of $(a\ does\ C)_2$—the guard $(a\ does\ C)$ as defined in OCCAM$_2$ to guarantee that only the *currAgent* can execute a step:

$$(a\ does\ C)_3 = (a = currAgent\ \textbf{and}\ cmd(pos(a)) = C)$$

There are three more refinements concerning *mode*.

- $mode(a) = running$ is refined to: a is in *agentQueue*.
- put a asleep at n is refined to put *currAgent* asleep at n that is defined as follows:

    > put *currAgent* asleep at $n =$
    > $pos(currAgent) := n$
    > $currAgent := nil$

Note that this update will usually be followed by a DEQUEUE step which activates the next queue element:

> DEQUEUE =
> **if** $currAgent = nil$ **and not** $agentQueue = [\,]$ **then**
> $currAgent := first(agentQueue)$
> $agentQueue := rest(agentsQueue)$

- Correspondingly STOP and WAKEUP(a) are refined to:

    > STOP$_3$ = **if** a does **stop then** $a := nil$

    > WAKEUP$_3(a)$ = ENQUEUE$(a, agentQueue)$

Refinement concerning *minTime*. *minTime* is refined to a list of agents with their waiting time (in the order of the time values).

$$minTime : Processor \rightarrow (Agent \times Nat)^* \text{ sorted by time}$$

Since we are concerned here with only one *processor* we simply write *minTime* instead of *minTime(proc)*. The definition requires a refinement of three rules where *minTime* appears:

- In ALTREGISTRATION$_3$ $minTime(a) := t_{min}$ is refined to an order-respecting *insertion* of (a, t_{min}) into the list *minTime*.

    > $minTime := insert((a, t_{min}), minTime)$
    > where *insert* is assumed to respect the time order

- Refinement of TIMEWAKEUP:

  TIMEWAKEUP$_3$ =
      if $minTime \neq [\ ]$ **then**
      let $minWait =$ minimal waiting time in $minTime$
      if forsome $(a, minWait) \in minTime$ $ReadyFor(altRunning, a)$
        then choose
          $(a, minWait) \in minTime$ **with** $ReadyFor(altRunning, a)$
          WAKEUP(a)
          $c\_mode(a) := altRunning$
          $minTime := delete((a, minWait), minTime)$
    where
      $ReadyFor(altRunning, a) =$
        $timer > minWait$ **and** $c\_mode(a) = altSleep$

- In ALTRULE$_1$ with time parameter add

  $minTime := delete((a, -), minTime)$

  to prevent a from being chosen once more (by DEQUEUE)

Refinement concerning sequential implementation of parallelism.
This refinement concerns the three rules related to Occam's parallelism.

The refinement of PAR (see Example 13, pg. 116) is part of the *mode* refinement in the sense that putting the created children into *running mode* becomes now to ENQUEUE them.

PAR$_3$$(a, n) =$ **if** $(a$ does $PAR \ n)_3$ **then**
  forall $i = 1, \ldots, n$ **let** $a_i =$ **new** $(Agent)$ **in**
    ENQUEUE$(a_i, agentQueue)$ -- in any order
                                -- *mode* update disappears
    $env(a_i) := env(a)$ -- initialize the state of a_i
    $pos(a_i) := next(pos(a), i)$ -- assign the subprogram S_i to a_i
    $parent(a_i) := a$
    $count(a) := n$ -- set running-children counter
    put a asleep at $next(pos(a))$

The refinement of CHILDTERMINATION is characterized by three features:

- at each moment only *one* agent $a = currAgent$ executes the rule
- no partial updates of $count(parent(a))$ are needed any more
- the PARENTWAKEUP rule is optimized away by including it into the CHILDTERMINATION$_3$ rule:

  CHILDTERMINATION$_3$$(a) =$
    if $(a$ does $end)_3$ **then**   -- only one agent $a = currAgent$
      $count(parent(a)) := count(parent(a)) - 1$ -- no partial updates
      if $count(parent(a)) = 1$ **then** WAKEUP$(parent(a))$
               -- the last one terminates the PAR implementation
    DELETE$(a, Agent)$

Thus we arrive at the sequential implementation model OCCAM$_3$. To let them stand out we indent the modified rules.

OCCAM$_3$ =
  SEQCMDS with refined STOP$_3$
  INIDLE
  OUTIDLE
  INREADY
  OUTREADY
  OUTALTWAKEUP
    PAR$_3$ -- put children into *agentQueue*
    CHILDTERMINATION$_3$ -- deleting PARENTWAKEUP
    ALTREGISTRATION$_3$ -- insert (a, t_{min}) into *minTime* sequence
    TIMEWAKEUP$_3$ -- *minTime* lookup for some *minWait* < *timer*
    ALTRULE$_3$ -- when selecting delete (a, t) from *minTime*
    DEQUEUE   -- to let *currAgent* = *nil* fetch the next *a* to execute

Theorem 4 (Sequential Implementation of Occam). *OCCAM$_3$ is a correct refinement of OCCAM$_2$ and also a complete one if there is no divergence (where one agent runs alone forever).*

Proof. As above we concentrate on the correctness part mapping OCCAM$_3$ runs to OCCAM$_2$ runs.

  CHILDTERMINATION$_3$ is mapped to CHILDTERMINATION$_2$
    if $count(parent(a)) > 1$
  CHILDTERMINATION$_3$ is mapped to
    CHILDTERMINATION$_2$ followed by PARENTWAKEUP
      if $count(parent(a)) = 1$
  TIMEWAKEUP$_3$ is mapped to the set of TIMEWAKEUP$_2(b)$
    forall b **with** $(b, minWait) \in minTime$

Each other OCCAM$_3$ rule R is mapped to the homonymous OCCAM$_2$ rule R. For proof details see [44, Sect. 4.3].

5.3.5 Time-Slicing Refinement

Time-slicing eliminates the divergence phenomenon from OCCAM$_3$. The simple refinement idea is that every agent a can be $a = currAgent$ only for a fixed *period*. When this time is *Elapsed a* is ENQUEUEd by a new rule TIMESLICE.

  TIMESLICE = **if** *Elapsed* **and** *currAgent* $\neq$ *nil* **then**
    ENQUEUE(*currAgent*, *agentQueue*)
    currAgent := *nil*
      where *Elapsed* = *timer* − *start* > *period*

The *start* time is updated when an agent becomes *Active*, so that this update is added to DEQUEUE$_3$:

DEQUEUE$_4$ =
    if *currAgent* = *nil* **and not** *agentQueue* = [ ] **then**
        currAgent := *first*(*agentQueue*)
        agentQueue := *rest*(*agentsQueue*)
        start := *timer*   -- refinement by begin of execution time

Executing a command is once more constrained, here by the time not yet being *Elapsed*:

    (*a* does *C*)$_4$ = (*a* does *C*)$_3$ **and not** *Elapsed*

The correctness and completeness of this model follow immediately.

Theorem 5 (Sequential Occam Model with Time-Slicing). *The refinement* OCCAM$_4$ *of* OCCAM$_3$ *by time-slicing is correct and complete.*

Methodological Remark. The first steps to go from OCCAM$_4$ via compilation to a proven-to-be-correct Transputer code model consist in linearizing the flowchart-based nondeterministic model, followed by a refinement to sequential search of the alternatives. For the details we must point the reader to [43]; here we could only illustrate by a real-life example how such stepwise refinements of complex models help the practitioner to build, check (validate and verify), modify, understand and document those models for reuse (see Sect. 7.2).

5.4 Concurrency, Parameterization, Context Awareness

Parameterization is a fundamental technique to define an abstract entity that can be instantiated into a variety of concrete instances by replacing the abstract parameters by concrete values. A well-known example is provided by the class concept in object-oriented programming languages. Abstracting from any language specific particularities one can view a class as given by an ASM *pgm* that defines a multi-agent ASM (*ag$_i$*, *pgm*)$_{i \in I}$ with a set of agents *ag$_i$* ($i \in I$ for some index set I) with same program *pgm*, same signature, maybe even same initialization but different evolution of their state, for example due to different environmental influences. Such a parameterization of *pgm* as *pgm*(*a*) is a special case of *pgm*(*params*) with arbitrary parameters, as used for example in the Call by Name mechanism defined in Sect. 2.3.

    Parameterization offers also a clean and simple way to explicitly define program environments that influence the execution of programs. This provides in particular a technique to efficiently design and analyze concurrent systems constructed out of single-agent subsystems. We illustrate this in Sect. 5.4.2 by a model for multithreaded Java, using the concept of context aware ambient ASMs defined in Sect. 5.4.1.

5.4.1 Context Aware Processes (Ambient ASMs)

In this section we sketch a general method to design and analyze context sensitive processes. We illustrate in Sect. 5.4.2 a typical application that refines the single-agent Java program interpreter from Sect. 3.2 to a truly concurrent thread model. Another application is in Sect. 8.4.1.1 where in recursive calls of an algorithm we must provide fresh instances with encapsulated states for the execution of the called algorithm. The reader might also recognize in the usage of a context k to parameterize operations of the Browser model (Sect. 5.2.1) an example of this common requirement.

One can specify and manage context sensitivity by introducing environment parameters with respect to which terms and rules are evaluated. For the sake of generality we do this via an extension of ASMs by rules of form **amb** exp **in** M where M is an ASM rule and exp an arbitrary expression. exp determines the level of abstraction of the considered $environment$.

Definition 38 (Semantics of Ambient ASMs). The behaviour of an $ambient$ ASM **amb** exp **in** M consists in evaluating exp and use the obtained value as $environment$ (passed by value) for the execution of M.

To define the meaning of executing M in an $environment$ we parameterise each context sensitive function f in the signature of M implicitly by env so that evaluating $f(t)$ in a state is turned into an evaluation of $f(env, t)$. Everything else in the behavioural definition of ASMs remains unchanged.

$f(env, t)$ is also denoted by $f_{env}(t)$ to stress that a context sensitive function f is turned into a family of independent functions f_{env}, separated one from the other by the specific $environment$. This feature permits to precisely describe widely used encapsulation techniques (for states, computations, patterns, etc.), as is illustrated in Sect. 5.4.2 by separating the states of independent threads in concurrent runs.

Therefore the interaction type definition of functions (Sect. 2.1.1) is extended by what we call $context$ $sensitive$ or $environment$ $dependent$ functions.

Exercise 25 (Reduction of Flat Ambient ASMs). In the general hierarchical form of the ambient ASM concept one can record environments in a stack; the whole stack then becomes an additional parameter to context-sensitive functions. In many applications the flat version of Ambient ASM we explain and use here suffices where at each moment only the most recent environment is used. Show how flat ambient ASMs can be transformed to equivalent ASMs without occurrences of **amb** exp **in** M rules. For a solution see [50, pg. 137].

5.4.2 From Sequential to Concurrent Runs (Java/C#)

In this section we first extend the imperative Java component JAVA_I and its procedural extension JAVA_C (Sect. 3.2) with the thread-handling component JAVA_T, which in the sequence of stepwise refined models of [159] completes the definition of a single-agent JAVA interpreter:

$\text{JAVA} =$
$\quad \text{JAVA}_I$ -- imperative instructions, Sect. **3.2.1**
$\quad \text{JAVA}_C$ -- procedural (class) instructions, Sect. **3.2.2**
$\quad \text{JAVA}_O$ -- object-oriented instructions, not shown here
$\quad \text{JAVA}_E$ -- exception handling instructions, not shown here
$\quad \text{JAVA}_T$ -- thread handling instructions

Then we use the concept of context sensitive processes (ambient ASMs) to specify truly concurrent Java program runs, namely as runs of the following Java program instances:

amb a **in**
   SYNCHRONIZE
   JAVA
where
   JAVA is the above single-agent interpreter of Java programs
   $a \in \textit{Thread}$ -- see below the definition of *Thread*

The component SYNCHRONIZE guarantees that the agents $a \in \textit{Thread}$ of the instances respect the Java synchronization discipline.

The thread instructions model JAVA_T. In Java threads are independent concurrently running processes within a single program. We view them as agents a equipped with a Java $pgm(a)$ to execute. They are represented as *References* in the *heap*—defined in JAVA_O, it records the $classOf(ref)$ of *Objects* together with the values of $instanceFields(C)$—and exchange data with other threads via the *heap* and the *globals* function of their class. The independence results from the fact that every thread executes an instance of the Java interpreter JAVA with its own frame stack and current frame, which we denote by a function *localState*. This function is local to the thread and cannot be accessed by other threads, a fact we model below by the ambient concept.

$localState : \textit{Thread} \rightarrow (\textit{Frame}^*, \textit{Frame})$

The thread extension (of JAVA_E) consists only of a rule for *synchronized statements* which allow one thread a at a time to exclusively execute a protected code area. To guarantee this, Java associates a unique lock to the target reference which must be grabbed by the thread that wants to execute the protected code and must be released upon completion of that code. A function $sync(a)$ records the sequence of all references grabbed by a thread a. Since a thread may hold multiple locks for the same object also a lock counter *locks* is needed.

$$sync : Thread \rightarrow Ref^* \qquad\qquad locks : Ref \rightarrow Nat$$

To execute a **synchronized** (*exp*) *stm* statement first the *exp*ression is evaluated: if the computed value *ref* is *null*, a *NullPointerException* is thrown (modeled in $JAVA_E$); otherwise it is checked whether the current *thread* already holds the lock of object *ref*. If it does, one more lock is grabbed and execution of the (protected) statement can be started. Upon return from the *stm* execution (whether *Norm*ally or with an *abr*uption) the thread must RELEASELOCK and passes control to the parent node. If the current *thread* does not yet hold the lock of *ref* it enters *exec*ution mode *Synchronizing* (from the normal *exec*(*thread*) = *Active*).[15] Thereby it becomes subject to be chosen by the synchronization management to grab the lock on its *syncObject* *ref* and to perform its next execution step in a given run. This explains the following definition of $JAVA_T$. For the special case of THREADABRUPTion see below.

$JAVA_T =$ **case** *context*(*pos*) **of**
   synchronized $(^\alpha exp)\ ^\beta stm \rightarrow pos := \alpha$ -- first evaluate *exp*
   synchronized $(^\triangleright ref)\ ^\beta stm \rightarrow$
     if *ref* = *null* **then** *failUp*(*NullPointerException*)   -- see $JAVA_E$
     else
       if *ref* $\in$ *sync*(*thread*) **then**   -- *thread* already holds a lock on *ref*
         sync(*thread*) := [*ref*] · *sync*(*thread*)   -- grab another lock
         locks(*ref*) := *locks*(*ref*) + 1   -- counter update
         pos := β -- enter protected *stm*
       else   -- become subject to being scheduled
         exec(*thread*) := *Synchronizing*
         syncObj(*thread*) := *ref*   -- record synchronization object
   synchronized $(^\alpha ref)^\triangleright Norm \rightarrow$ RELEASELOCK(*Norm*)
   synchronized $(^\alpha ref)^\triangleright abr \rightarrow$ RELEASELOCK(*abr*)
   THREADABRUPT
  where
   RELEASELOCK(*phrase*) =
    let [*r*] · *rest* = *synch*(*thread*)
    synch(*thread*) := *rest*
    locks(*r*) := *locks*(*r*) − 1
    yieldUp(*phrase*)

---

[15] Since we do not explain here the thread methods offered by Java (but see [159, Sect. 7.2.2]) we neglect here the other four *exec* mode values: *NotStarted* (when a thread is created, value that remains unchanged until the call of the thread's start method whereby the thread becomes *Active*), *Waiting* (entered by execution of Java's wait method), *Notified* (entered by execution of Java's notify method), and *Dead* (entered by killing the thread).

The rule THREADABRUPT refers to the abruption and the class initialization mechanism in Java. If during the execution of a **synchronized** statement an abruption occurs it is passed up by RELEASELOCK(*phrase*) except at a **synchronized** statement for which there is a special rule. That rule takes into account a constraint on class initialization explained below. Therefore *propagatesAbr* has to be refined as follows (we include the try/finally cases from JAVA$_E$).

> *propagatesAbr*(*phrase*) **iff** *phrase* is none of the following statements:
> labeled, static initializer, try, finally, synchronized stm

If an *abruption* reaches the beginning of a thread's program and its frame stack *frames* is null, then the thread is killed (after updating some wait mechanism data we are not going to explain here). So THREADABRUPT is defined as follows.

> THREADABRUPT =
>   **static** $\triangleright$ *abr* → *notifyThreadsWaitingForInitialization*
>   *abr* → **if** *pos* = *firstPos* **and** *frames* = [ ] **then** KILL(*thread*)
> **where**
>   KILL(*t*) =
>   **forall** $t' \in$ *waitSet*(*t*) *exec*(*t'*) := *Notified*
>   *waitSet*(*t*) := ∅
>   *exec*(*t*) := *Dead*

To explain what happens when a thread abrupts an initialization method we have to refine the INITIALIZE(*c*) machine: it must insert the condition that only one thread should execute the class initialization. Therefore we record it as *initThread* when it changes *classState*(*c*) from *Linked* to *InProgress* and calls the class initialization method. Other threads that try to initialize the class when its initialization is *InProgress* are suspended (put into *execution* mode *Waiting* so that they are not *Runnable*) and registered in a set *initWait* of all such threads by the following rule:

> **if** *classState*(*c*) = *InProgress* **and** *initThread*(*c*) ≠ *thread* **then**
>   *exec*(*thread*) := *Waiting*   -- exclude *thread* from *Runnable* ones
>   INSERT(*thread*, *initWait*(*c*))

Upon abruption of the initialization method the current thread must make all these waiting threads *Active* again; it sets *initThread* to *undef* and empties the *initWait* set.

> *notifyThreadsWaitingForInitialization* =
>   **let** *c* = *classNm*(*meth*)   -- the current class initialization *meth*
>   **forall** $t \in$ *initWait*(*c*) *exec*(*t*) := *Active*
>   *initWait*(*c*) := ∅
>   *initThread*(*c*) := *undef*

The concurrent Java thread model CONCURJAVATHREAD. The machine JAVA interpretes any Java program as executed by a single agent. Applying the concept of ambient ASM it is easy to use the interpreter to define a model for truly concurrent execution of a Java program with threads $(a, pgm(a))$ where $pgm(a)$ essentially is the parameterization of JAVA by a. More precisely each thread a is equipped with the following program. The SYNCHRONIZE component serves to grab the lock a has computed on a new $syncObj(a)$ and expects to be granted to continue its execution in the given run.

> **amb** a **in**
> SYNCHRONIZE
> JAVA
> **where** SYNCHRONIZE =
> **if** $exec(a) = Synchronising$ **then**
> $sync(a) := [syncObj(a)] \cdot sync(a)$ -- add the new lock
> $locks(syncObj(a)) := 1$ -- initialize the new lock counter
> $exec(a) := Active$

The environment sensitive functions are the frame stack function *frames* and the frame component functions *meth, restbody, pos, locals*. It means that these functions define the local state of a and are not accessible to any other thread. A concurrent run of threads $(a, pgm(a))_{a \in A}$ is then defined by Def. 36 (pg. 112) with the following additional synchronization management constraint on the set A_m of agents which make a step in state S_m:

- every chosen $a \in A_m$ is *Runnable* (i.e. *Active* or *Synchronising*),[16]
- no chosen thread $a \in A_m$ is *Synchronizing* on a $syncObj(a)$ that is locked by some other agent,
- if a thread $a \in A_m$ is *Synchronizing* no other thread $a' \in A_m$ is *Synchronizing* on the same $syncObj(a)$.

For a mathematical analysis of an interleaving version of this thread model see [159] and its analogue for C# in [158].

---

[16] We disregard here the Waiting mechanism implemented by Java's wait method. See [159] for the details about this and other thread methods of Java.

Chapter 6
Mixed Synchronous/Asynchronous Control Structures

In this section we explain two classes of computational processes with a mixed asynchronous/synchronous form of run control: *bulk synchronous parallel* and *streaming* algorithms (with neural networks, spreadsheets and the TCP/IP protocol as examples). Another outstanding example are recursive algorithms we analyze in Sect. 8.4.

6.1 Bulk Synchronous Parallel (BSP) Control

The *bulk synchronous parallel control* model[1] is a computation paradigm that is widely used for the analysis of parallel algorithms. The concurrent runs of processes connected via a communication network consist of alternating segments of either only local process steps or only communication steps and where the alternation is controlled by a synchronizer. We explain the Bulk Synchronous Parallel (BSP) paradigm of computing as an interesting refinement of the concept of concurrent computations (Def. 36, pg. 112).

A BSP system is a multi-agent system of finitely many sequential processes $(a_i, \mathcal{M}_i)$ with $1 \leq i \leq k$, to be executed asynchronously on k processors. Their local signatures Σ_i^{local} are disjoint. The processes can exchange data only via communication channels $c_{i,j}$ ($1 \leq i \neq j \leq k$). Such channels can be introduced as functions where for $\mathcal{M}_i$ each $c_{i,j}$ is declared as output function (to pass data from agent a_i to agent a_j) and each $c_{j,i}$ as monitored function (to read data passed by agent a_j to a_i), as depicted in Fig. 6.1.

Furthermore, phases where (in $mode_i = \mathsf{local}$) all processes perform only local actions of their $processPgm_i$ are separated from phases where (in $mode_i = \mathsf{comm}$) they all just exchange data following their $commPgm_i$. A synchronizer agent a_0 SWITCHes between the phases in such a way that if its $mode_0$ is local and coincides with the $mode_i$ of all processes, they can perform

---

[1] The model we explain here is taken from [76].

Fig. 6.1 Writing through channels from source to target

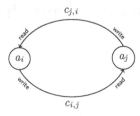

local $processPgm_i$-steps; the same way, if for every i $mode_0 = mode_i = $ comm, the processes can communicate using their $commPgm_i$. This is expressed by the following definition of BSP programs $\mathcal{M}_i$ the BSP agents are equipped with.

Definition 39 (BSP Process Rule). A BSP process rule is a rule of the following form:

> **if** $mode_i = $ local $= mode_0$ **then** $processPgm_i$
> **if** $mode_i = $ comm $= mode_0$ **then** $commPgm_i$

The *local BSP process rule* $processPgm_i$ is a PGA rule defined inductively starting from assignment instructions of one of the following two forms:

- $mode_i := $ comm, terminating the current local process phase of the i-th process, or
- $f(t_1, \ldots, t_n) := t$ **with** $f \in \Sigma_i^{local} \setminus \{mode_i\}$

The *communicating BSP process rule* $commPgm_i$ is a PGA rule defined inductively starting from assignment instructions of one of the two following two forms:

- $mode_i := $ local, terminating the current communication phase of the i-th process, or
- $c_{i,j}(t_1, \ldots, t_n) := t$.

In a run the synchronizer a_0 opens the next communication phase when the processes have terminated their current local computation phase and (via updates $mode_i := $ comm) are all ready for a communication phase; a_0 closes this communication phase (and reopens the next local process phase) when every process has terminated its communication steps for this phase (via an update $mode_i := $ local). Therefore the SWITCH action of the synchronizer is defined as follows:[2]

---

[2] Note that the quantifier stands for a conjunction of fixed length.

SWITCH =
   if $mode_0$ = local **and forall** $i = 1, \ldots, k$ $mode_i$ = comm **then**
      $mode_0$:= comm
   if $mode_0$ = comm **and forall** $i = 1, \ldots, k$ $mode_i$ = local **then**
      $mode_0$:= local

Summarizing we define:

Definition 40 (BSP-ASM). A BSP-ASM is a multi-agent ASM $\mathcal{B} = (a_i, \mathcal{M}_i)_{0 \le i \le k}$ where the synchronizer has the program $\mathcal{M}_0 = $ SWITCH and each process agent has as program $\mathcal{M}_i$ a BSP Process Rule with local BSP process rule $processPgm_i$ and communicating BSP process rule $commPgm_i$.

Every $\mathcal{B}$-computation leading from $mode_i$ = local (for all $i = 0, \ldots, k$) after a SWITCH step to a state with $mode_i$ = comm (for all $i = 0, \ldots, k$) and then by another SWITCH step back to a state with $mode_i$ = local (for all $i = 0, \ldots, k$) is called a *BSP-superstep*. It consists of a concurrent local computation segment of SWITCH and $processPgm_i$ $(i = 1, \ldots, k)$ followed by a concurrent communication segment of SWITCH and $commPgm_i$ $(i = 1, \ldots, k)$; both segments are terminated by a synchronization step. Runs of the BSP-ASM are sequences of such BSP-supersteps.

6.2 Streaming (Data Flow) Control

As for the BSP case in the preceding section, a *streaming* system is a multi-agent system but without central synchronizing agent a_0. The streaming (also called *dataflow*) computation paradigm is based on the idea that the agents are autonomous—meaning that potentially they can execute at any time—and that it is the availability of data which controls the execution of their otherwise asynchronous computation steps. Which agents are observed in any state S_m of a concurrent run to simultaneously perform a globally observable step—i.e. the elements of the set A_m in Def. 36 (pg. 112)— is not determined by program counters, but rather by the availability of the input data needed for the operation of each agent, in other words by the data flow rather than (or, in addition to) a control flow. Given that input data are provided by the environment or by other system components at maybe unpredictable times, streaming systems exhibit naturally the non-deterministic behaviour of concurrent systems. On the other hand, by the characteristic scheduling constraint to execute a computation step as soon as all input data is available, and no later, streaming systems provide efficient computation, which can be an advantage for certain classes of problems.

The streaming paradigm has been used in hardware implementations optimized to the processing of streams of data, e.g. in *digital signal processors* (DSP), including the common case of real-time encoding and decoding of multimedia data, as well as in specialized hardware for computer networks. It has also been used in software architectures, to efficiently process series of actions (e.g., transactions in an e-commerce system) or events (e.g., event-oriented programming in user interfaces). The streaming paradigm is also at the core of several computational models and languages, including Kahn's Process Networks [108], Hoare's Communicating Sequential Processes (CSP) [102] and later derivatives such as Occam (Section 5.3).

In this section we first define a stream control scheme in terms of three basic components READ, COMPUTE, WRITE with corresponding predicates *CanRead, DoneRead, CanWrite, DoneWrite, DoneCompute* (Sect. 6.2.1). The scheme is an example of the Look-Compute-Action pattern (pg. 27) which we instantiate in Sect. 6.2.2 by appropriate refinements of the components. The resulting modules can then be used to build concrete streaming machines by feature composition of basic components. We illustrate this by three well-known streaming machines: neural networks (Sect. 6.2.3), spreadsheets (Sect. 6.2.4), and streaming in computer networks, here illustrated by defining a rigorous high-level model of the TCP/IP protocol (Sect. 6.2.5). The last two examples exhibit a dynamic topological communication structure.

6.2.1 High-Level Streaming Model

A streaming system (also called streaming machine) is a multi-agent system of finitely many sequential processes $(a_i, \mathcal{M}_i)$ $(i = 1, \ldots k)$ that are connected by communication lines called *Channels*. Every channel behaves as FIFO buffer and can be connected to at most two agents, one which writes (its output) to the buffer and one which reads (its input) from the buffer, asynchronously.

Obviously only what has been written to a channel can then be read from that channel, but in streaming systems these two actions do not happen at the same time, differently from the instantaneous communication concept $\text{COM}(a, c, v; b, d, t)$ of Occam explained in Sect. 5.3. Here, we extend the BSP concept of channel $c_{i,j}$ by defining structured objects which provide queueing and addressing through three functions on a set *Chan* we leave abstract here:

$$buffer : Chan \to Buffer$$
$$reader : Chan \to Agent$$
$$writer : Chan \to Agent$$

When an agent a_i is connected as reader to a channel we say that this channel is an input channel of a_i and denote it by $in_{i,k}$ (for some k), denoting the finite set of input channels of a_i by $In_i = \{in_{i,1}, \ldots, in_{i,k_i}\}$ (for some k_i); analogously, when an agent a_i is connected as writer to a channel we say that this channel is an output channel of a_i and denote it by $out_{i,l}$ (for some l), denoting the finite set of output channels of a_i by $Out_i = \{out_{i,1}, \ldots, out_{i,l_i}\}$ (for some l_i). We say that $Connected(a_i, a_j)$ *via chan* holds—so that communication can happen between the agents a_i, a_j through this *channel*—if a_i is the writer of $chan$ and a_j its reader. We write $Connected(a_i, a_j)$ if for some channel $Connected(a_i, a_j)$ via $chan$ holds.

We abstract from various channel details such as whether the buffers are bounded or unbounded, what their maximum capacity may be, etc. by assuming that on each channel c we have two predicates $IsReadable(c)$ and $IsWriteable(c)$ that indicate whether the channel is readable by an agent (i.e., it contains some data) and whether it is writable (i.e., if the buffer is unbounded, or it is bounded and has not reached full capacity). In addition, we will assume that agents can **write** a value **to** a channel (thus enqueuing the value on the channel buffer) and **read from** a channel (thus removing a value from the queue of the channel buffer, which is returned as result of the read operation). Using the buffer representation of channel data we abstract from the finite but arbitrarily large transmission time of data from an output channel of one agent to an input channel of another agent. We assume that conflicting buffer updates are reconciled as to implement an atomic queue.[3] We abstract here also from the size of the concrete in-memory representations of a data item, and consider buffer positions as always holding a single logical data item.

Each streaming machine component $\mathcal{M}_i$ has the following Read-Compute-Write program structure (see also Fig. 6.2 below). It is an instance of the Look-Compute-Action pattern (pg. 27) with to-be-detailed stage components (PGA rules) READ_i, COMPUTE_i, WRITE_i, and for each stage Start/Termination predicates $CanRead_i/DoneRead_i$, $CanWrite_i/DoneWrite_i$ and $DoneCompute_i$. It is possible that different agents have different components and different predicates.

$\mathcal{M}_i =$
    if $mode_i =$ reading **and** $CanRead_i$ **then**
        READ_i
        if $DoneRead_i$ **then** $mode_i :=$ computing
    if $mode_i =$ computing **then**
        COMPUTE_i
        if $DoneCompute_i$ **then** $mode_i :=$ writing
    if $mode_i =$ writing **and** $CanWrite_i$ **then**
        WRITE_i
        if $DoneWrite_i$ **then** $mode_i :=$ reading

Each agent in every round goes sequentially over its three stage modes, which are not synchronized with those of other agents. In reading mode, an agent waits for the needed data to be available in its input channels, and if so reads the data. In computing mode the agent performs whatever computation is necessary to obtain the output values. In writing mode these values are written to output channels when possible, and the agent goes back to reading

---

[3] The operations can be seen as partial updates on the $buffer(c)$ associated to a channel c, see Section 4.1.

Fig. 6.2 Control State ASM Diagram for agents of a streaming system

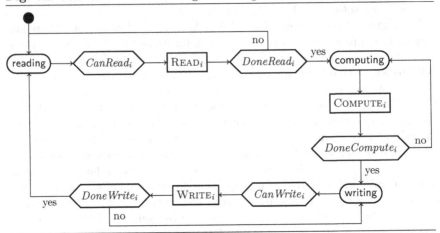

the next set of data. Each stage may consist of a single or of multiple steps, as controlled by the various *Done* predicates. Notice that for reading and writing (I/O operations which may depend on external events) we have symmetric controlling predicates *CanRead* and *CanWrite*, whereas for computing, which is a purely internal operation, there is no corresponding guard *CanCompute*.

6.2.2 Refined Streaming Variants

In this section we show how different refinements of the READ_i, COMPUTE_i, WRITE_i components and of the corresponding predicates, together with additional restrictions on how agents are connected through channels, yield well-known classes of streaming machines. We begin with a widely used functional refinement FCTALDATAFLOW that involves all components. Then we define a class STATEFULDATAFLOW of streaming machines by a refinement of the COMPUTE_i component, a class SELECTDATAFLOW of nondeterministic streaming machines by a refinement of the READ_i component, and a class NONSYSDATAFLOW of non-systolic streaming machines by a refinement of the WRITE_i component. We illustrate a further refinement to the class GUARDEDSELECTDATAFLOW where in addition to data availability also other conditions can be imposed on reading data. Then we briefly discuss systems with dynamic channel structure.

Functional Data Flow. The simplest case is purely functional and concerns all components. To trigger a Read-Compute-Write round all input arguments $(input_{i,1}, \ldots, input_{i,k_i})$ must be defined, so that all k_i input channels must be ready to be read together in one step (so that for the functional case no termination test $DoneRead_i$ is needed and can be assumed to be always true)[4]. Then all output locations $output_{i,j}$ are computed in parallel, simultaneously, as a function $f_{i,j}$ of the read input channel values (so that also the termination test $DoneCompute_i$ is not needed). Finally, all l_i output channels are required to be ready to write the functional output $output_{i,1}, \ldots, output_{i,l_i}$ of this round in one step (so that also the termination test $DoneWrite_i$ is not needed).

This yields the following refinement FCTALDATAFLOW$_i$ of program $\mathcal{M}_i$:

$CanRead_i = $ **forall** $c \in In_i$ $IsReadable(c)$

READ$_i = $ **forall** $1 \leq k \leq k_i$ **do** $input_{i,k} := $ **read from** $in_{i,k}$

COMPUTE$_i = $ **forall** $1 \leq l \leq l_i$ **do** $output_{i,l} := f_{i,l}(input_{i,1}, \ldots, input_{i,k_i})$

$CanWrite_i = $ **forall** $c \in Out_i$ $IsWriteable(c)$

WRITE$_i = $ **forall** $1 \leq l \leq l_i$ **do write** $output_{i,l}$ **to** $out_{i,l}$

By the synchronous parallelism in the component rules and predicates of FCTALDATAFLOW machines this computational paradigm realizes what is called a *systolic* behaviour, its results proceed in waves along the network. Kahn's Process Networks (KPN) [108] are of this form with unbounded channels (so that $CanWrite_i$ will always be true). This variant also models computations by feedforward neural networks [107], with appropriate $f_{i,j}$ (Sect. 6.2.3).

Stateful Data Flow. With a refinement of the COMPUTE$_i$ component one can support *stateful dataflow graphs*. Allow a refinement LOCCOMP$_i$ of COMPUTE$_i$ to maintain across different rounds a persistent local state, say of a finite set $locals_i$ of variables (0-ary functions). We can assume that the variables in $locals_i$ are appropriately initialized in the initial state of the agent, and can be both used and assigned during the computation (potentially, across multiple steps, depending on $DoneCompute_i$).

We also assume as before that by the time $DoneCompute_i$ becomes true, LOCCOMP$_i$ stores in $output_{i,l}$ any final results (which may depend on the value of $locals_i$) that should be written on output channels; for a stateful refinement of the functional machine FCTALDATAFLOW this implies that the functions $f_{i,l}$ have the local state $locals_i$ as further argument. The resulting refinement defines a class of STATEFULDATAFLOW machines.

Non-deterministic Data Flow. With a refinement of the READ$_i$ component one can enable agents to choose reading a selection of channels with available input. We call such a set P of input channels a *selection pattern*, and write $IsReadable(P)$ to mean that all channels in P are readable.

When a selection pattern P $IsReadable$, a round can be started with the data from the channels in P (i.e. without waiting for all other input channels to be readable).[5] To model this let $SelectPattern_i$ be a set of subsets $P_{i,s} \subseteq$

---

[4] This comes up to delete the stage termination test in Fig. 6.2

[5] Note that if rounds can be started with partial input without any fairness constraint among patterns, then some input channels may never be read.

$\{1, \ldots, k_i\}$ of indices k of input channels $in_{i,k}$ (for $1 \le s \le s_i$). In the reading phase an agent waits until some selection pattern P *IsReadable* and then performs its local computation (and writes corresponding results) depending on which pattern has been selected to activate the READ$_i$ component. This leads to a class SELECTDATAFLOW of streaming machines with the following refinement of READ$_i$ and *CanRead$_i$*. Note that, as for the data flow pattern, after a step of READ$_i$ for a chosen pattern the read step is done so that no further termination test *DoneRead$_i$* is needed and *DoneRead$_i$* can be assumed to be always true in this model.

$$CanRead_i = \textbf{forsome } P \in SelectPattern_i \; IsReadable(P)$$

READ$_i =$
> **choose** $P \in SelectPattern_i$ **with** $IsReadable(P)$
> **forall** $k \in P$ **do** $input_{i,k} := \textbf{read from } in_{i,k}$
> $actPattern_i := P$

In addition, if so desired, one can enable COMPUTE$_i$ to take advantage from the information on the chosen $actPattern_i$ by performing different computations depending on the value of $actPattern_i$. For the refinement of the functional model it suffices to provide $actPattern_i$ as an additional argument to the $f_{i,l}$ functions; in the general case one can explicitly distinguish in the COMPUTE$_i$ program what to do in the various cases of $actPattern_i$.

Similarly, at the writing stage one could select which channels to write to, based upon the information on the value of $actPattern_i$ or of the computed $output_{i,l}$ locations, as done for example in the non-systolic variant described below.

Exercise 26 (Ordered selection patterns). Replace the choice among multiple competing selection patterns by a rule that tests selection patterns in a fixed order, say $P_{i,1}, \ldots, P_{i,s_i}$. See the Appendix B.

It may be noted that the pure functional variant FCTALDATAFLOW$_i$ defined above is a special case of the non-deterministic activation pattern variant, with $SelectPattern_i = \{P_{i,1}\}$ and $P_{i,1} = \{1, \ldots, k_i\}$. At the other extreme, we have the special case with $s_i = k_i$ and $P_{i,s} = \{s\}$, i.e. input is handled separately for each channel as soon as it is available. This latter case is not frequently encountered in practical systems, although there are notable exceptions.[6]

Non-Systolic Data Flow. A non-systolic behaviour is characterized by a refinement of the WRITE$_i$ component, writing all defined outputs with writable corresponding channel as soon as there is some such output. This

---

[6] For example, the `select` or `poll` system calls in UNIX, used to suspend a process while waiting for at least one of a set of file descriptors to become ready. Another example is an agent merging individual data items from a number of input channels, in order of arrival, into a single output channel.

can be obtained by the following refinement $\textsc{NonSysWrite}_i$ of $\textsc{Write}_i$ and yields a class $\textsc{NonSysDataFlow}$ of streaming machines.

$CanWrite_i = true$

$\textsc{Write}_i =$
  forall $1 \leq l \leq l_i$ **with** $output_{i,l} \neq undef$ **and** $IsWriteable(out_{i,l})$ **do**
    write $output_{i,l}$ **to** $out_{i,l}$
    $output_{i,l} := undef$

$DoneWrite_i = $ **forall** $1 \leq l \leq l_i$ $output_{i,l} = undef$

Non-systolic systems tend to be more efficient (in fact, computations which need only some of the results of an agent can proceed immediately after the result is available), at the cost of loosing temporal coherence between the different results from the same computation. Streaming systems for which temporal coherence is important (e.g., multimedia processors) will usually implement systolic behaviour. Conversely, asynchronous systems (e.g., a packet switching network component) will implement non-systolic behaviour.

Exercise 27. Refine the non-systolic streaming model described above by introducing the concept of *output pattern*, so that partial results are written out to channels only when all outputs identified by one of a set of patterns can be written simultaneously (notice that this requires both the *output* variable to be defined, and the corresponding *out* channel to be writeable, for each output of the pattern).

Guarded Selection of Data Flow. Some programming and specification languages, e.g. the Language Of Temporal Ordering Specification (LOTOS) [24], or libraries that implement the streaming paradigm provide affordances to test additional conditions or guards (in addition to data being available) before proceeding with reading from a channel. For our models, it suffices to assume an additional function on channels, $peek(c)$, to return the same value that **read from** c would return if $IsReadable(c) = true$, and $undef$ otherwise. Guards can then be added in a refinement of $CanRead_i$ and $\textsc{Read}_i$ by a predicate $Guard_i$ which can examine the contents of channels via $peek$ and, in the case of stateful systems, the local state via $locals_i$.

To show a concrete example we formulate this for a $\textsc{SelectDataFlow}$ refinement by a machine we call $\textsc{GuardedSelectDataFlow}$. It suffices to refine $CanRead_i$ and correspondingly $\textsc{Read}_i$ by adding the $Guard_i$ to the readability test (in $CanRead_i$) and to the selection condition (in $\textsc{Read}_i$) as follows:

$CanRead_i =$
  forsome $P \in SelectPattern_i$
    $IsReadable(P)$ **and** $Guard_i(P, locals_i)$

$\text{READ}_i =$
  choose $P \in SelectPattern_i$ **with**
      $IsReadable(P)$ **and** $Guard_i(P, locals_i)$ **in**
      forall $k \in P$ **do** $input_{i,k} :=$ **read from** $in_{i,k}$
      $actPattern_i := P$

In the case of non-systolic systems, partially read input (in $input_{i,k}$) and partially computed outputs (in $output_{i,l}$) may also be available for testing by $Guard_i$. This is akin to the alternative statement in Occam (Example 10 pg. 64).

Static vs. Dynamic Network. In a streaming system the topology of the network of agents is determined by how channels are set up, with the same channel c appearing both in the Out set of one agent ($writer(c)$), and in the In set of another agent ($reader(c)$); the two agents thus share the same $buffer(c)$.

Most streaming systems (e.g., those implemented in hardware) have a static topology, where the set of agents and the structure of their connections is established at the beginning of the computation by having appropriate $reader()$, $writer()$ and $buffer()$ in the initial state, and is immutable thenceforth.

A streaming system with a dynamic topology can be modeled by allowing assignments to $reader(c)$ and $writer(c)$ during the computation, thus treating In_i and Out_i as dynamic sets. They can then be updated by each agent autonomously, based upon knowledge about other agents in the network, possibly by introducing in Fig. 6.2 (pg. 156) a fourth control state reconfigure between writing and reading, where communication structure updates can be programmed by a RECONFIGURE_i component. This is, for example, the case of a computer network where each host can dynamically open or close connections to other hosts it knows in the network (see the example in Section 6.2.5). For another example see the USERINTERFACE component of the spreadsheet machine (Sect. 6.2.4) which creates and deletes connections dynamically (but leaves the set of agents static). Note that with dynamic communication lines also the $SelectPattern$ concept becomes dynamic.

Modular ASM refinements and Feature-Oriented-Programming. The reader will have noticed that the ASM refinements defined in this section are *modular*, in that they can be combined in different ways to obtain composite behaviours. This is an example of how modularity in ASM refinements supports Feature-Oriented-Programming (FOP) techniques to define software product lines and prove for them behavioural properties (see [14, 13]).

6.2.3 Artificial Neural Network

Some particularly simple examples of streaming systems with however important practical applications are various classes of artificial neural networks (ANN). In Deep Neural Networks (DNN), there are multiple layers of computation elements called *neurons* (agents); each neuron applies a function to the values of its inputs, and produces a single value that is then provided as output. The values flow according to an interconnection structure (channels) that is fixed as part of the specific architecture.

Neurons in the first or input layer receive values from the environment; neurons in the output layer provide values to the environment; neurons in intermediate or "hidden" layers receive the output of preceding layers and provide input to the subsequent layers. In each layer, the result of the function computed by each neuron is provided to all connected nodes in the next layer.

An example of DNN is depicted in Fig. 6.3; the network in this concrete case computes a function $(y_1, y_2) = DNN_f(x_1, x_2, x_3, x_4)$, which is an approximation (learned from known individual examples presented to the DNN during training) of some unknown function $f(\cdot)$. Notice that while the network depicted in Fig. 6.3 is a complete layered acyclic directed graph (a common case in ANNs), this is not a requirement of the architecture. Other common cases include Recurrent Neural Networks (RNNs) which have cycles, and Convolutional Neural Networks (CNNs) in which each neuron is only connected to a limited number of *neighbours* in adjacent layers. Different arrangement of channels in a streaming system can of course model such architectural variants.

The kind of computation performed by a DNN can be expressed as a direct refinement of FCTLDATAFLOW, with the computation step refined as follows:

$\text{COMPUTE}_i =$
$\quad$ **forall** $1 \leq l \leq l_i$ **do**
$\quad\quad output_{i,l} := \tanh(\sum_{k=1}^{k_i} w_{i,k} \cdot input_{i,k})$

Fig. 6.3 A Deep Neural Network as a streaming system

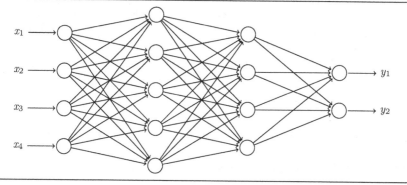

where $w_{i,k}$ are the *weights* associated to the various inputs of the i-th neuron; we use in the example the hyperbolic tangent function $\tanh(x)$ as the *activation function* of the neuron (a popular choice), but different applications might require different functions, e.g. $ReLU(x) = \max(0, x)$ or $sigmoid(x) = \frac{1}{1+e^{-x}}$. When executing a pre-trained model (a "forward" computation), the $w_{i,k}$ are constants, and thus the computation is purely functional.[7] The resulting behaviour is that of a functional, systolic, static streaming system.

If we want to also model the training phase, where weights are adjusted by gradient-controlled "backward" propagation of errors (that is, difference between the produced output and the expected output), then the $w_{i,j}$ weights become part of the local state of a neuron, which is preserved (and adjusted) across repeated forward and backward stages during the training. Hence, the complete trainable model is a stateful, systolic, static streaming system.

6.2.4 Spreadsheet Streaming Machine

In a typical spreadsheet application, *Cells*—arranged in a 2-dimensional matrix of R rows and C columns—can contain either literals, or formulas. Formulas are written in an expression syntax[8] which, among other things, permits to reference the value of other cells. The *localValue* of a cell is the result of *evaluating* its literal respectively formula, based on the current *localValue* of all referenced cells. Notice that it is possible to create circular references (e.g., when two cells contain formulas which reference each other); such cases are sometimes treated as an error.[9]

The user can directly enter a (new) formula or a (new) literal in any cell at any moment. When this happens at a cell c the *localValue* of c must be recomputed because the *localValue* of some cell b that is newly referenced by c (or the *localValue* of the cell c with the newly entered literal) may yield a value change.

We model the spreadsheet as a streaming control system, with an agent $a_{(r,c)}$ and program $\text{CELL}_{(r,c)}$ for each cell (r, c) (where r and c represent the row and column coordinates of the cell), and a single agent a_{UI} with program USERINTERFACE that implements the user interface of the spreadsheet. Initially, each cell is *Connected* only to the user interface, i.e. $In_{(r,c)} = \{ui_{(r,c)}\}$ and $Out_{(r,c)} = \{\}$, with the channel $ui_{(r,c)}$ modeling the connection between the user interface (the writer of the channel) and the individual cell (the reader of the channel).

---

[7] For some more details see the training refinement model in [57, Sect. 4].

[8] In most spreadsheet applications, a formula has to start with the character =.

[9] In some system, the user has the option of requesting a fixed point computation instead, providing additional parameters.

The user interface program. The operations of the user interface are as follows. An *inputEvent* signals when the user has committed a new text t into a particular cell c, where t can represent a formula or a literal. The set of cells referenced in t is obtained by a function *cellsReferencedIn(t)*. This will be the empty set in case t is a literal or a formula without references. Note also that this set may include some elements that are already connected to the cell c, because they were referenced in the previously entered text for c.

Channels among cells are then reconfigured: by DISCONNECT all channels are removed that connect c to previously referenced cells that are no longer *cellsReferencedIn* t; for the cells that are referenced in the new formula but not yet *Connected* with c, new channels are added to CONNECT them to c.

When a formula is entered in a cell c, USERINTERFACE also instructs (via their interface channels ui_b) all cells b referenced in the formula—those already *Connected* to c and those newly CONNECT*ed* to c—to send their *localValue$_b$* (even if unchanged) to c. Here again, if a literal was entered in c then no such cell b exists, and no message is sent. In c, the values received by the referenced b cells (if any) serve to update the *localValue$_c$*; this happens when in the *computing* phase c will DORECALCulation of *localValue$_c$*, see COMPUTE below.

In addition, USERINTERFACE informs c (via the interface channel ui_c) that its *localText$_c$* has changed and must be replaced by the newText t. The *inputEvent* is DISMISSed (read: becomes *undef*) by firing USERINTERFACE.

```
USERINTERFACE =
  if inputEvent ≠ undef then
    let c = cell(inputEvent), t = text(inputEvent),
        Refs = cellsReferencedIn(t) in
      forall a ∈ Cell \ Refs do
        DISCONNECT(a, c)        -- drop chans from no-longer ref'd cells
      forall b ∈ Refs do
        CONNECT(b, c)               -- add chans from newly ref'd cells
        write (update, c) to ui_b       -- ask b to send localValue_b to c
        write (newText, t) to ui_c        -- ask c to set localText_c to t
      DISMISS(inputEvent)                      -- event trigger done
  where
    DISCONNECT(a, c) =
      forall ch ∈ Chan with writer(ch) = a and reader(ch) = c do
        writer(ch) := undef
        reader(ch) := undef
    CONNECT(b, c) =
      if not Connected(b, c) then
        let ch = new Chan in
          writer(ch) := b
          reader(ch) := c
          buffer(ch) := new Buffer            -- initially empty buffer
```

In the above UserInterface model, we assume that the ui_c channels are unbound, i.e. always writeable. In practice, this is not a limitation as the rate at which the user can submit input events is much slower than that of the spreadsheet updates, hence the reader is much faster than the writer on those channels.

The cell program. The program $CELL_{(r,c)}$ (the same for all cells) is defined as in Fig. 6.2 (pg. 156) for generic streaming systems but instantiated with the following components $READ_{(r,c)}$, $COMPUTE_{(r,c)}$, $WRITE_{(r,c)}$ and respective guards $CanRead/Write$, $DoneRead/Write$, $DoneCompute$.

The $READ_{(r,c)}$ component distinguishes two different *activation* modes: the first (Ulevent) indicates that at the given cell new input is available from the user interface due to some user action, while the second (newValue) indicates that one or more cells on whose value the value of the given cell depends, may have a new value – so that the cell's own value may need to be updated. In both cases, after reading the corresponding *input* and recording the *activation* mode, the agent has $DoneRead_{(r,c)}$ and transitions to computing mode.

$CanRead_{(r,c)} = $ **forsome** $ch \in In_{(r,c)}$ $IsReadable(ch)$

$READ_{(r,c)} = $
    if $IsReadable(ui_{(r,c)})$ **then**   -- Read input from UserInterface
        $inputUI_{(r,c)} := $ **read from** $ui_{(r,c)}$
        $activation_{(r,c)} := $ Ulevent
    else   -- Read input from cells
        forall $ch \in In_{(r,c)}$ **with** $IsReadable(ch)$ **do**
            $input_{(r,c),writer(ch)} := $ **read from** ch
            $activation_{(r,c)} := $ newValue

$DoneRead_{(r,c)} = true$

It should be noted that in the **else** case ch cannot be $ui_{(r,c)}$, by the very case distinction.

The $COMPUTE_{(r,c)}$ component distinguishes three input cases: an update or a newText instruction from the UserInterface (two cases ① and ② that are handled by the component HandleUIEvent below) or the arrival (at some non-interface input channels of a cell (r, c)) of some newValues from some cells referenced by the formula in cell (r, c) (case ③ the component HandleNewValue below handles by triggering DoRecalc). DoRecalc tries to compute the new $localValue_{(r,c)}$ that must replace the previous (not any more valid) one. So we have the following definition for $COMPUTE_{(r,c)}$.

$COMPUTE_{(r,c)} = $
    HandleUIEvent   -- cases ① and ②
    HandleNewValue   -- case ③
    DoRecalc   -- case ④

It remains to define the submachine behaviour of these $\text{COMPUTE}_{(r,c)}$ components. We distinguish the three input cases and the work of the DoRECALCulation machine.

① Input of a dependent-cell-update request. If a request $inputUI_{(r,c)} = (\text{update}, d)$ to update a dependent cell d arrives from USERINTERFACE, the agent executes HANDLEUIEVENT: it sets $output_{(r,c),d}$ to a message with its own current $localValue_{(r,c)}$ and (due to the definition of $DoneCompute_{(r,c)}$ below) proceeds to writing. This is expressed by the following subrule of the HANDLEUIEVENT below:

> **if** $activation_{(r,c)} = \text{Ulevent}$ **then**
> **if** $kind(inputUI_{(r,c)}) = \text{update}$ **then**
> **let** $d = targetCell(inputUI_{(r,c)})$ **in**
> $output_{(r,c),d} := (\text{myValue}, localValue_{(r,c)})$

② Input of a newText. If the USERINTERFACE requests to enter a new-Text into the cell (r,c), this text is extracted from the $inputUI_{(r,c)}$ and stored by HANDLEUIEVENT in the local state (in $localText_{(r,c)}$). A TRIGGERRECALC is executed, which causes the current (the to-be-updated) $localValue_{(r,c)}$ of the cell to be invalidated; the value of $activation_{(r,c)}$ is also invalidated so that in the next step $\text{COMPUTE}_{(r,c)}$ tries to DoRECALC and (by the definition of $DoneCompute$ below) enters mode $writing$. This is expressed by the second subrule of the following HANDLEUIEVENT rule:

> HANDLEUIEVENT =
> **if** $activation_{(r,c)} = \text{Ulevent}$ **then**
> **if** $kind(inputUI_{(r,c)}) = \text{update}$ **then** -- ① dependant cell update
> **let** $d = targetCell(inputUI_{(r,c)})$ **in**
> $output_{(r,c),d} := (\text{myValue}, localValue_{(r,c)})$
> **if** $kind(inputUI_{(r,c)}) = \text{newText}$ **then** -- ② new text for this cell
> $localText_{(r,c)} := enteredText(inputUI_{(r,c)})$
> TRIGGERRECALC

③ Input of a newValue. If by some non-ui-input channel ch of a cell (r,c) some newValue arrives (from some cell that is referenced in the $localText$ of (r,c)), then as in the preceding case the agent will TRIGGERRECALC, i.e. invalidate the current $localValue_{r,c}$ (to-be-updated by the DoRECALC component below) and invalidate $activation_{r,c}$ to trigger DoRECALC. This explains the following rule HANDLENEWVALUE.

Note that the new value that arrives at (r,c) as input via a non-ui channel ch is stored in the corresponding input location $input_{(r,c),writer(ch)}$ where DoRECALC will check that it is available.

> HANDLENEWVALUE =
> **if** $activation_{(r,c)} = \text{newValue}$ **then** -- ③ new referenced cell value
> TRIGGERRECALC

④ The DORECALC component. In cases ② and ③, the current $localValue_{(r,c)}$ of the cell is no longer valid and has to be updated. This update consists in checking whether all input values for referenced cells are available. If so, the new $localValue$ is computed—by evaluating the $localText$ with all the various $input_{(r,c),w}$ for each referenced cell writer w (we denote this set as $\overline{input_{(r,c)}}$ for brevity). The $resul$ting value is assigned to the output variables $output_{(r,c),reader(ch)}$ for the $reader(ch)$ of any $ch \in Out_{(r,c)}$. In this way upon reaching the writing stage, all dependent cells will be updated (by receiving a newValue activation). In any case, the agent proceeds to writing (since $activation_{(r,c)}$ is $undef$ and thus $DoneCompute_{(r,c)}$ is true) so that any pending $outputs$ are written out. Then the agent proceeds to reading to wait for more argument values or input events to arrive.

> DORECALC =
>   **if** $activation_{(r,c)} = undef$ **then**   -- ④ attempt recalc this cell
>   **if** $allArgsAvail$ **then**
>   **let** $result = eval(localText_{(r,c)}, args)$ **in**   -- evaluate text
> $localValue_{(r,c)} := result$
>   **forall** $ch \in Out_{(r,c)}$ **do**   -- update dependants
> $output_{(r,c),reader(ch)} := (\mathsf{myValue}, result)$
>   UPDATEDISPLAY$((r, c), result)$

where the $allArgsAvail$ predicate checks whether all the arguments needed for the evaluation of the value of the current cell are indeed available; it is defined as follows:

> $allArgsAvail =$
>   **forall** $ch \in In_{(r,c)} \setminus \{ui_{(r,c)}\}$ $input_{(r,c),writer(ch)} \neq undef$

and $args$ is a map of cells mentioned in $localText_{(r,c)}$ (if any) to their current values, defined as

> $args = \{ref \mapsto v \mid \exists ch \in In_{(r,c)}$ **with** $writer(ch) = ref$
>   **and** $input_{(r,c),ref} = (\mathsf{myValue}, v)$ $\}$

TRIGGERRECALC causes a recalculation (in the next step) of the current cell value by the DORECALC rule; it is defined as

> TRIGGERRECALC =
> $localValue_{(r,c)} := undef$
> $activation_{(r,c)} := undef$

The termination predicate for the compute stage is refined as follows:

> $DoneCompute_{(r,c)} =$
> $(activation_{(r,c)} = \mathsf{Ulevent}$ **and** $kind(inputUI_{(r,c)}) = \mathsf{update})$ -- case ①
>   **or** $(activation_{(r,c)} = undef)$ -- case ④

Fig. 6.4 Possible paths in the execution of $\text{COMPUTE}_{(r,c)}$

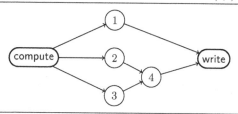

Notice that our definition of $DoneCompute_{(r,c)}$ guarantees that the compute stage will span exactly one step (in case ①) or two steps (in cases ② and ③, both followed by ④), as depicted in Fig. 6.4.

Finally, $\text{WRITE}_{(r,c)}$ is a pure data refinement (here just a renaming)[10] of the NONSYSWRITE_i streaming component defined above (pg. 159):

$$CanWrite_{(r,c)} = true$$

$\text{WRITE}_{(r,c)} =$
    forall $ch \in Out_{(r,c)}$ **with** $output_{(r,c),reader(ch)} \neq undef$ **do**
      if $IsWriteable(ch)$ **then**
        write $output_{(r,c),reader(ch)}$ **to** ch
        $output_{(r,c),reader(ch)} := undef$

$$DoneWrite_{r,c} = \textbf{forall } ch \in Out_{(r,c)} \; (output_{(r,c),reader(ch)} = undef)$$

Thus, our spreadsheet computation is an example of a stateful, non-deterministic, systolic, dynamic streaming system.

The combined behaviour of USERINTERFACE and CELL is depicted below as UML sequence diagrams. Fig. 6.5 shows the handling of an *inputEvent* generated by the user u. Fig. 6.6 and 6.7 show the handling of the remaining messages by any cell c.

---

[10] Define agent indeces i as matrix points (r, c), channels $out_{i,l}$ as channels $ch \in Out_{(r,c)}$, and the output locations $output_{i,l}$ as $output_{(r,c),reader(ch)}$.

Fig. 6.5 Handling of an input event by the user interface in the spreadsheet model

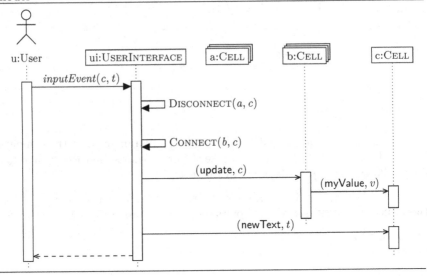

Fig. 6.6 Handling of incoming myValue messages by a cell in the spreadsheet model

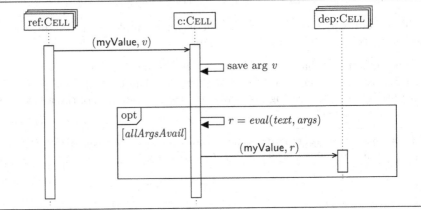

Fig. 6.7 Handling of incoming newText messages by a cell in the spreadsheet model

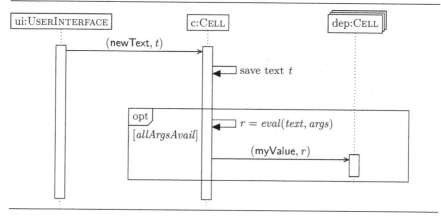

6.2.5 TCP/IP Streaming in Computer Networks

TCP/IP (the Transmission Control Protocol / Internet Protocol) [60] is one of the protocols used to implement host-to-host communication on the Internet. In its basic form, it implements two-way communication between a pair of hosts, one of which is designated as *server* (the one waiting for connection requests) and the other as *client* (the one initiating a connection request). Each host is identified by a unique *address*[11]; furthermore, it provides a number of *ports*[12] to indicate specific connection points. The pair ⟨*host, port*⟩ determines which agent, among all those executed by a given host, should handle the data transmitted over the connection. A connection is uniquely identified by two such pairs, one for each end of the communication channel. From the point of view of one of the participating agents, its own ⟨*host, port*⟩ address is the *local* one, whereas the other is the *remote* one. From the point of view of the other agent, these roles are switched. The roles of *source* (sender or writer) and *destination* (receiver or reader) are instead fixed, and depend on the direction of the data flow.

Following the style used in the Java networking library, we describe the workings of TCP/IP through operations grouped in two classes (in the sense of Section 3.2.2): *Socket* and *ServerSocket*. The latter provides operations used by a server when setting up to accept a connection request (open, accept,

---

[11] In IP implementation, Internet host addresses are encoded as 32 bit integers (for IP version 4) or 128 bit integers (for IP version 6), with certain ranges reserved or assigned to specific users.

[12] In TCP implementation, ports are encoded as 16 bit integers, with the first 1024 reserved for admin-level usage, and the remaining ones freely available to applications.

close), whereas the former provides operations used to establish a connection and transmit data (open, read, write, close).

The actions corresponding to the various operations are taken by agents of a streaming system. Agents residing on different hosts cannot share any state; but on each host h, a designated agent d_h which is part of the host's operating system and represents the driver handling the networking hardware, has access to a special pair of channels through which it can send and receive messages via the physical networking infrastructure. d_h can share some state with other agents $a_{h,i}$ on the same host; these agents are mutually isolated and don't share state among themselves. Moreover, each agent $a_{h,i}$ can invoke operations of the network driver via some here not furthermore specified CALL / RETURN mechanism.

The network driver $(d_h, \mathcal{D}_h)$ is defined according to our general model for streaming system agents, with the refinements below. We assume that in the initial state, $In_h = \{ihw_h\}$ and $Out_h = \{ohw_h\}$, where ihw_h and ohw_h are the I/O channels connecting the driver to the networking hardware. Agents $(a_{h,i}, \mathcal{A}_{h,i})$, representing OS processes running on h, will use other channels connected to d_h as needed (see Fig. 6.8, pg. 171). Thus at every moment the network driver d_h on host h is connected to the networking hardware (through the pair of channels ihw_h/owh_n) and to each agent $a_{h,i}$ corresponding to the OS processes on h that are accessing the networking functionality.

6.2.5.1 Networking driver

The networking driver can receive messages from the networking hardware of h or from any of the local processes on h; these messages are handled separately by the HANDLENETWORK and HANDLELOCAL components below. In keeping with common practice, we give priority to the handling of networking hardware (a shared resource) over that of local agents.

$CanRead_h = \textbf{forsome } c \in In_h \quad IsReadable(c)$

READ$_h =$
    choose $c \in In_h$ **with** $IsReadable(c)$ **do**
        $input_{h,c} :=$ **read from** c

$DoneRead_h = true$

COMPUTE$_h =$
    if $input_{h,ihw_h} \neq undef$ **then**
        HANDLENETWORK   -- handle messages from network
    else
        HANDLELOCAL   -- handle messages from local agents

$DoneCompute_h = true$

Fig. 6.8 Overview of the networking model

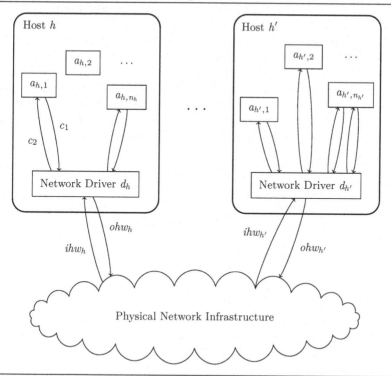

Incoming packets from networking hardware are of four kinds: inbound connection requests and corresponding connres responses, data packets to be delivered to some process on h, and disconnection signals. In all cases, the incoming data packet will carry additional information, that we will extract through appropriate background functions, abstracting from the details of the data format. In particular, beside addressing information (source and destination addresses, each composed of host and port numbers), a packet may carry a *payload* with arbitrary data (that is exchanged between processes on the network).

HANDLENETWORK =
  let $pkt = input_{h,ihw_h}$, $lh = dsthost(pkt)$, $lp = dstport(pkt)$,
    $rh = srchost(pkt)$, $rp = srcport(pkt)$ **in**
    case $kind(pkt)$ **of**
      connect $\rightarrow$ HNCONNECT   -- incoming connection request
      connres $\rightarrow$ HNCONNRES   -- outgoing connection response
      data $\rightarrow$ HNDATA   -- incoming data packet
      disconnect $\rightarrow$ HNDISCONNECT   -- connection closed

Each of the operations to be performed upon receiving the different kind of packets are detailed in the following. In case a connection request from a process on another host is incoming, the local agent responsible for the destination port (as established by SERVERACCEPT from Sect. 6.2.5.3) is identified, and if present a new pair of channels is set up[13] between that agent and the network driver, over which communications will be carried on (by HANDLELOCAL). In addition, a mapping is established linking the channels and the connection identity (as given by the two pairs of *host, port* addresses). Finally, confirmation that the connection is now established is sent, through the network, to the requesting host and any pending SERVERACCEPT call is completed.

> HNCONNECT =
>> **let** $a = accepting_h(lp)$ **in**
>>> **if** $a = undef$ **then**   -- no process waiting on port
>>>> $output_{h,ohw_h} := (rh, rp, lh, lp, \mathsf{connres}, \mathsf{ko}, \text{connection refused})$
>>> **else**
>>>> **let** $c_1 = $ **new** *Channel*, $c_2 = $ **new** *Channel* **in**
>>>>> CONNECT(c_1, a, d_h)
>>>>> CONNECT(c_2, d_h, a)
>>>>> $outbound_h(c_1) := (rh, rp, lh, lp)$
>>>>> $inbound_h(rh, rp, lh, lp) := c_2$
>>>>> $output_{h,ohw_h} := (rh, rp, lh, lp, \mathsf{connres}, \mathsf{ok}, \text{connection accepted})$
>>>>> RETURN$(pendingCall_h(lp), (\mathsf{success}, (c_1, c_2)))$ -- complete call

Dually, the connres packet that can be received when requesting an outgoing connection is handled by the following macro:

> HNCONNRES =
>> **if** $result(pkt) = \mathsf{ok}$ **then**   -- connection accepted
>>> **let** $a = callee(pendingCall_h(lp))$,
>>>> $c_1 = $ **new** *Channel*, $c_2 = $ **new** *Channel* **in**
>>> CONNECT(c_1, a, d_h)
>>> CONNECT(c_2, d_h, a)
>>> $outbound_h(c_1) := (rh, rp, lh, lp)$
>>> $inbound_h(rh, rp, lh, lp) := c_2$
>>> RETURN$(pendingCall_h(lp), (\mathsf{success}, (c_1, c_2)))$
>> **else**   -- connection refused
>>> RETURN$(pendingCall_h(lp), (\mathsf{fail}, \text{connection refused}))$

Notice that in the macro above, as elsewhere, we omit for brevity any check about the legality of the incoming packet (e.g., we do not explicitly check that there is indeed a pending CLIENTOPEN call from Sect. 6.2.5.4 for the

---

[13] Via CONNECT and DISCONNECT operations that we specify below.

given lp, which could be false if a forged connres packet is crafted and sent via the physical network infrastructure by a malicious actor).

If a data packet has been received, the payload is extracted and forwarded to the appropriate channel. Notice that the *payload* function is assumed to be defined in such a way that the receiving agent will only receive the data as posted by the sender agent (as if the two agents were communicating locally via channels).

HNDATA =
   let $c = inbound_h(rh, rp, lh, lp)$ **in**
      if $c = undef$ **then**   -- no process waiting on port
         $output_{h,ohw_h} := (rh, rp, lh, lp, \text{connres}, \text{ko}, \text{connection refused})$
      else
         $output_{h,c} := payload(pkt)$

A disconnection request causes the destruction of the corresponding channels, and the removal of mapping information. It an attempt is made to close a connection that had never been opened, the attempt is silently ignored.

HNDISCONNECT =
   let $a = accepting_h(lp)$ **in**
      if $a = undef$ **then**   -- no process waiting on port
      skip
      else
         forall $c \in Chan$ **with** $outbound_h(c) = (rh, rp, lh, lp)$ **do** -- one c
            DISCONNECT(c)
            $outbound_h(c) := undef$
         DISCONNECT($inbound(rh, rp, lh, lp)$)
         $inbound(rh, rp, lh, lp) := undef$

In the preceding macros, to set up and dispose of channels we use the following macros, variants of the CONNECT and DISCONNECT macros used in the USERINTERFACE machine above (pg. 163):

CONNECT(ch, a, b) =	DISCONNECT(ch) =
$writer(ch) := a$	$writer(ch) := undef$
$reader(ch) := b$	$reader(ch) := undef$
$buffer(ch) := \textbf{new } Buffer$	$buffer(ch) := undef$

In the model above, it should be remarked that a new pair of channels $\langle c_1, c_2 \rangle$ (providing for two-way communication) is established between the network driver and an agent for each network connection established by that agent. Each agent can in fact maintain an arbitrary number of connections open at the same time, and using separate channels ensures that the corresponding *buffers* are kept distinct. The functions $inbound_h$ and $outbound_h$ are used to map (local) addresses from incoming network packets to channels, and data to send from local channels to (remote) addresses to be inserted in outgoing network packets.

Any data written by a process to the outbound channel of a connection should be wrapped in a packet (as the packet's payload) and completed[14] with source and destination routing information. The packet is then sent to the networking hardware for physical transmission. The HANDLELOCAL macro below expresses these operations.

HANDLELOCAL =
    choose $c \in In_h$ **with** $input_{h,c} \neq undef$ **do**
      let $(rh, rp, lh, lp) = outbound_h(c)$,
          $pkt = (rh, rp, lh, lp, \mathsf{data}, input_{h,c})$ **in**
      $output_{h,ohw_h} := pkt$

This completes the computing stage. The writing stage of the network driver is a typical non-systolic variant, with a minor modification to accommodate the separate handling of the channel connected to the networking hardware from that of channels connected to local OS processes.

$Can\,Write_h = true$

WRITE$_h$ =
    if $output_{h,ohw_h} \neq undef$ **and** $IsWriteable(ohw_h)$ **then**
      write $output_{h,ohw_h}$ **to** ohw_h
      $output_{h,ohw_h} := undef$
    forall $c \in Out_h$ **with** $c \neq ohw_h$ **do**
      if $output_{h,c} \neq undef$ **and** $IsWriteable(c)$ **then**
          write $output_{h,c}$ **to** c
          $output_{h,c} := undef$

$Done\,Write_h =$ **forall** $c \in Out_h$ $output_{h,c} = undef$

6.2.5.2 Networking operations

As for the communication between agents $a_{h,i}$ (representing processes on host h) and the network driver d_h on the same host, we assume that some OS-provided mechanism allows the processes to cause the execution of certain rules in the context of d_h. Such rules correspond to operations that the processes request to d_h, and would be executed in alternative to the steps of the compute stage detailed above.

---

[14] We omit here other technical details, such as adding a checksum to ensure that data is not corrupted in transit.

One such mechanism could be the exchange of control messages between processes and the network driver via an additional per-process pair of channels, to be implemented as a separate pattern and activation mode. An accurate model need however be OS-dependant, as it should reflect the way user processes interact with system components on a particular environment.

Some of the operations can be completed in a single step, but others may have to wait on external events (e.g., waiting for a connection to arrive), and are thus naturally asynchronous. We do not specify here a particular call convention; depending on the language and operating system, these operations could be implemented as blocking calls, or as asynchronous invocations, with results to be fetched at some later time via some form of **await** operation. Here, we simply assume that each invocation of a method includes an additional parameter: a unique $call$ value that is used to associate invocations with corresponding results. A function $caller : Call \rightarrow Agent$ lets us identify the agent performing the call.

In particular, we assume that a new $Call$ is generated for each invocation, and provided to both the callee (the network driver) and the caller (the user process). When a call is completed, either synchronously or asynchronously, a RETURN macro referencing the corresponding $call$ will provide the user process with the operation's results. We also assume that a RETURN($call, returnValue$) executed by d_h, in addition to any OS-specific way of providing the $returnValue$ to $caller(call)$, also removes the $call$ from the range of $pendingCall_h(\cdot)$ (by setting the corresponding locations to $undef$). Using the conventions above, the effect of the various operations can be expressed succinctly as described in the next subsections.

Exercise 28. The OS-specific mechanism could be represented via monitored or shared variables, or via additional channels, or by using oracle functions, etc. Choose a particular mechanism, and then define the following three concepts accordingly.

1. Write a model for an asynchronous realization of the CALL/RETURN mechanism. Hints: define $state : Call \rightarrow \{new, pending, succeeded, failed\}$ and $result : Call \rightarrow Values$ (valid only when the $call$ is settled, i.e. $state(call)$ is either $succeeded$ or $failed$).
2. Define an **await** $call$ operation that suspends the executing agent until the $call$ is settled.
3. Define a synchronous realization of the CALL/RETURN mechanism. You can combine the asynchronous version with **await**, or write a different model.

You may want to compare your resulting models with the operations of *Promises*, *Futures* and *await/async* in popular programming languages such as Java, C++, JavaScript.

6.2.5.3 Server operations

A server on host h can open a specific *port* (provided that the port is not already in use by another agent), thus establishing ownership over that port:

SERVEROPEN($call, port$) =
    if $accepting_h(port) = undef$ **then**
       $accepting_h(port) := caller(call)$
       RETURN($call$, (success))
    else
       RETURN($call$, (fail, port already in use))

A server can invoke the SERVERACCEPT operation on a *port* it owns to indicate that it intends to receive connection requests for other agents on the network. The invocation of this operation can result in an immediate error, or leave the call suspended until a connection request arrives (the corresponding RETURN will then be performed by HNCONNECT):

SERVERACCEPT($call, port$) =
    if $accepting_h(port) = caller(call)$ **then**
       if $pendingCall_h(port) = undef$ **then**
          $pendingCall_h(port) := call$ -- defer till a connect arrives
       else
          RETURN($call$, (fail, already accepting))
    else
       RETURN($call$, (fail, not owner))

Closing the *port* has the effect of relinquishing ownership and interrupting any pending accept operation (notice how in this case *two* calls are completed at the same time; the pending SERVERACCEPT fails, while the current SERVERCLOSE succeeds):

SERVERCLOSE($call, port$) =
    if $accepting_h(port) = caller(call)$ **then**
       $accepting_h(port) := undef$
       if $pendingCall_h(port) \neq undef$ **then**   -- pending accept
          RETURN($pendingCall_h(port)$, (fail, port closed))
       RETURN($call$, (success))
    else
       RETURN($call$, (fail, not owner))

6.2.5.4 Client operations

As for client operations, only the opening and closing of the connection need to be specified, since reading and writing are realized by the native **read from** and **write to** operations on channels. We thus have,

CLIENTOPEN($call, rh, rp$) =
   choose lp **in** $availablePorts_h$ **do**
      $output_{h,ohw_h} := (rh, rp, h, lp, \mathsf{connect})$
      $pendingCall_h(lp) := call$ -- defer till a connres arrives
   ifnone
      RETURN($call$, (fail, no free ports))

where $availablePorts_h$ is the set of all ports that are available to the *agent* (depending on whether it is a user-mode process or a privileged process) that are not already in use, i.e. they do not appear in the domain of $inbound_h$ and the codomain of $outbound_h$.

Closing a connection is straightforward, as it only involves sending a disconnect packet over the network, aborting a possibly pending CLIENTOPEN call, and closing the corresponding channels:

CLIENTCLOSE($call, lp, rh, rp$) =
   $output_{h,ohw_h} := (rh, rp, h, lp, \mathsf{disconnect})$
   forall $c \in Chan$ **with** $outbound_h(c) = (rh, rp, h, lp)$ **do**   -- unique c
      DISCONNECT(c)
      $outbound_h(c) := undef$
   DISCONNECT($inbound(rh, rp, h, lp)$)
   $inbound(rh, rp, h, lp) := undef$
   if $pendingCall_h(lp) \neq undef$ **then**   -- pending CLIENTOPEN
      RETURN($pendingCall_h(lp)$, (fail, closed while connecting))
   RETURN($call$, success)   -- we ignore errors

This completes our example. From the point of view of the individual processes, once a connection is established via a successful SERVERACCEPT on host *server* by agent s and a corresponding CLIENTOPEN on host *client* by agent c, any data written on each agent's outbound channel will appear (through the physical network and the operations of the network driver) on the other agent's inbound channel, and vice versa, despite the two agents residing on different hosts and sharing no state and no direct channels.

Our computer network is an example of a stateful, non-deterministic, non-systolic, dynamic streaming system.

6.2.5.5 Completing the browser model

In Sect. 5.2.1.3 we presented a model for the Browser Transport Layer, where a TCPSEND macro was used in conjunction with abstract *Buffers* to express the actual network operations used to fetch data from a web server. We can now provide a possible realization of TCPSEND based on the networking model we just introduced, where we use an abstract **await** syntax to express asynchronous invocation of the client operations from Section 6.2.5.4.

Fig. 6.9 Realization of TcpSend(*host*, *payload*, *buffer*) in the networking model

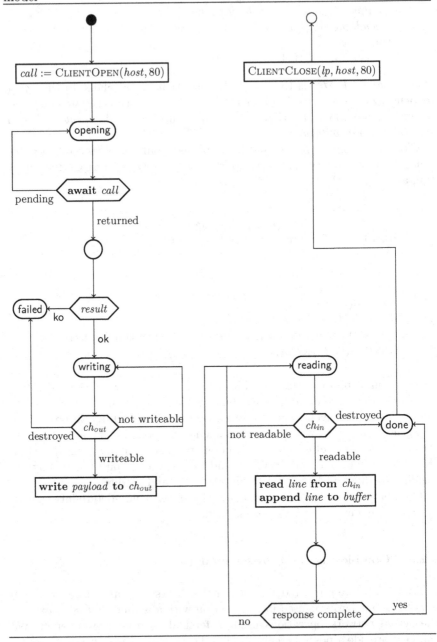

Our TCPSEND is implemented as a Control State ASM, represented in Fig. 6.9, that can be executed in parallel with the whole browser model, enqueuing fragments of the server response to the corresponding *Buffer* as they arrive from the physical infrastructure.

Notice that, although not detailed in the figure, we freely use return values from the CLIENTOPEN call once it has returned (namely: the success indicator *result* and the channel pair $\langle ch_{out}, ch_{in} \rangle$ from HNCONNRES, and the allocated local port lp from CLIENTOPEN).

Part II
Computational Paradigms: Analysis

Introduction and Survey of Part 2

Part 2 is devoted to three themes.

- Ch. 7 explains three fundamental complementary methods for the analysis of computations at different levels of abstraction: mathematical program **verification** (by proofs of properties), experimental program **validation** (by test suites), and professional program **inspection** (a direct comparison of the terms, properties and behavior of the program to the real world scenario they are intended to describe). These methods are applied in a *hierarchical process development*:
  - it starts with building precise requirements models, called **ground models** one can submit to inspection (Sect. 7.1),
  - it leads through verified and/or validated **model refinements** (which piecemeal implement the abstractions) to compilable code (Sect. 7.2).

  Such refinements yield pairs of stepwise refined process families which make implementation patterns explicit.
- Ch. 8 classifies some historically or conceptually outstanding classes of algorithmic processes, defined by instantiating the specific structure of their data, elementary actions and run control features. This makes the characteristic ingredients of each of these families explicit and ready for being studied as computational paradigm in a model theory of computing. We illustrate this for the historically first **sequential** (Turing machine or finite automata like) abstract model of computation with fixed program (Sect. 8.1) and its **arithmetical** instance (Sect. 8.2), as distinguished from multi-agent models of computation for **concurrent** (Sect. 8.3) and **recursive** (Sect. 8.4) algorithms.
- In Ch. 9 we illustrate the possibility ASMs offer to develop a practically useful rich algorithmic model theory that measures the complexity of runs in terms of items in the computational structure of abstract machines (Sect. 9.2). In Sect. 9.1 we use ASMs to succintly formulate and prove some classical **intrinsic limits** of computing.

Chapter 7
Correctness Analysis: Inspection, Validation, Verification

The two major properties of interest for algorithms are their correctness and their complexity. The complexity issue is addressed in Ch. 9. In this chapter we investigate the correctness problem with a focus on the code correctness problem: to make sure and to document that the executions of a proposed computer program perform what the program has been built for. It is characteristic for such system developments to involve descriptions at numerous levels of abstraction that have to be linked in an appropriate way, leading from what is called requirements capture through high-level design to programming and system maintenance. We explain here how the modeling concepts described in the previous chapters contribute to a reliable and practical design and analysis method for software system engineering.[1]

In Sect. 7.1 we describe how one can exploit the abstraction potential of ASMs to rigorously define the requirements (read: an elaborated consistent, correct and complete version of them) by an executable abstract model—called *ground model*[2]—that can be objectively checked for its adequacy ('domain-specific correctness'). In Sect. 7.2 we explain how using the ASM refinement method enables to rigorously formulate and apply every design and implementation decision taken on a stepwise-refinement-path from the abstract requirements model to the targeted efficiently runnable or compilable code and to check the refinement correctness.

For ground models as well as for their ASM refinements there are two complimentary methods to document the correctness of a component respectively of a refinement step (implementation of an abstraction) with respect to the design intentions:

- Model **validation** by experimental testing and comparison of runs of the abstract and the refined model, checking that the test results are as expected and related in the intended way.

---

[1] This chapter is based on [31, 34, 33, 35, 37, 38].

[2] In [31] they were called primary models.

© The Author(s), under exclusive license to Springer Nature Switzerland AG 2024
E. Börger, V. Gervasi, *Structures of Computing*,
https://doi.org/10.1007/978-3-031-54358-6_7

- Model **verification** by proving properties of interest for abstract and concrete runs and proving that the properties correspond to each other to establish correctness.

For this reason the abstract models must not only be *executable* but also come with a *mathematically analyzable* behavioural definition, as is the case for ASMs. Note that for every scientific discipline experiments and mathematical proofs must go together, as we have learnt from Galilei. In computer science this combination comes in the form of test suites put together with proofs of properties of model runs.

However, for the requirements model there remains a gap that for reasons of principle cannot be closed by mere programming constructs or model transformations. It concerns the relation between the ground model and the part of the real-world it describes. The characteristic (non-mathematical but scientifically rigorous) method to check the adequacy of the model with respect to its intended behaviour in the world is **model inspection**, a method that resembles the traditional code inspection (Sect. 7.1) but proceeds at an application-domain-determined level of abstraction. We explain below how ASMs by their abstract and rigorous character efficiently support model inspection.

In Sect. 7.3 we point out that the development of stepwise refined models provides a **documentation** that not only facilitates (and not only for newcomers!) the understanding of the final code but also adds to its reliability as well as resilience and enhances considerably the code maintenance (support for reuse and design for change).

7.1 Ground Models (Inspection)

To define what the software for a computer-based system is supposed to do is the role of the requirements which must provide the conceptual algorithmic core of the system prior to its implementation. Methodologically speaking this role is an epistemological one and resembles the role Aristotle assigned to axioms to ground science in reality, avoiding infinite regress. The requirements must relate real-world items and behavior (objects, events, actions) to corresponding descriptions of what in philosophical terms could be called the essence of the software, its process kernel. Unfortunately, too often the formulation of requirements is incomplete or on the contrary detailed beyond necessity, ambiguous, or even inconsistent. In addition, when the requirements are precise, complete and consistent they still may not reflect correctly the intended behaviour of the system to be built so that often the running code is proposed as the true definition of the system. But as we explain below this does not provide the epistemologically and pragmatically needed appropriate 'grounding' of the code in the real world where the system will work.

An efficient and reliable development method for software-intensive systems needs precise high-level models of (system and software) requirements—we call them *ground models*—that tackle three major problems in software engineering we describe in more detail below:

- The ground model must provide an **adequate understanding by all stakeholders** (customers, users, software experts) of what the system to-be-built should consist of. This involves a language and communication problem: domain experts and software developers must be enabled via the ground model to reach a common understanding of the desired behaviour of the system prior to its coding.
- Domain experts must be enabled to check—by a **repeatable and well-documented inspection** procedure applied to the ground model—that the requirements describe in an appropriate way what the to-be-designed system is supposed to do. This is also expressed by saying that the requirements are 'correct' and 'complete' (read: correspond to the desired system behaviour). This is an epistemological, not a mathematical problem the ground model must resolve, namely to directly and appropriately relate the conceptual linguistic terms of the model to the intended real world items or affaires. Leibniz called this *proportio quaedam inter characteres* ('symbols') *et res* ('things') and considered it as the foundation of truth: 'Et haec proportio sive relatio est *fundamentum veritatis*' [119].
- For system maintenance the ground model must enable the system developers to cope with ever-changing requirements by faithfully capturing and tracing them (in synchrony with the code) via **well-documented modeling-for-change** so that the models can be reused to extend them together with their implementation by new features (a process called horizontal refinement that supports also software product lines [14]).

Ground Model Language. To build a ground model—a precise system blueprint as used by architects—from given requirements usually consists not only in translating the possibly ambiguous natural-language terms by precise expressions but also in making the requirements consistent, correct, complete and minimal (abstracting from unnecessary implementation details). This is a difficult mediation task between domain experts and software experts and needs a description language both of them understand so that it solves the communication problem. In this language it must be possible to calibrate the degree of precision of expressions to describe the relevant domain-specific terms without ambiguity in a way the software experts understand. On the other side the language must come with a general conceptual data and operation model the application domain experts can grasp without becoming software experts themselves. Clearly, the language of ASMs is an easily extendable, not formal but rigorous language that satisfies these conditions, what explains its successful use to build ground models.

Ground Model Inspection. Given that a ground model starts with transforming informally-expressed requirements into something precise there are no mathematical means to prove the correctness (and analogously the completeness) of such a transformation, due to the lack of yet another mathematically precise model of the requirements the ground model could be compared to. To check the 'correctness' and 'completeness' of a ground model the only way to proceed is by model inspection. It resembles traditional code inspection,[3] where however the ground model inspection performs a direct comparison of model terms to the intentions the domain experts associate to the corresponding constructs in the real world (as described by the initially given informally expressed requirements) and to what is conveyed by the ground model to the software experts. This very serious and widely neglected problem is of epistemological (not mathematical) nature and is resolved if the inspection provides an appropriate 'evidence' for the desired correspondence between model terms and matters in the real world. This phenomenon is characteristic for scientific (not purely mathematical) theories and has been observed already by Aristotle in his *Analytica Posteriora*: to provide a foundation for a scientific theory no infinite regress is possible; in every chain of theories the first one must be justified by evident axioms (see [9]). Ground model inspection must provide such evidence that the terms and rules of the ground model are 'correct' and 'complete'.

Clearly, model inspection is enhanced by the two main complimentary and precise correctness checking methods, namely *experimental validation* by testing runs of a model and *mathematical verification* by proving model properties of interest. Therefore ground models must be not only mathematically precise, but also executable, as ASM ground models are (see [7] for tool support). The executability of ASM ground models offers to run use cases to systematically try to *falsify* the ground model in the Popperian sense [138]. It also permits to define, independently of the code, a system-acceptance test plan where executions of the still to-be-defined code are matched against runs of the ground model. Furthermore, it supports prototyping as well as the definition of reference implementations. Last but not least it permits early conceptual correctness checks and to establish explicit links between the traditional levels of testing: of the entire system, of its modules and of its code components (by unit tests). Concerning the verifiability of model properties, to verify ASMs covers the full range from proof sketches to mathematical proofs to formal deductions in logic calculi to computer-assisted proofs. Notably it permits to integrate domain-specific forms of reasoning that are not limited to formal deductions.

---

[3] We cannot do better than quote here Parnas' code inspection guidelines: 'the key to inspection of any complex product is a policy of *divide and conquer*, i. e., having the inspector examine small parts of the product in isolation, while making sure that 1) nothing is overlooked and 2) that the correctness of all inspected components implies the correctness of the whole product. The decomposition of the inspection into discrete steps must assure that each step is simple enough that it can be carried out reliably and that one inspection step can be carried out without detailed knowledge of the others.' [135]

There is a great variety of ASM ground models in the literature, some of them not surprisingly constructed to define various industrial standards.[4] The full value of ASM ground models becomes visible when they are linked by a chain of ASM refinements to preserve the behavioral correctness of the ground models in their implementation. This is the theme of the next section.

7.2 Model Refinements (Validation and Verification)

Refinement is a well-known general methodological principle to manage complexity by decomposing systems into parts whose details can be designed and analysed step-by-step. Refinement is intimately related to its inverse: abstraction. Thus it should not surprise that the abstract operational character of ASMs can be exploited to define a stepwise refinement concept that allows one to link ground model runs—piecemeal and in an effectively controllable manner—to executions of compilable code, offering at any intermediate level of abstraction to formulate, analyse, implement, and document in a precise way the underlying design decision for the further detailing of some abstraction. In this short section we explain the basic idea of the notion of ASM refinement and refer for small but characteristic examples to the machines we define in this book. For further extensions and more involved practical applications of the concept we provide references to the literature.

The ASM models in the literature and in this book illustrate how the abstraction potential of ASMs leads directly to a component-based system development approach. Furthermore, this potential permits to tailor abstraction/refinement pairs of components to meet any given design idea. In terms of ASMs that is a question of accurately linking not only abstract to corresponding refined data, but also corresponding abstract and refined operations in the runs of the to-be-related components. This is the reason why ASM-refinements offer more expressivity and flexibility than other refinement notions in the literature: an ASM-refinement step typically refines both data and flow of control (read: execution of rules) and thereby can be tailored to achieve the desired effect of corresponding actions on the values of corresponding locations in runs at the abstract and the refined level of abstraction.

More precisely stated, to define an ASM refinement M^* of a given ASM M the system designer is free to determine the following items to realize his design idea (see the illustration by Fig. 7.1).

- The definition of a *refined state* and a *refined program* M^*. The state refinement (change of signature) expresses the data part of the refinement

Fig. 7.1 The ASM refinement scheme.
© 2003 Springer-Verlag GmbH Berlin Heidelberg, reprinted with permission

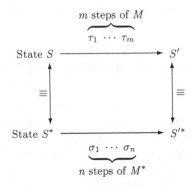

With an equivalence notion $\equiv$ between data in
locations of interest in corresponding states.

step (see below the required equivalence of locations of interest) whereas
the rule refinement takes care of the (possibly) refined flow of control.

- The definition of *corresponding computation segments*: abstract segments
  $\tau_1, \ldots, \tau_m$ where each τ_i represents a single M-step, and refined segments
  $\sigma_1, \ldots, \sigma_n$ of single M^*-steps σ_j. These segments reflect the refinement
  of the flow of control. Their initial and final state pairs S, S^* and S', S'^*
  are called *corresponding states of interest* because they are those the designer will compare to check the correctness of the refinement. In given
  runs these computation segments lead from corresponding states of interest to corresponding states of interest. The resulting diagrams are called
  (m, n)-diagrams and the refinements (m, n)-refinements. It is a distinctive
  feature of ASM-refinements—crucial for their practicality to decompose
  complex actions into simpler ones—that any pairs (m, n), $(*, n)$, $(m, *)$
  (where usually $*$ is some function of n or m) may appear, including opti-
  mization pairs (n, m) where $n > m$, not only the typical data refinements
  (of type $(1, 1)$) or procedural refinements (of type $(1, n)$ with $n > 1$) as
  one finds in compiler design where single source code instructions are
  compiled (read: refined) to target code [168, 87, 41][159, Sect. 14.2].
- The definition of *corresponding locations of interest*, i.e. pairs of (usually
  sets of) abstract and corresponding refined locations that must be checked
  (validated or verified) in corresponding states of interest to match the
  desired data refinement condition.

- The definition of the intended *preservation of the meaning of data* in abstract locations of interest by the data in the corresponding refined locations. Usually this defines an *equivalence* of the local data and these equivalences accumulate to the notion of the equivalence of corresponding states of interest.

It remains to define the precise meaning of refinement correctness, i.e. what it means if a refined run correctly simulates an abstract run.

Definition 41 (ASM Refinement Correctness). Choose any notion $\equiv$ of equivalence of states and of initial and final states. An ASM M^* is a correct refinement of an ASM M **iff** each concrete run $S_0^*, S_1^*, \ldots$ (of M^*) has a corresponding abstract run $S_0, S_1, \ldots$ (of M) such that

- their corresponding states of interest S_{i_k} and $S_{j_k}^*$ are equivalent

  - where $i_0 < i_1 < \ldots$ and $j_0 < j_1 < \ldots$ are index sequences with $i_0 = j_0 = 0$

- and either both runs terminate and their final states are equivalent,
- or both runs and both sequences $i_0 < i_1 < \ldots, j_0 < j_1 < \ldots$ are infinite.

Remark on design and verification. Perhaps already the few small but characteristic examples for ASM refinements in this book (Sect. 3.2.2 (Java), 4.4 (Prolog), 4.6 (RAM to reflective RASP), Sect. 5.3 (Occam), 6.2.2 (streaming machines), 9.2.1 (universal machine)) let the reader grasp the potential of the concept. Numerous examples in the literature show the practicality of the ASM refinement method, a result of the freedom it offers the practitioner to **choose an appropriate abstraction level** to implement a design idea **and an adequate reasoning method** for its verification coupled with experimental validation. We cannot show it here but want to point out that this freedom helps to not only construct stepwise refined design chains, but to accompany these definitions with (even machine-assisted) correctness-proof chains (see for example [52, 148, 149, 43, 159, 59, 14]). Furthermore, the above defined notion of ASM refinement has been extended and implemented in KIV (Karlsruhe Interactive Verifier) by Schellhorn [143, 144, 146, 145, 147, 150] and is used by the KIV group in Augsburg for challenging applications, e.g. security critical protocols in e-commerce [94], an electronic purse [96, 152, 95] with a verified Java implementation [90] and an underlying Java calculus [160] that has been influenced by the ASM models in the Jbook [159], a verified flash file system [151, 70, 23], and much more. Also in the Verifix project on compiler verification [85, 86, 87] refinement-correctness theorems have been proved using the interactive theorem prover of the PVS system (https://pvs.csl.sri.com/).

7.3 The Role of Documentation

Too often when a software project ends there is no interest any more to provide a documentation of what has been done. But this makes it difficult a) to maintain the code (including bug correction) or b) to reuse the code to respond to requirements changes that show up during the maintenance period. In both cases a refinement chain that links in a provably correct way a ground model to compilable code is of intellectual help and reduces the cost of code maintenance. Such a documented refinement chain provides what in requirements engineering is called *traceability*, both between requirements and implementation, and at different levels of implementation. Practical experience shows that such a documentation makes it possible to quickly localise the conceptual origin of a bug, probably at some higher level of abstraction than that of the final code, to repair the bug there and to insert the change along the refinement chain from there to the final code. A similar situation arises when for a running system additional requirements show up: find their level of abstraction in the refinement hierarchy, introduce the new requirements there by a model refinement that is followed by an appropriate refinement in the lower-level models down to the compilable code. Consider that at the level of abstraction of requirements it is usually easier than in efficient code to detect inconsistency issues among different requirements.

The basic reason in both cases a) and b) is that a model refinement chain facilitates the understanding of the system behaviour,[5] providing the designer with handles that are intimately associated with the design steps that were taken to implement the requirements and can be used to massage the implementation when some changes have to be made.

It is important to realize that ASM models—pseudo-code with a precise meaning—if used in the right way are not unrelated to the writing of final code but represent parts of it. During the software development process every design decision does appear anyway (even if not explicitly formulated in rigorous terms), whether on the blackboard or articulated during a team meeting or described by a prototype or inserted as comment into the code. What an ASM definition of a design idea does is a) to formulate the idea precisely as a piece of pseudo-code that later refinement steps fill up, and b) to systematically keep such information in a digital document instead of erasing it when the corresponding chunk of code has been written. It has been proven that this can be done in practical cases, and at the scale of real-life systems[6] and it helps (also economically to reduce maintenance expenses and system failures, see [49] for an industrial example).

---

[5] Note that even the quality of manuals can be improved if the manual writers can access a good documentation.

[6] See for example the reuse of the Prolog/WAM models and of their compilation correctness proof [52, 51] for the compilation of CLP(R) programs to code running on IBM's Constraint Logic Arithmetical Machine (CLAM) [53] or for the compilation of PROTOS-L programs to code running on IBM's Protos Abstract Machine (PAM) [16, 15] or the

Fig. 7.2 Process Structure of the ASM Development Method.
© 2003 Springer-Verlag GmbH Berlin Heidelberg, reprinted with permission

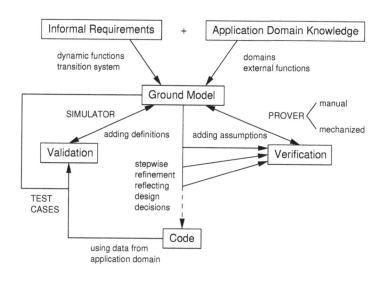

Remark on the modeling process. A refinement chain leading from a ground model to compilable code has often a sequential character, but the development *process* is by no means linear. Typically the construction is a back and forth because frequently during the design and programming phases issues show up that belong to higher levels of abstraction but had been overseen. This is illustrated by Fig. 7.2. In a sense the final ground model is defined only once the coding has been finished and no further change is to be expected. But as explained above, in the maintenance phase the game starts again because to let the method work the models and the final code must remain in sync.

---

reuse of the Java interpreter ground model in [58] for an interpreter ground model of C# programs in [45, 59].

Chapter 8
Characterization of Process Families

In this chapter we characterize some historically or conceptually outstanding classes $\mathcal{P}$ of algorithmic processes in terms of the structures over which they operate: their architectural background, the type of their data, operations, control constructs and runs. As examples we consider sequential (Sect. 8.1) and in particular arithmetical algorithms (Sect. 8.2) and their runs for the case of single-agent (thereby input-driven) processes; for multi-agent processes we investigate the case of concurrent algorithms (Sect. 8.3) and for mixed synchronous/asynchronous systems the case of recursive algorithms (Sect. 8.4).[1]

The epistemological claim for each of these axiomatically defined classes $\mathcal{P}$ to represent a fundamental intuitive computational paradigm is formulated as a **thesis** and supported by a **characterization theorem**. For each characterization theorem a class $\mathcal{ASM}(\mathcal{P})$ of concrete ASMs is defined and proved to **capture the computational paradigm**; by this it is expressed that the following two two properties hold:

- **completeness property**: for each axiomatically described process in $\mathcal{P}$ with its runs one can construct a machine in $\mathcal{ASM}(\mathcal{P})$ with computationally equivalent runs,
- **correctness property**: each machine in $\mathcal{ASM}(\mathcal{P})$ with its runs satisfies the axioms for machines in $\mathcal{P}$ with their runs and thus is an element of $\mathcal{P}$.[2]

Such characterizations of algorithmic processes over abstract data types have an ancestor in Turing's epistemological (but not axiomatic) analysis in [162] of processes that can be carried out (in principle) by a single (human or mechanical) calculator using paper and pencil, investigation that led to

---

[1] For a recent survey of various other computational paradigm characterizations and open questions (e.g. concerning unbounded nondeterminism or bounded nondeterminism with unbounded parallelism) see [153, Sect. 7].

[2] In the literature the term 'plausibility' is used for the correctness property and 'characterization theorem' for the completeness property.

E. Börger, V. Gervasi, *Structures of Computing*,
https://doi.org/10.1007/978-3-031-54358-6_8

Turing's model of computation and to what in the literature is called Turing's Thesis (for computable numerical functions)[3]. See Sect. 8.2 for more details on Turing's Thesis.

Why ASMs. As concrete machines over abstract structures we use in this book ASMs instead of descriptions in other equally comprehensive state-based specification frameworks (notably (Event-) B [2, 3] or TLA [118]). The main reason is the greater flexibility ASMs offer, in two ways:

- ASM design is focused on the dynamic state-change aspects—lifting them in a natural way (see Sect. 8.1.1) and term-for-term (see pg. 237) from Turing's tape cells with symbol content to sets of locations containing arbitrary structured data.
- ASM design is not constrained by (though compatible with) a particular verification framework.

A second pragmatic reason is that ASMs come with a simple and intuitive behavioural semantics that provides rigour to pseudo-code (see Def. 14, pg. 32), the prevailing form in which algorithms are described in the literature and in textbooks on algorithms and data types.

Furthermore, as we will see in the next chapter, the update-based ASM computation model enriches the set of possible complexity measures, simplifies numerous classical recursion-theoretic arguments and by investigating computation directly over structures opens the door for a complexity discipline which is based on machine concepts that are relevant for the practice of computing and not blurred by coding or proof system details (see Sect. 9.2).

8.1 Single-Agent Sequential Algorithms

We first explain (in Sect. 8.1.1) how Turing machines (TMs) as mathematical model for 'sequential' computations of intuitively computable functions—i.e. algorithmic input-driven processes executed by a single agent that stepwise executes a fixed program—are naturally extended to the Parallel Guarded Assignment (PGA) rules. In doing this we also show how some of the intuitive arguments Turing provides in [162]—to justify the thesis that TMs are an epistemologically reasonable mathematical substitute for computing numerical functions by single-agent algorithms in the intuitive sense of the term—can be extended by three precise Sequential Postulates that Gurevich [93] proposed to mathematically characterize *single-agent input-driven stepwise algorithmic processing of abstract data by abstract operations using a fixed program*. In fact the class **PGA** of PGA rules—the historically first form of ASMs—captures the paradigm of single-agent input-driven stepwise data processing using a fixed-program that is described by those Sequential Postulates:

---

[3] We disregard here the distinction between functions over *Nat* respectively strings.

Theorem 6 (A Characterization of a Class of Sequential Algorithms). *Let* Seq *be the class of algorithms that satisfy the Sequential Postulates defined below.* Seq *is captured by the class* PGA *of Parallel Guarded Assignment rules (Def. 12, pg. 24) with respect to input-driven runs of single-agents which stepwise execute a fixed program.*

Proof: for the correctness property see the end of Sect. 8.1.1, for the completeness property see Sect. 8.1.2.

The theorem also holds for non-deterministic sequential algorithms and bounded-choice PGAs (Def. 29, pg. 63), see Corollary 1 (pg. 202). As Corollary 2 we obtain in Sect. 8.2 an axiomatic characterization of Turing-Computability.

Remark Thesis versus Characterization Theorem. It remains for the reader to accept or to disagree with the various theses discussed in this chapter. For example, Ch. 4 (on reflective algorithms) and Sect. 8.4 (on recursive algorithms) investigate two classes of algorithms one would probably want to consider as sequential, but they are not captured by the Sequential Postulates. In this book we stick to the technical content of the characterization theorems and leave the interesting epistemological evaluation of axiomatic descriptions of computational paradigms for another occasion.

8.1.1 From Turing Machines to PGAs

In [162] Turing investigated which data, operations and forms of control are needed for a single agent—a human or mechanical calculator—to compute number theoretic functions using paper and pencil. The signature of Example 5 (pg. 26) shows the computational ingredients Turing identified: a *tape* of (at least potentially infinitely many) squares (read: memory locations (*tape, int*) where without loss of generality the *tape* is mathematically described as function *tape* : *Integer* → *Alphabet*) containing a (almost everywhere the blank) symbol *tape(int)* of a finite *Alphabet*, a 'scanned square' (read: 0-ary function) *head* that is currently observed (but can be moved) by the machine to read or modify the square's current content *tape(head)*, and a current control (read: a 0-ary function) *ctl* with finitely many possible values (named by Turing *condition* or *machine-configuration* or *state of mind*). Thus a TM-state consists of the values of the dynamic functions *tape, head, ctl* together with the static functions *write, nextCtl, moveDir*ection (with $+1, -1$ for shifting the *head* to the right/left) and in the background the set *Integer* of integer numbers and the *Alphabet*.[4] The pair (*ctl, tape(head)*) determines which state-changing actions (read: assignments) the machine can possibly perform simultaneously in one step: to read and update the content of the

---

[4] Remember that we treat sets via their characteristic function.

scanned square, to move its *head* to the right or left of the scanned square, and to change its current *ctl* value.

These TM-state functions together with the TM-step transition function defined by the 3 parallel assignments determine the level of abstraction of TM-computations. If one wants to express algorithmic steps at different (any higher or lower) levels of abstraction it comes natural to generalize the TM-items (TM-state and TM-step function) in two ways for computations over abstract data:

- Allow any memory for the definition of abstract states, i.e. any set of locations $(f, args)$ containing any objects as their value, where f belongs to a finite set of dynamic or static functions. From Sect. 1.1.2 we know that mathematically such states are Tarski structures.
- Allow for the one-step transition executed by a single agent any state-transition function; formulated in terms of machines and memory locations this comes up to generalize the three simultaneous (synchronous parallel) TM-step assignments to the simultaneous execution (as one-step) of any finite set of guarded assignments (PGAs).

To guarantee that the level of abstraction at which an algorithm operates is fixed it is required that the algorithm does not distinguish between isomorphic states. This leads to the first two postulates for single-agent (also called sequential) algorithmic processes.

Definition 42 (Sequential Step Postulate). A single-agent (also called sequential) algorithmic process P is a state-transition system, i.e. it comes with:

- a set $State(P)$ of states,
- a subset $Init(P) \subseteq State(P)$ of initial states,
- a one-step transition function $step_P : State(P) \to State(P)$

This suffices to define single-agent sequential process runs as a sequence of discrete computational steps (see Def. 22, pg. 40).

Definition 43 (Abstract State Postulate). For a single-agent algorithmic process P

- the states are Tarski structures (see Def. 2, pg. 10), all of the same finite signature Σ,
- the one-step transition function does not change the superuniverse (so that in a given run all states have the same superuniverse),
- isomorphy constraint: the sets of states resp. initial states are closed under isomorphism and every isomorphism between two states S, S' is also an isomorphism between their next states $step_P(S), step_P(S')$ (if they are defined).

By Definition 10 (pg. 19) the difference between a successor state $step_P(S)$ (if defined) and its predecessor state S—i.e. the (as effect of the step) fresh part of the successor state—is a consistent set of non-trivial[5] updates denoted by $\Delta(P, S) = step_P(S) - S$. When it is fired in S the successor state $step_P(S)$ is obtained: $S + \Delta(P, S) = step_P(S)$.

To make the steps of a sequential process 'effective' it remains to require an appropriate finiteness condition. In [162] Turing requires for effective processes (to be reducible to TMs) a finite set of symbols (to appear in 2-dimensional memory or on the tape), a finite set of 'states of mind' and a bound on the number of symbols or squares which the process can 'immediately recognize' (observe and possibly modify) at any one moment. This makes every step depending only on an a priori bounded (algorithm-specific but run-independent) number of state elements.

Following Turing's analysis an algorithmic process can access elements of the superuniverse only via ground terms, like $tape(head)$. One can obtain a bound on the number of elements an algorithm can examine in each step by bounding the number of ground terms on which every step of the algorithm depends. This leads to the following Definition.

Definition 44 (Bounded Exploration Postulate). For every single-agent algorithmic process P there is a finite set T of so-called *critical terms* such that if two states S, S' agree on[6] the evaluation $eval(t, S) = eval(t, S')$ of every critical term $t \in T$, then the process computes for both states the same Δ-set $\Delta(P, S) = \Delta(P, S')$ leading to their successor states.

This postulate implies that the elements $a_1, \ldots, a_n, a$ of non-trivial updates $((f, (a_1, \ldots, a_n)), a)$ in $\Delta(P, S)$—involved in the state change from S to its successor state S'—are values of critical terms $t_1, \ldots, t_n, t$ respectively; therefore $\Delta(P, S)$ can be calculated as yield of a difference calculator rule $rule_P^S$, hence $\Delta(P, S) = \Delta(rule_P^S, S)$, of all those assignments $f(t_1, \ldots, t_n) := t$ with state-change-involved critical terms (see Lemma 4 below).

Example 14. Critical TM terms are the following: $head$, $write(ctl, tape(head))$, $move(ctl, tape(head))(head)$, $nextCtl(ctl, tape(head))$ (see Example 5, pg. 26).

Definition 45 (Sequential Thesis). Following [93] we call the above three postulates the *Sequential Postulates* and call *Sequential Thesis* the statement that every single-agent algorithmic process in the intuitive meaning of the term satisfies the Sequential Postulates.

The above formulated Characterization Theorem 6 (pg. 197) we are going to prove now is presented in [93] to support the thesis. Note that the mathematical proof of the theorem is independent of whether one accepts the epistemological thesis or not.

Proof of the PGA correctness property. By the semantics of PGA rules (Def. 14, pg. 32) each PGA rule (equipped with a set of initial states)

---

[5] See the footnote to the definition of $\Delta(P, S)$ on pg. 33.

[6] We also say 'coincide for'.

satisfies the Sequential Step Postulate (with $step_P(S) = S + eval(P, S)$) and the Abstract State Postulate; for the isomorphy constraint see Exercise 2 (isomorphy of state updates, pg. 20) and Exercise 7 (isomorphic yields, pg. 33). For the Bounded Exploration Postulate use as set of critical terms the set of all (ground) terms that appear in the PGA rule in an assignment $f(t_1, \ldots, t_n) := t$ as argument or value term t_i or t or in a formula b_i of a guard if b_i.[7]

8.1.2 The PGA Theorem

The PGA completeness property can be formulated as follows:

Theorem 7 (PGA Theorem). *If a process P satisfies the Sequential Postulates, then its step function can be computed by a PGA (with the same signature, the same sets of states and initial states as P) in normal form (see Def. 12, pg. 24):*

$$\textbf{if } \varphi_1 \textbf{ then } f_1(s_{1,1}, \ldots, s_{1,n_1}) := t_1$$

$$\vdots$$

$$\textbf{if } \varphi_k \textbf{ then } f_k(s_{k,1}, \ldots, s_{k,n_k}) := t_k$$

where the guards φ_i are Boolean combinations of term equations.

Proof. The proof is done in three steps. Let T be a set of critical terms of P. **Step 1.** For every state S with well-defined successor state S' the difference set $\Delta(P, S) = S' - S$ is shown to depend only on the values of critical terms so that it can be computed by an ASM as its update set in S, here a PGA $rule_P^S$ consisting of a parallel composition of assignments with critical terms (Critical Terms Lemma 4). **Step 2.** The difference calculators $rule_P^S$ for S are shown to depend only on which equations between critical terms hold in state S (Critical-Terms-Similarity Lemma 5). **Step 3.** The finitely many Critical-Terms-Similarity types can be axiomatized as guards φ_{S_i}—conjunctions of equations and inequalities between critical terms in some state S_i—which yield finitely many guarded difference calculators **if** φ_{S_i} **then** $rule_P^{S_i}$ whose parallel combination PGA_P computes $\Delta(P, S)$ for every state S (Similarity Type Formalization Lemma 6).

Lemma 4 (Critical Terms). 1. For every state S of P and for every (non-trivial) to-be-executed update $((f, (a_1, \ldots, a_n)), a_0)$ in $\Delta(P, S)$ the arguments $a_1, \ldots, a_n$ read and the computed new value a_0 are values of critical terms.

---

[7] If the **seq** operator (Def. 24, pg. 53) and the **let** construct (Def. 15, pg. 34) are added to PGAs the resulting class of ASMs still satisfies the bounded exploration postulate, but this does not hold any more if the **forall** construct is added. See [58, Sect. 7.2.3] for a proof.

2. Therefore every $upd \in \Delta(P, S)$ can be computed by an $assignInstr_{upd} = f(t_1, \ldots, t_n) := t$ with critical terms t_i, t of P so that all together $\Delta(P, S)$ can be computed by the parallel combination $rule_P^S$ of all $assignInstr_{upd}$ for $upd \in \Delta(P, S)$, i.e. $\Delta(P, S) = \Delta(rule_P^S, S)$. $rule_P^S$ is called an ASM difference calculator for state S.

Proof. The first claim is proved by contradiction. Suppose one of the elements of the given update u, say $x = a_i$, is not the value of a critical term. Map S by an isomorphism α to a new state S' (by the isomorphy closure) that is identical to S except for x which is replaced by and mapped by α to a new fresh element y. By the isomorphy constraint α is also an isomorphism between the successor states $step_P(S)$, $step_P(S')$ so that the image $((f, (\alpha(a_1), \ldots, \alpha(a_n))), \alpha(a))$ of the update u in $\Delta(P, S)$ is an update in $\Delta(P, S')$. Now, S and S' coincide on critical terms since only x and no critical term value v is mapped by α to y, so that $\alpha(v) = v$. By the bounded exploration postulate it follows that $\Delta(P, S) = \Delta(P, S')$ so that y which occurs in the elements of the update image of u in $\Delta(P, S')$ occurs also in an update of $\Delta(P, S)$: a contradiction to the freshness of y.

The second claim follows from the definitions.

Lemma 5 (Critical-Terms-Similarity). If two states S, S' satisfy the same equations between critical terms—called critical-terms-similarity—then their ASM difference calculators $rule_P^S$ and $rule_P^{S'}$ are the same.

Proof. First construct an isomorphism α from S to a state S^* that agrees with S' on the evaluation of critical terms (see below). By the isomorphy constraint in the Abstract State Postulate it follows that $\alpha(\Delta(P, S)) = \Delta(P, S^*)$ so that (see Exercise 1) $rule_P^S = rule_P^{S^*}$. Since S^* and S' agree on the evaluation of critical terms the bounded exploration postulate implies that $\Delta(P, S^*) = \Delta(P, S')$ so that $rule_P^{S^*} = rule_P^{S'}$ and thereby $rule_P^S = rule_P^{S^*} = rule_P^{S'}$.

To construct such a state S^* assume that the base sets of S and S' are disjoint (otherwise take an isomorphic copy of S without elements from S'). Map by a function α the value $eval(t, S)$ of every critical term in S to its corresponding value $eval(t, S')$ in S' and every other element (of the base set of S) to itself. By the disjointness of the base sets of S, S' and by the critical-terms-similarity of the two states the function is well-defined and bijective. The isomorphic α-image say S^* of S agrees with S' on the evaluation of critical terms t because by the homomorphy property $eval(t, S^*) = \alpha(eval(t, S))$ holds and by definition of α also $\alpha(eval(t, S)) = eval(t, S')$.

Lemma 6 (Similarity Type Formalization). Each of the finitely many Critical-Terms-Similarity types can be formalized as property of some state S_i $(1 \leq i \leq n)$ and used as guard φ_{S_i} of $rule_P^{S_i}$ such that the parallel combination of these guarded difference calculators computes $step_P$.

Proof. By finiteness of T there are only finitely many Critical-Terms-Similarity types. Each of them is described by a Boolean combination of equations between critical terms as follows: for a state S let φ_S be the conjunction of all equalities $s = t$ and all inequalities $s \neq t$ that hold in S between critical terms s, t. There are finitely many states $S_1, \ldots S_n$ of P such that every state S of P satisfies the same equations between critical terms as one of the S_i and thus satisfies φ_{S_i}. Therefore to compute the step function $step_P$ we define:

$$\mathrm{PGA}_P = $$
$$\textbf{if } \varphi_{S_1} \textbf{ then } rule_P^{S_1}$$
$$\vdots$$
$$\textbf{if } \varphi_{S_n} \textbf{ then } rule_P^{S_n}$$

Let S be any state of P. By Lemma 4 on Critical Terms $\Delta(P, S) = \Delta(rule_P^S, S)$. Since by the Critical-Terms-Similarity Lemma 5 $rule_P^S = rule_P^{S_i}$ (for some i where S satisfies φ_{S_i}) it follows that PGA_P executing $rule_P^{S_i}$ in state S yields the update set $\Delta(P, S)$, simulating the move of P from S to the successor state $step_P(S) = S + \Delta(P, S)$.

Corollary 1 (Bounded-Choice PGA Theorem). *If a process P satisfies the postulates for non-deterministic sequential algorithms, then its step relation can be computed by a bounded-choice PGA (with the same signature, the same sets of states and initial states as P) in normal form as described in Def. 29 (pg. 63).*

Proof. The nd-Sequential Postulates for non-deterministic sequential algorithmic processes P are the Sequential Postulates with the following adaptations:

- In the Sequential Step Postulate (Def. 42, pg. 198) $step_P$ is a relation so that a state S may have more than one successor state S' (i.e. with $(S, S') \in step_P$).
- In the Abstract State Postulate (Def. 43, pg. 198) the second condition in the isomorphy constraint is changed to require that every isomorphism α from a state S_1 to a state S_2 maps every pair (S_1, S_1') in the successor relation $step_P$ to a pair (S_2, S_2') in the successor relation such that α is an isomorphism from S_1' to S_2'.

Correspondingly instead of one update set $\Delta(P, S)$ we have to consider the set $\boldsymbol{\Delta}(P, S)$ of all such difference sets $\Delta_P(S, S') = S' - S$ between every successor state S' of S and S, i.e.

$$\boldsymbol{\Delta}(P, S) = \{S' - S \mid (S, S') \in step_P\}.$$

The Bounded Exploration Postulate is formulated with $\boldsymbol{\Delta}(P, S)$ instead of $\Delta(P, S)$.

If P satisfies these postulates for non-deterministic sequential algorithms, then there exists a bound for the number of possible successor states of any state S of P. In fact, by the Critical Terms Lemma every element that occurs in an update of an update set in $\Delta(P, S)$ is value of a critical term so that by the finiteness of the set of critical terms there is a bound for the number of update sets in $\Delta(P, S)$ that depends only on P and not on S. Therefore the same arguments as for the PGA Theorem apply if in the definition of PGA_P the difference calculators $rule_P^{S_i}$ are replaced by the following bounded-choice PGA rule:

> **choose** $rule \in \{rule_{i,1}, \ldots, rule_{i,l_i}\}$ **do** $rule$
> **where**
> $\quad rule_{i,j}$ consists of finitely many parallel assignment instructions

8.2 Arithmetical Algorithms and Turing's Thesis

Since in Sect. 8.1.1 we have described algorithmic single-agent processes with abstract data and operations as generalization of numerical algorithms, the latter appear as instances of the former. Therefore it comes natural to refine the Sequential Thesis to an Arithmetical Thesis for computations over *Nat*. Doing this one obtains via the PGA Theorem an axiomatic characterization of Turing machine computability, as we are going to show in this section.

Call a process numerical if its operations apply arithmetical functions to natural numbers. The Arithmetical State Postulate we are going to define requires a numerical algorithmic process to use as auxiliary functions only some clearly computable static background functions. This is what we used already for Definition 26 of Structured Input/Output ASMs (pg. 55).

Definition 46 (Arithmetical State Postulate). A single-agent algorithmic numerical process P satisfies the Arithmetical State Postulate if it has as base set the set *Nat* plus the two truth values and *undef*. Furthermore, as background functions it has only the following ones: the usual Boolean operations, finitely many initial functions of recursion theory (see Def. 26, pg. 55) including C_0^1 (the unary constant 0 function), $+1$ (the successor function), and the characteristic function of the $<$ relation. It also has a 0-ary function in_P (whose value is a finite input sequence of natural numbers, to be provided as arguments to P) and a dynamic function out_P (for the computation result, in case of i/o-algorithms). P has exactly one initial state per input value and in each initial state only in_P and none of its dynamic functions are defined (i.e. $\neq undef$).

Corollary 2 (Axiomatic characterization of Turing computability).
Every function that is computed by a single-agent algorithmic numerical process that satisfies the Sequential Postulates and the Arithmetical State Postulate is Turing machine computable.

Proof. Let a function f be computed by a single-agent algorithmic numerical process P that satisfies the Sequential Postulates and is therefore equivalent to some PGA_P (by the PGA Theorem, pg. 200). Since by the Arithmetical State Postulate P, and therefore PGA_P, works over natural numbers using only μ-recursive static background functions, the PGA_P-computations can be Gödelized in a standard way[8] implying that PGA_P computes a μ-recursive function. In Sect. 3.3.1 we have proved these functions to be computable by structured i/o-ASMs (Structured Programming Theorem 1, pg. 56). By a simple exercise this proof can be rephrased in terms of structured function-computing Turing machine programs.[9]

Exercise 29 (Characterization of Arithmetical Algorithms). Denote by **ArithAlg** the class of algorithms that satisfy the Sequential Postulates and the Arithmetical State Postulate. Explain why the restriction **ArithPGA** of **PGA** to PGAs that satisfy the Arithmetical State Postulate captures **ArithAlg**.

Epistemological status of TM/ASM. Obviously there can be an epistemological disagreement on whether a specific set of mathematical axioms (e.g. the Sequential Postulates) 'captures' the targeted intuitive concept (e.g. sequential algorithm) and thus justifies a corresponding thesis. Turing used three kinds of argument for his widely shared answer (known as Turing's Thesis) to the question "What are the possible processes which can be carried out in computing a number?" (intended with pencil and paper) [162, pg. 249]:

(a) A direct appeal to intuition.

(b) A proof of the equivalence of two definitions (in case the new definition has a greater intuitive appeal).

(c) Giving examples of large classes of numbers which are computable.

Gurevich [91] asked a more general question for *any* "processes which can be carried out in computing":

Every computational device can be simulated by an appropriate dynamic structure [read: ASM] – of appropriately the same size – in real time; a uniform family of computational devices can be uniformly simulated by an appropriate family of dynamic structures [read: ASMs] in real time.

---

[8] For example, formalize instead of register machine steps (see [29, pg. 52]) the update set computation by *eval* (Def. 14) and the *apply* function $\mathfrak{A} + U$ (Def. 9) of PGAs (Def. 12), exploiting that by the Arithmetical State Postulate in initial states $\mathfrak{A}$ only the *input* location has a defined value so that in each state of the computation started with $\mathfrak{A}$ there are only finitely many dynamic locations with defined content. For a comparison see the Gödelization of RAMs and their runs in Fig. 4.7, pg. 102.

[9] For a technically very elegant definition of such structured TM programs see Rödding's Turing operators in [29, pg. 20].

The large variety of system descriptions by ASMs in the literature[10] provides an argument of kind (c) for various instances of an ASM thesis, typically extensions of PGAs by specific further constructs—for example more or less restricted forms of selection functions, of quantifiers (e.g. in BSP-ASMs, see Sect. 6.1) and more generally of other logical operators (e.g. Hilbert's ϵ and ι operators), of memory management (e.g. by **import**), of dynamic program change constructs (see Ch. 4), of application-domain functions, etc.

Various theorems (some of them explained in this chapter) that characterize well-known computational paradigms in terms of corresponding instances of ASMs provide an argument of kind (b), where the 'greater intuitive appeal' stems from the combination of simplicity and generality of the ASM concept.

Concerning argument (a) it looks like we should not expect *just one* new thesis that is supported by 'a direct appeal to intuition'. Even in the restricted sequential case the claim in [93] that PGAs—misleadingly called there sequential ASMs—capture sequential algorithms *tout court* does not match different intuitive understandings of sequentiality; *a fortiori* such disagreements can be observed when it comes to capture more involved concepts, for example unbounded parallelism (see the discussion in [77]), recursion ([130, 20, 39, 55]), or reflectivity (see [153] and Ch. 4 in this book). Another interesting example is the discussion in [156] about whether Turing's Thesis can be derived as a corollary from the PGA Theorem (Sect. 8.1.2) or whether we should content ourselves with the proof that the class **ArithPGA** captures **ArithAlg**. What we see showing up are various classes of ASMs each of which can be proved to provide practical mathematical machine models for a specific class of (possibly axiomatically described) computing devices; in the case of **PGA** those which satisfy the Sequential Postulates. This belongs to a new computation theory over structures we discuss in Ch. 9.

8.3 Concurrent Algorithms

In this section we investigate whether Def. 5.1 (pg. 111) of multi-agent ASMs and their concurrent runs captures an epistemologically satisfying machine-independent axiomatic description of the concurrency paradigm. We build upon the classification of the interaction type of locations (Sect. 2.1.1) and the characterization of sequential algorithms by PGAs (Theorem 6, pg. 197) to formulate the following conditions proposed in [54] as an extension of PGAs for practical use in design and analysis of concurrent processes:

Definition 47 (Concurrency Postulate).

1. The actors of a concurrent process P are finitely many agents a, each equipped with a fixed sequential algorithm $alg(a)$ and its own clock.

---

[10] There are more than seven hundred references in [58, 50] and `https://abz-conf.org/method/asm/`.

2. Concurrent runs of P are sequences of interaction states, started in some initial state.
3. In each interaction state S_m the agents which are ready to execute a step in S_m form a subset $A_m \subseteq A$. Each $a \in A_m$ performs one of the following actions, simultaneously with the other agents in A_m.

- a can be in global or local *mode*; in global *mode* it has read/write access to the interaction data (shared or monitored locations), in local *mode* it can access only its own local locations.
- In global *mode* a can do two things:
    - it performs a simultaneous read/write step, remaining in global *mode*,
    - it can decide to switch to local *mode*, making a local copy of the current value of the interaction data.
- In local *mode* a can perform a subcomputation that may end up in a write back *mode* = wb in which a switches back to global *mode* and the evaluation of $pgm(a)$ contributes to the next interaction state by an update of (some) interaction locations. For this reason A_m is required to be a subset of agents with *mode* $\in \{$global, wb$\}$.

Theorem 8 (A Characterization of Concurrency). *Concurrent ASMs with concurrent runs (Def. 36, pg. 112) capture the computational paradigm of concurrency.*

Proof. For the algorithms executed by the agents of a concurrent run one cannot simply invoke the characterization of sequential single-agent input-driven algorithms by PGAs (Theorem 6, pg. 197), a problem that is due to the presence of input/output and shared locations in concurrent runs. Such locations make it possible that in a concurrent run some states become reachable for an agent although in its isolated mono-agent runs they are unreachable. One can however strengthen the proof arguments to include the presence of input/output and shared locations when describing by updates of an ASM rule the update sets $\Delta(alg(a), S)$ a given sequential algorithm generates in a concurrent run. This exploits that those ASM rules depend only on the updates that establish the relation between a state and its successor state via the algorithmic transition function. To simplify the exposition we restrict here the attention to deterministic component computations (which satisfy the Sequential Postulates).

Concurrent ASMs and their runs satisfy the conditions of the Concurrency Postulate due to the definition of concurrent ASM runs (Def. 36, pg. 112) and the characterization Theorem 6 for sequential algorithms (pg. 197). This establishes the correctness property. Therefore it remains to check the following:

Completeness property: Let P be a concurrent process with a finite set A of agents $a \in A$ each equipped with an algorithm $alg(a)$ that satisfies the Sequential Postulates. If P satisfies the Concurrency Postulate, then its runs can be simulated step-by-step by corresponding runs of a concurrent ASM $Concur(P) = \{(a, pga(a)) \mid a \in A\}$ with the same sets A_m of agents and the same states and initial states.

We paraphrase the proof of Theorem 7 (pg. 200) to define for each agent a the desired PGA component $pga(a)$ of $Concur(P)$ to simulate the behaviour of the given component algorithm $alg(a)$ of P. The signature $\Sigma_{alg(a)}$, the states, the initial states, the $step_{alg(a)}$ function and a set T_a of critical terms are determined for every agent a by the Sequential Postulates. Let $S_0, S_1, \ldots$ be the interaction state sequence with agent sequence $A_0, A_1, \ldots$ of an arbitrary concurrent P-run where (by the Concurrency Postulate) for every m the following equation holds (if the successor state of S_m is defined):[11]

$$S_{m+1} = S_m + \bigcup_{a \in GoGlobal} \Delta(alg(a), S_m) \downarrow \Sigma_{alg(a)}).$$

$S \downarrow \Sigma$ denotes the restriction of state S to the signature Σ.

Paraphrasing the proof of the PGA Theorem 7 (Sect. 8.1.2) we show below:

Lemma 7 (PGA Components of $Concur(P)$). For each agent $a \in A$ there is a PGA rule $pga(a)$ such that

forall a, S holds $\Delta(alg(a), S) = \Delta(pga(a), S)$.

The lemma extends the above equation for P-runs to $Concur(P)$-runs:

$$
\begin{aligned}
S_{m+1} \\
&= S_m + \bigcup_{a \in GoGlobal} \Delta(alg(a), S_m) \downarrow \Sigma_{alg(a)}) \\
&= S_m + \bigcup_{a \in GoGlobal} \Delta(pga(a), S_m) \downarrow \Sigma_{alg(a)})
\end{aligned}
$$

where $Concur(P)$ is defined by $(a, pga(a))_{a \in A}$.

Proof of the lemma. We invite the reader to read once more the proof in Sect. 8.1.2 with $alg(a)$ in mind in place of the process P. The construction of a PGA $rule_{alg(a)}^S$ (consisting of assignments with critical terms) to compute $\Delta(alg(a), S) = \Delta(rule_{alg(a)}^S, S)$ in the proof for the Critical Terms Lemma 4 (pg. 200) goes through verbatim[12] for all states S of a, which includes shared, monitored and output locations with corresponding critical terms. Also the proof that $rule_{alg(a)}^S$ works unchanged for every critical-term-similar state S' (Lemma 5, pg. 201) goes through verbatim for all states S of a. Therefore, by the Similarity Type Formalization Lemma 6 (pg. 201)—exploiting the finiteness of the set T_a of critical terms and thereby of similarity types—the PGA$_P$ defined for the PGA Theorem works also for $pga(a)$, replacing $rule_P^{S_i}$ by $rule_{alg(a)}^{S_i}$.

---

[11] In the non-deterministic case one has to consider here a relation between state and successor state instead of an equation and the corresponding set $\Delta(alg(a), S)$ of update sets $alg(a)$ can yield in S.

[12] Just replace P by $alg(a)$ and T by T_a.

8.4 Recursive Algorithms

Recursion plays a major role in computing, but the concept is not well captured by the single-agent sequential computation model because a recursive call may involve multiple agents to independently perform some subcomputations, segments of computation that can be single-agent sequential or multiagent concurrent runs. On the other side, the interaction between a caller and a callee of a recursive call is restricted to passing input and returning a result, which is more restrictive than the interaction between components of concurrent processes. So the paradigm of recursive computations stands in the middle between sequential and concurrent computations and the question arises whether there is a mathematical definition that closely expresses the intuitive meaning of recursion and is captured by an appropriate class of abstract machines.

In this section we explain a positive answer proposed in [55]. In Sect. 8.4.1 we distill what we consider as essential properties of the intuitive notion of recursive algorithms into two Recursion Postulates, a Call Step Postulate and a Recursive Run Postulate. They support a conservative extension of nondeterministic sequential algorithms and their runs into recursive algorithms and their runs. Guided by this intuition and trying to turn it into an adequate machine concept we extend in Sect. 8.4.2 bounded-choice PGAs by a Call rule to recursive ASMs with recursive runs. This allows us to prove in Sect. 8.4.3 an extension of the characterization theorem from non-deterministic sequential to recursive algorithms.

Theorem 9 (A Characterization of Recursive Algorithms). *Recursive algorithms—those satisfying the non-deterministic Sequential and the Recursion Postulates—are captured by recursive ASMs.*

8.4.1 Recursion Postulates

The characteristic property of a recursive algorithm is that it can call (some instances of) itself or some other (recursive) algorithms—triggering the callees to perform some input/output subcomputation—and remain waiting until the callee returns the output computed for the given input. Furthermore, in one step a caller may trigger finitely many independent i/o-algorithms, for example *mergesort* calls two copies of itself to independently sort each one half of a given list. Due to the callees' independence (which must be guaranteed by an appropriate state encapsulation, in particular for different calls of a same algorithm but with different input), the called component processes can be executed in any sequential order or in parallel or even asynchronously. This illuminates the position of recursive algorithms as multiagent algorithms between single-agent sequential and concurrent algorithms.

Furthermore, it lets it appear as reasonable to consider recursive algorithms with non-deterministic component processes.

In a recursive call we view the caller as parent algorithm and the callees as child algorithms. Caller and callee are used as i/o-algorithms (Def. 23, pg. 52); their input/output locations for the parent/child interaction must satisfy the following (recursive) call relationship.

Definition 48 (Call Relationship of Interaction Functions). A (recursive) call relationship holds between the interaction functions of two (instances of) i/o-algorithms $\mathcal{A}^p$ (parent) and $\mathcal{A}^c$ (child) if they satisfy the following:

- The signature of the caller—the parent—comprises the input and output functions of the callee—the child—but none of the child's controlled functions.
- The parent algorithm, when calling the child algorithm and only then, assigns some input to monitored locations of the child and thereby defines an initial state of the child, but it never reads the child's input locations.
- The parent algorithm never updates but can read the output locations of its child algorithm, namely when the latter has *Terminated* its computation (read: has reached a final state with defined output).
- To simplify the exposition but without loss of generality we assume that in the state where a callee by its last move reaches its final state it does not call a new child.[13]

Remember that by the function classification (Sect. 2.1.1) monitored locations of $\mathcal{A}$ are read by $\mathcal{A}$, but never updated by $\mathcal{A}$, whereas output locations of $\mathcal{A}$ are never read by $\mathcal{A}$, but can be written by it. By the Call Relationship the initial states of a callee are input-dependent. This reflects a common understanding of parameter passing in recursive calls.

The following postulate describes the characteristic properties of call steps by which sequential algorithms become recursive algorithms.

Definition 49 (Recursive-Call-Step Postulate).
When an i/o-algorithm p (the caller, viewed as parent algorithm) calls a finite number of i/o-algorithms $c_1, \ldots, c_n$ (the callees, viewed as child algorithms $CalledBy(p)$), then the Call Relationship of Interaction Functions holds between the caller and each callee. For each callee c_i the caller activates a fresh instance of the algorithm and updates the *input*, thereby defining the initial state from where the requested subcomputation can start. These subcomputations are independent of each other and the caller remains waiting—i.e. performs no step—until each of its callees has terminated its computation. To simplify the exposition we assume, as is done usually, that every called i/o-algorithm eventually terminates its run and updates as its last move its

---

[13] In other words we require that a *Terminated* and therefore no longer *Active* algorithm is not *Waiting* for computations of still *Active* child algorithms.

output; so this output becomes available to the caller in the callee's final state.

Definition 50 (Recursive Algorithm). A *(sequential) recursive algorithm* $\mathcal{R}$ is a finite set of i/o-algorithms which satisfy the non-deterministic Sequential Postulates and whose transition relation may comprise call steps all of which satisfy the Recursive Call Step Postulate. One of these i/o-algorithms is distinguished as *main* algorithm. The elements of $\mathcal{R}$ are also called components of $\mathcal{R}$.

Since a recursive call may trigger multiple component algorithms to independently perform some subcomputations, runs of recursive algorithms are multi-agent runs: not sequential single-agent but also not concurrent runs. The called component processes can be executed in any sequential order or in parallel or even asynchronously. So we need a definition of what constitutes runs of a recursive algorithm. Whether an instance of a component algorithm can participate in a run step depends on whether

- it is still *Active*, i.e. has been *Called* but has not yet *Terminated* its run
- and it is not *Waiting* for a callee to return.

We therefore collect in a dynamic set *Called* the instances of component algorithms that are called in a run, similarly we collect in *CalledBy*(P) the children called by process P, so that in every state of the run *Called* = $\bigcup_P$ *CalledBy*(P) holds. Obviously in initial states only *main* is *Called* and *CalledBy*(P) is empty for every P. We define below a precise meaning of 'instance' of an i/o-algorithm we use in the Call Step and the Recursive Run postulates.

Definition 51 (Recursive-Run Postulate). For a recursive algorithm $\mathcal{R}$ with main component *main* a *recursive run* is a sequence $S_0, S_1, S_2, \ldots$ of states together with a sequence $C_0, C_1, C_2, \ldots$ of sets of instances of components of $\mathcal{R}$ which satisfy the Recursive Run Constraint:

Recursive-Run Constraint.

- the run starts with an instance *Main* of *main*, i.e. $C_0 = \{Main\}$,
- every C_i is a finite set of instances of components of $\mathcal{R}$ that are *Active* and not *Waiting* in S_i, where in S_i we define:

  $Active(P)$ **iff** $P \in$ *Called* **and not** $Terminated(P)$
  $Waiting(P)$ **iff forsome** c $c \in$ *CalledBy*(P) **and** $Active(c)$

- every S_{i+1} is obtained in one $\mathcal{R}$-step by performing in S_i simultaneously one step of each i/o-algorithm in C_i. Such an $\mathcal{R}$-step is also called a *recursive step* of $\mathcal{R}$.

8.4.1.1 Fresh Instances of i/o-Algorithms

In the Call Step and the Recursive Run Postulates we refer to 'fresh instances' of i/o-algorithms to guarantee the independence of recursively called subcomputations. This notion can easily be described more precisely using parameterization, as explained for ambient ASMs in Sect. 5.4.1. Here it suffices to equip a called i/o-algorithm $\mathcal{A}$ and its functions with a new parameter (read: a child executing agent) c so that the following holds:

- The interpretation of a function symbol f of $\mathcal{A}$ yields different specimens of functions $f_c, f_{c'}$ for different agents c, c'.
- In the run of $\mathcal{A}_c$ the child interpretation f_c of each input or output function f is the same as the parent interpretation $f_c = f_p$ (due to the call relationship of interaction functions).

Therefore one can express the meaning of "activate a fresh instance of each callee c_i" more precisely as follows: if in a state S with successor state S' a parent i/o-algorithm instance $\mathcal{A}_p$ calls i/o-algorithms $\mathcal{A}^1, \ldots, \mathcal{A}^n$, then create for each i a fresh child instance $\mathcal{A}^i_{c_i}$ of $\mathcal{A}^i$ with input locations $input_i$ so that in the successor state S' the child algorithm instance $\mathcal{A}^i_{c_i}$ is $CalledBy$ the caller instance $\mathcal{A}_p$ and is $Initialized(\mathcal{A}^i_{c_i}, input_i)$ so that it is ready to start its computation, whereas the parent algorithm instance $\mathcal{A}_p$ becomes $Waiting$.[14] For every algorithm $\mathcal{B}$, $Initialized(\mathcal{B}, input_i)$ expresses that the restriction $S' \downarrow \Sigma^{\mathcal{B}}$ of S' to the signature of $\mathcal{B}$ is an initial state of $\mathcal{B}$ determined by $input_i$.

8.4.2 Recursive ASMs

We now define recursive ASMs as a multi-agent extension of bounded-choice PGAs by a recursive ASM call construct of form $t_0 \leftarrow M(t_1, \ldots, t_n)$. The construct is used as an i/o-machine and therefore called ASM i/o-rule. For notational convenience we include into the definition the **let** construct, without loss of generality (see footnote 7 on pg. 200).

Definition 52 (Recursive ASM). A recursive ASM $\mathcal{R}$ is a finite set of recursive ASM rules, called components of $\mathcal{R}$, with one rule declared as main rule. Recursive ASM rules are defined by adding to the inductive definition of bounded-choice PGAs (including the **let** construct) a clause for ASM i/o-rules $t_0 \leftarrow M(t_1, \ldots, t_n)$ for given recursive ASM rule M. In an ASM i/o-rule the outermost function symbol of t_0 is an output function for M (an element of Σ_{out}) and the sequence $\langle t_1, \ldots, t_n \rangle$ is the value of an input function for M (an element of Σ_{in}).

---

[14] Except the trivial case that all $\mathcal{A}^i_{c_i}$ are already $Terminated$ when $Called$ in S'.

Since recursive ASMs are particular recursive algorithms (as we will prove in Sect. 8.4.3), their runs have the structure we have distilled into the Recursive Run Postulate for recursive algorithms (Def. 51, pg. 210). To guarantee the independence of component runs we use agents a equipped with ambient ASM programs **amb** a **in** *rule* (Def. 38, pg. 145) so that each agent executes its *rule* instance in its own state space, independently of the other agents.

Definition 53 (Recursive ASM run). A *recursive ASM run*—i.e. a run of a recursive ASM $\mathcal{R}$ with main component *main*—is a sequence $S_0, S_1, S_2, \ldots$ of states together with a sequence $A_0, A_1, A_2, \ldots$ of subsets of a dynamic set of *Agents*, where each $a \in Agent$ is equipped with a $pgm(a)$ that is the instance **amb** a **in** r of a rule $r \in \mathcal{R}$, such that the following holds:

- The run starts with an instance of *main*, i.e. in the initial state S_0 there is only one agent ($A_0 = \{root\} = Agent$). It is initially *Active* and not *Waiting*; it is equipped with $pgm(root) = $ **amb** *root* **in** *main*.
- Every A_i is a finite set of in S_i *Active* and not *Waiting* agents, where we define in S_i:

  $Active(a)$ **iff** $a \in Agent$ **and not** $Terminated(pgm(a))$
  $Waiting(a)$ **iff forsome** $a' \in CalledBy(a)$ $Active(a')$

- Every S_{i+1} is obtained in one $\mathcal{R}$-step by performing in S_i for each agent $a \in A_i$ one step of its $pgm(a)$. Such an $\mathcal{R}$-step is called a recursive step of $\mathcal{R}$.

Called and *CalledBy(parent)* are defined as for recursive algorithms. The input/output interaction between a caller and a callee satisfies the following **Recursive Call Parameter Constraints**:

- The caller can update but never read any input location of the callee.
- The caller can read but never update any output location of the callee.
- Caller and callee have no other common locations and the initial state of a callee computation is determined by the value of its input locations.

It remains to define the semantics of single ASM i/o-rules $r = t_0 \leftarrow M(t_1, \ldots, t_n)$. Let $M(x_1, \ldots, x_n) = q$ be the declaration of M, with all free variables of q among $x_0, x_1, \ldots, x_n$. The caller program r triggers the creation of a new agent c and an instance $pgm(c)$ of the body q of M and its initialization by the values of the input terms $t_1, \ldots, t_n$, so that the initial state is input-dependent. For the callee the sequence $\langle t_1, \ldots, t_n \rangle$ of the input terms t_i ($1 \le i \le n$) is classified as value of the input function and the outer function symbol of the output term t_0 as output function. So to establish the Call Relationship for caller and callee (Def. 48, pg. 209) we define the interaction function types of the caller correspondingly and make the corresponding input/output locations interpreted in the same way in both state spaces. Caller and callee have no other functions in common since both are defined as ambient ASMs. The new callee agent c becomes $Active$[15] whereas, by INSERTing it into $CalledBy(p)$, the parent agent p becomes $Waiting$.

Definition 54 (Semantics of i/o-rule). The semantics of the i/o-rule $t_0 \leftarrow M(t_1, \ldots, t_n)$ is the singleton set $\Delta(r, S)$[16] containing the unique update set that is computed in state S by the following deterministic ASM rule $\text{CALL}(t_0 \leftarrow M(t_1, \ldots, t_n))$.[17]

$\text{CALL}(t_0 \leftarrow M(t_1, \ldots, t_n)) =$
    let $c = $ **new** $(Agent)$
    $pgm(c) :=$
        let $x_1 = t_1, \ldots, x_n = t_n$ -- evaluate input passed by value
           amb c **in** P -- equip callee with its initialized pgm instance
        $\text{INSERT}(c, CalledBy(\textbf{self}))$ -- child becomes $Active$, parent $Waiting$
        $CalledBy(c) := \emptyset$
    where $M(x_1, \ldots, x_n) = P$ -- declaration of M

Note that during the entire computation of the callee the value of the input terms t_i does not change: the caller does not update them because it is $Waiting$, the callee cannot update them because they are monitored for the callee.

It remains to check that the Recursive Call Parameter Constraints are satisfied. In $pgm(c)$ the outer function symbols of t_i for $1 \leq i \leq n$ are classified as input functions (which are not read but can be written by the caller program); the outer function symbol f of t_0 is classified as output function (which is not updated but can be read by the caller program). The in/out-function symbols can be considered as belonging to the signature of caller and callee and to be interpreted the same way in the states of caller and callee. Therefore the first two of the Recursive Call Parameter Constraints can be assumed without loss of generality for caller and callee programs. The third condition too is satisfied, because the ambient ASM mechanism separates the state spaces of different agents. It turns each local function symbol f of arity n in a program instance implicitly into an $(n+1)$-ary function symbol, namely by adding the additional agent as environment parameter for the evaluation of terms with f as leading function symbol. Therefore, each local function of the callee resolves into locations that are different from those of each local function of the caller.

Remark on Call Trees. Starting with the initial tree $Agent = \{root\}$, every recursive run begins with a segment of steps that is under the control

---

[15] Since the initial state of the callee is input-dependent, initially the predicate $Terminated$ is completely $undef$ined.

[16] Remember that $\Delta(P, S)$ defines in the non-deterministic case the set of update sets which change state S into a successor state S'.

[17] The **new** construct can be avoided by introducing instead a counter c which for each recursive call is incremented by 1 in a partial update (sequentially, one by one, if there are finitely many simultaneous calls each of which needs a different $pgm(c)$, see Sect. 4.1).

of a single agent, namely of *root* with an instance of program *main*. We call such a segment a sequential run segment. If in a step of a sequential run segment the executing agent makes exactly one recursive call (Fig. 8.1), this triggers a new sequential run segment that is under the control of the callee.

If in a step of a sequential run segment the executing agent makes more than one recursive call, this triggers a finite branching of the call tree. It creates new leaf nodes of *Active* and not *Waiting* agents, and passes control from the caller to a multi-agent concurrent run segment of *Active* and not *Waiting* agents.[18] If an *Active* but *Waiting* agent a is the last node of a sequence $root, a_1, \ldots, a_n$ of *Waiting* agents in the caller/callee relation and the computations of all *child*ren of this node a are *Terminated*, control goes back (by the definition of *Active*) from the concurrent run segment of the callees to their caller a, starting a new sequential run segment. In this way from a *Terminated* (and thereby not any more *Active*) callee control goes back to its caller when all its siblings are also *Terminated*. When the run terminates the tree will be without *Active* agents.

Fig. 8.1 Recursive call nesting in state S with successor state S'

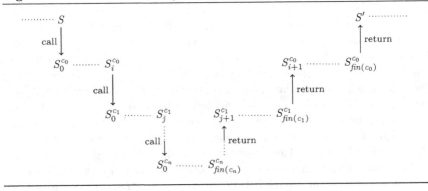

8.4.3 Proof of the Recursive ASM Theorem

In this section we prove Theorem 9 (see statement on pg. 208). The first half of it is the **correctness property**: each recursive ASM $\mathcal{M}$ defines a recursive algorithm $\mathcal{M}_{alg}$ such that the terminating recursive runs of $\mathcal{M}$ can be step-by-step simulated by the runs of $\mathcal{M}_{alg}$.

Proof. First we show that every terminating recursive ASM $\mathcal{M}$ satisfies the non-deterministic Sequential Postulates and the Recursion Postulates.

---

[18] As with communicating ASMs, due to the separate states of the agents these concurrent run segments can also be interpreted as parallel interleaving runs (Sect. 5.2).

The signature of the PGA and the i/o-components of $\mathcal{M}$ define the states as required by the non-deterministic Abstract State Postulate. The non-deterministic Sequential Step Postulate is satisfied by the definition of recursive ASM runs. For the Bounded Exploration Postulate use that each PGA component of $\mathcal{M}$ and the body of each of the finitely many i/o-rules of $\mathcal{M}$ components (together with their input parameters) have a set of critical terms. Their union provides a set of critical terms for $\mathcal{M}$. The Recursive-Call-Step Postulate is satisfied (for terminating runs) due to Def. 54 of the recursive ASM CALL(i/o-rule). For the Recursive Run Postulate the recursive run constraint is satisfied by Def. 53 of recursive ASM runs.

Let $\mathcal{M}_{alg}$ be the recursive algorithm that shows up by the analysis of $\mathcal{M}$. Their recursive runs as defined by Def. 51 and Def. 53 are structurally identical, step by step, only the wording ('instances of components' versus 'agents associated with component program instances') is different. Furthermore, each single step of $\mathcal{M}_{alg}$ in any state S is defined by an update set computed by the rules of $\mathcal{M}$ to define a successor state S'.

For the other half of Theorem 9 we must prove the **completeness property**: for each recursive algorithm $\mathcal{R}$ one can construct a recursive ASM $\mathcal{ASM}(\mathcal{R})$ such that the (terminating) recursive runs of $\mathcal{R}$ are step-by-step simulated by (terminating) recursive runs of $\mathcal{ASM}(\mathcal{R})$.

Proof. By the Recursive-Run Postulate every step of $\mathcal{R}$ leading from any state S to a successor state S' is the result of one step of each of finitely many *Active* and not *Waiting* $\mathcal{R}$-component instances $\mathcal{A}_a$. By the Recursive-Call-Step Postulate these instances are fresh and come with disjoint signatures Σ_a and subrun states $S \downarrow \Sigma_a$, $S' \downarrow \Sigma_a$ with difference set $\Delta_{\mathcal{A}_a}(S \downarrow \Sigma_a, S' \downarrow \Sigma_a)$. Consider any $\mathcal{A}_a$ and let $\mathcal{A}$ be the $\mathcal{R}$-component of which $\mathcal{A}_a$ is an instance. By definition of fresh instances (see Sect. 8.4.1.1), modulo the parameterization by agent a, a fresh instance $\mathcal{A}_a$ and its original $\mathcal{A}$ perform the same steps. Therefore it suffices to show that every $\mathcal{A}$-step leading from S to S' via a difference set $\Delta_{\mathcal{A}}(S, S') \in \Delta(\mathcal{A}, S)$ in a given run of $\mathcal{R}$ can be described as equivalent step of a recursive ASM rule $r_{\mathcal{A}}$. This is expressed by the following lemma.

Lemma 8 (Construction of Recursive ASM Components). For each $\mathcal{R}$-component $\mathcal{A}$ one can construct a recursive ASM rule $r_{\mathcal{A}}$ which computes $\Delta(\mathcal{A}, S)$, i.e. such that $\Delta(r_{\mathcal{A}}, S) = \Delta(\mathcal{A}, S)$ for all states S appearing in a recursive run of $\mathcal{R}$ where (any given instance $\mathcal{A}_a$ of) $\mathcal{A}$ makes a step.

Due to the lemma the required recursive ASM $\mathcal{ASM}(\mathcal{R})$ can be defined by replacing in $\mathcal{R}$ the (instances of) i/o-components $\mathcal{A}$ by (instances of) $r_{\mathcal{A}}$.

Proof of the lemma. We adapt the arguments used for sequential algorithms in the proof of the PGA Theorem (Sect. 8.1.2, Steps 1–3) to the case of sequential algorithms extended by call rules. Let T be a set of critical terms for $\mathcal{A}$. We distinguish the following three cases with arbitrary given states S and some successor state S': in state S $\mathcal{A}$ either makes no recursive call

and no return step or a call step or a return step. In each case we construct
in step 1 a bounded-choice PGA $rule_{\mathcal{A}}^{S}$ (instead of a deterministic $rule_{P}^{S}$)
that computes a set of update sets (not only one set of updates) satisfying
$\Delta(rule_{\mathcal{A}}^{S}, S) = \Delta(\mathcal{A}, S)$. In step 2 we show that $rule_{\mathcal{A}}^{S}$ depends only on the
equations between the critical terms in S. In step 3 we apply the similarity
type argument to turn $rule_{\mathcal{A}}^{S}$ into a rule $r_{\mathcal{A}}$ that works for every state S.

Case 1: In state S of the given run $\mathcal{A}$ makes no recursive call and no final
(return value *outputting*) step. In this case no update of $\mathcal{A}$'s *input* or *output*
function appears in any $\Delta_{\mathcal{A}}(S, S') \in \Delta(\mathcal{A}, S)$. Therefore, for $\mathcal{A}$ the first claim
of the Critical Terms Lemma 4 holds (pg. 200) for every update in any update
set $\Delta_{\mathcal{A}}(S, S') \in \Delta(\mathcal{A}, S)$. Then to define $r_{\mathcal{A}}$ one can paraphrase as follows
the three steps explained for the proof of Theorem 7 and Corollary 1.

Step 1: By the Critical Terms Lemma for every update set $\Delta_{\mathcal{A}}(S, S') \in$
$\Delta(\mathcal{A}, S)$ we obtain a parallel combination $rule_{\mathcal{A}}^{S,S'}$ of all assignment instructions with critical terms for updates in $\Delta_{\mathcal{A}}(S, S')$. Then the bounded choice
composition of these rules for all (nota bene finitely many) successor states
S' defines a rule $rule_{\mathcal{A}}^{S}$ with $\Delta(rule_{\mathcal{A}}^{S}, S) = \Delta(\mathcal{A}, S)$.

Step 2: We adapt the proof for the Critical-Terms-Similarity Lemma
(pg. 201) to $rule_{\mathcal{A}}^{S}$, applying the arguments in the lemma to every differ-
ence set in $\Delta(rule_{\mathcal{A}}^{S}, S)$ and $\Delta(\mathcal{A}, S)$ showing that $rule_{\mathcal{A}}^{S}$ depends only on the
equations between critical terms in S.

Step 3: We apply the proof for the Similarity Type Formalization lemma
to the rules $rule_{\mathcal{A}}^{S}$ to establish the lemma with $r_{\mathcal{A}}$ defined as follows:

$$r_{\mathcal{A}} =$$
$$\textbf{if } \varphi_1 \textbf{ then } rule_{\mathcal{A}}^{S_1}$$
$$\vdots$$
$$\textbf{if } \varphi_n \textbf{ then } rule_{\mathcal{A}}^{S_n}$$

Case 2: in state S of the given run $\mathcal{A}$ makes some recursive calls. Again
in a first step we construct a bounded-choice PGA $rule_{\mathcal{A}}^{S}$ that computes a set
of update sets satisfying $\Delta(rule_{\mathcal{A}}^{S}, S) = \Delta(\mathcal{A}, S)$.

To do this, consider any update $(l, v_0) \in \Delta_{\mathcal{A}}(S, S') \in \Delta(\mathcal{A}, S)$ at any
location $l = (f, (v_1, \ldots, v_n))$. Then the update cannot be a final value return
move (i.e. updating an *output* function) of $\mathcal{A}$ because otherwise in state S'
$\mathcal{A}$ would be *Terminated* but also *Waiting* (having just called some child),
contradicting the Recursive-Call Relationship (pg. 209). But f could be the
input function of a called child. So we have two subcases to consider.

- Case 2.1. f is not an *input* function of some child algorithm.

Then all elements v_i of the given update are critical values and there exist
critical terms t_i of $\mathcal{A}$ with $eval(t_i, S) = v_i$ (as in Case 1) so that we can use
the assignment rule $f(t_1, \ldots, t_n) := t_0$ to yield the update (l, v_0) $\mathcal{A}$ generates
in state S.

- Case 2.2. f is an *input* function of a child algorithm $\mathcal{C}$.

In this case we construct an i/o-PGA rule whose call yields the input defining update $((f, (v_1, \ldots, v_n)), v_0)$ and creates a new child ASM to perform the subcomputation. To do this we proceed as follows.

By the Recursive-Call-Step Postulate (pg. 209) with the Call Relationship, $\mathcal{A}$ in state S is just calling the child algorithm $\mathcal{C}$ so that $\mathcal{C}$ becomes *Active* and $\mathcal{A}$ becomes *Waiting*. Let $S_i^{\mathcal{C}}$ with $i = 1, \ldots, k$ for some k be the subcomputation triggered by $\mathcal{C}$ (including all its subcomputations) with final state $S_k^{\mathcal{C}}$. Consider the recursive calls made in this subcomputation: their nesting depth is smaller (by 1) than the nesting depth of the recursive calls made in the run segment from S to S'. This is illustrated in Fig. 8.1 (pg. 214): in state S the algorithm calls $c_0 = \mathcal{C}$ and defines its initial state $S_0^{c_0}$. The subcomputation of c_0 ends in state $S_{fin(c_0)}^{c_0}$ and during this subcomputation the depth of nesting of recursive calls is one less than the nesting depth of recursive calls between S and S'.

Therefore by induction on the depth of nesting of recursive calls there is a recursive ASM component rule $r_{\mathcal{C}}$ that simulates $\mathcal{C}$'s subcomputation, i.e. satisfies $\Delta(r_{\mathcal{C}}, S_i^{\mathcal{C}}) = \Delta(\mathcal{C}, S_i^{\mathcal{C}})$ for every subcomputation state $S_i^{\mathcal{C}}$ where $(i = 1, \ldots, k)$ for some k with final state $S_k^{\mathcal{C}}$ of $\mathcal{C}$. With this rule we can define the desired recursive i/o-rule *output* $\leftarrow M(t_1, \ldots, t_n)$ and its parameters as follows.

- The body of M is the recursive rule $r_{\mathcal{C}}$, declared by $M(x_1, \ldots, x_n) = r_{\mathcal{C}}$ where x_i are the input variables of $r_{\mathcal{C}}$.
- By the Recursive-Call-Step Postulate the input value v_0 at location $l = (f, (v_1, \ldots, v_n))$ for $\mathcal{C}$ is passed to the child but defined by an update made by the parent so that the v_i appear in S as values of critical terms t_i of $\mathcal{A}$.
- The *output* locations of $\mathcal{C}$ are shared with $\mathcal{A}$ as critical read-only terms of $\mathcal{A}$ (by the Call Relationship).

Therefore the recursive ASM i/o-rule $out \leftarrow M(t_1, \ldots, t_n)$ (where out is an output location of $\mathcal{C}$) yields the update $((f, (v_1, \ldots, v_n)), v_0)$ in state S (and creates the new child). Nota bene that by the CALL semantics of recursive i/o-rules (Def. 54, pg. 213) the input assignment $f(t_1, \ldots, t_n) := t_0$ (which yields the update (l, v_0)) is integrated into the clauses **let** $x_i = t_i$ (for $1 \leq i \leq n$) that pass the input to the body $r_{\mathcal{C}}$ of the child.

The parallel composition of all the assignment instructions and i/o-rules defined in cases 2.1 or 2.2 for each $(l, v_0) \in \Delta_{\mathcal{A}}(S, S')$ yields $\Delta_{\mathcal{A}}(S, S')$ in state S. Therefore the bounded-choice composition of these rules for all successor state S' of S defines a recursive ASM $rule_{\mathcal{A}}^S$ with $\Delta(rule_{\mathcal{A}}^S, S) = \Delta(\mathcal{A}, S)$.

Then we apply step 2 (introducing critical terms similarity) and step 3 (exploiting finiteness of critical terms) as in Case 1 to refine $rule_{\mathcal{A}}^S$ to $r_{\mathcal{A}}$ satisfying $\Delta(r_{\mathcal{A}}, S) = \Delta(\mathcal{A}, S)$ for every state S.

Case 3. In state S $\mathcal{A}$ makes a final step to return the value computed by its subcomputation. In step 1 consider any update $(l, v_0) \in \Delta_{\mathcal{A}}(S, S') \in \mathbf{\Delta}(\mathcal{A}, S)$ at any location $l = (f, (v_1, \ldots, v_n))$. There are again two cases to consider.

- Case 3.1. f is an *output* function symbol of $\mathcal{A}$. The values v_i have been computed by the subcomputation of $\mathcal{A}$, therefore they are values of critical terms t_i of $\mathcal{A}$ so that the assignment rule $f(t_1, \ldots, t_n) := t_0$ yields the output update $l = ((f, (v_1, \ldots, v_n)), v_0)$.
- Case 3.2. Otherwise. Since $\mathcal{A}$ in state S makes its final move, it cannot simultaneously make a new recursive call (because otherwise in its final state, when *Terminated* with defined *out*put, it would have some *Active* children, something we excluded by the Call Relationship (pg. 209). Therefore f is not an *in*put function and the Critical Terms Lemma provides critical terms $t_0, t_1, \ldots, t_n$ of $\mathcal{A}$ with values $v_0, v_1, \ldots, v_n$ (as in case 1) such that the assignment $f(t_1, \ldots, t_n) := t_0$ yields the given update (l, v_0).

The parallel composition of the assignment instructions defined in cases 3.1 and 3.2 for each $(l, v_0) \in \Delta_{\mathcal{A}}(S, S')$ yields $\Delta_{\mathcal{A}}(S, S')$ in state S. Therefore the bounded-choice composition of these rules for all successor state S' of S defines a recursive ASM $rule_{\mathcal{A}}^{S}$ with $\mathbf{\Delta}(rule_{\mathcal{A}}^{S}, S) = \mathbf{\Delta}(\mathcal{A}, S)$.

Then we apply again step 2 (introducing critical terms similarity) and step 3 (exploiting finiteness of critical terms) as in Case 1 to refine $rule_{\mathcal{A}}^{S}$ to $r_{\mathcal{A}}$ satisfying $\mathbf{\Delta}(r_{\mathcal{A}}, S) = \mathbf{\Delta}(\mathcal{A}, S)$ for every state S.

Remark on termination. Theorem 9 characterizes a wide class of recursive algorithms, but there are other classes of interest that wait for an abstract characterization, for example recursive algorithms whose computations are intended to not terminate. A famous example is the *Sieve of Eratosthenes*; using ASMs it can be defined in three lines: starting with $sieve = \{n \in Nat \mid n \geq 2\}$ it inserts step by step the current minimum p of *sieve* into the set of *Primes* and deletes any multiple of p from *sieve*.

> SIEVEOFERATOSTHENES =
>   **let** $p = min(sieve)$ -- initially $min(sieve) = 2$
>   INSERT$(p, Prime)$
> $sieve := \{n \in sieve \mid p \text{ does not divide } n\}$

Remark on structures. In keeping with the traditional view on recursion, we have formulated the postulates in Section 8.4.1 in functional terms, i.e. for the case when the callee computes a function based on the provided arguments and returns the resulting value to the caller.

The underlying computational model of ASMs would however lend itself well to defining a more general notion, where entire parts of the state—possibly expressing complex structures with all the corresponding algebraic properties—are exchanged between caller and callee, either as arguments (to define the initial state of the callee) or as results (to extract from the final state of the callee those parts that are of interest to the caller).

Such an approach would provide a characterization of encoding-free recursive computations on structures, thus simplifying the investigation of properties in those practical cases which are not naturally framed as computation of recursive functions.

Chapter 9
Complexity Analysis

This chapter is devoted to the second important property of algorithms (besides their correctness, theme we investigated in Ch. 7), namely their complexity. Different algorithms may compute the same desired result but differ in efficiency. This triggers the analysis of the complexity of algorithmic behaviour in terms of various complexity measures. In Sect. 9.1 we illustrate the power of universal (programmable) machines and of recursion, but also some intrinsic computational limits and their impact on fundamental issues in computation theory and logic; these limits separate a) algorithmically unsolvable (computational or logical) problems from those that have an algorithmic solution, and similarly b) problems that cannot be solved efficiently from those that have efficient solutions. In Sect. 9.2 we point to the role of a modern complexity theory that investigates algorithms which work on appropriate structures (not only numbers or strings) and are executed by networks of corresponding abstract machines (not Turing machines), measuring complexity in terms of a great variety of concrete structural parameters that are of practical relevance.

9.1 Power and Limits of Computation

In this section we explain four fundamental concepts that determine the power as well as the intrinsic limits of algorithms: (*un*)*decidability* (with its recursive enumerability companion), the *diagonalization* and *reduction* method, and *universal* (programmable) machines. The reader will find here no new result but can experience the simplifying effect of dealing with computational issues at appropriate levels of abstraction, in particular dealing directly with programs instead of their numerical encoding (Gödelization).

Decidability and Recursive Enumerability. Once one has a notion of algorithms $a \in Alg$ and of algorithmically computable functions $f \in AlgFct$ one can define the fundamental concept of *decidability* and of *recursive enu-*

E. Börger, V. Gervasi, *Structures of Computing*,
https://doi.org/10.1007/978-3-031-54358-6_9

merability of sets or relations. A set X (or its defining property) is called *Alg*orithmically decidable—i.e. decidable by algorithms in *Alg*—if its characteristic function ξ_X is an *Alg*-computable total function $\xi_X \in AlgFct$; it is called *Alg*-undecidable (or unsolvable) if it is not *Alg*-decidable. X is called recursively enumerable by algorithms in *Alg* if it is empty or coincides with the range $f(0), f(1), \ldots$ of an *Alg*-computable (possibly partial) function $f \in AlgFct$. The terms decidable or recursively enumerable are normally used without further specification if they are intended to relate to the intuitive meaning of the underlying sets *Alg* and *AlgFct* or if these sets are clear from the context, as happens in classical recursion theory that is about partial recursive (i.e. Turing computable) functions over *Nat*. The idea for these definitions can be traced back to Leibniz' definition of *ars iudicandi* (a method to decide the truth of given scientific statements) and *ars inveniendi* (a method to list all true scientific statements) (see [97]).

Exercise 30 (Aristoteles). Show that if a set and its complement are both recursively enumerable, then they are decidable.[1] Below we will see that not every recursively enumerable set is recursive.

Diagonalization. A property of the intuitive notion of algorithm is that any algorithm comes with a finite (usually thought to be textual) description. As a consequence there are only denumerably many algorithms so that for set-theoretic cardinality reasons **there are more problems (sets) than decidable problems**. In fact, Cantor's diagonal argument shows that there is no enumeration $C_0, C_1, \ldots$ of all subsets of the *Nat*ural numbers because otherwise the diagonal set $D = \{n \in Nat \mid n \notin C_n\}$ would be one set C_k of the list which implies the contradiction

$$k \in C_k \underset{\text{(by } C_k = D)}{\textbf{iff}} k \in D \underset{\text{(by Def. of } D)}{\textbf{iff}} k \notin C_k.$$

This argument is visualized (in the form known as Richard's paradox [142]) by Fig. 9.1 where for every list of monadic functions (say 0-1-valued characteristic functions $c_0, c_1, \ldots$ of subsets C_i of *Nat*) one obtains a new diagonal function d (the characteristic function of the diagonal set D) by defining

$$d(n) = 1 - c_n(n) \neq c_n(n).$$

From a constructive point of view Cantor's diagonalization argument defines for each denumerable list of objects of a given type—here sequences $C_0, C_1, \ldots$ of sets $C_i \subseteq Nat$ or $c_0, c_1, \ldots$ of functions $c_i : Nat \to \{0, 1\}$— some new object of the given type (here $D \neq C_i$ because $i \in D$ iff $i \notin C_i$ respectively d because $d(i) \neq c_i(i)$), showing thereby that such lists cannot

---

[1] Aristoteles was the first to develop a calculus which enumerates the set of valid syllogisms together with a calculus to enumerate the set of fallacies; the latter is not complete but has been completed in [157, 123] showing that the Aristotelian syllogistic is decidable. See [26, 27] with further references there.

Fig. 9.1 Richard's paradox. © 1985 (Vieweg-Verlag now) Springer-Verlag GmbH Berlin Heidelberg, reprinted with permission

arg / fct	0	1	2	...	n	...
c_0	$c_0(0)$	...	...	...	...	...
c_1	⋮	$c_1(1)$				
c_2	⋮		$c_2(2)$			
⋮	⋮			⋱		
c_n	⋮				$\boxed{c_n(n) \neq 1 - c_n(n)}$	
⋮	⋮					⋱

exhaust the class of considered objects. A similar use of diagonalization can be made for various decision procedures or computing machines, establishing some limits for them: given a (maybe hypothetical) problem solving machine P use it to construct another machine D that inverts the result of the problem solver, thus generating a contradictory behaviour if D is applied to itself. We show below a few examples that establish by diagonalization some fundamental limits of computational methods (Sect. 9.1.1). On the positive side, the diagonalization method is frequently used in complexity theory to prove hierarchy theorems.[2] It also provides a theoretical foundation for the meaning of recursion which is related to universal (programmable) machines we explain in general ASM terms in Sect. 9.1.2.

Reduction Method. Once one has an undecidable (or a lower bound for the computational complexity of a) property P one can use it to show the undecidability (or a lower complexity bound) of other problems Q by reducing Q algorithmically to P instead of producing a specialized diagonalization argument for Q. The reduction method has innumerable applications for proving undecidability and more generally complexity limits of given problem classes. We illustrate as outstanding example an undecidability proof for the *Entscheidungsproblem* (the decision problem of first order logic) (Sect. 9.1.3) that has a complexity theoretic analogue, namely that the satisfiability problem of propositional logic is NP-complete (Sect. 9.1.3.2), where NP is the class of problems that can be decided by a nondeterministic Turing machine in polynomial time.

---

[2] For an example see the universal ASM in Sect. 9.2.1: applying to it a diagonalization establishes a linear time hierarchy for RAMs and a class of ASMs.

9.1.1 Undecidable Computational Problems (Diagonalization)

In [162] Turing used a diagonalization argument to prove the undecidability (by Turing Machines) of various TM properties (e.g. whether a TM is circle-free or not, whether it ever prints a particular symbol, etc.). In this section we illustrate the method by two examples: proving the undecidability of the *Halting* problem of arithmetical PGAs (see Exercise 29, pg. 204) and more generally of any other non-trivial computational problem for them, as expressed by the Theorem of Rice below. The proof of this theorem uses the Recursion Theorem we explain in Sect. 9.1.2.2.

To remain close to the formulation of Cantor's and Richard's diagonal argument we define

$$Halt = \{M \in \mathsf{ArithPGA} \mid M(M) \downarrow\}$$

to be the set of (Gödel numbers of)[3] arithmetical PGAs M which, started with their own description M as input $in_M = M$, eventually terminate their input-driven computation, property usually denoted by $M(M) \downarrow$. As usual for ASMs we use as termination criterion whether a state is reached that yields an empty update set. The following theorem shows that $Halt$ is undecidable (by arithmetical PGAs or computationally equivalent algorithms).

Theorem 10 (Halting Problem). *It is undecidable by arithmetical PGAs whether any arithmetical PGA M started with its own description M as input eventually terminates its input-driven computation.*

Proof by contradiction. Assume that there is an arithmetical PGA H that decides $Halt$, i.e. started in any initial state with input $M \in \mathsf{ArithPGA}$, H eventually reaches a state with defined output, namely yes or no, *answer*ing the question whether $M \in Halt$ or not. Then H is easily changed to an input-driven arithmetical PGA D as defined by Fig. 9.2. The machine D first uses H to compute the (initially undefined output) *answer* to the question whether $M \in Halt$ is yes or no. Then the control flow is changed to invert the answer: if $answ = $ no holds (i.e. $M \notin Halt$) we trigger the termination of D by letting D in $ctl = $ halt generate the empty update set; if $answ = $ yes holds (i.e. $M \in Halt$) we trigger a not terminating computation of D by letting D in $ctl = $ loop continue ad infinitum to generate some update without changing the state (namely the update (ctl, loop) by the definition of the FSM scheme with $cond = true$ and $rule = $ **skip**, see pg. 28).

As a result, letting D work with itself as input implies a contradiction:

$$D \in Halt \quad \underset{\text{(by Def. of } Halt)}{\textbf{iff}} \quad D(D) \downarrow \quad \underset{\text{(by Def. of } D)}{\textbf{iff}} \quad D \notin Halt.$$

---

[3] To let the algorithmic features discussed in this chapter stand out *expressis verbis*, we consider programs as numbers, abstracting from the particular Gödelization of programs by natural numbers that remains implicit.

Fig. 9.2 Diagonal Machine D for Halt (with Input Machines M)

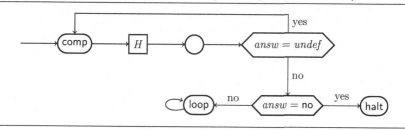

In [141] it has been shown that undecidability holds not only for *Halt* but for every class of numerical algorithms that compute a non-trivial algorithmic property or relation. We prove this here for arithmetical PGAs. We borrow the recursion-theoretic notation $[M]$ to denote the function computed by (the ASM with Gödel number) M (Def. 26, pg. 55).

Theorem 11 (Theorem of Rice). *Let C be a non-trivial class of* **ArithPGA**-*computable functions, where non-trivial means that $C \neq \emptyset$ and C is not the class of all* **ArithPGA**-*computable functions. It is undecidable by arithmetical PGAs whether an arithmetical PGA M computes a function in C, formally stated:* $\{M \in \textbf{ArithPGA} \mid [M] \in C\}$ *is* **ArithPGA**-*undecidable.*

Proof by contradiction. The proof uses the Recursion Theorem 15 (proved in Sect. 9.1.2 below) that every computable function f has a 'fixpoint' program M in the sense that M computes the same function as $f(M)$, i.e. such that $[M] = [f(M)]$ holds. We apply this to a recursive diagonalization function d that changes the behaviour of a decision procedure we assume to be given for the set $\{M \in \textbf{ArithPGA} \mid [M] \in C\}$.

Let M_0 be some arithmetical PGA with computed function $[M_0] \notin C$ and M_1 some arithmetical PGA with computed function $[M_1] \in C$. Define the diagonalization d as follows (see Fig. 9.3):

- Map every arithmetical PGA M with $[M] \in C$ to the machine M_0—which computes a function that is not in C.
- Map every arithmetical PGA M with $[M] \notin C$ to the machine M_1—which computes a function that is in C.

This function d is (by the assumption) clearly **ArithPGA**-computable.

$$d(M) = \begin{cases} M_0 & \text{if } [M] \in C \\ M_1 & \text{else} \end{cases}$$

Therefore by the Recursion Theorem 15 d has a 'fixpoint' program M satisfying $[M] = [d(M)]$. Then the function computed by M must be element of C or not.

Fig. 9.3 Fixpoint for Rice's Theorem. © 1985 (Vieweg-Verlag now) Springer-Verlag GmbH Berlin Heidelberg, reprinted with permission

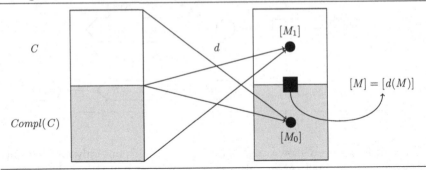

- Case 1: $[M] \in C$. Then $d(M) = M_0$ so that $[M] = [d(M)] = [M_0] \notin C$ and thus $[M] \notin C$.
- Case 2: $[M] \notin C$. Then $d(M) = M_1$ so that $[M] = [d(M)] = [M_1] \in C$ and thus $[M] \in C$.

So $[M] \in C$ **iff** $[M] \notin C$, a contradiction. Therefore the assumption that the set $\{M \in \mathsf{ArithPGA} \mid [M] \in C\}$ has a decision procedure is false and the theorem is proved.

Exercise 31. To prepare the ground for the next exercise we remind the reader that every n-registers machine M can be simulated by a register machine M' with only two registers [129, 155]. Hint: using prime number encoding of register contents define M' such that for control states i, j, i', j' and register contents x_l, y_l the following holds:

$$(i, x_1, \ldots, x_n) \overset{1}{\Rightarrow}_M (j, y_1, \ldots, y_n) \textbf{ iff}$$
$$(i', \langle x_1, \ldots, x_n \rangle, 0) \Rightarrow_{M'} (j', \langle y_1, \ldots, y_n \rangle, 0)$$

Exercise 32 (2-RM Halting Problem). Apply the proof for Theorem 10 above to the following halting problem for 2-register machines (see the preceding Exercise 31). Call a control state *halting* state of M if M has no RM-instruction for $mode = \mathsf{halt}$ (so that M yields the empty update set once it entered this $mode$): $Halt_{2-RM} = \{M \in 2\text{-}RM \mid (0, 0, 0) \Rightarrow_M (\mathsf{halt}, 0, 0)\}$.

9.1.2 Universality and Recursion

Turing's discovery in [162] of the existence of universal programmable machines brought the stored-program digital computer model that changed our world. The recursion theorem is a cornerstone of classical recursion theory. In this section we formulate these two fundamental concepts in terms of ASMs so that the recursion-theoretic results stand out directly, in their algorithmic nature, abstracting where possible from the details of a number encoding of computational features of algorithms that work on non-numeric objects of algorithmic nature.

9.1.2.1 Universal Machine and Enumeration Function

To formulate directly and in some detail a universal Turing machine that can simulate every TM computation is technically rather involved, given the (intended!) rudimentary signature of TMs (see [162]). But on a higher level of abstraction the intuitive concept of simulation of a class of machines can be expressed in a rather simple yet concise way. We illustrate this here with ASMs, exploiting that their comprehensive state concept (if we abstract from finiteness and implementation concerns) permits to incorporate the states and the program of any ASM directly, without encoding, into the current states of a universal machine. In Sect. 9.2.1 we show how this abstract concept of a UNIVERSALASM can be refined (in the sense explained in Sect. 7.2) to a universal machine for ASMs of a fixed finite signature.

Here is the classical definition Turing gave of the concept of a "universal computing machine" $\mathcal{U}$:

> If this machine $\mathcal{U}$ is supplied with a tape on the beginning of which is written the S.D [Standard Description] of some computing machine $\mathcal{M}$, then $\mathcal{U}$ will compute the same sequence as $\mathcal{M}$. [162, pg. 241]

In other words a (single-agent) universal ASM needs as input (say in a 0-ary function $simPgm$) a description of the to-be-simulated machine M together with a description (say in a 0-ary function $simState$) of an initial state where to start the M-sequence (read: M-computation) and its simulation. We provide this by an *initial* step of the universal machine: in $mode =$ init it loads the $pgm(M)$ into $simPgm$ and one of M's *InitialStates* into $simState$ and goes into $mode =$ simulate. For simplicity of exposition we make the notational assumption made already for reflective ASMs (Sect. 4.3), namely that all declared submachines of M are put into its *main* program, replacing every occurrence of a call rule $N(t_1, \ldots, t_n)$ in the $main(M)$ program by the rule body $N'(x_1/t_1, \ldots, x_n/t_n)$ where $N(x_1, \ldots, x_n) = N'$ is the rule declaration. Therefore $pgm(M) = main(M)$.

For the simulation steps let us restrict our attention for the moment to steps of deterministic ASMs (without **choose** construct), as done by Turing for TMs; for the extension to nondeterministic ASMs see Exercise 33. In $mode =$ simulate the universal machine uses the function $eval$ (Def. 14, pg. 32) to compute the update set $U = eval(simPgm, simState)$, the very same update set the to-be-simulated (deterministic) machine computes in its state $simState$. If U is consistent the universal machine uses the *apply* function (Def. 9, pg. 19) to *apply* U to the current $simState$.

This explains the following definition of a UNIVERSALASM rule that simulates computations of deterministic ASMs. Obviously we assume without loss of generality that $mode \notin \Sigma(M)$ for every simulated M.

UNIVERSALASM =
    if $mode =$ init **then**   -- initialize the simulation
        choose $M \in \{M \mid M$ is a deterministic ASM$\}$
        choose $S \in InitialState(M)$
        $simPgm := main(M)$ -- load M's main program
        $simState := S$ -- load an initial state of M
        $mode :=$ simulate   -- start the simulation
    if $mode =$ simulate **then**
        let $U = eval(simPgm, simState)$ -- compute M's updates
        if $Consistent(U)$ **then** $simState := apply(simState, U)$
    where $apply(S, U) = S + U$

Remark on unbounded choice. To express which program (with an arbitrary signature!) and which initial state are selected to be loaded for the simulation by the universal machine we make use of the unbounded **choose** operator. Sure the resulting machine UNIVERSALASM is not what in the literature is called a sequential ASM (a PGA in our terminology). For a refinement to a machine UNIVERSALASM(Σ) that simulates every ASM over the given fixed signature Σ see Sect. 9.2.1.

Exercise 33 (Universality for Nondeterminism). Refine the machine UNIVERSALASM to work for nondeterministic ASMs. For a solution see Appendix B.

A theme that is about an instance of 'universal' machines is that of *computable enumeration functions* e, i.e. computable functions where every computable (without loss of generality 1-argument) function f satisfies for some k the equation $f(x) = e(k, x)$ for all x. Kleene [112] investigated such enumeration functions in terms of μ-recursive functions[4] which led to a normal form for such functions we shortly present here abstractly, in terms of ASM-computable functions (think about k as some ASM rule). The normal form is used in the Recursion Theorem in Sect. 9.1.2.2. For the notion of ASM-computability with arbitrary (not necessarily structured) deterministic i/o-ASMs M over *Nat* we refer to Def. 23 (pg. 52) and Def. 26 (pg. 55).

Theorem 12 (Kleene Normal Form Theorem). *There exists a binary enumeration function e of all unary **ArithPGA**-computable functions that is **ArithPGA**-computable, i.e. for every **ArithPGA**-computable f there is an arithmetical PGA M such that for all arguments x holds $f(x) = e(M, x)$. Traditionally the function $e(M, x)$ of x computed by M is denoted by $[M](x)$.*

---

[4] Note that Kleene submitted his article 2 years before Turing's article [162] was published.

Proof. We define four **ArithPGA**-computable functions whose composition specifies an interpreter model for arithmetical PGAs and thus yields the desired enumeration function e. The four functions specify the interpreter components, each of them corresponding to a fundamental conceptual ingredient of computing functions. We remind the reader that by definition the machines to compute functions are i/o-machines that interact with the environment only to determine the initial state and to output the result of their computation.

- An **input function** $input(M, x)$ defines the initial state of M with input x, i.e. the state where $in = x$ and pgm is (the program of) M.
- A **1-step transition function** $step_{pgm}$ whose iteration $iterate(pgm, n) = step^n_{pgm}$ describes the state reached (if defined) after n steps of pgm.
- A **stop criterion** $Stop(S)$ expresses a termination property, for example that in state S the pgm generates an empty update set.

  Exercise 34. Show that one can equivalently use the criterion that in the given computation the initially undefined output location out is for the first time defined in state S (formally that for the first time $out^S \neq undef$ holds). For a hint see the Appendix B.

- An **output function** $output(S)$ extracts the value out^S.

These four functions imply that the following equation holds for all x if f is computable by an arithmetical i/o-PGA M. Kleene's termination predicate $T(pgm, x, n)$ expresses that starting in the initial state S_0 (with $in = x$ and loaded program pgm) after n pgm-steps a state S is reached (i.e. $S_0 \overset{n}{\Rightarrow}_{pgm} S$) in which the $Stop(S)$ predicate is satisfied:

$(*) \quad f(x) = output(\; iterate\;(pgm, \mu n(\,T(pgm, x, n)))\;(input(M, x))\;)$

Intuitively, these four functions and the T-predicate are clearly **ArithPGA**-computable (in fact μ-recursive, see Theorem 1, pg. 56). That the composition (here e) of **ArithPGA**-computable functions is **ArithPGA**-computable has been shown already in Theorem 1. We recall the iterative definition of $step^n_{pgm} = iterate(pgm, n)$ (see Def. 25, pg. 54).

$$step^0_{pgm}(S) = S$$

$$step^{n+1}_{pgm}(S) = \begin{cases} step^n_{pgm}(S) & \text{if } eval(pgm, step^n_{pgm}(S)) = \emptyset \\ \text{not defined} & \text{if } eval(pgm, step^n_{pgm}(S)) \text{ is} \\ & \text{inconsistent} \\ step_{pgm}(step^n_{pgm}(S)) & \text{otherwise} \end{cases}$$

Remark on Universality. The composition of four functions for input, output, a 1-step transition and a termination criterion to a universal (read: a computable enumeration) function defined by $(*)$ represents abstractly Kleene's normal form for computable numeric functions and can be rephrased in terms of any standard computation model. As an interesting example see Moschovaki's *iterator* definition in terms of in/output, transition and termination functions to formally define the meaning of algorithms [131, pg. 11]. An instance of the equation (∗) for the register machine model can be found in [29, Ch. AII1]: using an explicit Gödelization just instantiate the definition of the four functions in terms of RM-programs working with *Natural* number registers (see Exercise 5). For Buchberger's analysis of those functions that can play the role of one of the four components of 'universal' computation models and for references on this theme see [29, Ch. BIII3].

9.1.2.2 Recursion Theorem

The Recursion Theorem of classical recursion theory is based upon a simple program transformation technique known as S_n^m−Theorem in logic, as Parameterization Lemma in computing where it found an interesting application for partial evaluation of programs. We first describe this parameterization technique.

The partial evaluation interpretation of the parameterization lemma reads as follows: consider programs M to be given with a sequence y of m input variables for static input and a sequence x of n input variables for dynamic input. The idea is that the static input is the part of the input data that can be precomputed because known at compile time. For every m, n one can compute a program called S_n^m that takes as input any program M together with any values $y_1, \ldots, y_m$ for its static input variables and generates a hopefully more efficient 'residual program' $S_n^{m+1}(M, y_1, \ldots, y_m)$ that computes for every dynamic input $x_1, \ldots, x_n$ the same result as M for the entire input $y_1, \ldots, y_m, x_1, \ldots, x_n$. A particularly interesting case is where M is a programming language interpreter ([81]). In abstract terms this specification of the program transformer S_n^m is easily stated and proved to work correctly.

Theorem 13 (S_n^m−Theorem). *For every m, n one can construct an arithmetical PGA S_n^{m+1} such that for every arithmetical PGA M and every input sequence y, x (with y of length m and x of length n) the following equation holds:*

$$[M](y, x) = [S_n^{m+1}(M, y)](x).$$

Usually the indices m, n are omitted if they are clear from the context.

Proof. Define $S_n^{m+1}(M, y)$ by $in := (y, in)$ **seq** M, an ASM which for every input x (of length n) first copies y (of length m) into the input in and then executes M with $in = y, x$.

The recursion theorem is easily proved using the S_n^m−theorem. We first prove a form of the theorem for monadic **ArithPGA**-computable functions.

Theorem 14 (Fixpoint Theorem). *Each **ArithPGA**-computable function f has a program fixpoint M such that $[f(M)] = [M]$.*

Proof. Let f be **ArithPGA**-computable. Then also the function $[f(S(j,j))](x)$ of j, x is **ArithPGA**-computable so that for some arithmetical i/o-PGA M and every j, x holds

$$[M](j,x) = [f(S(j,j))](x)$$

so that by this equation for $[f(S(j,j))](x)$ and the S_n^m-theorem holds

$$[f(S(M,M))](x) = [M](M,x) = [S(M,M)](x)$$

establishing the fixpoint $[f(S(M,M))] = [S(M,M)]$.

Slightly modifying this proof one obtains a proof for the recursion theorem.

Theorem 15 (Recursion Theorem). *For each **ArithPGA**-computable function f (of arity $n+1$) there is an i/o-**ArithPGA** M such that $[M](x) = f(M,x)$ holds for every argument tuple x of length n.*

Proof. For **ArithPGA**-computable function f also the function $f(S(j,j),x)$ is **ArithPGA**-computable so that for some arithmetical i/o-PGA M and all j, x holds

$$[M](j,x) = f(S(j,j),x).$$

By the S_n^m-theorem and the definition of the function $f(S(j,j),x)$ it follows that for every x the following equation holds:

$$[S(M,M)](x) = [M](M,x) = f(S(M,M),x).$$

Remark. The recursion theorem allows one to define a computable function g of n arguments by an equation $f(M,x) = t$ for an $n+1$-ary computable function f where in the defining term t occurrences of $[M](x)$ (read: of recursive calls of M) are allowed to stand for the intended $g(x)$.

9.1.3 Undecidable Logic Problems (Reduction Method)

In this section we illustrate the reduction method to derive impossibility results for a set P of problems by translating into P in an effectively computable manner a set of problems Q which are already know to share this impossibility property.

As application examples we prove the complexity of two outstanding logical decision problems: the undecidability of the *Entscheidungsproblem* (the decision problem of first-order predicate logic, Sect. 9.1.3.1) and the NP-completeness of the satisfiability problem of propositional logic (Sect. 9.1.3.2). We prove both results by refinements of Turing's method [162] to describe the semantics of machine programs by logical formulae, used as reduction method for establishing complexity relations between logic and computing.

There is a great variety of reducibility concepts (see [29]). The following standard notion from recursion theory suffices for our illustrative purposes here.

Definition 55 (Many-One Reduction). A set A is called m-reducible[5] to a set B, denoted $A \leq_m B$, if there is an algorithmically computable function f (called a *reduction function*) such that for all x holds $x \in A$ **iff** $f(x) \in B$.

Lemma 9 (Many-One Reduction Property). If $A \leq_m B$ and A is algorithmically undecidable, then B is algorithmically undecidable.

9.1.3.1 Entscheidungsproblem

A century ago Hilbert presented the *Entscheidungsproblem* as 'the main problem of mathematical logic' [100, pg. 74], hoping that one would find an algorithm for deciding the truth or falsity of any mathematical statement.[6] Church and Turing proved independently that this is not possible (see [62, 162]). Turing's proof introduced a method to effectively reduce machine problems—specifically an unsolvable word problem for TMs—to logical decision problems for the class of formulae that describe the machine problem. It has numerous variations and became a fundamental method of complexity theory.

For the decision problem of first-order logic we illustrate the method by a frugal and particularly simple logical description of the semantics of 2-register machines.[7]

Theorem 16 (Logical Interpretation of 2-Register Machines). *One can define the semantics of 2-register machines M by predicate logic program formulae* STEP$_M$ *with atomic formulae* $\overline{C}$ *representing states C of M such that the following equivalence holds:*

Lemma 10 (2-RM Simulation). *For all states C, D of any 2-RM M holds*

$$C \Rightarrow_M D \text{ iff } \overline{C} \wedge \forall x \forall y \text{STEP}_M \to \overline{D} \text{ is a logically valid formula}$$

where logical validity means that the formula is true for every (not only for the intended) interpretation of its predicate and function symbols.[8]

---

[5] Many-One refers to the fact that the reduction function is not necessarily injective (one-to-one).

[6] That logic would be of help to define problem solving methods was known for centuries, but Leibniz seems to be the first who understood the need of a comprehensive language (*characteristica universalis*) and a mechanical procedure (*calculus ratiocinator*) to resolve mechanically any question formulated in the *characteristica universalis*. It was Frege who defined a concrete universal (symbolic) language for mathematics on the basis of which Russell and Whitehead could formalize the mathematics of their time.

[7] This logical encoding has been developed in [1, 25] with the goal to obtain classes of syntactically severely restricted formulae with unsolvable decision problem.

[8] When writing logical formulae we use the traditional symbols $\forall$ instead of **forall**, $\exists$ instead of **forsome**, $\wedge$ instead of **and**, $\to$ for implication, etc.

Proof. 2-RM states are triples (i, m, n) of control state i and register content m, n one can describe by an atomic logical formula $K_i mn$, denoted as (i, m, n). Due to a theorem of Skolem one can identify numbers m with the logical term built up from 0 by applying m times the successor function $'$ to 0. The intended interpretation of the atomic formulae $K_i mn$ is that from some start state (see START_M below) M can reach the state (i, m, n). Each machine step $C \xrightarrow{1}_M D$—determined by the execution of an M-instruction— can be 'simulated' as a logical deduction step: it deduces (read: applies the rules of logic to derive) $\overline{D}$ from $\overline{C}$ and a program formula $\forall x \forall y \text{STEP}_M$. To achieve this define STEP_M as the conjunction of the following implications for each instruction-determined possible step of M.

- For addition instructions $(i, 1, +1, l)$ concerning the first register define $K_i xy \to K_l x' y$, similarly for addition instructions concerning the second register (inverting the role of x and y).
- For subtraction instructions $(i, 2, -1, l)$ concerning the second register define $K_i yx' \to K_l yx$ and $K_i y0 \to K_l y0$ (remember that for natural numbers the function $x - 1$ is defined to satisfy $0 - 1 = 0$), similarly for subtraction instructions concerning the first register (inverting the role of x and y).
- For 0-test instructions $(i, 1, test, l)$ concerning the first register define $K_i 0y \to K_l 0y$ and $K_i x'y \to K_{i+1} x'y$, similarly for subtraction instructions concerning the second register (inverting the role of x and y).

Then the simulation lemma follows by an induction on M-runs. As a corollary one obtains the Church-Turing theorem.

Theorem 17 (Church, Turing). *The* Entscheidungsproblem—*even the decision problem of the class of (syntactically rather restricted) reduction formulae* α_M *of 2-Register Machines* M—*is algorithmically undecidable.*

Proof. Take in the 2-RM simulation as START_M and STOP_M formulae $K_0 00$ respectively $K_{halt} 00$. This provides an m-reduction of $Halt_{2-RM}$ to the class of reduction formulae $\alpha_M = K_0 00 \land \forall x \forall y \text{STEP}_M \to K_{halt} 00$ for 2-RM machines M; in fact $(0, 0, 0) \Rightarrow_M (halt, 0, 0)$ iff α_M *is valid*. This proves the theorem because the halting problem $Halt_{2-RM}$ is known to be algorithmically undecidable (see Exercise 32 on pg. 226 and [129, 155]).

9.1.3.2 NP-Completeness of Propositional Logic

In this section we explain a frugal parameterized scheme (discovered in [28]) for logical descriptions of time-restricted or space-restricted Turing machine runs that establish strong links between computational complexity of machines and expressibility of logical formulae. We illustrate the method by a

234 9 Complexity Analysis

proof for the NP-completeness of SAT, the well-known satisfiability problem of propositional logic.[9]

First of all we must refine the reducibility concept to take time restrictions for the computation of reduction functions into account.

Definition 56 (Polynomial Time Reduction). A set A is called *p-time* (or polynomial-time) *reducible* to a set B, denoted $A \leq_p B$, if $A \leq_m B$ via a reduction function f that is computable by a deterministic Turing machine in polynomial time (in the length of the input).

For the logical interpretation of 2-RMs in Theorem 16 above, given the simple structure of 2-RMs and the goal to obtain syntactically rather restricted reduction formulae, we defined for each M a fixed program formula STEP_M and for each state C a fixed atomic state formulae $\overline{C}$. For (in this section possibly non-deterministic) Turing machines M we define a scheme for composing in different logics program and state formulae STEP_M and $\overline{C}$ to the intended reduction formula out of the following parameterized basic formulae with the indicated intended interpretation:

- $H(t, x)$ to express that the head position at time t is the tape cell x. For notational simplicity the tape is assumed to consist of cells numbered $0,1,\ldots$.
- $T_j(t, x)$ to express that at time t the tape cell x contains the letter j.
- $I_i(t)$ to express that at time t the control state is i.
- $S(t, t')$ to express that the successor of t is t'.

Note the time parameter t that is needed in general to express time constraints (but was not needed to describe the not time-restricted 2-RM halting problem). Note also the presence of the successor relation that is needed in general (but in the case of register machines became a function symbol S to represent numbers as $S^m 0$).

Assume any state C_t of M at time t to be expressed in terms of basic formulae by a formula $\overline{C_t}$. Then one can define the program formula STEP_M in terms of basic formulae such that the following holds.

Lemma 11 (TM Simulation). Let $\mathfrak{A}$ be a model that satisfies $\overline{C_0} \wedge \text{STEP}_M$. If M started in C_0 can make t steps and $\mathfrak{A}$ provides enough time and space parameters to describe those steps—i.e. in $\mathfrak{A}$ there are S-chains of length t of time and tape cell parameters—then for some C_t holds $C_0 \overset{t}{\Rightarrow}_M C_t$ along those chains and $\mathfrak{A}$ satisfies $\overline{C_t}$.

STEP_M is defined as (finite or infinite, depending on the time and space resources) conjunction of the following formulae for every M-instruction $(i, j, k, move, l)$ (see Example 5 on pg. 26 and the tuple-notation for instructions on pg. 12) for all parameters i, l (for control states), j, k (for tape

---

[9] Numerous instantiations of the method are applied in [48] for a systematic investigation of the complexity of logical decision problems.

letters) and all t, t', x, x', y concerned according to the underlying time and space bounds. Without loss of generality assume that instructions with same pair i, j make the same *move*.

- for right move instructions $(i, j, k, +1, l)$ define:

$$I_i(t) \wedge H(t, x) \wedge T_j(t, x) \wedge S(t, t') \wedge S(x, x')$$
$$\rightarrow \bigvee_{(i,j,k,+1,l) \in M} T_k(t', x) \wedge H(t', x') \wedge I_l(t')$$

- the same with $H(t', x)$ in the conclusion for no-move instructions
- for left move instructions $(i, j, k, -1, l)$ define:

$$I_i(t) \wedge H(t, x') \wedge T_j(t, x') \wedge S(t, t') \wedge S(x, x')$$
$$\rightarrow \bigvee_{(i,j,k,-1,l) \in M} T_k(t', x') \wedge H(t', x) \wedge I_l(t')$$

- for no change outside the current head position define:

$$H(t, x) \wedge y \neq x \wedge T_j(t, y) \wedge S(t, t') \rightarrow T_j(t', y))$$

Exercise 35. Convince yourself by an induction on run time t that the TM-simulation holds. Consider halting instructions with control state *halt* to be of form $(halt, j, j, 0, halt)$ (stay idle).

A propositional logic instantiation of program and state formulae $\text{STEP}_M, \overline{C}$ proves the following theorem.

Theorem 18 (Cook, Levin). *SAT, the satisfiability problem of propositional logic, is NP-complete, i.e. it is an element of NP and every $X \in NP$ is p-time reducible to it.*

Proof. $SAT \in NP$ holds because for some nondeterministic TM M, after guessing a truth value assignment to the propositional variables occurring in a given input formula α in conjunctive normal form, M computes the resulting truth value v of α in polynomial time in the length of the input and accepts α if and only if $v = 1$.

To polynomial-time reduce the acceptance problem of any nondeterministic p-time bounded TM M it suffices to appropriately instantiate STEP_M to a propositional formula in conjunctive normal form and to add two state formulae for START and an ACCEPTing halt such that the following time-restricted reduction property follows from the above TM-Simulation Lemma 11 (where for brevity we write s for the polynomial bound of the number of steps in the length of the input and use 1 as accepting control state). Clearly the reduction function is TM-computable in polynomial time.

Time-Restricted Reduction Property:
M *accepts input* $v_0 \dots v_{n-1} \in \{0, 1\}^n$ *in s steps* **iff**
$(\text{START}_{n,s} \wedge M\text{-STEP} \wedge \text{ACCEPT}_{s,1})(x_0/v_0, \dots, x_{n-1}/v_{n-1})$ *is satisfiable*

M-STEP is defined by an instantiation of the schema STEP$_M$: interpret the basic formulae (deleting those with symbol S) as pairwise different propositional variables with natural number parameters $t, t', x, x', y \leq s$ for time and space. $S(t, t')$ is interpreted as $t' = t + 1$ (the same for $S(x, x')$) and is treated not as part of the formula but as condition on the admitted parameters, the same for $y \neq x$.

The initial M-states are $(0, v_0)v_1 \ldots v_{n-1}b \ldots b$ (of length s) where b is the blank tape symbol (say $b = 2$), 0 the initial control state and the initial head position. Therefore the start formula is defined by:

START$_{n,s} =$
$\quad I_0(0) \wedge H(0, 0) \wedge \bigwedge_{0 \leq j < n} \text{INPUT}_j \wedge \bigwedge_{n \leq j \leq s} T_b(0, j)$
$\quad$ **where**
$\qquad \text{INPUT}_j = (T_1(0, j) \leftrightarrow x_j) \wedge (T_0(0, j) \leftrightarrow \neg x_j)$

Note that due to the formulation of INPUT$_j$ the start formula depends only on the length n of the input, not on the concrete input values $v_0 v_1 \ldots v_{n-1}$.

The stop formula ACCEPT$_{s,1}$ must express that the final control state, the one at time s, is the accepting control state 1. Since the TM-simulation lemma only guarantees that in the final state at least one control state i is reached we formulate the ACCEPTance condition by stating that in the final state no control state formula $I_i(s)$ different from $I_1(s)$ is true.

ACCEPT $= \bigwedge_{i \neq 1} \neg I_i(s)$

Exercise 36. Instantiate the above TM formalization scheme by first-order formulae to derive an alternative proof for the unsolvability of the *Entscheidungsproblem*.

9.2 Complexity of Computing over Structures

In this section we explain how replacing Turing Machines by Abstract State Machines leads to a complexity theory for computations on structures (not only numbers or strings) that has the potential to become useful also for the practice of today's computing. Such investigations are related to the classical study of the relations between algorithms and data structures with respect to their complexity [6, 133] as well as to a major theme in finite model theory, namely the relations between logic languages and complexity classes they capture [68, 121]. Given the extraordinary richness of the ASM world compared to Turing's world [12] one would have expected a huge theoretical interest to explore this new world,[10] but up to today there is only a comparatively small number of papers in this challenging area of research, to mention

---

[10] Already in 1982, long before the final definition of ASMs in [92], it had been asked in [61] whether the complexity class P can be characterized by a model of computation over

some of the first ones [21, 22, 18, 19]. Here we illustrate the potential of such ASM-based complexity studies by two examples: the construction of a universal ASM over a fixed signature which leads to a linear hierarchy for ASMs and RAMs (Sect. 9.2.1) and the investigation of distributed Look-Compute-Move algorithms (Sect. 9.2.2) which operate and move in discrete graphs or in Euclidean spaces.

We have explained in Sect. 8.1.1 how Turing's model of computation is generalized in a natural way by a simple class of ASMs, namely Parallel Guarded Assignments. In fact, not only are TM programs literally PGAs (as shown by Example 5, pg. 26), but the normal form of PGAs

if φ_1 **then** $f_1(s_{1,1}, \ldots, s_{1,n_1}) := t_1$

$\vdots$

if φ_k **then** $f_k(s_{k,1}, \ldots, s_{k,n_k}) := t_k$

(see Theorem 7, pg. 200)—a parallel composition of guarded assignments where the guards φ_i are Boolean combinations of term equations—generalizes directly, term-by-term, the usual behavioural description of TM-instructions (i, a, b, m, j):

if $ctl = i$ **and** $tape(head) = a$ **then** $tape(head) := b$	-- print
if $ctl = i$ **and** $tape(head) = a$ **then** $head := m(head)$	-- move
if $ctl = i$ **and** $tape(head) = a$ **then** $ctl := j$	-- proceed

Remember that each TM-step can be seen as a condensed form of the omnipresent Look-Compute-Action pattern (pg. 27). Furthermore, as we know from Theorem 7, the PGA model captures at any level of abstraction the computational paradigm of the Sequential Postulates, i.e. of single-agent input-driven stepwise data processing using a fixed program.

This means that TMs are a particular subclass of PGAs so that nothing is lost in passing the investigation from TMs to PGAs and more generally to ASMs, but a lot can be gained. Already the few but characteristic examples in Sect. 9.1.1 (Halting Problem and Theorem of Rice) and Sect. 9.1.2 (Kleene Normal Form Theorem and the Recursion Theorem) illustrate how the high level of abstraction ASMs support lets algorithmic phenomena and arguments stand out explicitly in a technically simple manner. This holds also for the idealized computer models in terms of which traditional complexity theory works, in particular the TM model, the Random Access Machine (Exercise 14, pg. 59) with its reflective RASP version (Sect. 4.6, pg. 101), the Bulk Synchronous Parallel Control model (Sect. 6.1) for the design and analysis of parallel algorithms, and many others most of which satisfy the postulates for a class of ASMs that captures those idealized paradigms of computing (see the examples illustrated in Ch. 8).

---

structures (instead of Turing machines working on strings). In view of the successful use of ASMs in the practice of computing the theme of a computation theory over structures has been proposed again in [58, pg. 310] (Problem 26), see also [125].

There is a large variety of concepts to measure the computational complexity of (classes of) algorithms by the amount of resources required to run the algorithms. In the traditional complexity theory mostly used are bounds on computation time and space, e.g.:

- the number of steps or of basic (arithmetical, communication, load/store, read/write, move, etc.) operations that are performed in an appropriate unit of time,
- the amount of memory required to store the arguments on which operations are applied.

Other types of resources have recently become important in practical cases, e.g. energy consumed by the execution of algorithms on battery-powered devices or in very large data centers.

Since such measures of complexity depend on the underlying model of data, operations and memory, it is to be expected that investigating computations directly over the structures of interest opens the door for a rich computational complexity discipline with underlying machine concepts that are relevant for the practice of today's computing, whether generic or domain-specific. Practitioners typically measure concrete data and operations directly, at the genuine level of abstraction of the investigated algorithms; to mention two among a myriad of examples in the area of algorithms and data structures: the number of comparisons of keys and the number of shifts of to-be-sorted data in sorting algorithms [133] or the structural complexity of non-numeric objects of computation (e.g. syntactically restricted forms of logical formulae when analysing their decision problems [48]).

In terms of the ASM framework this comes rather natural: it means to take into account the signature (data structure) and in particular the background of algorithms or classes of machines when investigating their complexity properties. In Sect. 3.1.1 we have observed that the ASM-computability concept is first of all a notion of relative computability where, logically speaking, the background plays the role of an oracle so that even the impressive research on degrees of unsolvability [120] can be uniformly expressed in terms of ASMs. What is important for the practice of computing is that one can tailor the concept of ASM-computation by appropriate constraints on the background (for an example see the Arithmetical State Postulate in Def. 46, pg. 203) which result in corresponding parameters for complexity measures. We list here some typical complexity measures ASMs do support explicitly and directly:

- cost of data access
- cost of background operations
- cost of term evaluation
- cost of computing updates (assignments) and more generally of instructions (e.g. ASM rules in terms of the size of their parse tree)
- cost of single computation steps or of tasks involving objects and actions

- maximum number and size of the content of used locations in a run
- cost of runs (depending on the underlying control structure or scheduling scheme)
- cost of refinement, measuring the complexity of macro versus micro steps (i.e. abstract versus refined and in particular implemented steps on given hardware)

Note that the listed parameters refer to structural features and not to their encoding by computable numbers. It might be worth to stress that since the cost of encoding and decoding is in itself variable, and comes with its own complexity, when discussing the complexity of an algorithm (or problem) with that encoding in mind it may be difficult or impossible to separate the complexity which is proper of the problem, from that which comes from the encoding. With ASMs, and more general when computing on structures directly, it is natural to skip the encoding altogether, so it is easier to focus on the proper complexity of the solution.

9.2.1 Universal ASM over Fixed Signature

An interesting application of ASMs in complexity theory appeared in [17] where a linear time hierarchy theorem is proved for (a class of) ASMs and analogously for RAMs. The result is obtained by applying the diagonalization technique to the runs of a universal ASM with fixed signature Σ and fixed program. This construction is a refinement UNIVERSALASM(Σ) of the UNIVERSALASM in Sect. 9.1.2.1. It implements the choice of a to-be-simulated machine M (with an initial state S_0) by starting with a given encoding of M (and S_0) to first construct a copy that is then used to directly read and write the data during the stepwise simulation, without modifying the initial encoding of M. In this section we explain such a simulator $U = $ UNIVERSALASM(Σ) for a class of ASMs with fixed signature Σ.

Signature. The ASMs we consider in this section are input/output control state PGAs M (i.e. interacting with the environment only for input/output), extended by **import** rules. The latter are used to build a data copy of the to-be-simulated machines M. For simplicity of exposition the machines M are assumed to have no static functions (except the logical ones *true*, *false*, *undef*), but they may have any finite number of dynamic functions. The signature Σ is assumed to contain in particular the following dynamic functions that are used to construct and traverse a parse tree representation of any M (the analogue of the standard description of a TM program on the TM tape in Turing's definition of universal machines, pg. 227):

- Functions *parent*, *fstChild*, *nxtSibl* (to build the parse tree) and tree labeling functions *type*, *nomen* we call PT-functions.

- Five PT-traversal functions:

  – a *cursor* function to denote the currently visited parse tree node,
  – a function *val* used to assign computed results to nodes,
  – two functions *lastUpdNode* and *nxtUpdNode* to construct linked lists of visited nodes in the parse tree where some updates have been computed that will be applied at the end of the parse tree traversal,
  – a 0-ary Boolean-valued *error* function assumed to be initially *false* and to become *true* when during the **apply** phase the simulator detects an update inconsistency.[11]

- Functions *ctl*, 0, *succ*. Initially the simulator is in *ctl*-state 1 and finds an encoding of the parse tree of the given program M in an initial segment $[0, n)$ of *Nat*, so that besides 0 there is the standard *succ*essor function restricted by $succ(n-1) = undef$.

Architectural Component Structure. The strategy of the simulation is to first CopyParseTree of M to provide space (the analogue of the TM tape) for the universal machine U to record the intermediate data M needs during the computation of its updates for a step. Each M-step (as long as the *Sim*ulation is not *Finished*) is performed by the ParseTreeEvaluation component. ParseTreeEval starts in a given simulation state S (where *ctl* = SimStep) a traversal of M's parse tree in mode *ctl* = down. U moves down in depth-first manner and then moves up again, recording (where needed) at the currently visited node *cursor* the computed subtree evaluation result as *val*(*cursor*). When eventually the *cursor* comes back to the parse tree root and U enters mode *ctl* = apply, the third component ApplyUpdates finds at the UPDATE nodes the values computed for the update elements: it checks them for consistency and applies them if they are consistent. This finishes the current simulation step and lets U enter the computed successor state S' of S (if defined) with mode *ctl* = SimStep.

The just described architectural view of U = UniversalAsm(Σ) is rigorously defined by the control state ASM in Fig. 9.4 and the definition below of its components.

Here we anticipate the definition for the termination condition and the initialization of the linked list of update nodes. This list will be extended by *nxtUpdNode* upon encountering during the parse tree traversal a *node* with label *type*(*node*) = UPDATE. The Gödelization function *ordinal* defined below is used to describe the termination condition.

---

[11] Since we explain here only the universal machine and not its diagonalization feature that serves to prove the linear time hierarchy, we disregard the i/o-functions of the simulated machines and the particular role assigned to the 0-ary output function *out* in [17] concerning the diagonalization. A similar role is played by the *error* function we introduce as element of Σ for the consistency check after the parse tree evaluation. The input function *in* is also not mentioned explicitly as element of Σ, but its functionality is present via the parse tree encoding, see below.

Fig. 9.4 UNIVERSALASM(Σ) Component Structure

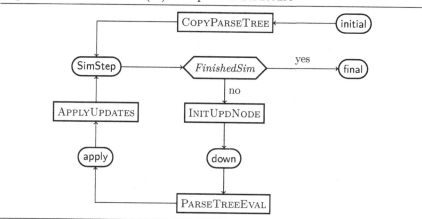

$$FinishedSim \text{ \textbf{iff} } val(ordinal(ctl)) = \mathsf{final}$$
$$\text{INITUPDNODE} = (lastUpdNode := 0)$$

It remains to define and explain the three components COPYPARSETREE (a preprocessor that constructs the initial simulation state of U providing a copy of the parse tree where to record step-simulation data), the PARSETREEEVAL to compute the updates of M in the current simulation state, and the final application of the computed update set Upd (if consistent) by APPLYUPDATES. Note the precisely defined splitting of the simulator into components which interact as expressed by the architectural design of the main component UNIVERSALASM(Σ); the splitting satisfies the principle that to be satisfactorily inspectable for a correctness check, a component (specification or piece of code) should fit a page or two.

Path Tree and COPYPARSETREE **Preprocessor.** The role of the submachine COPYPARSETREE is to produce a copy of the (Gödelization of the) input parse tree formed by the initial state elements in $[0, n)$ together with $succ$ and the PT-functions. The elements of initial states are called original elements of the simulation states, i.e. of those states where $ctl = \mathsf{SimStep}$. The Gödelization we describe below is done in such a way that the copies of the first nodes $succ^i(0)$ with $i = 0, 1, 2, \ldots, m$ are reserved to contain the current values of the i-th 0-ary non-logical function $nullary_i$, listing that by definition starts with $succ^0(0) = 0$, $succ^1(0) = ctl = \mathsf{initial}$.

$$0 \xrightarrow{succ} 1 \xrightarrow{succ} 2 \ldots succ^i(0) \ldots (n-1)$$
$$val \downarrow \quad \downarrow \quad \downarrow \quad \downarrow \quad \quad \downarrow$$
$$0' \xrightarrow{succ} 1' \xrightarrow{succ} 2' \ldots nullary_i \ldots (n-1)'$$

This explains the definition in Fig. 9.5 with the following definition of the macros.

Fig. 9.5 COPYPARSETREE Component

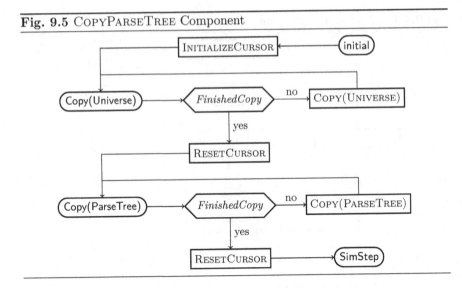

INITIALIZECURSOR = RESETCURSOR = $(cursor := 0)$
FinishedCopy **iff** *cursor* = **undef** -- *cursor* reached $succ(n-1) =$ *undef*

COPY(UNIVERSE) =
    import *node* **do** *val(cursor)* := *node* -- clone the visited node *cursor*
    cursor := *succ(cursor)*   -- visit next node

COPY(PARSETREE)[12] =
    forall $f \in \{succ, parent, fstChild, nxtSibl, type, nomen\}$
      $f(val(cursor)) := val(f(cursor))$ -- copy parse tree structure
    cursor := *succ(cursor)*   -- visit next node

The definition of the parse tree $PT(M)$ of M by induction on M follows the usual pattern (see the figures at the beginning of Sect. 4.3) but with two particular labeling functions *type* and *nomen*. Fig. 9.6 shows the trees for terms $f(t_1, \ldots, t_r)$ (with *type* FUN and *nomen* f for the outer function symbol) which includes the case of 0-ary functions ($r = 0$), for assignment instructions $f(t_1, \ldots, t_r) := t_{r+1}$ (with *type* UPDATE and *nomen* f for the outer function symbol), conditional instructions **if** *cond* **then** N (with *type* COND) and parallel instructions **par** $M_1, \ldots, M_n$ (with *type* PAR).

Fig. 9.7 shows the trees for the **import** v **do** N construct and for variables. The parse tree for a variable v is a one-node tree with *type* VAR and *nomen* v.

To construct $PT(\textbf{import } v \textbf{ do } N)$ with variable v a new node x is introduced as *parent* of the *root* of $PT(N)$; its *type* is defined as IMPORT and its

---

[12] The use of **forall** stands here as abbreviation for six parallel PGA assignments.

Fig. 9.6 ParseTree for PGA Constructs

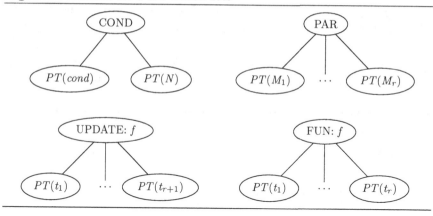

Fig. 9.7 Parse Tree for Variables and Imports

update binding $nomen(node) := x$
wherever $nomen(node) = v$ in $PT(N)$ N.B. x is the root node for
for rule **import** v **in** N the two constructs.

$nomen$ as x. In addition, for every occurrence of a $node$ with $nomen(node) = v$
in $PT(N)$ the binding is updated to $nomen(node) = x$.

Initial states $I(M, \Sigma)$ of U are defined as states that satisfy the following
conditions.

- $ctl = $ initial $= succ(0)$,
- the *regular* elements (i.e. those that are in *Workspace*, see Sect. 2.3.2) form
  an initial segment $[0, n)$ of *Nat* with $n \geq 2$ and standard interpretation of
  0 and $succ$ (including $succ(n-1) = undef$) the simulator will not change,
- the regular elements together with the restriction of the PT-functions to
  regular elements form a (Gödelization defined below for the) parse tree
  $PT(M + m)$ of a notationally slightly modified but equivalent program
  $M + m$ (where m is the number of non-logical 0-ary function symbols
  in Σ); also this parse tree will only be read but never be changed by U
  during the simulation,

- every $f \in \Sigma$ (except 0, *succ*, *ctl* and the PT-functions) is interpreted as *undef* resp. *false* (for every argument). This comes up to assume (without loss of geneality) that M starts in a blank state.

The program extension $M + m = \mathbf{par}\ \mathbf{par}\ \dots\ \mathbf{par}\ M$ (m times) has the effect to create in the parse tree m initial nodes, as illustrated by Fig. 9.8, that are used only for recording the current value of the non-logical 0-ary functions.

Fig. 9.8 Parse Tree Extension $PT(M + m)$

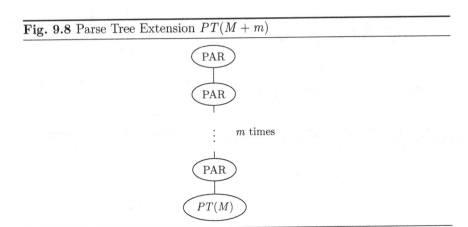

For this reason the Gödelization of $PT(M + m)$ is defined as follows:

- Starting with 0 perform a depth-first numbering (Gödelization) of all parse tree nodes and replace them by their Gödel number. Note that as a consequence, in the parse tree for $M + m$ every $succ^i(0)$ for $i < m$ is a node of type PAR.
- Number (Gödelize) all function names $f \in \Sigma$ as f_i where all non-logical 0-ary function names $nullary_i$ come first and in particular 0 receives number 0 and *ctl* receives number 1. Represent f_i by the term $succ^i(0)$, denoted as $ordinal(f)$. Thus the initial PAR nodes in $PT(M + m)$ can be used to record the current value of a 0-ary non-logical function as $val(ordinal(nullary_i)) = val(succ^i(0))$.
- To complete the Gödelization replace the labels PAR, COND, FUN, IMPORT, UPDATE, VAR in the *type* function by the respective number 0,1,...,5, replace every value f of the *nomen* function by $ordinal(f)$, and replace the *ctl*-values of U by some numbers.

Component PARSETREEEVAL. We are now ready to explain the component for the PARSETREEEVALuation of the universal machine U. Starting in mode $ctl = $ down with $cursor = 0$ (due to the last RESETCURSOR step of the COPYPARSETREE component) the machine moves down in the depth-first manner to reach a leaf. At each node of $type(cursor) = $ IMPORT it records a new element as $val(cursor)$; at each node of $type(cursor) = $ UPDATE it extends the linked list of encountered update nodes by

$$nxtUpdNode(lastUpdNode) := cursor$$
$$lastUpdNode := cursor$$

(list that had been initialized in mode SimStep when entering mode down). When U reaches a leaf (i.e. a node without child so that $fstChild(cursor) = undef$) it switches to $ctl := \text{up}$.

This and the following definition of the used macros explain the moving-down part of the ParseTreeEvaluator in Fig. 9.9.

Fig. 9.9 ParseTreeEval Component

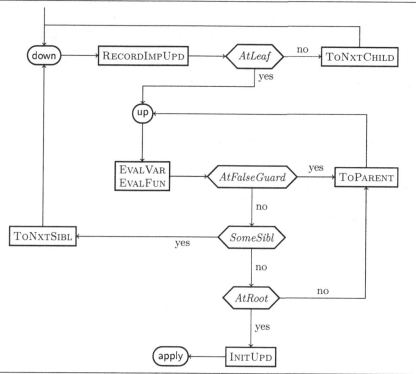

RecordImpUpd =
  if $type(cursor) = \text{IMPORT}$ **then**
    import $node$ **do** $val(cursor) := node$ -- record new node
  if $type(cursor) = \text{UPDATE}$ **then**   -- extend list of update nodes
    $nxtUpdNode(lastUpdNode) := cursor$
    $lastUpdNode := cursor$
ToNxtChild = $(cursor := fstChild(cursor))$ -- depth-first traversal
$AtLeaf$ **iff** $fstChild(cursor) = undef$ -- there is no child

As to the moving up segments of the tree traversal, in mode up the simulator visits for each node the next sibling except when it is *AtFalseGuard*, i.e. at the root of the guard child of a COND node with guard evaluated to *false*; in that case U can move to the *parent* node because is not necessary to evaluate the body of that conditional rule. Otherwise U moves *ToNxtSibl*ing, assuming there is some, and reenters mode $ctl =$ down. If there is no sibling U moves to the *parent* node unless it reaches the root of the parse tree. In the latter case U enters $ctl =$ apply (and initializes for the consistency check the auxiliary set Upd of already applied updates). This calls the APPLYUPDATE component to check the computed updates for consistency and in the positive case to apply them to the current M-state.

Wherever in a moving up step the *cursor* visits a VAR: x or a FUN: f node, the simulator must EVALVARiable respectively EVALFUNction.

EVALVAR finds (via *nomen*(*cursor*) in the parse tree definition for variables and import constructs in Fig. 9.7) the IMPORT node x where the current M-value of x is recorded as *val*(x). Therefore one can define EVALVAR as follows:

> EVALVAR =
>> **if** *type*(*cursor*) = *VAR* **then** *val*(*cursor*) := *val*(*nomen*(*cursor*))

EVALFUN is a PAR rule of (finitely many) rules for $f \in \Sigma$, so it is a PGA though for notational convenience we formulate it using the **forall** construct. Clearly at each FUN node only the rule guarded by the ordinal number of its *nomen* applies.

> EVALFUN =
>> **if** *type*(*cursor*) = *FUN* **then**
>>> **forall** $f \in \Sigma$
>>>> **if** *nomen*(*cursor*) = *ordinal*(f) **then**   EVALUATE$_f$

To define EVALUATE$_f$ there are two cases, depending on whether f is 0-ary or not. Let $r = arity(f)$.

Case 1: $r > 0$ or f is a 0-ary logic function.[13] Then we define:

> EVALUATE$_f$ =   -- record current f-value on computed arguments
>> *val*(*cursor*) := f(*val*(*child*$_1$), . . . , *val*(*child*$_r$))
>
> **where**
>> *child*$_1$ = *fstChild*(*cursor*)
>> *child*$_{i+1}$ = *nxtSibl*(*child*$_i$)   **forall** $i < r - 1$

Case 2: f is a non-logic 0-ary function. Then the current M-value of f is kept as *val*(*ordinal*(f)) at *ordinal*(f) = $succ^i(0)$ for some $i < m$ so that we define:

---

[13] We do not need to consider *error* here since it is used by the simulator only once and only to get a defined value, namely if and when during the apply phase an inconsistent update set is discovered.

EVALUATE$_f$ = $(val(cursor) := val(ordinal(f)))$ -- record current f-value

Together with the following definition of the other macros this explains the moving-up part of Fig. 9.9.

TOPARENT = $(cursor := parent(cursor))$ -- go to *parent* node
SomeSibl **iff** $nxtSibl(cursor) \neq undef$ -- visited node has some sibling
TONXTSIBL = $(cursor := nxtSibl(cursor))$
AtRoot **iff** $cursor = 0$ -- entire parse tree has been traversed
INITUPD = $(Upd := \emptyset)$ -- initialize set of applied updates

Exercise 37 (AtFalseGuard). Define the (intuitively clear but verbose) property *AtFalseGuard*. Hint: reformulate part of the definition above for EVALUATE$_f$. For a definition see the Appendix B.

Component APPLYUPDATES. In $ctl =$ apply mode the machine, starting with $cursor = 0$, checks at each $nxtUpdNode(cursor)$ in the computed list whether the update recorded there is consistent with those already applied in the (initially empty) set Upd. In case U detects an inconsistency it sets $error := true$ so that *FinishedApply* becomes true and the simulation stops with $ctl =$ final. Otherwise U will APPLY the update and add it to Upd (if it is new) so that it can go TONXTUPDNODE (if there is one) or otherwise enter mode $ctl =$ SimStep and reset the *cursor* for the next simulation step. This explains Fig. 9.10 and its macros (where again for notational convenience we use **forall** instead of the bounded **par**-notation with finally many arguments).[14] The submachine CHECKAPPLYUPD$_f$ of CHECKAPPLYUPD is explained below.

Fig. 9.10 APPLYUPDATES Component

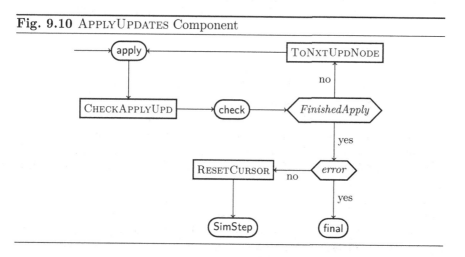

---

[14] Note that when initially $cursor = 0$, none of the CHECKAPPLYUPD rules fires since 0 is not an UPDATE node.

CHECKAPPLYUPD =
    forall non-logical $f \in \Sigma$ **with** $f \neq error$
      if $nomen(cursor) = ordinal(f)$ **then** CHECKAPPLYUPD$_f$
FinishedApply **iff** $nxtUpdNode(cursor) = undef$ **or** $error = true$
TONXTUPDNODE =
    $cursor := nxtUpdNode(cursor)$
    $nxtUpdateNode(cursor) := undef$
RESETCURSOR = $(cursor := 0)$

For CHECKAPPLYUPD$_f$ we must distinguish whether the $arity(f)$ is positive or 0 to correctly identify the location for the computed and to-be-checked and possibly applied update. The elements of the update have been computed by the subtrees t_i of the current node and are recorded there as $val(root(t_i))$.

CHECKAPPLYUPD$_f$ =
    let $child_1 = fstChild(cursor)$ -- access subtrees for *upd* elements
    if $arity(f) > 0$ **then**
      forall $1 \leq i \leq r$ **let** $child_{i+1} = nxtSibl(child_i)$
      let $arg = (val(child_1), \ldots, val(child_r))$ -- computed arguments
      let $upd = ((f, arg), val(child_{r+1}))$
             -- retrieve *upd* elements computed by subtrees
        CHECKAPPLY(upd)
    if $arity(f) = 0$ **then**
      CHECKAPPLY$((val, ordinal(f)), val(child_1))$
    where
      CHECKAPPLY$((g, a), b)$ =
        if $((g, a), b) \in Upd$ **then skip**   -- same update already applied
        elseif forsome $c \neq b$ $((g, a), c) \in Upd$ **then**
         $error := true$ -- two inconsistent updates detected
        else   -- new update is consistent with those already made
         $g(a) := b$ -- apply the update
         INSERT$(((g, a), b), Upd)$ -- record applied update

Analysis of Simulation as Refinement. To prove the correctness of the simulation of runs of ASMs M with signature Σ by runs of the simulator $U =$ UNIVERSALASM(Σ) we describe the relation between the computations using the refinement scheme of Sect. 7.2, an interesting and frequently encountered $(1, c)$ refinement type with a small constant c. Such simulations are called lock-step simulation.

For every M-computation $S_0, S_1, \ldots$ there is an U-computation with corresponding states $\overline{S_0}, \overline{S_1}, \ldots$ of interest such that the M-locations in S_i (the locations of interest) have the same value as their corresponding U-locations. We call these corresponding states of interest $\overline{S_i}$ simulation states (where $ctl = $ SimStep). The first one of them is reached by the preprocessing U-computation segment by which COPYPARSETREE leads from U's initial state $I(M, \Sigma)$ described above to the first state with $ctl = $ SimStep, the state $\overline{S_0}$.

For S_0 and $\overline{S_0}$ the correspondence between the locations of interest (initially the blank M-locations and their counterpart in U) holds by definition of I and the fact that the preprocessor CopyParseTree does not touch the M-locations.

For each M-step leading from S_i to S_{i+1} U starts the three-phase-simulation of this step in $\overline{S_i}$ with $cursor = 0$. In a first phase it moves down from the parse tree root to the leafs, recording at each IMPORT: x node the newly imported element and extending at each UPDATE: f node the list of encountered UPDATE nodes (that is needed for the application of the computed updates performed at the end of this simulation round by the ApplyUpdates component). We visualize these actions as follows:

$$\text{IMPORT} : x \quad \xrightarrow{val} \quad \textbf{import } new \textbf{ do } val(cursor) := new$$

$$\text{UPDATE} : f \quad \xrightarrow{val} \quad \begin{array}{l} nxtUpdNode(lastUpdNode) := cursor \\ lastUpdNode := cursor \end{array}$$

In a second phase U moves up from the leafs to the root of the parse tree visiting however sibling nodes it encounters (from where it may again move down to the leafs and then return up again). In the ascending phase U records at each VAR: x node the S_i-value of x (where by the binding defined by IMPORT nodes in the parse tree, x denotes an IMPORT: x node). At each FUN: f node it records the S_i-value of f applied to the S_i-values computed at the node's children. We visualize these actions as follows:

$$\text{VAR} : x \quad \xrightarrow{val} \quad val(cursor) := val(nomen(cursor))$$

$$\text{FUN} : f \quad \xrightarrow{val} \quad val(cursor) := \begin{cases} val(ordinal(f)) & \text{if } f \text{ is 0-ary} \\ f(val(children)) & \text{otherwise} \end{cases}$$

In phase 3 by the ApplyUpdates component U traverses the list of the visited updates nodes to check at each node of the list whether the update recorded there is consistent with the already applied updates (those in the set Upd initialized by the empty set) and in the positive case to apply that update, thus updating the concerned M-locations to their value in state S_{i+1}; in case of an encountered inconsistency U stops its computation.

The reader will have observed that this rather typical ASM refinement scheme not only allows one to prove runtime properties by induction on runs (here of M and its simulation by U), but the component structure of the refined machine (here of U) permits to split the major proof steps into a series of lemmas, one per component, fighting this way complexity (of both design and verification).

Remark on completeness. In the presentation above we have closely followed the approach presented in [17], where the theorem establishing the linear time hierarchy was first stated and proved. While that approach suffices to prove the theorem, some aspect of the construction might appear rather artificial (e.g. creating additional PAR nodes in the syntax tree to store parts of the state, or the somewhat contrived treatment of VAR and IMPORT). Moreover, the construction only considers the most basic ASM constructs.

For a complete model of an ASM interpreter with variable signature, which more directly express the operations of an ASM run by means of appropriate structures, rather than by making recourse to unnatural encoding, the reader may refer to [75] where also non-determinism, partial updates and arbitrary backgrounds are allowed. The model of the interpreter in [75], which is itself specified as an ASM, constitutes a full specification of the universal ASM concept.

9.2.2 Look-Compute-Move Algorithms

Distributed systems of mobile agents that operate in complex topological environments provide an interesting example for modern complexity investigations of computations over structures. In this section we explain the basic concepts of one such example, surveyed in [80]: the class of Look-Compute-Move (LCM) algorithms which operate in a spatial universe—a graph (a discrete version) or an Euclidean space (a continuous version)—using various resources and forms of communication and interaction that lead to a variety of models of computation with rich structural complexity properties.

9.2.2.1 Signature of LCM algorithms

An LCM algorithm is a pair (Ag, LCMPGM) of a team Ag of finitely many *agents* (also called robots) and a program LCMPGM each *agent* executes. The structure where an LCMPGM operates is typically either a finite connected undirected graph G (with a universe V of vertices and a set E of edges) or an Euclidean space (with a universe $U \subseteq Real^n$ for some finite dimension n). At each moment every *agent* is *positioned* in a point *pos* of the universe (called its current *pos*ition). In rounds, based on an observation of its current environment, each *agent* computes a *destination* point and then (if *dest* $\neq$ *pos*) moves towards this *dest*ination—each time the *agent* is activated to execute such an LCM round (also called LCM cycle). The LCM control structure is similar to the one for streaming systems (see Fig. 6.2, pg. 156).

The LCMPGM describes the sequential execution of the three steps LOOK, COMPUTE and MOVE an agent performs in the corresponding *mode* $\in$ {*look, compute, move*} once it has been activated for an LCM round. Activation of agents to make them run requires some START mechanism we formulate using an additional *mode* value *sleep*. LCM algorithms come with a variety of notions of run we analyze in more detail in Sect. 9.2.2.3. In [80, pg. 4-7] they are formulated in terms of scheduling policies where agents are

activated by a scheduler (expressed as setting *Active* for the considered agent
to true). We reflect this by a START step that wakes up (read: calls) the
activated agent to sequentially execute its three LCM cycle steps.[15]

At this point we can define LCMPGM by the following abstract scheme of
four round components that are guarded by their *mode* value so that they
are executed in sequential steps (see below). They are open to refinements by
adding details characterizing various classes of LCM algorithms we explain
below.

LCMPGM =
   START
   LOOK
   COMPUTE
   MOVE

To equip each *agent* with its own separate state we use the **ambient** notation (see Sect. 5.4.1) declaring the agent-sensitive locations (like *pos*, *Active*,
mode, etc.) as implicitly instantiated per *agent*. Thus each *agent* is equipped
with the following program:

$$pgm(a) = \textbf{amb } a \textbf{ in } \text{LCMPGM}$$

9.2.2.2 Discrete LCM Algorithms over Graphs (LCMGRAPHPGM)

To illustrate in more detail the four LCMPGM components we consider the
case of graph algorithms where the robots interact only through (global or
local) shared memory or by face-to-face communication (of pairs of robots positioned on the same node and both reading the partner's memory) or by wire-
less communication and can move only to neighbouring nodes of their current
position. We focus the attention on algorithms with local shared memory that
is accessible for *agents* on a mutual exclusion basis, say as *nodeInfo(pos)* at
their current *position* where they can read, record and update the information. We denote this LCMPGM refinement by LCMGRAPHPGM.

To abstract from the details of mutual exclusion we let the START component REQUESTACCESS(*nodeInfo(pos)*) and guard the LOOK component
by a *HasAccessTo(nodeInfo(pos))* predicate. Robots also may use some own
*workMem*ory (that is RESET at the beginning of a new round) and have some
*privateMem*ory that is persistent (i.e. it does not change when *mode = sleep*).

---

[15] Concerning scheduling it is assumed (see [139]) that once the execution of an LCM-
cycle by an *agent* is started (triggered by an activation of the *agent*) its three program
components LOOK, COMPUTE and MOVE will immediately be executed and their executions will terminate regularly, except in the continuous model where moves of agents
(differently from the graph model) are not atomic and a *mobility scheduler* may stop
a moving agent. But it is the scheduler's role to deactivate an agent (by an update
Active(ag) := false) where desired.

This explains in more detail the role of the START and LOOK component for LCM graph algorithms. When an agent becomes *Active* it STARTs one LCM cycle: it requests a mutual exclusion access to the local memory *nodeInfo*(*pos*) that is available at its current *position*, refreshes its work memory and goes to *mode* = *look* (where by the fairness assumption it will eventually receive access to the local *nodeInfo*rmation).

> START =
>   **if** *Active* **and** *mode* = *sleep* **then**
>   RESET(*workMem*)   -- clean working memory
>   REQUESTACCESS(*nodeInfo*(*pos*))   -- require exclusive access
>   *mode* := *look*   -- wake up the agent

In *look mode* a robot, when it *HasAccessTo* the local memory *nodeInfo* at its current *position*, takes a *snapshot* of it, updates it, RELEASEs the lock and enters the *compute mode*.

> LOOK =
>   **if** *mode* = *look* **then**
>   **if** *HasAccessTo*(*nodeInfo*(*pos*)) **then**
>   *snapshot* := *nodeInfo*(*pos*)   -- record current observation
>   WRITETO(*nodeInfo*(*pos*))   -- interact with env
>   RELEASE(*nodeInfo*(*pos*))   -- release lock
>   *mode* := *compute*

With LCM algorithms working in an Euclidean space the observation in *look mode* of the environment does not manage any data (so that the START rule contains no REQUESTACCESS) but only takes a *snapshot* of the positions of those other robots it can *observe* (determined in terms of its specific local coordinate system with *origin* = *pos*) within its *visibility* range. This operation is considered as instantaneous.

Details on local memory. A frequently used refinement of the local memory function *nodeInfo* is to a *whiteboard* with mutual-exclusion constraint for reads and writes on this *whiteboard* by any agent visiting the node in question. Analogously, *nodeInfo* can be refined to communication via a token-count in the mutual-exclusion-constrained Petri net fashion: nodes and agents can hold tokens; when an agent visits a *node* it records in *info* the number of tokens found on the *node* and may change *nodeInfo* by adding some of its own tokens to those found on the *node* and/or vice versa by picking up some of the tokens from the *node*.

Exercise 38 (LCM with face-to-face communication). Refine LOOK for face-to-face communication. See the Appendix B.

The COMPUTE component executes a PROTOCOL we do not specify further here. It is assumed to be the same for each agent but it is called with the agent's current *snapshot* value[16] and calculates in particular whether and where to move to in the next step. We assume the result of that computation to be recorded in a location *dest*; in the graph model it is either a neighbouring node of *pos* in the graph—i.e. the destination for the next move to perform— or *undef*, indicating that the decision is to not move. In the Euclidean model the result may include also a trajectory to the destination and the robots are capable to perform infinite precision real arithmetic operations.

COMPUTE =
    if *mode* = *compute* then
        PROTOCOL(*snapshot*)   -- compute *dest* where to move to
        mode := *move*

In the graph model, differently from an Euclidean model, "The MOVE operation is considered instantaneous" [80, pg. 12] so that it can be described by an update of the agent's *position* to the computed *destination*—if the PROTOCOL decided to request a move from *pos* to *dest*. If however the PROTOCOL has computed *dest* = *undef* the agent remains in its current *position*. In both cases the agent is set to *mode* = *sleep* (cycle termination) so that it becomes ready to be activated for a next LCM cycle. In general, for backtracking purposes an agent records the information on the port from which it came (described by labeling the edges incident to a node).

MOVE =
    if *mode* = *move* then
        if *dest* ∈ *V* then
            pos := *dest*   -- perform the move to vertex *dest*
            RECORDBACKTRACK(*Info*(*pos*, *dest*))
        elseif *dest* =*undef* then skip   -- stand still
        mode := *sleep*   -- terminate the LCM cycle

Remark on termination. "At the end of a cycle a robot may either start a new cycle or become inactive (sleep)" [80, pg. 9], but "The choice of which robots are activated ... is assumed to be made by *the activation scheduler*" [80, pg. 6]. This is the reason why in the graph model at the end of a cycle we let the agent go to sleep (from where it may START immediately a new LCM cycle if it is still (or again) *Active*).[17]

Note that in an Euclidean model the MOVE rule is more complex. There the robots can turn and move in any direction and use these motorial capabilities to move towards the computed *dest*ination (possibly along a computed trajectory). Furthermore, a *mobility scheduler* controls the move speed, may

---

[16] Obviously PROTOCOL is assumed to be designed such that two executions by different agents generate no inconsistency.

[17] If one wants to allow that the agent can try to deactivate itself it suffices to add a partial update (see Def. 33) *Active* :=$_{schedPriority}$ *false* where to resolve a possible update conflict the action *schedPriority* gives priority to the scheduler's update of the location *Active*.

impose for moves a maximal length γ if the distance to the *destination* is greater than this constant γ and may interrupt the move. Therefore, instead of updating the computed *destination* the *mode* is updated for the move phase to *motile* ("not necessarily moving, but capable of moving" [111, pg. 9]) with an additional rule for the termination of the move phase we do not formalize here.

9.2.2.3 LCM Runs and Complexity

In applications, for each robot each round, each component computation and each inactivity segment (where *mode = sleep*) may have its particular duration (and in case of an Euclidean structure also its rate of motion in every move phase). Any constraint made on their timing can affect the computational capabilities of LCM algorithms. In this section we use the control structures explained in Ch. 3–5 to describe the major notions of run that are used for LCM graph algorithms, essentially variations of synchronous or asynchronous protocol executions.

Synchronous LCM runs come with a specific robot activation schedule and a specific timing of the robot components. Formally these runs are sequences $R_1, R_2, \ldots$ of rounds; in each round R the activated agents execute one by one each of their sequential components in parallel (simultaneously)

Fig. 9.11 LCMSYNCROUND simulator for LCMGRAPHPGM

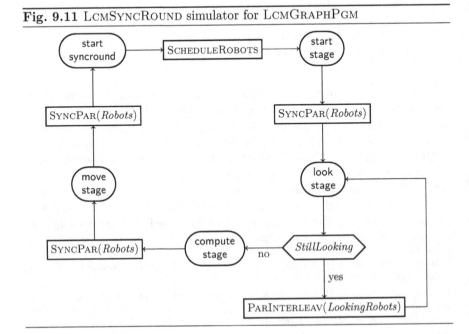

and terminate their activity at the end of the round. The role of the *activation scheduler* to determine in a fair way[18] for each round the team of *Active* agents becomes explicit in the synchronous LCM run simulator LCMSYNCROUND defined by Fig. 9.11 for LCM algorithms with LCMGRAPHPGM (where each component can be viewed as an atomic action).

LCMSYNCROUND is a single-agent sequential ASM. In each round it first schedules a set *Robots* of $pgm(a)$ (for some agents $a \in Ag$ that form the *RoundTeam*). Then in its start stage the simulator executes simultaneously (in parallel) one step for every $pgm(a) \in Robots$, using for the synchronization the SYNCPAR module defined on pg. 68, and proceeds to its look stage. Assuming that initially all agents are in *mode* = *sleep*, after the first simulation step the *RoundTeam* agents are all in *mode* = *look*. In the look stage where (due to the mutual exclusion scheme for the local communication) in each moment at each node at most one team member can make a step, instead of SYNCPAR the parallel interleaving paradigm PARINTERLEAV(*Process*) is applied (see pg. 69) with $ReadyToExec(pgm(a))$ meaning that the robot a $HasAccessTo(nodeInfo(pos(a)))$. Assuming a fair mutual exclusion, eventually there will be no more *RoundTeam* agent with $mode(a) = look$ so that also the simulator enters its compute stage. In that stage the simulator executes again simultaneously for every $pgm(a) \in Robots$ one step, the same in its move stage, namely the COMPUTE respectively the MOVE component of $pgm(a)$, applying again the SYNCPAR operator to *Robots*. This terminates the round. The macros for Fig. 9.11 are defined as follows.

SCHEDULEROBOTS =
  choose $A \subseteq Ag$[19]   -- select round team
    forall $a \in A$ $Active(a) := true$
    $RoundTeam := A$
    $Robots := \{pgm(a) \mid a \in A\}$
  $LookingRobots = \{pgm(a) \mid a \in RoundTeam$ **and** $mode(a) = look\}$
  $StillLooking$ **iff** $LookingRobots \neq \emptyset$
  $ReadyToExec(pgm(a))$ **iff** $HasAccessTo(nodeInfo(pos(a)))$

The definition in Fig. 9.11 satisfies the requirement that only at the end of a round execution a new round can be started. The two well-known border cases of synchronous runs are where the activation scheduler selects for each round the *RoundTeam* of all agents respectively for each round a *RoundTeam* of only one agent, called in [80, pg. 6] *fully synchronous* respectively *centralized* LCM activation model.

Asynchronous LCM runs. For LCM graph algorithms with atomic sequentially executed components one can specify an asynchronous execution model by the notion of concurrent ASM runs (see Definition 36, pg. 112).

---

[18] Fairness is meant as usual that in an infinite run every robot is activated infinitely many times.

[19] This stands for **choose** A **in** $\mathcal{P}(Ag)$

To show this we define a concurrent run simulator LCMASYNCROUND for LCMGRAPHPGMs which in each step activates a (constrained to be fairly selected) set of robots for one round execution and at the same time executes for some already activated robots their current component (as determined by their current *mode*).[20] In the concurrent ASM run each simulated component step can be interpreted as a GLOBALSTEP (see Fig. B.1, pg. 266).[21] Initially all robots are assumed to be in *mode* = *sleep* and not *Active*.

> LCMASYNCROUND =   -- simulator for LCMGRAPHPGM
>   ACTIVATESOMEROBOTS
>   EXECSOMEACTIVATEDROBOTS
> **where**
>   ACTIVATESOMEROBOTS =
>   **choose** $A \subseteq$ *SleepingNotActiveAgents*
>   **forall** $a \in A$ *Active*(a) := *true*
>   EXECSOMEACTIVATEDROBOTS =
>   **choose** $^{22} A \subseteq \{a \in Ag \mid Active(a)\}$
>   **forall** $a \in A$ **do** *pgm*(a)
> **where**
>   *SleepingNotActiveAgents* =
> $\{ag \in Ag \mid mode(ag) = sleep$ **and not** $Active(ag)\}$

In this way every robot can be activated independently of other robots and the executions of components by different activated robots may happen at arbitrary (same or different) moments.

Exercise 39 (Eager LCM Round Execution). If one wants the components of every activated robot to be executed without delay (as is expressed in [139], see footnote at the end of Sect. 9.2.2.1) it suffices to constrain the selection in EXECSOMEACTIVATEDROBOTS by stipulating that if in a concurrent run a robot is activated at time t by ACTIVATESOMEROBOTS, then its program instance will be selected by EXECSOMEACTIVATEDROBOTS in the next four steps of the concurrent run to execute the robot's components. Show that the resulting LCMASYNCROUND program is equivalent to the following scheduler:

> ACTIVATESOMEROBOTS
> SYNCPAR$(\{pgm(a) \mid a \in Ag$ **and** $Active(a)\})$

Bounded asynchronous LCM runs. In LCM algorithms working in an Euclidean space the intrinsically durative MOVE component requires an ASYNCLCM run concept where robots can be activated independently and

---

[20] For simplicity but without loss of generality we assume here that *Active* agents remain *Active* at least until their current round is terminated.

[21] A durative component version can be captured by a sequence of LOCALSTEPs.

[22] This stands for **choose** A **in** $\mathcal{P}(\{a \in Ag \mid Active(a)\})$.

the duration of their component executions and inactivity periods is finite but arbitrary and may even change from round to round and may differ from robot to robot. As a consequence the activity rounds of different robots may overlap arbitrarily; for example during one robot's round another robot could execute any finite number of rounds. This leads to the interesting subclass of bounded asynchronous LCM runs: a $k -$ ASYNCLCM run is an ASYNCLCM run where during the time interval of any round execution by any robot r every other robot r' can be activated at most k times. In [111] it is shown that LCM algorithms running under $k -$ ASYNCLCM scheduling can solve certain problems LCM algorithms executed under unbounded ASYNCLCM scheduling cannot solve.

The coordination of teams of agents is but one example of interesting computational complexity parameters which come into view when investigating computations over structures instead of numerical computations. For LCM structures various intensively investigated parameters to measure the complexity of LCM algorithms concern background functions and operations, for Euclidean spaces for example the local coordinate system of robots, visibility features (visibility range, visibility obstructions, multiplicity detection, collision handling), forms of measurement inaccuracy (when computing distances or angles), motorial capabilities (mobility scheduling), etc. (see [80, 111]).

Appendix A
ASM Behaviour in a Nutshell

Definition of: N generates (U, η') (in $\mathfrak{A}$ with parameters ζ, η)

- **Assignment rule:** $N = (f(t_1, \ldots, t_n) := t_0)$. N generates (U, η) with update set $U = \{((f, (\overline{t_1}, \ldots, \overline{t_n})), \overline{t_0})\}$ and $\overline{t_i} = eval(t_i, \mathfrak{A}, \zeta)$
- **Import rule:** $N = \mathbf{import}\ x\ \mathbf{do}\ M$. N generates some (U_α, η')
  - if M generates it in $\mathfrak{A}$ with parameters $\zeta[x \mapsto \alpha]$ and $\eta \cup \{\alpha\}$
    - for an arbitrary element $\alpha \in Heap \setminus (Workspace(\mathfrak{A}) \cup range(\zeta) \cup \eta)$

- **Conditional rule:** $N = \mathbf{if}\ Cond\ \mathbf{then}\ M$.
  - Case 1. N generates $(\emptyset, \eta)$ if $eval(Cond, \mathfrak{A}, \zeta) = false$
  - Case 2. otherwise, N generates some (U, η') if M does it

- **Parallel rule:** $N = \mathbf{par}\ (M_1, M_2)$. N generates $(U_1 \cup U_2, \eta_2)$ if
  - M_1 generates some (U_1, η_1) and
  - M_2 generates some (U_2, η_2) in $\mathfrak{A}$ with parameters ζ, η_1

- Let $range(x, \varphi, \mathfrak{A}, \zeta)$ be $\{a \in Workspace(\mathfrak{A}) \mid eval(\varphi, \mathfrak{A}, \zeta[x \mapsto a]) = true\}$
  - **Choose rule:** $N = \mathbf{choose}\ x\ \mathbf{with}\ \varphi\ \mathbf{do}\ M$
    - Case 1: N generates $(\emptyset, \eta)$ if $range(x, \varphi, \mathfrak{A}, \zeta) = \emptyset$
    - Case 2: otherwise N generates some (U_a, η') if M does it with $\zeta[x \mapsto a], \eta$ for any $a \in range(x, \varphi, \mathfrak{A}, \zeta)$
  - **Forall rule:** $N = \mathbf{forall}\ x\ \mathbf{with}\ \varphi\ \mathbf{do}\ M$
    - Case 1: N generates $(\emptyset, \eta)$ if $range(x, \varphi, \mathfrak{A}, \zeta) = \emptyset$
    - Case 2: otherwise N generates (U, η') if the following holds:
      $\{a_1, a_2, \ldots\}$ is any enumeration of $range(x, \varphi, \mathfrak{A}, \zeta)$
      M generates (U_n, η_n) with parameters $\zeta[x \mapsto a_n], \eta_{n-1}$
      for every a_n with some (U_n, η_n) and $\eta_0 = \eta$
      $U = \bigcup_n U_n$ and $\eta' = \bigcup_n \eta_n$

- **Let rule:** $N = (\mathbf{let}\ x = t\ \mathbf{in}\ M)$. N generates some (U, η')
  - if M does it with parameters $\zeta[x \mapsto eval(t, \mathfrak{A}, \zeta)], \eta$

© The Author(s), under exclusive license to Springer Nature Switzerland AG 2024
E. Börger, V. Gervasi, *Structures of Computing*,
https://doi.org/10.1007/978-3-031-54358-6

In this list we use for single-agent ASMs the expression

$$M \text{ generates a pair } (U, \eta')$$

(in $\mathfrak{A}$ with parameters ζ, η) to stand for $evalCand(M, \mathfrak{A}, \zeta, \eta, (U, \eta')) = true$ used in the book. The wording should help to support a quick but correct intuitive understanding of the procedure M performs to compute for every given state $\mathfrak{A}$ with initially empty parameters ζ, η every update set candidate (each of which—if consistent—can then be used to transform the given $\mathfrak{A}$ into a possible successor state).

Technically this means the following. Denote by $UpdSets(M, \mathfrak{A})$ the set of update sets $U = Upd(M, \mathfrak{A})$ in pairs (U, η') generated by M in $\mathfrak{A}$ started with empty parameters ζ and η. The definition of

$$M \text{ can make a move from state } \mathfrak{A} \text{ to } \mathfrak{B}$$

from pg. 32 reads now that there is a consistent update set $U \in UpdSets(M, \mathfrak{A})$ so that $\mathfrak{A} + U$ is one of the possibly multiple successor states $\mathfrak{B}$. The wording of the corresponding extended definition of single-agent ASM runs (Def. 22, pg. 40) remains unchanged.

Appendix B
Solutions of Selected Exercises

4 Solution of exercise 4 from pg. 27. **2-dimensional Turing Machine interpreter.** Just replace *Nat* by *Plane* (*Integer* × *Integer*), correspondingly replace *tape* by *plane* : *Plane* → *Alphabet* (so that the *head* positions become pairs $(x, y) \in Plane$) and extend the allowable *moveDir*ections by 'up' and 'down':

$$moveDir(ctl, tape(head)) \in \{right, left, up, down\}$$

The rule TURINGMACHINE defined in the main text remains unchanged (modulo the new interpretation of *Square*)

2-DIMENSIONALTM(*write, nextCtl, move*) =
 plane(*head*) := *write*(*ctl, plane*(*head*))   -- *tape* replaced by *plane*
 ctl := *nextCtl*(*ctl, plane*(*head*))
 shift *head* **to** *moveDir*(*ctl, plane*(*head*)) -- four move directions
where
 let *head* = (x, y) **in**
  shift *head* **to** *right* = (*head* := $(x + 1, y)$)
  shift *head* **to** *left* = (*head* := $(x - 1, y)$)
  shift *head* **to** *up* = (*head* := $(x, y + 1)$)
  shift *head* **to** *down* = (*head* := $(x, y - 1)$)

5 Solution of exercise 5 from pg. 31. **Register Machine interpreter.** Use indexed registers r_j as dynamic 0-ary functions (with values in *Nat*).

RM(*reg, oper, nextCtl*) =
 let $i = ctl, j = reg(ctl), op = oper(ctl), l = nextCtl(ctl)$
  if *op* = *test* **then**
   if $r_j = 0$ **then** *ctl* := *l* **else** *ctl* := $i + 1$
  if *op* ≠ *test* **then**
   $r_j := op(r_j)$
   ctl := $i + 1$

© The Author(s), under exclusive license to Springer Nature Switzerland AG 2024
E. Börger, V. Gervasi, *Structures of Computing*,
https://doi.org/10.1007/978-3-031-54358-6

Since a register machine is supposed to work on natural numbers it uses the modified subtraction operation where $0 - n$ is defined as 0.

The three parameters $reg, oper, nextCtl$ (here static functions of control states) define the pgm of register machine instructions. They determine for each instruction label i (e.g. $i \in Nat$) a register (which we denote by $r_{reg(i)}$), an operation to be performed on that register, and a label of the next to-be-executed instruction (which may depend on the current content of register $r_{reg(i)}$.

This formulation of the RM-rule is intended to make it explicit that variations of RM-machines can be defined depending a) on the register data (natural numbers, real numbers, bit-sequences, words, trees, etc.) and the corresponding set of operations on register contents and b) on the way to access registers, whether statically or dynamically. The above RM-interpreter has finitely many registers that are provided by a static function $r(reg(ctl))$. To determine a register dynamically one can define its index k as the content of some register r_j, writing r_k where $k = content(r_j)$ (assuming that indices are natural numbers). This is called indirect register addressing and is supported by the view of registers as 0-ary dynamic functions. A widely used example is provided by the Random Access Machine model (see Exercise 14, pg. 59).

---

8 Solution of exercise 8 from pg. 41. **Interactive Turing Machine interpreter.** Introduce a monitored location *envInput* and an additional program function *output* to write on an output location *outputToEnv* read by the environment.

$$\text{TURINGMACHINE}(write, nextCtl, move, envInput) =$$
$$in(head) := write(ctl, in(head), envInput) \qquad \text{-- param for } envInput$$
$$head := move(ctl, in(head), envInput)(head)$$
$$ctl := nextCtl(ctl, in(head), envInput)$$
$$outputToEnv := output(ctl, in(head), envInput)$$
where
$$move(ctl, in(head), envInput) \in \{right\text{-}move, left\text{-}move, no\text{-}move\}$$

11 Solution of exercise 11 from pg. 55. **Understanding of while.**

while *cond* **do skip**	If *cond* is false, the **while** terminates immediately with success. If *cond* is true, then the **skip** is executed, which produces an empty update set and again the **while** terminates with success.
while *false* **do** *M*	Since the condition is false, the **while** terminates immediately with success.
while *true* **do** *a* := *a*	Diverges, since the update set produced by the assignment is never empty nor inconsistent.
while *true* **do** $\begin{array}{l} a := 1 \\ a := 2 \end{array}$	Terminates (with failure) since the two updates produced by the assignments are mutually inconsistent.

13 Hint for exercise 13 from pg. 58. **PGA programs for structured machines.** Use control-state ASMs. For M_1 **seq** M_2 the PGA M defines a $(1,2)$-refinement (see Fig. 7.1). Assume M_1 and M_2 to have sufficiently disjoint signatures.

$M =$ -- triggered by $mode = start_M$
   if $mode = start_M$ **then**
     M_1
     $mode := start_{M_2}$ -- switch to M_2
   if $mode = start_{M_2}$ **then**
     M_2
     $mode := stop_M$ -- finished executing **seq**

For **while** *cond* **do** N the PGA M defines a $(1, *)$-refinement where $*$ is determined by the length of the simulating computation.

$M =$ -- triggered by $mode = start_M$
   if $mode = start_M$ **and** *cond* **then**   -- *cond* is true, proceed to N
     $mode := start_N$
   if $mode = start_M$ **and not** *cond* **then**   -- *cond* is false, stop
     $mode := stop_M$
   if $mode = start_N$ **then**   -- execute N and repeat
     N
     $mode := start_M$

14 Solution of exercise 14 from pg. 59. **Interpreter for Random Access Machine programs.** Let *pgm* be the given program of instructions *instr*(l), use *ctl* as instruction counter (initialized by *ctl* = 0) with the abbreviation *currInstr* = *instr*(*ctl*). For the arithmetical operations denote by *meaning*(*opCode*) the corresponding arithmetical function (where for division x/y is cut off to its integer part, i.e. the greatest integer equal to or less than x/y). Represent registers r_n as 0-ary dynamic functions.

RamInterpreter =
  let $cmd = opCode(currInstr)$, $arg = operand(currInstr)$ **in**
    if $cmd \in \{Load, Store, Add, Sub, Mult, Div\}$ -- check failures
      and $WrongAddr(arg)$ **then** Halt($WrongAddr$)
    if $cmd = DIV$ **and** $operandVal(arg) = 0$ **then** Halt($DivBy0$)
    else   -- regular behaviour
      if $cmd = Load$ **then** $acc := operandVal(arg)$
      if $cmd = Store$ **then**
        if $arg = reg\ n$ **then** $r_n := acc$
        if $arg = addr\ n$ **let** $k = r_n$ **in** $r_k := acc$
      if $cmd \in \{Add, Sub, Mult, Div\}$ **then**
        $acc := meaning(cmd)(acc, operandVal(arg))$
      if $cmd = Jump$ **or**   -- Jump instructions
        $(cmd = Jump(> 0)$ **and** $acc > 0)$ **or**
        $(cmd = Jump(= 0)$ **and** $acc = 0)$
          then $ctl := arg$ -- Jump to label arg
      if $cmd \notin \{Jump, Jump(> 0), Jump(= 0), Halt\}$
        or $(cmd = Jump(> 0)$ **and not** $acc > 0)$
        or $(cmd = Jump(= 0)$ **and not** $acc = 0)$
          then $ctl := next(ctl)$ -- Go to next instruction
      if $cmd = Read$ **then**
        if $arg = reg\ n$ **then** $r_n := inTape(headIn)$
        if $arg = addr\ n$ **then let** $k = r_n$ **in** $r_k := inTape(headIn)$
        Move($headIn, inTape$)   -- move to next square
      if $cmd = Write$ **then**
        $outTape(headOut) := operandVal(arg)$
        Move($headOut, outTape$)   -- move to next square
where
  $currInstr = instr(ctl)$
  $WrongAddr(arg)$ **iff**
    $arg = addr\ n$ **and** $r_n < 0$
  Halt($Reason$) =   -- $Reason \in \{WrongAddr, DivBy0\}$
    $ctl := halt$ -- enter control state $halt = 1$
    ReportError($Reason$)
  $next(l) = l + 1$ -- compute the label of the next instruction
  $meaning(Add) = +$
  $meaning(Sub) = -$
  $meaning(Mult) = \times$
  $meaning(Div) = /$ -- modified to yield integers
  $operandVal(int\ i) = i$
  $operandVal(reg\ n) = r_n$
  $operandVal(addr\ n) = \begin{cases} undef & \text{if } r_n < 0 \\ r_{r_n} & \text{else} \end{cases}$

For uniformity of notation we consider *Labels* as *operands* of jump instructions. If the machine reaches $ctl = halt$, by definition the command of $instr(halt)$ is *Halt*, but the RAMINTERPRETER has no rule with $cmd = Halt$ so that the machine halts and the RAMINTERPRETER generates the empty update set.

18 Solution of exercise 18 from pg. 85. **Backtracking Scheme.** Let a set $\mathcal{M}$ of machines be given with a function $alternatives(M)$ that assigns to machines M a subset of alternative machines in $\mathcal{M}$. Unexplained macros are identical to those of PUREPROLOG.

> BACKTRACKSCHEME =
> LAYOUTALTS
> TRYNEXTALT
> ALTTERMINATION

The component machines are defined as follows:

> LAYOUTALTS =
> **if** $mode = layoutAlts$ **and** OK **then**
> EXTENDTREEBY $node_1, \ldots, node_m$ **with**
>   -- machine alternatives
> **forall** $i = 1, \ldots, m$ $pgm(node_i) := M_i$
>   -- one node per to-be-tried-out machine alternative
> $mode := tryNextAlt$ -- switch to try the alternatives
> **where**
> $[M_1, \ldots, M_m] = alternatives(pgm(currnode))$

> TRYNEXTALT =
> **if** $mode = tryNextAlt$ **and** OK **then**
> **if** $cands(currnode) = [\,]$ **then**   -- no candidate left
> BACKTRACK
> **else**
> TRYNXTCAND

> TRYNXTCAND =
> $currnode := first(cands(currnode))$
> $mode := execute$ -- start next machine
> $cands(currnode) := rest(cands(currnode))$ -- update candidates

> ALTTERMINATION =   -- upon termination of a machine
> **if** $mode = successful$ **then**
> $stop := success$
> **if** $mode = unsuccessful$ **then**
> BACKTRACK
> $mode := tryNextAlt$

$\boxed{19}$ Solution of exercise 19 from pg. 85. **Prolog rule asking for one more solution.**

NEXTSOLUTION =
    if $stop = success$ **and** $AnotherSolutionWanted$ **then**
        BACKTRACK
        $stop := 0$

$AnotherSolutionWanted$ is a monitored 0-ary predicate, typically representing a user request for an alternative solution.

$\boxed{22}$ Solution of exercise 22 from pg. 113.

$$S_{m+1} = S_m + \bigcup_{a \in GoGlobal} U_a$$

where U_a is an update set candidate generated by agent a in this run in state S_m.

$\boxed{24}$ Hint for exercise 24 from pg. 116. **Concurrent Step with Local Computation Segments.** The program is defined by Fig. B.1 below.

Fig. B.1 CONCURSTEP with Local Computation Segments

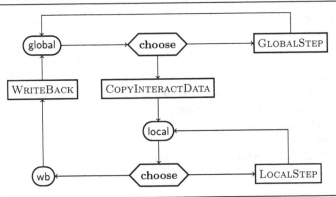

$\boxed{26}$ Solution of exercise 26 from pg. 158. **Ordered Selection Patterns.** Denote by $P_{i,1}, \ldots, P_{i,s_i}$ the given static selection pattern order. Denote by ACTION$_{i,s}$ the body of the READ$_i$ component in the main text:

ACTION$_{i,s}$ =
    forall $k \in P_{i,s}$ **do** $input_{i,k} :=$ **read from** $in_{i,k}$
    $actPattern_i := P_{i,s}$

Then refine READ$_i$ to the following rule:

$\text{READ}_i =$
$\quad$ **if** $IsReadable(P_{i,1})$ **then** $\text{ACTION}_{i,1}$
$\quad$ **elseif**
$\qquad \vdots$
$\quad$ **elseif** $IsReadable(P_{i,s_i})$ **then** ACTION_{i,s_i}

---

33 Solution of exercise 33 from pg. 228. **Universal ASM for nondeterministic ASMs.** It suffices to replace in UNIVERSALASM the line

$\quad$ **let** $U = eval(simPgm, simState)$

by the line

$\quad$ **choose** $U \in UpdSet$ **with** $evalCand(simPgm, simState, U)$

---

34 Solution of exercise 34 from pg. 229. **Stop Criterion.** Modify the given i/o-*pgm* to a program that generates in every state an update (e.g. an initially undefined signal to still be active) unless *out* is defined. Then *pgm* reaches a stop state S in terms of $out^S \neq undef$ if and only if the program

$\quad$ **while** $out = undef$ **do**
$\quad$ *pgm*
$\quad$ *stillActive* := 1

reaches a stop state S in terms of generating in S an empty update set.

---

37 Solution of exercise 37 from pg. 247. **Definition of** *AtFalseGuard*. Compare the description below with the definition of EVALUATE$_f$ in the PARSETREEEVAL component (pg. 246).

$\quad$ *AtFalseGuard* **iff**
$\qquad$ $cursor = fstChild(parent(cursor))$ **and**
$\qquad$ $type(cursor) = \text{FUN}$ **and** $type(parent(cursor)) = \text{COND}$ **and**
$\qquad$ **let** $f = nomen(cursor)$, $r = arity(f)$
$\qquad\quad$ $((r > 0$ **or** f is a nullary logic function)
$\qquad\qquad$ **and** $f(val(child_1), \ldots, val(child_r)) = false)$
$\qquad\quad$ **or** (f is a non-logic nullary function
$\qquad\qquad$ **and** $val(ordinal(f)) = false)$
$\qquad$ **where**
$\qquad\quad$ $child_1 = fstChild(cursor)$
$\qquad\quad$ $child_{i+1} = nxtSibl(child_i)$ **forall** $i < r - 1$

---

38 Hint for exercise 38 from pg. 252. Denote by $robotInfo(a)$ the information an *agent* obtains from any other agents a at the same node $pos(ag)$. This notation implies that in face-to-face communication an *agent* can see and distinguish the other agents a that currently have the same $pos(a) = pos(ag)$.

Look =
   if $mode = look$ then
      $snapshot := \{(a, robotInfo(a)) \mid a \in Ag \text{ and } pos(a) = pos(\mathbf{self})\}$
      $mode := compute$

Obviously for face-to-face communication there is no memory access request in the START component.

References

1. Aanderaa, S.: On the decision problem for formulas in which all disjunctions are binary. In: 2nd Scandinavian Logic Colloquium Symp., pp. 1–18 (1971) 232
2. Abrial, J.R.: The B-Book. Cambridge University Press, Cambridge (1996) 196
3. Abrial, J.R.: Modeling in Event-B: System and Software Engineering. Cambridge University Press, Cambridge (2010) 196
4. Ackermann, W.: Begründung des "tertium non datur" mittels der Hilbertschen Theorie der Widerspruchsfreiheit. Mathematische Annalen **93**, 1–36 (1924) 60
5. Agha, G.: Actors: a model of concurrent computation in distributed systems. MIT Press (1986) 118
6. Aho, A.V., Hopcroft, J.E., Ullman, J.D.: The design and analysis of computer algorithms. Addison-Wesley (1974) 101, 105, 107, 236
7. ASM method: tool support. `https://abz-conf.org/method/asm/` (2023) 188
8. Avigad, J., Zach, T.: The Epsilon Calculus. In: E.N. Zalta (ed.) The Stanford Encyclopedia of Philosophy, Fall 2020 edn. Metaphysics Research Lab, Stanford University (2020) 60
9. Barnocchi, D.: L'"evidenza" nell'assiomatica aristotelica. Proteus **5**, 133–144 (1971) 188
10. Barros, A., Börger, E.: A compositional framework for service interaction patterns and communication flows. In: K.K. Lau, R. Banach (eds.) Formal Methods and Software Engineering. Proc. 7th International Conference on Formal Engineering Methods (ICFEM 2005), *LNCS*, vol. 3785, pp. 5–35. Springer (2005) 131
11. Barwise, J., Etchemendy, J.: Tarski's World. CSLI, Stanford (CA) (1993). See 2008 edition by D. Barker-Plummer and J. Barwise and J. Etchemendy 11
12. Barwise, J., Etchemendy, J.: Turing's World 3.0 for Windows. Cambridge University Press (2001) 236
13. Batory, D.: Science of Software Product Lines (in preparation). ACM publishers (2025) 160
14. Batory, D., Börger, E.: Modularizing theorems for software product lines: The Jbook case study. J. Universal Computer Science **14**(12), 2059–2082 (2008). URL `http://www.jucs.org/jucs_14_12/modularizing_theorems_for_software`. Extended abstract "Coupling Design and Verification in Software Product Lines" of FoIKS 2008 Keynote in: S. Hartmann and G. Kern-Isberner (Eds): FoIKS 2008 (Proc. of *The Fifth International Symposium on Foundations of Information and Knowledge Systems*), Springer LNCS 4932, p.1–4, 2008 160, 187, 191
15. Beierle, C., Börger, E.: Refinement of a typed WAM extension by polymorphic order-sorted types. Formal Aspects of Computing **8**(5), 539–564 (1996) 192
16. Beierle, C., Börger, E.: Specification and correctness proof of a WAM extension with abstract type constraints. Formal Aspects of Computing **8**(4), 428–462 (1996) 192

E. Börger, V. Gervasi, *Structures of Computing*,
https://doi.org/10.1007/978-3-031-54358-6

17. Blass, A., Gurevich, Y.: The linear time hierarchy theorems for Abstract State Machines. J. Universal Computer Science **3**(4), 247–278 (1997) 239, 240, 249

18. Blass, A., Gurevich, Y.: The logic of choice. J. Symbolic Logic **65**(3), 1264–1310 (2000) 237

19. Blass, A., Gurevich, Y.: New zero-one law and strong extension axioms. Bull. EATCS **72**, 103–122 (2000) 237

20. Blass, A., Gurevich, Y.: Algorithms vs. machines. Bull. EATCS **74**, 96–118 (2002). 205

21. Blass, A., Gurevich, Y., Shelah, S.: Choiceless polynomial time. Annals of Pure and Applied Logic **100**, 141–187 (1999) 237

22. Blass, A., Gurevich, Y., Shelah, S.: On polynomial time computation over unordered structures. J. Symbolic Logic **67**(3), 1093–1125 (2001) 237

23. Bodenmüller, S., Schellhorn, G., Bitterlich, M., Reif, W.: Flashic: Modular verification of a concurrent and crash-safe flash file system. In: A. Raschke, E. Riccobene, K.D. Schewe (eds.) Börger Festschrift, vol. LNCS 12750, pp. 239–265. Springer (2021) 191

24. Bolognesi, T., Brinksma, E.: Introduction to the ISO specification language LOTOS. Computer Networks and ISDN Systems **14**(1), 25–59 (1987) 159

25. Börger, E.: Reduktionstypen in Krom- und Hornformeln. Ph.D. thesis, Institut für Mathematische Logik und Grundlagenforschung der Universität Münster i.W. (1971) 232

26. Börger, E.: Per una teoria delle fallacie dal punto di vista della logica simbolica. Proteus **III**(7), 11–23 (1972) 222

27. Börger, E.: Überlegungen zur Aristotelischen Irrtumslehre vom Standpunkt der mathematischen Logik. In: E. Börger, D. Barnocchi, F. Kaulbach (eds.) Zur Philosophie der mathematischen Erkenntnis. Königshausen und Neumann (Würzburg) (1981). ISBN: 978-3-8847-9022-9 222

28. Börger, E.: Decision problems in predicate logic. In: Logic Colloquium 82, pp. 263–301 (1984). Elsevier (North Holland) 233

29. Börger, E.: Computability, Complexity, Logic (English translation of "Berechenbarkeit, Komplexität, Logik", Vieweg-Verlag 1985), *Studies in Logic and the Foundations of Mathematics*, vol. 128. North-Holland (1989). Italian Translation "Computabilità Complessità Logica", Vol. 1 Teoria della Computazione. Bollati Boringhieri 1989 204, 230, 231

30. Börger, E.: A logical operational semantics of full Prolog: Part 2. Built-in predicates for database manipulations. In: B. Rovan (ed.) Mathematical Foundations of Computer Science 1990, pp. 1–14 (1990). Springer LNCS 452 82, 90

31. Börger, E.: Logic programming: The Evolving Algebra approach. In: B. Pehrson, I. Simon (eds.) IFIP 13th World Computer Congress, vol. I: Technology/Foundations, pp. 391–395. Elsevier, Amsterdam (1994) 185

32. Börger, E.: Evolving Algebras and Parnas tables. In: H. Ehrig, F. von Henke, J. Meseguer, M. Wirsing (eds.) Specification and Semantics. Dagstuhl Seminar No. 9626, Schloss Dagstuhl, Int. Conf. and Research Center for Computer Science (1996) 11

33. Börger, E.: The ASM ground model method as a foundation of requirements engineering. In: N. Dershowitz (ed.) Verification: Theory and Practice, *LNCS*, vol. 2772, pp. 145–160. Springer-Verlag (2003) 185

34. Börger, E.: The ASM refinement method. Formal Aspects of Computing **15**, 237–257 (2003) 185

35. Börger, E.: Construction and analysis of ground models and their refinements as a foundation for validating computer based systems. Formal Aspects of Computing **19**, 225–241 (2007) 185

36. Börger, E.: Modeling distributed algorithms by Abstract State Machines compared to Petri Nets. In: M.B. et al (ed.) ABZ 2016, *Lecture Notes in Computer Science*, vol. 9675, pp. 3–34. Springer-Verlag (2016). DOI: 10:1007/978-3-319-33600-8.1 119

37. Börger, E.: Why programming must be supported by modeling and how. In: T. Margaria, B. Steffen (eds.) ISOLA 2018, *Lecture Notes in Computer Science*, vol. 11244, pp. 89–110. Springer-Verlag (2018). `https://doi.org/10.1007/978-3-030-03418-4_6` 185

38. Börger, E.: The role of executable abstract programs in software development and documentation. `http://arxiv.org/abs/2209.06546` (2022). Originally prepared and accepted for presentation to (but then withdrawn from) ISOLA 2022, track *Programming - What is Next: The Role of Documentation* 185

39. Börger, E., Bolognesi, T.: Remarks on turbo ASMs for computing functional equations and recursion schemes. In: E. Börger, A. Gargantini, E. Riccobene (eds.) Abstract State Machines 2003 – Advances in Theory and Applications, *Lecture Notes in Computer Science*, vol. 2589, pp. 218–228. Springer-Verlag (2003) 205

40. Börger, E., Craig, I.: Modeling an operating system kernel. In: V. Diekert, K. Weicker, N. Weicker (eds.) Informatik als Dialog zwischen Theorie und Anwendung, pp. 199–216. Vieweg+Teubner, Wiesbaden (2009) 130

41. Börger, E., Del Castillo, G.: A formal method for provably correct composition of a real-life processor out of basic components (The APE100 Reverse Engineering Study). In: B. Werner (ed.) Proc. 1st IEEE Int. Conf. on Engineering of Complex Computer Systems (ICECCS'95), pp. 145–148. IEEE (1995) 190

42. Börger, E., Demoen, B.: A framework to specify database update views for Prolog. In: J. Maluszynski, M. Wirsing (eds.) Programming Language Implementation and Logic Programming, pp. 147–158. Springer LNCS 528 (1991) 82, 90

43. Börger, E., Durdanović, I.: Correctness of compiling Occam to Transputer code. Computer Journal **39**(1), 52–92 (1996) 144, 191

44. Börger, E., Durdanović, I., Rosenzweig, D.: Occam: Specification and compiler correctness. Part I: Simple mathematical interpreters. In: U. Montanari, E.R. Olderog (eds.) Proc. PROCOMET'94 (IFIP Working Conf. on Programming Concepts, Methods and Calculi), pp. 489–508. North-Holland (1994) 130, 138, 140, 143

45. Börger, E., Fruja, G., Gervasi, V., Stärk, R.: A high-level modular definition of the semantics of C#. Theoretical Computer Science **336**(2–3), 235–284 (2005) 43, 52, 189, 193

46. Börger, E., Glässer, U., Müller, W.: The semantics of behavioral VHDL'93 descriptions. In: J. Mermet (ed.) EURO-DAC'94. European Design Automation Conference with EURO-VHDL'94, ISBN 0-89791-685-9, pp. 500–505. IEEE Computer Society Press, Los Alamitos, California (1994) 189

47. Börger, E., Glässer, U., Müller, W.: Formal definition of an abstract VHDL'93 simulator by ea-machines. In: C. Delgado Kloos, P.T. Breuer (eds.) Formal Semantics for VHDL, pp. 107–139. Kluwer Academic Publishers (1995) 189

48. Börger, E., Grädel, E., Gurevich, Y.: The Classical Decision Problem. Perspectives in Mathematical Logic. Springer (1997) 234, 238

49. Börger, E., Päppinghaus, P., Schmid, J.: Report on a practical application of ASMs in software design. In: Y. Gurevich, P. Kutter, M. Odersky, L. Thiele (eds.) Abstract State Machines: Theory and Applications, *Lecture Notes in Computer Science*, vol. 1912, pp. 361–366. Springer-Verlag (2000) 192

50. Börger, E., Raschke, A.: Modeling Companion for Software Practitioners. Springer (2018). ISBN 978-3-662-56641-1. For Corrigenda and lecture material on themes treated in the book see `http://modelingbook.informatik.uni-ulm.de` 24, 28, 75, 119, 131, 145, 205

51. Börger, E., Rosenzweig, D.: A mathematical definition of full Prolog. Science of Computer Programming **24**, 249–286 (1995) 82, 189, 192

52. Börger, E., Rosenzweig, D.: The WAM – definition and compiler correctness. In: C. Beierle, L. Plümer (eds.) Logic Programming: Formal Methods and Practical Applications, *Studies in Computer Science and Artificial Intelligence*, vol. 11, chap. 2, pp. 20–90. North-Holland (1995) 82, 191, 192

53. Börger, E., Salamone, R.: CLAM specification for provably correct compilation of CLP($\mathcal{R}$) programs. In: E. Börger (ed.) Specification and Validation Methods, pp. 97–130. Oxford University Press (1995) 192

54. Börger, E., Schewe, K.D.: Concurrent Abstract State Machines. Acta Informatica **53**(5) (2016). http://link.springer.com/article/10.1007/s00236-015-0249-7, DOI 10.1007/s00236-015-0249-7. Listed as Notable Article in ACM 21th Annual BEST OF COMPUTING, see www.computingreviews.com/recommend/bestof/notableitems.cfm?bestYear=2016. 112, 205

55. Börger, E., Schewe, K.D.: A behavioural theory of recursive algorithms. Fundamenta Informatica **177**(1), 1–37 (2020) 205, 208

56. Börger, E., Schewe, K.D., Wang, Q.: Serialisable multi-level transaction control:a specification and verification. Science of Computer Programming **131**, 42–85 (2016). http://authors.elsevier.com/sd/article/S0167642316300041, DOI 10.1016/j.scico.2016.03.008 29, 30, 125

57. Börger, E., Sona, D.: A neural abstract machine. J. Universal Computer Science **7**(11), 1007–1024 (2001) 162

58. Börger, E., Stärk, R.F.: Abstract State Machines. A Method for High-Level System Design and Analysis. Springer (2003) 20, 24, 31, 35, 53, 55, 193, 200, 205, 237

59. Börger, E., Stärk, R.F.: Exploiting Abstraction for Specification Reuse. The Java/C# Case Study. In: M. Bonsangue (ed.) Formal Methods for Components and Objects: Second International Symposium (FMCO 2003 Leiden), *Lecture Notes in Computer Science (ISBN 3-540-22942-6, ISSN 0302-9743)*, vol. 3188, pp. 42–76. Springer (2004). 191, 193

60. Cerf, V.G., Dalal, Y., Sunshine, C.: RFC675: Specification of internet Transmission Control Program (Dec 1974) 124, 169

61. Chandra, A.K., Harel, D.: Structure and complexity of relational queries. J.Comp.Syst.Sci. **25**(1), 99–128 (1982) 236

62. Church, A.: A note on the Entscheidungsproblem. J.Symbolic Logic **1**, 40–41 (1936) 232

63. Claverini, C.: Tommaso Campanella in difesa di Galileo Galilei. "Libertas philosophandi" e concordanza dei libri di Dio. Giornale Critico di Storia delle Idee **12/13** (2014-2015) V

64. CoreASM Contributors: ASM interpreter: The CoreASM Project. https://github.com/coreasm/ (since 2005) 69

65. Craig, I., Börger, E.: Synchronous message passing and semaphores: An equivalence proof. In: M. Frappier, U. Glässer, S. Khurshid, R. Laleau, S. Reeves (eds.) Abstract State Machines, Alloy, B and Z, *Lecture Notes in Computer Science*, vol. 5977, pp. 20–33. Springer-Verlag (2010) 130

66. Daessler, K.: Prolog. Part 1. General Core (1992). ISO IEC JTCI WG17 Committee Draft 1.0, N.92. 82, 90, 189

67. Dijkstra, E.W.: Guarded commands, non-determinacy and formal derivation of programs. Commun. ACM **18**(8), 453–457 (1975). Also available as EWD 472. 64

68. Ebbinghaus, H.D., Flum, J.: Finite Model Theory. Perspectives in Mathematica Logic. Springer (1995) 236

69. Ericsson-Zenith, S.: Occam 2 reference manual (1988). Prentice-Hall. ISBN 0-13-629312-3 28, 64

70. Ernst, G., Pfähler, J., Schellhorn, G., Reif, W.: Modular, crash-safe refinement for ASMs with submachines. Science of Computer Programming **131**, 3–21 (2016) 191

71. Eschbach, R., Glässer, U., Gotzhein, R., Prinz, A.: On the formal semantics of SDL-2000: A compilation approach based on an abstract SDL machine. In: Y. Gurevich, P. Kutter, M. Odersky, L. Thiele (eds.) Abstract State Machines: Theory and Applications, *Lecture Notes in Computer Science*, vol. 1912, pp. 242–265. Springer-Verlag (2000) 189

72. Farahbod, R.: CoreASM: An extensible modeling framework & tool environment for high-level design and analysis of distributed systems. Ph.D. thesis, Simon Fraser University, Burnaby, Vancouver, Canada (2009) 273

73. Farahbod, R.: Design and Specification of the CoreASM Execution Engine and Plugins. https://github.com/CoreASM/coreasm.core/raw/master/org.coreasm. engine/rsc/doc/CoreASM-DesignDocumentation.pdf (2010). See also [72]. 75

74. Farahbod, R., Dausend, M.: CoreASM Language User Manual. https://github.com/CoreASM/coreasm.core/raw/master/org.coreasm.engine/rsc/ doc/user_manual/CoreASM-UserManual.pdf (2016) 75

75. Farahbod, R., Gervasi, V., Glaesser, U.: CoreASM: An extensible ASM execution engine. Fundamenta Informaticae pp. 71–103 (2007) 250

76. Ferrarotti, F., Gonzalez, S., Schewe, K.D.: Bsp abstract state machines capture bulk synchronous parallel computations. Science of Computer Programming **184** (2019) 151

77. Ferrarotti, F., Schewe, K.D., Tec, L., Wang, Q.: A new thesis concerning synchronised parallel computing – simplified parallel ASM thesis. Theor. Comp. Sci. **649**, 25–53 (2016) 205

78. Fleischmann, A.: Distributed Systems. Software Design and Implementation. Springer-Verlag, Berlin Heidelberg New York (1994) 7

79. Fleischmann, A., Schmidt, W., Stary, C., Obermeier, S., Börger, E.: Subject-Oriented Business Process Management. Springer, Heidelberg (2012). www.springer.com/978-3-642-32391-1 (Open Access Book) 7

80. Flocchini, P., Prencipe, G., Santoro, N.: Distribute Computing by Mobile Entities. Current Research in Moving and Computing. Springer-Verlag (2019). LNCS 11340 250, 253, 255, 257

81. Futamura, Y.: Partial evaluation of computation process–an approach to a compiler-compiler. Systems, Computers, Controls **2**, 721–728 (1971) 230

82. Galilei, G.: Le opere di Galileo Galilei. In: Volume IV. Edizione Nazionale, Firenze (1894) V

83. Gervasi, V., Börger, E., Cisternino, A.: Modeling web applications infrastructure with ASMs. Science of Computer Programming **94**(2), 69–92 (2014). DOI http://dx.doi.org/10.1016/j.scico.2014.02.025. URL http://www.sciencedirect.com/science/article/pii/S0167642314000926 119

84. Gödel, K.: Über formal unentscheidbare Sätze der Principia Matematica und verwandter Systeme I. Monatshefte Math.Physik **38**, 173–198 (1931) 101

85. Goerigk, W., Dold, A., Gaul, T., Goos, G., Heberle, A., von Henke, F.W., Hoffmann, U., Langmaack, H., Pfeifer, H., Ruess, H., Zimmermann, W.: Compiler correctness and implementation verification: The Verifix approach. In: P. Fritzson (ed.) Int. Conf. on Compiler Construction, Proc. Poster Session of CC'96. IDA Technical Report LiTH-IDA-R-96-12, Linköping, Sweden (1996) 191

86. Goos, G., Zimmermann, W.: Verification of compilers. In: E.R. Olderog, B. Steffen (eds.) Correct System Design, *Lecture Notes in Computer Science*, vol. 1710, pp. 201–230. Springer-Verlag (1999). https://doi.org/10.1007/3-540-48092-7_10 191

87. Goos, G., Zimmermann, W.: Verifying compilers and ASMs. In: Y. Gurevich, P. Kutter, M. Odersky, L. Thiele (eds.) Abstract State Machines: Theory and Applications, *Lecture Notes in Computer Science*, vol. 1912, pp. 177–202. Springer-Verlag (2000) 190, 191

88. Gosling, J., Joy, B., Steele, G.: The Java™ Language Specification. Addison Wesley (1996) 45

89. Gosling, J., Joy, B., Steele, G., Bracha, G.: The Java™ Language Specification, 2nd edn. Addison Wesley (2000) 43

90. Grandy, H., Bischof, M., Schellhorn, G., Reif, W., Stenzel, K.: Verification of Mondex Electronic Purses with KIV: From a Security Protocol to Verified Code. In:

FM 2008: 15th Int. Symposium on Formal Methods. Springer LNCS 5014 (2008) 191

91. Gurevich, Y.: A new thesis. Abstracts, American Mathematical Society **6**(4), 317 (1985) 204

92. Gurevich, Y.: Evolving algebras 1993: Lipari Guide. In: E. Börger (ed.) Specification and Validation Methods, pp. 9–36. Oxford University Press (1995) 236

93. Gurevich, Y.: Sequential Abstract State Machines capture sequential algorithms. ACM Trans. Computational Logic **1**(1), 77–111 (2000) 24, 42, 196, 199, 205

94. Haneberg, D., Grandy, H., Reif, W., Schellhorn, G.: Verifying smart card applications: An ASM approach. In: Proc. Conference on Integrated Formal Methods (iFM 2007), *LNCS*, vol. 4591. Springer (2007). URL http://www.informati.uni-augsburg.de/lehrstuehle/swt/se/projects/gocard 191

95. Haneberg, D., Moebius, N., Reif, W., Schellhorn, G., Stenzel, K.: Mondex: Engineering a provable secure electronic purse. International Journal of Software and Informatics **5**(1), 159–184 (2011). http://www.ijsi.org 191

96. Haneberg, D., Schellhorn, G., Grandy, H., Reif, W.: Verification of mondex electronic purses with KIV: From transactions to a security protocol. Formal Aspects of Computing **20**(1) (2008) 191

97. Hermes, H.: Ideen von Leibniz zur Grundlagenforschung: die *ars inveniendi* und die *ars iudicandi*. In: Studia Leibnitiana. Akten des Internationalen Leibniz-Kongresses, Hannover, pp. 78–88 (1966) 222

98. Hewitt, C., Bishop, P., Steiger, R.: A universal modular ACTOR formalism for artificial intelligence. In: Proceedings of the 3rd International Joint Conference on Artificial Intelligence San Francisco/CA (IJCAI'73), pp. 235–245. Morgan Kaufmann (1973) 118

99. Hilbert, D.: Die logischen Grundlagen der Mathematik. Mathematische Annalen **88**, 151–165 (1923) 60

100. Hilbert, D., Ackermann, W.: Grundzüge der theoretischen Logik. Springer (1928, 1938) 232

101. Hilbert, D., Bernays, P.: Grundlagen der Mathematik I,II. Springer (1934, 1939) 60

102. Hoare, C.A.R.: Communication sequential processes. Communications of the ACM **21**(8), 666–677 (1978). DOI doi:10.1145/359576.359585 154

103. Hoyte, D.: Let Over Lambda: 50 Years of Lisp. Doug Hoyte/HCSW and Hoytech production (2008). URL https://books.google.it/books?id=vbTONwAACAAJ 101

104. Inmos: Transputer instruction set—a compiler writer's guide (1988). INMOS document 72TRN 119 05, Prentice-Hall, Englewood Cliffs, NJ. 132

105. Inmos: Transputer implementation of Occam (1989). In: Communication Process Architecture, Prentice-Hall, Englewood Cliffs, NJ. 132

106. ITU-T: SDL formal semantics definition. ITU-T Recommendation Z.100 Annex F http://www.sdl-forum.org, International Telecommunication Union (2000) 189

107. Ivakhnenko, A.G., Lapa, V.G.: Cybernetic Predicting Devices. U.S. Department of Commerce, Join Publications Research Service, Washington, D.C., USA (1966). (English version of the original: Kiberneticheskiye Predskazyvayushchiye Ustroystva, Kiev, USSR, 1965) 157

108. Kahn, G.: The semantics of a simple language for parallel programming. In: J.L. Rosenfeld (ed.) Proceedings of the IFIP Congress on Information Processing, pp. 471–475. North Holland Publishing Company (1974) 154, 157

109. Kari, J.: Theory of cellular automata: A survey. Theoretical Computer Science **334**, 3–33 (2005) 69

110. Kirkpatrick, D., Kostitsyna, I., Navarra, A., Prencipe, G., Santoro, N.: Separating bounded and unbounded asynchrony for autonomous robots: Point convergence with limited visibility. In: Proceedings of the 2021 ACM Symposium on Principles of Distributed Computing, PODC'21, p. 9–19. Association for Computing

Machinery, New York, NY, USA (2021). DOI 10.1145/3465084.3467910. URL https://doi.org/10.1145/3465084.3467910 275

111. Kirkpatrick, D., Kostitsyna, I., Navarra, A., Prencipe, G., Santoro, N.: On the power of bounded asynchrony: convergence by autonomous robots with limited visibility (2023). Submitted, extended version of [110] 254, 257

112. Kleene, S.C.: General recursive functions of natural numbers. Mathematische Annalen **112**, 727–742 (1936) 56, 228

113. Kossak, F., Illibauer, C., Geist, V., Kubovy, J., Natschläger, C., Ziebermayr, T., Kopetzky, T., Freudenthaler, B., Schewe, K.D.: A Rigorous Semantics for BPMN 2.0 Process Diagrams. Springer (2015) 189

114. Kossak, F., Illibauer, C., Geist, V., Natschläger, C., Ziebermayr, T., Freudenthaler, B., Kopetzky, T., Schewe, K.D.: Hagenberg Business Process Modelling Method. Springer (2016) 189

115. Lamport, L.: A new solution of Dijkstra's concurrent programming problem. Commun. ACM **17**(8), 453–455 (1974) 112

116. Lamport, L.: How to make a multiprocessor computer that correctly executes multiprocess programs. IEEE Trans. Computers **28**(9), 690–691 (1979) 67

117. Lamport, L.: On interprocess communication. Part I: Basic formalism. Part II: Algorithms. Distributed Computing **1**, 77–101 (1986) 112

118. Lamport, L.: Specifying Systems: The TLA+ Language and Tools for Hardware and Software Engineers. Addison-Wesley (2003). Availabel at http://lamport.org 196

119. Leibniz, G.W.: Dialogus de connexione inter res et verba. G. W. Leibniz: Philosophische Schriften (1677). Edited by Leibniz-Forschungsstelle der Universität Münster, Vol.4 A, n.8. Akademie Verlag 1999 187

120. Lerman, M.: Degrees of Unsolvability: Local and Global Theory. Cambridge University Press (2017). DOI 10.1017/9781316717059. Perspectives in Logic 238

121. Libkin, L.: Elements of Finite Model Theory. Springer (2012) 236

122. Lindholm, T.G., O'Keefe, R.A.: Efficient implementation of a defensible semantics for dynamic prolog code. In: Proceedings of the Fourth International Conference on Logic Programming, pp. 21–39 (1987) 90

123. Lukasiewicz, J.: Aristotle's Syllogistic. From the Standpoint of Modern Formal Logic. Clarendon Press (Oxford) (1954) 222

124. Lynch, N.: Distributed Algorithms. Morgan Kaufmann (1996). ISBN 978-1-55860-348-6 119

125. Makowski, J.A.: Some thoughts on computational models: from massive human computing to Abstract State Machines. In: A. Raschke, E. Riccobene, K.D. Schewe (eds.) Logic, Computation and Rigorous Methods (Börger Festschrift), *LNCS*, vol. 12750, pp. 172–186. Springer (2021) 237

126. McCarthy, J.: Recursive functions of symbolic expressions and their computation by machine, part I. Communications of the ACM **3**(4) (1960) 91

127. Mealy, G.H.: A method for synthesizing sequential circuits. Bell System Technical J. **34**, 1045–1079 (1955). DOI 10.1002/j.1538-7305.1955.tb03788.x 10

128. Memon, M.: Specification language design concepts: Aggregation and extensibility in coreasm. Master thesis, Simon Fraser University (2006) 75

129. Minsky, M.: Recursive unsolvability of Post's problem of 'tag' and other topics in the theory of Turing machines. Annals of Mathematics **74**, 437–455 (1961) 226, 233

130. Moschovakis, Y.N.: What is an algorithm? In: B. Engquist, W. Schmid (eds.) Mathematics Unlimited – 2001 and beyond, pp. 919–936. Springer-Verlag (2001) 205

131. Moschovakis, Y.N.: On founding the theory of algorithms (2002). URL https://www.math.ucla.edu/~ynm/papers/foundalg.pdf. Preprint, February 12, 2002 230

132. N., N.: Some catalogues of Conway's Game of Life patterns. https://conwaylife.
     com/wiki/, https://catagolue.appspot.com/home, https://conwaylife.com/
     ref/lexicon/lex_home.htm. Consulted on May 31, 2023. 71
133. Ottmann, T., Widmayer, P.: Algorithmen und Datenstrukturen.   BI Wis-
     senschaftsverlag (1993). Reihe Informatik Band 70 236, 238
134. Parnas, D.L.: Tabular representation of relations (1992). CRL Report 260, Mc-
     Master University 11
135. Parnas, D.L., Lawford, M.: The role of inspection in software quality assurance.
     IEEE Transactions on Software engineering 29(8), 674–676 (2003) 188
136. Pitman, K.M.: Special forms in Lisp. In: Proceedings of the 1980 ACM Confer-
     ence on LISP and Functional Programming, LFP '80, p. 179–187. Association for
     Computing Machinery, New York, NY, USA (1980). DOI 10.1145/800087.802804
     97
137. P.Michell, D.A., Thompson, J.A.: Inside the Transputer. Blackwell Scientific Pub-
     lications (1990) 137
138. Popper, K.: Logik der Forschung. Zur Erkenntnistheorie der modernen Naturwis-
     senschaft. Springer-Verlag Wien, Wien (1935) 188
139. Prencipe, G.: e-mail to Egon Börger (13.3.2023). Cc to pflocchi@uottawa.ca and
     santoro@scs.carleton.ca 251, 256
140. Rabin, M., Scott, D.: Finite automata and their decision problems. IBM J.Research
     3, 114–125 (1959) 26, 63
141. Rice, H.G.: Classes of recursively enumerable sets and their decision problems.
     Trans.AMS 89, 25–59 (1953) 225
142. Richard, J.: Les principes des mathématiques et le problème des ensembles. Revue
     Générale des Sciences Pures Et Appliquées 12(16), 541–543 (1905) 222
143. Schellhorn, G.: Verification of ASM refinements using generalized forward simula-
     tion. J. Universal Computer Science 7(11), 952–979 (2001) 191
144. Schellhorn, G.: ASM refinement and generalizations of forward simulation in data
     refinement: A comparison. J. of Theoretical Computer Science 336(2-3), 403–436
     (2005) 191
145. Schellhorn, G.: ASM refinement preserving invariants. J. UCS 14(12), 1929–1948
     (2008) 191
146. Schellhorn, G.: Completeness of ASM refinement. Electr. Notes Theor. Comput.
     Sci. 214, 25–49 (2008) 191
147. Schellhorn, G.: Completeness of fair ASM refinement. Sci. of Computer Program-
     ming 76(9), 756–773 (2011). URL https://kiv.isse.de/projects/Refinement/
     ASM-Refinement-complete.html 191
148. Schellhorn, G., Ahrendt, W.: Reasoning about Abstract State Machines: The WAM
     case study. J. Universal Computer Science 3(4), 377–413 (1997) 191
149. Schellhorn, G., Ahrendt, W.: The WAM case study: Verifying compiler correctness
     for Prolog with KIV. In: W. Bibel, P. Schmitt (eds.) Automated Deduction – A Ba-
     sis for Applications, vol. III: Applications, pp. 165–194. Kluwer Academic Publish-
     ers (1998). URL http://www.informatik.uni-augsburg.de/lehrstuehle/swt/
     se/publications 82, 191
150. Schellhorn, G., Ernst, G., Pfähler, J., Bodenmüller, S., Reif, W.: Symbolic execu-
     tion for a clash-free subset of ASMs. Science of Computer Programming 158, 21–40
     (2018). DOI 10.1016/j.scico.2017.08.014. URL https://www.sciencedirect.com/
     science/article/pii/S0167642317301739 191
151. Schellhorn, G., Ernst, G., Pfähler, J., Haneberg, D., Reif, W.: Development of a
     verified flash file system. In: ABZ 2014, LNCS, vol. 8477, pp. 9–24. Springer (2014)
     191
152. Schellhorn, G., Grandy, H., Haneberg, D., Moebius, N., Reif, W.: A System-
     atic Verification Approach for Mondex Electronic Purses Using ASMs. In: J.R.
     Abrial, U. Glässer (eds.) Rigorous Methods for Software Construction and Anal-
     ysis (Börger Festschrift), LNCS, vol. 5115, pp. 93–110. Springer (2009). URL
     http://www.informatik.uni-augsburg.de/swt/projects/mondex.html 191

153. Schewe, K.D., Ferrarotti, F.: Behavioural theory of reflective algorithms I: Reflective sequential algorithms. Science of Computer Programming **223** (2022) 78, 81, 195, 205
154. Schewe, K.D., Wang, Q.: Partial updates in complex-value databases. In: A. Heimbürger, et al. (eds.) Information and Knowledge Bases XXII, pp. 37–56. IOS Press (2011). Vol. 225 of Frontiers in Artificial Intelligence and Applications 75
155. Shepherdson, J., Sturgis, H.: Computability of recursive functions. J. Association for Computing Machinery **10**, 217–255 (1963) 226, 233
156. Sieg, W.: Axioms for computability: Do they allow a proof of Church's thesis? In: H. Zenil (ed.) Computation in nature and the nature of computation, pp. 332–341. College Publications (2012) 205
157. Slupecki, J.: Z badan nad Sylogistyka Arystotelesa. Travaux de la Société des Sciences et des Lettres **B6**, 5–30 (1948) 222
158. Stärk, R.F.: Formal specification and verification of the C# thread model. Theoretical Computer Science **343**, 482–508 (2005) 149
159. Stärk, R.F., Schmid, J., Börger, E.: Java and the Java Virtual Machine: Definition, Verification, Validation. Springer-Verlag (2001) 43, 52, 81, 146, 147, 149, 189, 190, 191
160. Stenzel, K.: A formally verified calculus for full Java card. In: C. Rattray, S. Maharaj, C. Shankland (eds.) AMAST 2004, *LNCS*, vol. 3116, pp. 491–505. Springer (2004) 191
161. Tarski, A.: Der Wahrheitsbegriff in den formalisierten Sprachen. Studia Philosophica **1**, 261–405 (1936) 11
162. Turing, A.M.: On computable numbers, with an application to the Entscheidungsproblem. Proceedings of the London Mathematical Society **s2-42**(1), 230–265 (1937). https://doi.org/10.1112/plms/s2-42.1.230 23, 26, 39, 52, 195, 196, 197, 199, 204, 224, 226, 227, 228, 231, 232
163. W3C Consortium: HTML 5: A vocabulary and associated APIs for HTML and XHTML (2010). URL http://www.w3.org/TR/html5. W3C Working Draft, October 19 129
164. Wallace, C., Tremblay, G., Amaral, J.N.: An Abstract State Machine specification and verification of the location consistency memory model and cache protocol. J. Universal Computer Science **7**(11), 1089–1113 (2001) 116
165. Wirth, N.: The development of procedural programming languages personal contributions and perspectives. In: W. Weck, J. Gutknecht (eds.) Modular Programming Languages, pp. 1–10. Springer Berlin Heidelberg, Berlin, Heidelberg (2000) 5
166. Wolfram, S.: Cellular Automata And Complexity: Collected Papers. CRC Press (2002). ISBN-10: 0201626640, ISBN-13: 978-0201626643, https://www.stephenwolfram.com/publications/cellular-automata-complexity/ 71
167. Wolfram, S.: A new kind of science. Wolfram Media (2002). ISBN: 1-57955-008-8, https://www.wolframscience.com/nks/ 18, 71
168. Zimmerman, W., Gaul, T.: On the construction of correct compiler back-ends: An ASM approach. J. Universal Computer Science **3**(5), 504–567 (1997) 190

Index

Printed in the United States
by Baker & Taylor Publisher Services